Cities, Change, and Conflict

A Political Economy of Urban Life

Cities, Change, and Conflict

A Political Economy of Urban Life

FOURTH EDITION

NANCY KLENIEWSKI
SUNY College at Oneonta

ALEXANDER R. THOMAS
SUNY College at Oneonta

WADSWORTH
CENGAGE Learning™

Australia • Brazil • Japan • Korea • Mexico • Singapore • Spain • United Kingdom • United States

WADSWORTH
CENGAGE Learning™

**Cities, Change, and Conflict,
Fourth Edition**
Nancy Kleniewski and
Alexander R. Thomas

Publisher/Executive Editor:
Linda Schreiber

Acquisitions Editor: Erin
Mitchell

Assistant Editor: Rachael Krapf

Editorial Assistant: Pamela
Simon

Media Editor: Melanie Cregger

Marketing Manager: Andrew
Keay

Marketing Assistant: Jillian
Myers

Marketing Communications
Manager: Laura Locallio

Content Project Management:
Pre-Press PMG

Creative Director: Rob Hugel

Art Director: Caryl Gorska

Print Buyer: Paula Vang

Rights Acquisitions Account
Manager, Text: Don Schlotman

Rights Acquisitions Account
Manager, Image: Leitha
Etheridge-Sims

Production Service: Pre-Press
PMG

Copy Editor: Pre-Press PMG

Cover Designer: Riezebos
Holzbaur/Christopher Harris

Cover Image: ©Michael Bishop/
Illustration Works/Corbis

Compositor: Pre-Press PMG

For product information and technology assistance, contact
us at **Cengage Learning Customer & Sales Support,
1-800-354-9706**.
For permission to use material from this text or product,
submit all requests online at **www.cengage.com/permissions**.
Further permissions questions can be e-mailed to
permissionrequest@cengage.com.

Library of Congress Control Number: 2010922637

ISBN-13: 978-0-495-81222-7

ISBN-10: 0-495-81222-6

Wadsworth
20 Davis Drive
Belmont, CA 94002-3098
USA

Cengage Learning is a leading provider of customized learning
solutions with office locations around the globe, including
Singapore, the United Kingdom, Australia, Mexico, Brazil, and
Japan. Locate your local office at **www.cengage.com/global**.

Cengage Learning products are represented in Canada by
Nelson Education, Ltd.

To learn more about Wadsworth, visit **www.cengage.com/
Wadsworth**.

Purchase any of our products at your local college store or at our
preferred online store **www.CengageBrain.com**.

Printed in the United States of America
1 2 3 4 5 6 7 8 13 12 11 10

Contents

Preface

Nancy Kleniewski originally wrote this book for two reasons: her love of cities and her love of teaching. Her love of cities dates back to her childhood, growing up in the small city of Pawtucket, Rhode Island, when a trip to the big city of Providence, Boston, or New York carried the promise of a parade, baseball game, or stage play. As she made her way through college (in Boston) and graduate school (in Philadelphia), she gained a deeper understanding of both the pleasures and the problems of urban life. In her studies, she found that social scientists were asking some exciting questions about the nature of cities and urban living, and that, although they had been investigating cities for more than a century, they were still making new discoveries. So, she decided to join in their project.

Alex Thomas met Nancy Kleniewski when she interviewed to be president at SUNY College at Oneonta. As the Sociology Department chair, he asked her to teach urban sociology, "as long as you use the same books I do: my book and your book." He, too had a love of cities dating back to his childhood. Born in the suburbs of New York City, by the end of high school he had also lived in Ocala, Florida, and a small town south of Utica, New York. Switching schools several times, from an early age he noticed cultural differences and similarities, and was excited to discover that sociologists seek answers to the types of questions he had considered from his youth.

The result of this new partnership is a comprehensive textbook that reflects the newest research in the discipline. It is written by two scholars who bring their own unique perspectives that reflect when and how they encountered the now-dominant paradigm in urban sociology. Nancy Kleniewski and Alex Thomas share a passion for the feel of cities—whether they're walking down a street or driving through an expressway—and it is this enthusiasm that their book conveys to students.

NEW IN THIS EDITION

The fourth edition of *Cities, Change, and Conflict* contains a number of modifications based on readers' and reviewers' suggestions. In addition to a thorough updating of statistics and references, the most significant changes are:

- A new beginning to Chapter 1, focusing on definitions of "city" and "urban"
- A new discussion of the postmodernist approach to urban sociology and the "L.A. School"
- Substantial revision of Chapter 3 on cities in world history, incorporating new research on the earliest cities
- Revision of Chapter 5 on metropolitan areas, including discussions of sprawl and gentrification
- An update and refocus of Chapter 7 to explore cities in the developing world, including discussion of several cities in different parts of the world
- Incorporation of recent developments, including the HOPE VI housing program, immigration policies, and terrorism
- New boxes on bank consolidation, the subprime mortgage crisis, "sundown towns," the Villaraigosa administration in Los Angeles, and other timely issues

PART I

Thinking About Cities

1

Examining Urban Issues

The city magnifies, spreads out, and advertises human nature in
all its various manifestations. It is this that makes the city
interesting, even fascinating. It is this, however, that makes it of
all places the one in which to discover the secrets of human
hearts, and to study human nature and society.

ROBERT PARK

"THE CITY AS A SOCIAL LABORATORY"

This book is about cities, one of the most widespread features of modern life.
Cities are exciting, vital, and diverse—sometimes to the point of bewilderment. They contain the sights, sounds, and smells of humanity and the many
products of human activity. People seek cities for jobs, to buy goods, to have
experiences, and to be with other people. They are also places where the inequalities of wealth and poverty, the contradictions of growth and deterioration,
the contrasts between social cooperation and competition are evident on a daily
basis. Cities contain in magnified form many of the best—and worst—features of
our society.

This chapter is an introduction to the kinds of questions and issues that will
be raised later on; it is a sampler, preview, and synopsis of some major issues in
urban sociology. In this chapter we will begin by exploring two issues:

1. How do we North Americans regard cities, and how do we define cities?

2. What does it mean to study cities from the perspective of political economy?

After discussing these two issues, we will analyze contemporary urban issues,
as previews of some of the important points we will explore in more depth later
in the book.

WHAT ARE CITIES?

Maybe it's the rush as you exit the Allston toll plaza in Boston and see the entire skyline in front of you, or the thrill of the Chicago skyline as you enter the "loop" from I-290, or Los Angeles as seen from I-10. Or it may be the sense of smallness you experience as you emerge from the Midtown Tunnel in Manhattan or walk toward City Hall on Market Street in Philadelphia. It could be the irritation of traffic as you travel the Washington Beltway or circle Atlanta on I-285. Cities exasperate and exhilarate. We all think we know what they are, but do we?

Cities are defined in many different ways, but the definitions that most people know are cultural definitions. A cultural definition is a social construction of what people in a given society think of as a "city," and as such cities vary from place to place and from time to time. At the end of the *Epic of Gilgamesh*, for instance, King Gilgamesh looks upon the walls of his home city of Uruk with great pride: for people in ancient Mesopotamia three thousand years ago, the city wall was the symbol of urban greatness. In contrast, many nineteenth-century paintings of American cities highlight not the city wall—there were none—but the great smokestacks and plumes of soot reaching into the atmosphere. Although today most Americans would see such a scene as a symbol of environmental degradation, at the time it was perceived as a symbol of industrial and urban greatness.

The task of the sociologist interested in researching the city is to define the city with enough precision to distinguish between individual cities and between cities and noncities. Although our cultural concepts are important in generating such definitions, we nevertheless find that there is no one satisfactory way to define the city. Consider, for instance, a metropolitan area of about 1.2 million people, such as New Orleans, Louisiana; Rochester, New York; or Salt Lake City, Utah. A visitor from one of the three largest metropolitan areas, New York, Los Angeles, or Chicago, respectively, might perceive each of these cities to be quite small and unsatisfying. In contrast, someone who grew up in a small agricultural town might find them to be large and exciting. In other words, the cultural definition of a city depends in part on where an individual was raised. This complicates the definition of a "city" for social science research. Nevertheless, there are ways of discussing cities in ways that account for the subjectivity inherent in such an exercise.

The Urban–Rural Continuum

One way of accounting for the subjectivity inherent in defining cities is to place urban settlements on a continuum of developed versus undeveloped space called the **urban–rural continuum**. At the rural end of the continuum are spaces that have not been developed at all, such as open prairie, forest, and desert environments. Their opposite at the urban end of the continuum are spaces that are completely developed, as in such urbanized environments as downtown Chicago's "loop" and Midtown Manhattan. These are spaces where nearly every inch has been planned and developed as part of the city, even in parks such as Grant Park in Chicago and Central Park in New York. Between the most urban and most rural spaces are the vast majority of places where people live. Agricultural towns are rural, for instance, but normally have a small village that in its fundamental landscape is urban. Smaller cities and large towns typically extend their development over large areas but are also surrounded by agricultural landscapes.

Sociologists refer to the differing types of development found in urban and rural areas as "combined and uneven development" (O'Connor 1998). Derived from a Marxist perspective, this refers to the tendency of economic development to take place in certain areas, such as manufacturing in cities and agriculture in rural places. The level of wealth is typically affected by the pattern of development, and historically urban areas have had more concentrated wealth than rural areas. Within metropolitan areas, however, the pattern of wealth distribution can vary considerably. In some metropolitan areas, for instance, downtown areas and suburbs attract considerable wealth—this is evident by a stroll through New York's Upper East Side and a drive through its wealthy suburbs in Westchester County. In other metropolitan areas, however, much of the wealth is found primarily in the ring of suburbs surrounding the city, such as in metropolitan Detroit.

The concentration of development, both economic and residential, that characterizes cities is a central concept in defining cities. One economic characteristic of a city is that it exhibits **economies of scale**. This means that as the size of a place, just as the size of a company or other economic unit, increases, the cost per unit of providing services decreases. In cities, this often refers to certain types of municipal services. For instance, assuming that the cost of maintaining a mile of roadway is constant, the higher the number of taxpayers paying to maintain the road, the lower the cost is for each individual taxpayer. If mile A of a highway has one hundred taxpayers and mile B has only fifty, it would cost taxpayers of mile A half as much per year for maintenance as mile B taxpayers. Companies in cities also benefit from economies of scale, and this is evident in the fact that very large cities also tend to have very large supermarkets and very large malls. The scale of a city is also related to such issues as crime, cultural creativity, and entrepreneurialism with larger cities often (but not always) attracting more of each (Bettencourt et al. 2007).

Cities also exhibit **economies of agglomeration**. This refers to the benefits that accrue to companies located in cities where similar firms also exist. For instance, the American automobile industry has historically been concentrated in the region near Detroit, Michigan. Although the "big three" automakers—Chrysler, Ford, and General Motors—compete against one another, being concentrated near one another gives each firm access to a specialized workforce and suppliers competing for their business. Similar concentrations of industry are found in such metropolitan areas as San Francisco (computers) and Seattle (aerospace). We will examine this further in Chapter 4.

Cities are not simply places of business and residence, however. Cities are also "nodes" in a global network of cities, each interconnected to the other through the various transactions that characterize human life, whether financial, cultural, or otherwise (Sassen 2002). In fact, cities have always been characterized by a "global" system. The earliest cities were participants in a "global" system that extended from southern Mesopotamia, in present day Iraq, to what is today southern Turkey (Algaze 1993). The system included a relatively well-developed urban economy centered on the cities of southern Mesopotamia, the largest of which was Uruk at nearly fifty thousand residents, and a wider region with which people traded manufactured goods for raw materials. A similar system was found during the Middle Ages in Europe that set the stage not only for modern nation states but for the current global economy (Sassen 2008). In our current global system almost the entire planet is a participant, but the basic structure is similar. There are at the top of the hierarchy global cities, the "big three" being New York, London, and Tokyo (Sassen 2001). There are also cities of a national or regional importance, and further down the hierarchy cities of a more local importance. Smaller towns and agricultural villages are also part of the global system. This hierarchy of places with the global system exhibits a **rank-size order**. According to rank-size pattern, the population of a town multiplied by its rank will be equal to the population of the largest city in a nation or territory. For instance, the population of Los Angeles (population 3,834,340 in 2007), the nation's second largest city, is about half of the population of the nation's largest city, New York (population 8,274,527 in 2007). In many regions, however, particularly in developing nations, there is a very sharp drop off in population after the largest city, a condition called primacy, in which case the largest city is referred to as a primate city.

The rank-size order of a given region or country is in part the result of other functions of cities. Cities act as administrative centers both in and out of government. This could involve the administration of policies or the maintenance of infrastructure. For example, New York City is the global city *par excellence*, but its suburbs are spread across multiple counties in four different states. Further afield, cities of national importance such as Philadelphia and Boston are the "cultural capitals" of their own regions of Pennsylvania and New England, respectively. Within New York State there are several large metropolitan areas that administer particular regions, such as Albany (New York's capital) and Buffalo. There are also a number of smaller metropolitan areas that also have their own spheres of influence, plus a number of small towns and agricultural villages.

Cities typically provide **central place functions** to the people who live in the surrounding area (Christaller 1966 (1933)). A small agricultural village, for instance, may have a gas station, a hardware store, a supermarket, a bank, a post office, and perhaps a few retail shops. According to central place theory, certain places provide services that are important to the overall functioning of a system, and those places that provide these "higher order" services tend to have more population and a larger market. If we consider that an agricultural village may provide a limited number of function to its residents, then those residents must travel to other places for higher order services, and this relationship is found in places across the urban-rural continuum. For instance, a small metropolitan area might provide most of the shopping that an individual will want, but some items might only be available in a very large metropolitan area. Consider that Toys 'R' Us is found in nearly every major metropolitan area in America, but F.A.O. Schwartz is not.

TABLE 1.1   **The Ten Largest Cities and Census Statistical Areas in the United States, 2007**

City	Population	CSA	Population
1. New York	8,274,527	1. New York	21,961,994
2. Los Angeles	3,834,340	2. Los Angeles	17,755,322
3. Chicago	2,836,658	3. Chicago	9,745,165
4. Houston	2,208,180	4. Washington-Baltimore	8,241,912
5. Phoenix	1,552,259	5. Boston-Worcester	7,476,689
6. Philadelphia	1,449,634	6. San Jose-San Francisco	7,264,887
7. San Antonio	1,328,984	7. Dallas-Fort Worth	6,498,410
8. San Diego	1,266,731	8. Philadelphia	6,385,461
9. Dallas	1,240,499	9. Houston	5,729,027
10. San Jose	939,899	10. Atlanta	5,626,400

SOURCE: U. S. Census Bureau, 2009a.

Defining Cities

Defining the city is a difficult task, not only because of cultural definitions and the continuum of types of urban places, but because the sociological definition is by its nature imprecise. Corporate boundaries typically do not encompass the entire developed area of a city, for instance, and so most cities have surrounding urbanized regions referred to as suburbs. As such, using the legal definition of a city will typically leave out a large geographic area and, in many cases, the majority of a region's residents. Similarly, choosing a population "cut off" above which a place is a "city" and below which it is not is not particularly useful either: is a place with fifty thousand residents any more of a city than a place with 49,999? Nevertheless, in order to study cities it is also necessary to somehow measure their characteristics: population, land area, economy, etc.

In the United States, it is typically the Office of Management and Budget (OMB) that defines how to measure cities and metropolitan areas (U.S. Census Bureau 2009a). Normally, when possible, the OMB uses the legal definitions of places: cities, towns, borroughs, counties, parishes, and states. In terms of whether a place is considered urban, however, the OMB uses a population cutoff of 2,500 residents in a densely settled area. Sometimes the urban place aligns with the legal boundaries, but often it does not.

The current definitions also distinguish between **urbanized areas** and **urban clusters**. In an urbanized area, there is an urban "core" that has a population density of at least one thousand residents per square mile, and can include a surrounding "fringe" with a population density of at least five hundred residents per square mile. To qualify as an urbanized area, the population must be at least fifty thousand, but not all of those residents need to live in the same city as defined legally. In fact, in 2007 there were 152 urbanized areas that did not contain a single city of fifty thousand people! In contrast, an urban cluster is defined the same way but has a total urbanized population of less than fifty thousand residents (USDA 2009). Urbanized areas and urban clusters are collectively called urban areas. In 2000, 68 percent of Americans lived in urbanized areas and another 11 percent lived in urban clusters.

Urban areas are used by the U.S. Office and Management and Budget (OMB) to define **core-based statistical areas**, which are divided into **metropolitan areas** and **micropolitan areas** (USOMB 2000). Core-based statistical areas are defined not only by urban areas but by the level of integration measured by commuting patterns found in a region, and except in New England are grouped by counties. (In New England they are grouped by townships, and a separate county-level definition called a New England County metropolitan area is also used). If a core-based statistical area has at least fifty thousand residents in an urban area, it is called a metropolitan area (MA). In a metropolitan area, a county that contains an urbanized area is referred to as the "central" county. There can be more than one central county in a metropolitan area. A nearby county in which 25 percent of workers commute into a central county, even if the county does not contain an urban area, is classified as an "outlying" county in the metropolitan area. The same definitions are used to define a micropolitan county, except that a micropolitan area has an urban cluster of at least ten thousand residents but no more than fifty thousand residents. Micropolitan areas are by definition "nonmetropolitan areas," and are sometimes grouped with other nonmetropolitan counties that do not have urban clusters. Figure 1.1 shows the distribution of core-based statistical areas in the United States.

In particularly large metropolitan areas, those with at least 2.5 million residents, there are further definitions. In such places as Boston, New York, and San Francisco the suburban region surrounding the city has grown so large as to exhibit a degree of independence from the central city, and in those cases portions of the region may be grouped into **metropolitan divisions** that are integrated with one another as measured by commuting patterns. For instance, the New York-Northern New Jersey-Long Island Metropolitan Area is divided into four metropolitan divisions: New York-White Plains-Wayne, Newark-Union, Edison-New Brunswick, and Nassau-Suffolk. Each division has communities that are strongly tied to one another economically yet are also integrated into the larger metropolitan area. Prior to 2003 these were called primary metropolitan statistical areas (PMSA).

Another type of core based statistical area, and the largest in geographic terms, is the **census statistical area** (CSA). A CSA represents the entire region that is integrated with the central city and is composed of all the metropolitan and micropolitan areas in the region. For example, the New York CSA includes the New York MA (and all of its metropolitan divisions) plus the Bridgeport-Stamford-Norwalk, Kingston, New Haven-Milford, Poughkeepsie-Newburgh-Middletown, and Trenton-Ewing metropolitan areas as well as the Torrington micropolitan area. It stretches from the southern tip of New Jersey 250 miles north to the village of Saugerties, New York, and 184 miles from Trenton, New Jersey to eastern Long Island (see Box 1.1). Prior to 2003 these were called consolidated metropolitan statistical areas (CMSA).

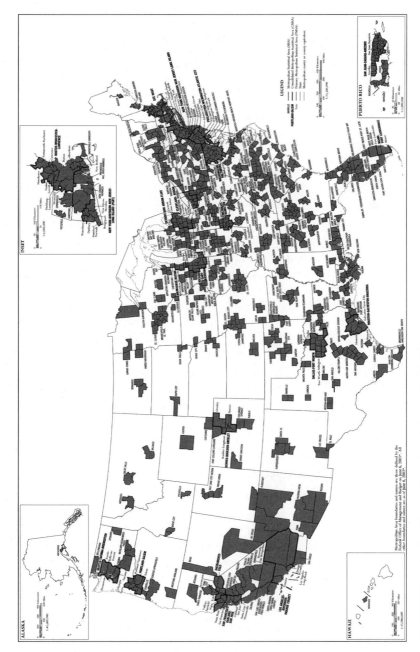

FIGURE 1.1 Core Based Statistical Areas in the United States.

9

B o x 1.1 • Case Study
How Big Is New York City?

New York, is the largest city in the United States, but exactly how big it really is depends on how you define "New York." The city of New York was home to 8,274,527 residents in 2007, a population larger than thirty-eight states. New York is also part of the New York-White Plains-Wayne metropolitan division, what previous scholars called a primary metropolitan statistical area, with a population of 11,607,843, greater than that of Ohio and forty-three other states. Although Long Island is immediately east of New York, it is considered part of its own metropolitan division, and so the nearly 2.8 million residents are not included in the above figure. However, Long Island, as well as large areas of New Jersey, Connecticut, and Pennsylvania are included in the New York census statistical area, what used to be called a consolidated metropolitan statistical area, which stretches from the southern tip of New Jersey to Saugerties, New York, and was home to 21,961,994 people in 2007.

A final type of urban agglomeration does not have an "official" definition but is nonetheless of increasing importance worldwide. It is a string of large metropolitan areas referred to collectively as a "megalopolis" (Gottman 1964). The term was originally coined to refer to region in the northeastern United States that extends from Washington, D.C., through Philadelphia and New York to Boston, Massachusetts, but it can be applied to highly urbanized regions of the world as well, such as the Los Angeles-San Diego-Tijuana corridor in California and Mexico that contains over 20 million residents or the western end of Lake Ontario stretching from Toronto, Canada, to Buffalo, New York, and contains over 11 million residents. Other megalopoli include the Taiheiyō Belt in Japan that includes that country's two largest cities, Tokyo and Osaka, the Rhine-Ruhr region of Germany that includes Cologne and Düsseldorf, and the Sao Paulo-Rio de Janeiro corridor in Brazil.

CITIES, CHANGE, AND CONFLICT:
THREE APPLICATIONS

This book is titled *Cities, Change, and Conflict* because the political economy approach stresses how societies change and how conflict between and among social groups plays a role in that change. Sometimes the changes and conflicts are right out in the open—for example, a debate in the city council over property taxes, a public hearing on a proposed highway, a sit-in challenging a landlord, or a strike against an employer. Other examples of change and conflict are more subtle, gradual, or even hidden—the members of one ethnic group in a neighborhood are being replaced by those of another group; one community's schools deteriorate while a neighboring community gets a new school; a developer buys an apartment house, evicts the tenants, and demolishes the building. Although more subtle, these changes and conflicts are also real.

We will look briefly at three contemporary issues that illustrate several of the key concepts we will return to in later chapters. These examples, although describing a specific set of events, represent social processes that are spread throughout the urban areas of our society.

The Forbidden City Within Los Angeles

Every city has a characteristic **built environment**, consisting of buildings, roads, bridges, and other structures. One of the key issues in urban sociology is how the built environment relates to the ways in which people use the city. The human–environment interaction is reciprocal: people build cities to fulfill certain purposes, and once the cities are built, they influence how people live in them. As Winston Churchill said, "We shape our buildings, and afterwards, our buildings shape us" (quoted in Michelson 1970, 168).

How does the built environment relate to other features of urban life? An issue we will explore in Part III of this book is the way in which different social groups are spatially divided in cities. People of different ethnicities, races, income levels, and even gender differ in where and how they live in the city. How does this social differentiation relate to the built environment? Let us begin with a proposition that we will explore later:

A city's built environment is a reflection of its social structure.

This proposition means that we can see the existence and interaction patterns of different social groups reflected in the physical structure of the city. For example, are the social groups very different from each other or not so different? Do they mix freely or are they separated? Are the spaces that different groups use similar or are they dramatically different from each other? For each city, we may find somewhat different answers to these questions, depending on the city's history and its current social structure.

To begin our exploration of the relationship between the built environment and the social structure, we can consider Mike Davis's analysis of the new downtown of Los Angeles in his book, *City of Quartz* (1990). Davis indicates that the architecture and design of the new downtown both reflect the separation of social groups in Los Angeles and help to enforce their separation from each other.

Davis calls the new downtown "The Forbidden City," a reference to Beijing's Forbidden City, the walled compound within which the emperors of China lived for hundreds of years until they were overthrown by a series of revolutions and wars in the twentieth century. Because it was thought to be important for royalty to be separated from ordinary people, the Forbidden City contained all of the necessities of life for the emperor's extended family as well as for the many nobles, retainers, and servants attached to the court. The Forbidden City thus encompassed several city blocks in size, and contained dozens of dwellings, ceremonial halls, schools, kitchens, stables, and gardens, all surrounded by a formidable wall that separated the court from its subjects.

Los Angeles's new downtown, built since the early 1980s, consists of a series of linked megastructures, or large, multipurpose buildings, including office

FIGURE 1.2 Downtown L. A. Tourist-oriented spaces such as the "Spanish Steps" help to remove pedestrian traffic from the streets and create a separate reality for affluent shoppers and tourists. Critics of contemporary city planning claim that new cities are creating a separate world for the wealthy.

towers, hotels, shopping centers, and entertainment facilities, all connected by a system of multilevel highways, access ramps, elevated pedestrian walkways, and parking garages. Although not literally walled in, Los Angeles's new downtown is difficult to enter, particularly on foot, and consists almost entirely of privately owned spaces, such as shops, hotels, and health clubs, that are monitored through the control of access. Once people gain entrance, Davis says, their experience is a "seamless" transition from work to shopping to play, allowing them to move from one activity to another without leaving the complex and without ever having to see a Latino teenager or a homeless person on the streets outside. This new downtown was built to accommodate white-collar office workers and to attract tourists, convention-goers, and suburban shoppers; and, not surprisingly, those are the groups normally found in the district. (See Figure 1.2.)

By way of contrast, Davis describes the old downtown of Los Angeles, which is just six blocks from the new downtown. Here, sidewalks teem with pedestrians, buses deposit shoppers on every corner, and the doors of business establishments open directly onto the street. Here also is where Latinos, African Americans, and poor people shop, eat, and play, in distinct contrast to the decidedly white and affluent clientele of the new downtown.

Davis relates that the city of Los Angeles planned and carried out the downtown's separation of the rich from the poor, of white Anglos from Latinos and African Americans, through its Redevelopment Agency. The architectural features of multilevel ramps, skyways, and blank concrete walls separating the new downtown from the rest of the city and making it a Forbidden City are designed to exclude the less affluent. The philosophy behind such reconstruction of urban space, Davis argues, is that middle-class whites gain a sense of security from being separated from people who are poor or are members of racial and ethnic minority groups. Thus, replacing openly public spaces with controlled-access semipublic spaces leads to a feeling of spatial security for white middle-class residents.

Lest we think that the separation of social groups is inevitable, Davis reminds us (1990, 231) that in the past century, planners such as Frederick Law Olmstead emphasized providing public amenities—parks, playgrounds, and plazas owned and operated by local governments—that would bring different social groups together. Olmstead thought public mixing of the classes would democratize cities and prevent the extreme social class polarization that was occurring in Europe. In recent years, however, city planners have more commonly adopted the fortress approach seen in Los Angeles. Detroit's Renaissance Center was the first example of this approach to gain national prominence, followed by numerous other downtown redevelopment projects that, rather than welcoming the public inside, have presented the architectural message that the public is not invited (Whyte 1988). If our built environment does indeed reflect our social structure, what we are seeing in the new downtowns is literally a "concrete" statement about the increasing separation of rich and poor in contemporary cities.

Criminalizing Homelessness

What rights do people have to use public space? Who has the power to define what constitutes appropriate or inappropriate public behavior? From a political economy point of view, those with the most power usually get to dominate the policy-making process. Yet, political decisions about urban issues result in different policies from one community to another. Let us use the case of homeless policy to examine the following proposition:

> Local laws and public policies can differ from one place to another based on the political and economic climate of different communities.

As we will see in Chapter 10, homelessness has been on the rise in the United States since 1980. In response, many cities have established positive programs such as emergency housing, soup kitchens, and clinics to help deal with the problem. Other cities have tried to drive homeless people away, or to make them less visible. Unfortunately, one increasingly common tactic cities use to deal with homelessness is to pass ordinances that punish or harass homeless individuals, in effect making it illegal to be homeless.

The National Law Center on Homelessness and Poverty tracks how cities and towns criminalize **homelessness**. The Center's 1999 report, *Out of Sight, Out of Mind*, provides grim evidence of how elected officials sometimes choose

Barry Lewis/Documentary/Corbis

F I G U R E 1.3 Is Homelessness a Crime? Although most homeless people do not live on the streets, some cities have criminalized public homelessness as a way of hiding the problem from sight.

to fight the homeless people themselves rather than the causes of homelessness. The Center's survey of fifty cities shows that officials may take one of these four different types of approaches toward criminalizing homelessness:

- Enacting legislation that limits the use of public space for living activities such as sleeping or sitting

- Enforcing existing restrictions on begging

- Conducting police "sweeps" to remove homeless people from specific areas

- Targeting homeless people for selective enforcement of generally applicable laws

Several cities have passed legislation that, although ostensibly prohibiting "unsafe" activity, actually target the street dwellers who make up the most visible segment of the homeless. (See Figure 1.3) Philadelphia, for example, passed a Sidewalk Behavior Ordinance that prohibits lying on public sidewalks; only a last-minute lobbying effort by homelessness advocates prevented the bill from carrying a jail sentence for violation. (See Box 1.2) In Tucson, the city council not only passed a law against sitting or lying on the sidewalks, but also attempted to lease the sidewalks to adjacent businesses, thus making the sidewalks private property and allowing the businesses to control access to them. Milwaukee has an "antiscavenging" law that prohibits people from looking through trash cans and dumpsters. New Orleans has an "unauthorized public habitation" law. Memphis prohibits people from owning shopping carts. San Diego passed a law

---

B o x 1.2 • Case Study
Project H.O.M.E.'s Campaign Against Homelessness

For the past few years, homeless advocates in Philadelphia have made some remarkable strides in pushing for solutions to homelessness. Several distinct but overlapping campaigns have worked to bring homelessness back into the public arena—and into the minds of elected officials.

A central struggle was the battle over a proposed Sidewalk Behavior Ordinance.... By banning lying on public sidewalks, the bill potentially criminalized homeless people on the streets. An ad hoc group of service providers and advocates, working under the name Open Door Coalition, cooperated in a multifaceted campaign of opposition to the Sidewalk Behavior Ordinance....

Just as the fight was raging in City Council, an important document was released, *Our Way Home: A Blueprint to End Homelessness* in Philadelphia ... [which] outlined concrete policy recommendations for a range of areas, including housing, jobs, shelter and services, and homelessness prevention. Thousands of copies were sent to elected officials, as well as the media. By releasing the Blueprint during the sidewalk ordinance debate, we were able to offer City Council practical, concrete alternatives that would help get people off the streets and into services—without policing or criminalizing them.

As the vote approached, coalition members packed City Council chambers with hundreds of people for three stormy public hearings. Ultimately, the bill passed, but it was significantly amended to include noncriminal penalties and stronger provisions for police to work with outreach teams instead of simply arresting homeless people. In addition, in response to our pressure, the city committed $5 million in new mental health and substance abuse services for those on the street....

[T]hrough another campaign, we are continuing the push for solutions to homelessness. Many of the same organizations that fought the sidewalk ordinance formed a nonpartisan coalition called Election '99: Leadership to End Homelessness. Building on the Blueprint, we developed a set of policy recommendations for all the mayoral candidates and began a broad effort to raise issues of homelessness during the election campaign. [This strategy] has put homeless advocates in Philadelphia in a strong position to affect homeless policies in the city during the next administration....

The success of these efforts was due to several factors. We had a strong coalition, the result of years of working together and building solid, trusting relationships. We ... learned to combine various advocacy strategies ...including street protests and even civil disobedience.... At the same time, though, we worked with city officials and the business community to find common ground.... We have also consistently stressed positive, concrete solutions, not just negative protests.... Finally, we have sought to meet the hardest challenge of any advocacy community: not simply to react to bad policies but to proactively develop and promote solutions and set the agenda.

SOURCE: William O'Brien, "Philadelphia Campaign Reshapes Homelessness Debate," *Shelterforce* No. 106 (July–August, 1999), pp. 8–9.

---

against storing property in public. Who else but homeless people would need to sit or lie down, store their possessions, or scavenge for food and clothing in public?

Restrictions on begging, usually termed "aggressive panhandling," are also numerous. New York City, Miami, and Milwaukee reportedly enforce these laws routinely. In cities such as Boston, Buffalo, Chicago, Los Angeles, Pittsburgh, St. Louis, and Tulsa, antipanhandling laws are selectively enforced.

Another common practice is the "sweep," in which police raid an area known to harbor homeless people, arrest them or chase them away, and confiscate or destroy their property in the process. Sweeps are often used to "clean up" particular districts, such as the Rhine neighborhood of Cincinnati, downtown Nashville, downtown Tucson, and the ballpark areas in Phoenix and San Diego. Police sweeps are sometimes prompted by a high-profile political or sporting event expected to attract large numbers of visitors. Chicago did a sweep of lower Wacker Drive when President Clinton visited in 1997; Milwaukee conducted one in 1998 just before the National Governors' Conference at the city's new Convention Center; Philadelphia conducted a sweep in conjunction with the Major League Baseball All-Star Game; Jacksonville swept the downtown prior to the arrival of the Jaguars; and San Antonio reportedly conducts sweeps prior to most professional sports events and political conventions.

Some laws on the books are rarely enforced but can be selectively enforced against homeless people. This gives elected officials and law enforcement agencies a tool to control where homeless people go and what they do. Such laws include prohibitions against sleeping on the subway (New York), urinating in public (Tucson), loitering (Los Angeles, Cleveland), jaywalking (Milwaukee), public intoxication (Tucson), littering (Tucson), and camping within the city (Austin, Texas). In some cities, officials have declared "zero tolerance" policies for homelessness under the theory that any public disorder contributes to crime. Thus, they react very strongly against minor offenses. San Francisco police, for example, issued sixteen thousand "quality of life" violation tickets, primarily to homeless people, in the first ten months of 1998. In New York, enforcement of "quality of life" violations has escalated from a summons to appear in court to jail time. Long Beach, California, officials pick up homeless people under vagrancy laws, drive them out of town, and leave them there; they also offer homeless people one-way bus tickets to other locations (National Law Center on Homelessness and Poverty 1999). Although large cities have received the most press attention for such policies, a 2006 report highlighted three smaller cities as being among the "meanest:" Sarasota, Florida; Lawrence, Kansas; and Little Rock, Arkansas (National Law Center on Homelessness and Poverty 2006, 24). A listing of the report's top 20 cities is shown in Table 1.2.

Contrary to these "ineffective, counterproductive, and inhumane" policies, the National Law Center on Homelessness and Poverty (1999) reports that several cities have adopted policies that can offer long-term help, both for assisting individual homeless people and for addressing the long-term causes of the homelessness problem. In its report, the Center cites the example of Portland, Oregon, which has adopted a two-pronged strategy. In addition to an outreach program that contacts homeless people and provides services for them, Portland has instituted a policy guaranteeing that more affordable housing units are constructed in the city. Another positive policy is the creation of a Business Improvement District in Times Square, New York City. This group of private businesses collaborates with a social service provider to hire homeless people who work twenty

T A B L E 1.2 The twenty meanest cities?

The National Law Center on Homelessness & Poverty selected the twenty "meanest" cities toward the homeless based on the number of antihomelessness laws, the enforcement of the laws and severity of the penalties associated with them, the general political climate toward the homeless, the city's history, both long term and recent, of dealing with the homeless, and the opinions of local activists for the homeless. In 2005, the twenty "meanest" cities were:

1. Sarasota, FL
2. Lawrence, KS
3. Little Rock, AR
4. Atlanta, GA
5. Las Vegas, NV
6. Dallas, TX
7. Houston, TX
8. San Juan, PR
9. Santa Monica, CA
10. Flagstaff, AZ
11. San Francisco, CA
12. Chicago, IL
13. San Antonio, TX
14. New York City, NY
15. Austin, TX
16. Anchorage, AK
17. Phoenix, AZ
18. Los Angeles, CA
19. St. Louis, MO
20. Pittsburgh, PA

SOURCE: National Law Center on Homelessness and Poverty, 2006, 24

hours a week cleaning the streets of Times Square and spend the remaining twenty work hours in group treatment or other self-improvement programs. In another positive step, citizens of Miami, Florida, voted to impose a 1 percent sales tax on restaurant meals that is designated for the use of the Dade County Homeless Trust. The tax raises some $6 million a year for shelters and supportive services (National Law Center on Homelessness and Poverty 1999).

What must be done to address the problem of homelessness? If policies are not put in place to prevent homelessness, we will continue to see a steady increase in the number of homeless families and individuals. As we will see in Chapter 10, a broad range of policies is needed, including affordable housing, improved mental health treatment, accessible and effective substance abuse programs, decent jobs, and livable wages. Through the political process, some local areas are addressing comprehensive policies, including assistance for people who are already homeless, and help for people at risk of becoming homeless.

Communities have the choice of turning the homeless into criminals or attempt-ing to address homelessness as a community problem.

Environmental Racism and Environmental Justice

Does every citizen have equal access to a safe and healthy living space? Are the dangers and difficulties of urban life spread evenly throughout cities and metro-politan areas? Or are some groups more likely than others to be exposed to pro-blems and hazards? By examining the case of the environment, we can explore the following proposition:

> The ability of a community to control its fate is related to its political
> and economic power.

During the 1980s, many people of color, including African Americans, Latinos, and Native Americans, began to recognize and rally against environmental threats to their neighborhoods. Until that time, the environmental movement was over-whelmingly made up of white, middle-class activists. As we will see in Chapter 9, the fact that lower-income people of color are especially subject to environmental hazards prompted new discussions of environmental issues in communities of racial minorities.

One of the earliest incidents to expose this pattern of the concentration of hazards in minority communities occurred in 1982, when officials decided to locate a toxic PCB landfill in a predominantly African-American area of North Carolina. Residents organized to stop its construction. The following year, the federal government's General Accounting Office reported that three of the four major hazardous landfills in the South were located in predominantly African-American communities. Shortly afterward, a national study found that the proportion of racial minorities in communities with hazardous waste facilities was double that of communities without such facilities. The authors concluded that they were observing a nationwide pattern of environmental racism (Bryant and Mohai 1992). Subsequent research has largely confirmed the earlier reports (Bullard and Waters 2005).

According to the Movement for Environmental Justice website (http://www.ejrc.cau.edu), "**environmental racism** refers to any policy, practice, or directive that differentially affects or disadvantages (whether intended or unin-tended) individuals, groups, or communities based on race or color. Environ-mental racism combines with public policies and industry practices to provide benefits for whites while shifting costs to people of color. Environmental racism is reinforced by government, legal, economic, political, and military institutions."

Environmental racism is not confined to decisions about locating hazardous waste facilities. Several other environmental threats face communities of color far more frequently than they do white communities. Lead poisoning, caused by eating or inhaling lead paint particles, eating vegetables grown in lead-polluted soil, and drinking water from lead plumbing, is rampant in the older sections of cities. Lead poisoning is the number one health problem for children nationwide, affecting millions of inner-city children, a high proportion of them African

American or Latino (Dolbeare and Ryan 1997). Cancer rates among residents of communities near polluting industries, such as petrochemical plants, are also far higher than the average. A string of African-American towns along the Mississippi River from Baton Rouge to New Orleans is called "Cancer Alley" because of the high rates of cancer among the residents (Bullard 1993).

Once activists and scholars began studying nationwide patterns of race and environmental hazards, they noticed a definite relationship between the two. Then they asked whether the high levels of exposure to environmental hazards in minority communities were due simply to poverty, or if there was a distinct relationship with race. Researchers have statistically disentangled the effects of income and race on environmental hazards (Bryant & Mohai 1992; Krieg 1998; Pastor 2001). They found that both factors contribute to the high incidence of hazards in minority communities. Low incomes and low property values in poor communities make it cheap for industries or government agencies to acquire land for environmentally questionable purposes. But members of racial and ethnic minority groups, independent of their incomes, have a limited number of residential choices compared to whites. This makes it more difficult for them to flee contaminated neighborhoods. Furthermore, whites dominate the political leadership of most communities, allowing them to take the stand of "not in my backyard." Thus elected officials often end up siting hazardous land uses among politically less powerful minority residents. After studying all of the available evidence, Bryant and Mohai (1992) concluded that race has more of an effect than income on influencing the level of environmental hazards in a given neighborhood.

Throughout the nation, the environmental justice movement combines the approaches of both the environmental movement and the civil rights movement. Grassroots groups have sprung up to address such issues as waste facility siting, lead contamination, pesticides, water pollution, air quality, nuclear products, and workplace health. Groups such as Brooklyn's Toxic Avengers, West Harlem Environmental Action, Mothers of East Los Angeles, and Concerned Citizens of South Central Los Angeles have used confrontational direct-action tactics similar to those used by civil rights groups in the 1950s and 1960s. In addition, however, the movement includes professional and workplace groups such as labor unions, community garden groups, and business–environmental forums that help activists make connections between their local struggles and related state or national issues (Taylor 1993).

One of the obstacles the movement has encountered is that members of low-income minority groups sometimes think their only choices are between a hazardous job or no job. They may seek work in workplaces (such as uranium mines or pesticide factories) that are shunned by whites because of the health risks. They may be convinced by authorities that a landfill or industrial plant is safe and will bring jobs to the community, only to learn after it is built that it poses threats to their families (Bailey, Faupel, and Gundlach 1993). The overwhelming need for employment and investment in low-income communities of color can make environmental concerns seem less important in comparison. The many environmental justice groups that have been formed, however, have had a number of significant successes in addressing both high-profile environmental problems such as industrial pollution, and less obvious but still pervasive problems such as asthma and lead poisoning.

CONCLUSION

Cities are contradictory places, reflecting the many currents and contradictions of contemporary society. Which of the following statements about cities is true?

- Cities are growing.
- Cities are shrinking.
- Cities are similar to each other.
- Cities are different from each other.
- Cities are orderly.
- Cities are in upheaval.
- Cities are exciting and vibrant places.
- Cities are the dumping grounds for many societal problems.
- Cities are overly influenced by wealthy and powerful groups.
- Ordinary people can affect what happens in cities.

As we will see in subsequent chapters, all of these statements are true—for some cities at some point in time. The point of studying about cities is to discover the circumstances under which each of these generalizations is true.

DISCUSSION QUESTIONS

1. Think of a mall or shopping center with which you are familiar. What space is public? What space is private? Now think of a city shopping street. How do the use of space and the demarcation of public and private differ from that of the mall? Who is allowed to use spaces in the two settings, and how is the use of the space controlled?

2. Examine a week's worth of listings of prime-time television shows in the local newspaper. How many shows take place in cities? How many portray a mostly positive view, a mostly negative view, or a balanced view of cities? Do you think television shows influence viewers' attitudes toward cities? Why or why not? What else influences beliefs and attitudes about cities?

3. In your community, what public policies or programs exist regarding housing and homelessness? What happens to hazardous waste generated by residents and industry? Are the patterns similar to or different from those described in this chapter? How?

4. What type of community do you live in, city, suburb, or rural town? Do people commute to your town or to another town? How does your community relate to other communities in the area?

2

Theoretical Perspectives
on the City

One day I walked with one of these middle-class gentlemen into
Manchester. I spoke to him about the disgraceful unhealthy slums
and drew his attention to the disgusting condition of that part of the town
in which the factory workers lived. I declared that I had never seen
so badly built a town in my life. He listened patiently and at the
corner of the street at which we parted company, he remarked: "And
yet there is a great deal of money made here. Good morning, Sir!"
FRIEDRICH ENGELS
THE CONDITION OF THE WORKING CLASS IN ENGLAND

Whenever researchers set out to study anything, from atomic structure to
international investment patterns, they begin with a set of questions. These
questions orient them to the object of their study. It should not be surprising that,
given a number of different researchers, each one might ask different questions
about the phenomenon under scrutiny. Although they may be studying the same
problem, they will probably investigate or at least emphasize different aspects of it.

Sociological studies can be grouped together on the basis of the main questions or assumptions that guide different research projects. These broader sets of
assumptions, methodologies, and key questions are often related to the investiga-
tor's theoretical approach to the subject. In urban studies, researchers with similar
overall theories about how urban society works will usually be interested in
asking similar questions. This chapter will explore how urban sociologists use
theory in their research, focusing on four questions:

1. Why do sociologists use theories to shape their research?

2. What theories do urban sociologists use and where do their theories
   come from?

3. What are the different assumptions and approaches that accompany different theories?

4. How do theories affect the research topics that urban sociologists select to study?

THEORIES AND PARADIGMS

Let us say that four sociologists set out to study housing problems in urban areas of the United States. They might take a number of different approaches, and the questions they ask at the outset will determine the direction of each researcher's study. One researcher might look for spatial patterns in the location of adequate and inadequate housing, mapping the areas with different housing conditions. A second might investigate the relationship between the incomes of residents and the quality of the housing in which they live, analyzing how residents as consumers spend their resources. A third might describe the mechanisms by which property is bought, sold, and financed, asking about the role of banks, realtors, and other individuals who make their living from buying and selling property. A fourth researcher might investigate the local, state, and federal government's policies regarding the supply and adequacy of housing.

How do investigators decide on the objects and methods of their studies? Aside from the obvious limitations of time, place, and costs of the research, social scientists choose their research questions based on fundamental assumptions about the operation of the social world. These assumptions are tentative answers to a set of overarching questions about the nature of society. For example, are societies and social institutions orderly systems composed of interdependent parts? Researchers who answer "yes" to this question tend to emphasize the ways in which the urban social system is integrated or the way that the parts fit together to make the whole city work smoothly. They tend to see changes in cities as evolutionary, being driven by predictable factors such as population growth. Researchers answering "no" to the question may see societies as composed of competing groups, each struggling to gain advantages over the others. They tend to look for the ways in which urban patterns reflect the power of some groups over other groups within the community and to see changes in urban patterns as the product of groups' struggles to gain and keep resources.

Researchers are also guided in their subject areas by different **paradigms**. A paradigm is a set of related concepts, research questions, and theories that a group of researchers find most useful for understanding the world (Pickvance 1984). Researchers using different paradigms will probably ask different questions, examine different data, and interpret their findings in different ways. In urban studies the dominant paradigm for the first half of the twentieth century was **urban ecology** (Flanagan 1993). Urban ecology shares many assumptions with theories of social organization and structural functionalism, stressing the orderly interaction of interdependent parts of social systems—in this case, of cities. Since the 1970s, a second paradigm, called **urban political economy**, has emerged; it stresses the use of power, domination, and resources in the shaping of cities. The new paradigm has helped focus researchers on several different questions and concerns within the field (Walton 1993).

So how do researchers adopt a theoretical orientation and choose a paradigm to guide their work? One influence is the nature of the social world surrounding the researchers: What problems, issues, and phenomena do they observe? Another is the academic milieu in which they work: How can their research build on the foundations laid by other investigators? Still another source contributing to the formation of a theoretical approach is the researchers' personal value systems: What do they think is good or bad about current social arrangements?

Every theorist and researcher who has asked questions about urban society has had to confront these questions. In this chapter we will examine the two most important paradigms within urban studies—urban ecology and urban political economy—to understand why the proponents have asked the questions they have, and what contributions their research has made to understanding cities. In each case we will first examine the theoretical antecedents or ancestors of the theory, then look at the theory when it was first developed, and finally examine its contributions and problems.

URBAN ECOLOGY PARADIGM

Antecedents: Tönnies, Durkheim, and Simmel

The growth of cities and the growth of sociology were intertwined in the history of the nineteenth century. From the beginning, sociologists were interested in urbanization because of the immense impact it was having on European societies. Throughout Europe, cities were growing rapidly. The main cause of this urbanization was the migration of large numbers of people from the rural countryside to urban areas. The classical theories of the city linked urban living to other changes occurring in European society, especially industrialization, secularization, and modernization. Thus, many early theorists asked questions about the transformation from traditional village life to modern urban life.

One of the first sociologists to set out a systematic theory of this transformation to urban life was the German writer Ferdinand Tönnies (1855–1936). His book *Gemeinschaft und Gesellschaft (Community and Society)* (1963, originally published in 1887) asked the question: What is the difference between life in a small town and life in a large city? He pictured the **gemeinschaft** (traditional, small community) as made up of people who cooperated with each other very closely, this behavior being determined by their kinship ties and reinforced by the social control of their neighbors and of the church. In contrast, Tönnies saw the **gesellschaft** (modern urban society) as made up of individuals acting for their own self-interest, cooperating only as much as required by the laws, contracts, or public opinion that constrained their actions. Tönnies's work set the stage for further theorizing about the links between the type of community in which people lived and their daily experiences, social ties, and even their self-concept. To Tönnies, the societal changes of industrialization and urbanization were linked to the changing nature of the local community. In the society of his time, he perceived that large and impersonal cities gradually superseded small, close, traditional family-oriented communities, and he feared that the transition from rural to urban life could threaten the very existence of society.

The French sociologist Émile Durkheim (1858–1917) followed a similar line of inquiry but arrived at a somewhat different answer to his question. Durkheim was aware that the rapid social change of the rural-to-urban transition had worried some social critics who thought that as the close ties of village-based, *gemeinschaft*-type societies dissolved, the society itself might dissolve. Durkheim wrote *The Division of Labor in Society* (1964, originally published in 1893) to investigate how changes in society would affect social cohesion, or, as he called it, social solidarity.

Durkheim's main line of argument is that "simple" societies (like the *gemeinschaft*) derive their cohesiveness from the similarities among their members. Everyone in a village knows or is even related to everyone else; most everyone practices the same religion and has a similar worldview. Not much variation exists in social and cultural values, ethnic background, or occupational distribution. Thus, what binds the group is the sameness of their makeup. In the more complex, modern, urban setting, people are very different from each other. They may have different religious, political, ethnic, and family backgrounds that make them very unlike each other. Because they all have different occupations, however, they are bound to each other out of necessity. The social solidarity of the modern city, Durkheim argued, is based not on the similarities among residents but on the interdependence born of the social and occupational differences among people. Durkheim called this **organic solidarity** (as opposed to the **mechanical solidarity** of the rural village), likening the specialization of different individuals to the specialization and interdependence of different parts of a living organism. This key insight into how societies work guided sociology for a century and was particularly important in future ecological research on cities.

While Tönnies and Durkheim had different responses to the changes that had occurred in the development of modern cities, their theories were similar in the sense that both emphasized the macrosocial (or large scale) level of culture and social institutions. In contrast to this macrosocial approach, the German theorist Georg Simmel (1858–1918) focused on the effects that city life, especially life in a large industrial metropolis, had on the individual. Simmel's theorizing initiated a social psychology of urban life, launched by his famous essay on cities, "The Metropolis and Mental Life" (1905). The starting point of Simmel's analysis was the observation that people living in a city must interact frequently with strangers. He thought that these frequent interactions overstimulated the nervous systems of urban dwellers, causing them to withdraw mentally as a kind of self-preservation technique. Simmel argued that urban interactions thus tended to be colder, more calculating, more based on rationality and objectification of others than relationships in smaller communities. Simmel did not think that urban social life was all bad; on the contrary, he seemed to prefer city life with its reserved and blasé outlook to the close ties and lack of privacy that village life represented. Analysts who built on Simmel's work, however, tended to stress the negative aspects of the density and impersonality of city life.

The classical theories of the city were important in establishing a foundation for urban sociology. They proposed an initial set of research questions and provided a common theoretical perspective on the city. As we have seen, the classical writers' theories emerged from their own social experiences in the massive transformation of Europe from rural and village-based feudalism to urban, industrial capitalism. Not surprisingly, Tönnies, Durkheim, and Simmel stressed questions of social order, social cohesion, community ties, and social differentiation. To their credit, they saw urbanization as only one aspect of a large-scale change that was engulfing European societies.

When urbanists in the United States later applied the classical theories to North American cities, they found the classical concepts useful as a foundation for their work. They also found that they had to go beyond the work of these early theorists, for two reasons. First, the classical theorists had provided little empirical evidence for their theories. Of course, the broad historical nature of their questions prevented some of these questions from being investigated in detail. But later researchers wanted more detailed information about how specific cities worked, to get a more bottom-up rather than top-down view of urban processes. Second, the classical theorists had not tried to unravel the various strands of social change that were occurring simultaneously. How was it possible to distinguish between the effects of urbanization and those of industrialization? Or between the effects of industrialization and those of the changing economic order? How many of the characteristics that were attributed to urban living were actually due to industrial capitalism? For example, Simmel stated that urban dwellers lived by the clock and judged each other by how much money they made. He never tried to establish, however, whether those attitudes derived from the urban environment itself or from the structure of the workplace or the changing structure of social classes. The earliest urban sociologists in the United States, the Chicago School, addressed itself to the first if not to the second of those problems.

The Chicago School

Just as sociology in Europe was growing up in the midst of social change, sociology in the United States was born in the midst of social change and urban growth. The sociology department that served as the cradle of urban studies was located at the University of Chicago, within the most rapidly growing city in the United States. Chicago was such a boomtown that the growth of new areas happened almost literally overnight. Sociologists working at the University of Chicago were directly confronted by the diversity, liveliness, and apparent fragmentation of urban life.

From the classical theorists, the urban sociologists of the Chicago School drew a concern for order, cohesion, and social relationships. The classical theorists were not their only influence, however. The Chicago School was both interdisciplinary and empirical, borrowing concepts and methods from a wide range of sources. One of the most important of these was botany, or the study of plant life and plant communities. The Chicago School theorists hoped to be able to find the same kinds of regular patterns in the social world as botanists had found in the natural world of plants.

The founder of the Chicago School of urban sociology was Robert E. Park (1864–1944), who established the discipline and collaborated with several generations of student scholars. Although Park shared the theoretical perspective of Tönnies, Durkheim, and Simmel, he did not share their reliance on the power of theory alone to explain social life. Rather, Park believed that the social world had to be investigated through direct observation. As a former newspaper reporter, Park had an interest in and a knowledge of many of the aspects of city life normally hidden from view. His research and that of his students included descriptions of these pockets of urban life, such as dance halls and ethnic ghettos. Park insisted that research should do more than describe pieces of the city; he saw the city as a laboratory for investigating the relationships of one facet of urban life to another. In his essay "The City: Suggestions for the Investigation of Human Behavior in the Urban Environment," Park (1915) argues that cities are like living organisms, composed of interconnected parts. The urban sociologist's task, he instructs, is to understand how each part relates to the structure of the city as a whole and to the other parts.

Robert Park called his approach to urban life human ecology, patterning it on the new biological science of ecology. Like biological ecology, human ecology studies the relationship between populations (in this case, human rather than animal or plant populations) and the environments or territories they inhabit. Park (1936) used the metaphor of "the web of life" to show how the different parts of the city depend on each other. He encouraged his students to look for social equivalents of ecological concepts such as niches, which the human ecologists renamed **natural areas**. One of Park's students, for example, studied the relationship between the high-rent Gold Coast neighborhood of Chicago and a nearby slum, pointing out that a symbiotic relationship existed between the two areas. Each neighborhood gained something from the proximity of the other: the poor residents of the slum obtained jobs as maids and handymen in Gold Coast households, and the wealthy Gold Coast residents had access to the illegal alcohol, drugs, and prostitution they wanted—but wanted to keep out of their neighborhood (Zorbaugh 1929).

Park's student and collaborator, Ernest W. Burgess, shared his mentor's quest to find the regularities and patterns in social life that natural scientists were discovering in the natural world. In his 1925 essay, "The Growth of the City: An Introduction to a Research Project," Burgess laid out a hypothesis that provided social scientists with research material for several decades thereafter. Burgess's hypothesis was that the purposes for which urban land was used (business, manufacturing, housing of different social classes, and so on) would follow a regular pattern. The very center of the city, Burgess reasoned, would be occupied by high-priced land uses such as businesses and entertainment, which could afford to pay for, and which could benefit financially from, a central location. Residential neighborhoods would be located further from the center, in waves according to the expense of commuting to the center from different distances.

Thus, the outskirts of the city would be dominated by high-priced residential neighborhoods, whereas middle-class and working-class families would live closer to the center. Between the center and the residential districts, Burgess contended, would lie an area of deteriorating housing and disreputable businesses. He called this area the **zones in transition** because he believed that city growth occurred outward from the center and that the central business district would always be expanding. Thus, the area just outside the center (wherever that boundary happened to be) would over time be bought up by businesses moving outward from the center. As potentially but not currently valuable land, Burgess reasoned, these marginal properties would be allowed to deteriorate, because their owners were holding them only until the sale price was favorable.

In Burgess's work we see an additional influence on the theory of urban ecology, namely, the **neoclassical school of economics**. This approach explains the location of various land uses in the city (business, industry, or residential) by the ability to pay for land. It attempts to predict the location of a particular land use by understanding what its needs are (e.g., a central location enables good business contacts, whereas a peripheral location offers a quiet place to sleep) and what its resources are (how much the purchaser can spend for a certain quantity of land). In other words, the neoclassical approach sees the use of a given piece of land as a result of competition between groups who would want to use it for different reasons and who have different abilities to pay for the space. This competition within the land market should result in each group getting the best location it can afford. Thus, similar land-use patterns will arise in cities, because the results of the competition for land should be similar from one city to another.

The overall pattern that Burgess sketched out for city growth was a series of concentric circles, with the central business district (or Loop, as it is called in Chicago) surrounded by the zone in transition, followed by the homes of the different social classes, in order of income. Superimposed over these concentric zones that designated social class or land prices were other belts and patches of ethnic neighborhoods, such as the Black Belt, the Jewish Ghetto, Little Sicily, Chinatown, and Deutschland, the home of German immigrants (see Figure 2.1). The **concentric zone model**, one of the most famous theoretical models in all of sociology, worked as a description of the pattern of land-use in Chicago and a few other North American cities of the 1920s.

In attempting to generalize the concentric zone model to other cities, however, subsequent researchers found that other patterns emerged. In his study of some 250 cities in the United States, Chicago School economist Homer Hoyt (1939) found a pattern of wedges, or sectors, rather than concentric zones and thus developed his **sector model** theory, as shown in Figure 2.2. Researchers Chauncey Harris and Edward Ullman (1945) subsequently found a mosaic pattern they called **multiple nuclei**. The only similarity between Burgess's model and Harris and Ullman's is that the central business district is located in the center. Other than that, Harris and Ullman found different land uses clustered together in different ways in different cities (see Figure 2.3). Thus, the ecologists' search for a model to describe "The City" was frustrated by the complexity of

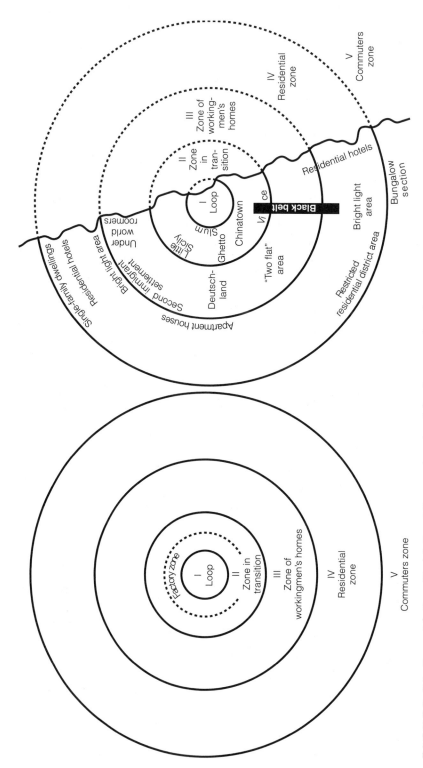

FIGURE 2.1 Concentric Zone Model. Ernest Burgess thought of the city as a series of concentric rings, or zones, used for different purposes and inhabited by different social groups. Left: the general concentric zone model; Right: Chicago in the 1920s. (Loop is Chicago's name for the central business district; the irregular line bisecting the circle is the shore of Lake Michigan.

SOURCE: Ernest Burgess, "The Growth of the City: An Introduction to a Research Project." In *The City*, edited by R. Park, E. W. Burgess, and R. D. McKenzie. Chicago: University of Chicago Press, 1925. Reprinted by permission.

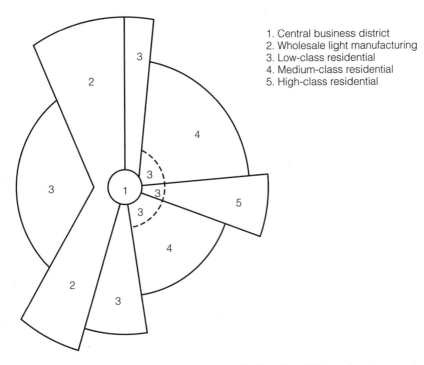

1. Central business district
2. Wholesale light manufacturing
3. Low-class residential
4. Medium-class residential
5. High-class residential

F I G U R E 2.2   Sector Model. Homer Hoyt, finding that different land uses and social groups clustered in wedge-shaped sectors based on the location of main roads and transportation routes, arrived at a variation on the Burgess model.

SOURCE: Chauncey Harris and Edward Ullman, "The Nature of Cities," *Annals of the American Academy of Political and Social Science*, Vol. 242, p. 13, copyright © 1945 by Sage Publications, Inc. Reprinted by permission of Sage Publications, Inc.

actual cities. When researchers began to investigate cities on other continents and in previous time periods, the search for a uniform model of urban growth grew even more complicated.

Besides questions about the location and growth of different areas of cities, the early human ecologists were also interested in the social life of urban areas. They believed, as did Tönnies and Simmel, that social interaction in cities was different from social interaction in rural areas or small communities. They shared with the classical theorists the notion that social relations in modern industrial cities were impersonal and fragmented. Louis Wirth did the most prominent work on this topic; he wrote the classic article "Urbanism as a Way of Life" in 1938.

Wirth set out to explain why social life in cities differed from life in smaller communities. The concept he called **urbanism** was similar to Simmel's and Tönnies's observations about urban social relations: Contacts among urban dwellers tend to be impersonal, superficial, utilitarian, and transitory. Unlike Simmel, however, Wirth did not attribute these social relations to a psychological cause (the individual's withdrawal from an overly stimulating environment) but to social and ecological causes. Wirth argued that three factors about the

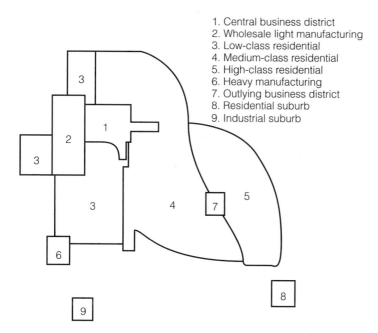

1. Central business district
2. Wholesale light manufacturing
3. Low-class residential
4. Medium-class residential
5. High-class residential
6. Heavy manufacturing
7. Outlying business district
8. Residential suburb
9. Industrial suburb

F I G U R E   2.3   Multiple Nuclei Model. Chauncey Harris and Edward Ullman found that, other than a central business district, there was little predictability about where different land uses and social groups would be found in different cities.

SOURCE: Chauncey Harris and Edward Ullman, "The Nature of Cities," *Annals of the American Academy of Political and Social Science*, Vol. 242, p.13, copyright © 1945 by Sage Publications, Inc. Reprinted by permission of Sage Publications, Inc.

population of cities were responsible for the social relations found in cities: the size, density, and heterogeneity of the population. He argued that, as communities became larger and denser and as more different kinds of people moved into them, the communities fragmented into smaller, more homogeneous groupings and the residents' orientation to people outside of the smaller group became less personal.

Wirth's theory is a good example of one of the underlying assumptions of human ecology: that social norms (the **moral order**) are rooted in the relationship between a population and the territory in which it lives (the **biotic order**). Thus, human ecology's scope spans both the spatial patterns of urban form and the social patterns of morality and norms. Wirth's theory makes explicit the connections between the two types of studies being done within the school of human ecology: studies of human behavior (such as the lives of gang members, homeless people, and immigrants) and studies of changing land-use patterns. The overarching theme is that both the social norms of a neighborhood and its changing land uses over time are different expressions of the same underlying principle: *how the different populations of the city adapt to (and compete for) territories.*

Contributions and Critique

The Chicago School's influence on urban studies in the United States cannot be overstated. Urban ecology was virtually synonymous with urban sociology for over fifty years and contributed heavily to urban geography, economics, and planning. After 1950, ecologists branched out into studies that, while building on the earlier works, took the discipline in new directions. One branch of ecology that grew up in the 1950s was **social area analysis**, or factorial ecology, an application of the statistical technique of factor analysis to urban questions. Applying this newly invented statistical technique, researchers Eshref Shevky and Wendell Bell (1955) discovered many regularities in the population characteristics of different urban neighborhoods. They combined similar variables until they reduced population differences to three dimensions: one reflecting the average socioeconomic status of households in the area, a second reflecting family size and structure, and the third reflecting the area's racial or ethnic makeup. They showed that knowing how one neighborhood differed from another on just these three basic population characteristics could help researchers predict many other features of life in those different settings. Studies using social area analysis have provided us with a great deal of information on social class and household patterns in cities.

Another direction the later ecologists followed is exemplified in the work of Otis D. Duncan (1961), who took literally the early ecologists' notion that the behavior of human populations is related to the natural environment. Duncan created a theoretical system in which both humans and the natural environment contribute to urban events. Duncan's model of the city shows how population, social organization, environment, and technology (POET) all interact with and influence each other, forming a changing ecosystem.

Other ecologists have shown that ecological theory could be broadened to apply to all social phenomena. Perhaps Amos Hawley (1944, 405) has used ecological theory most ambitiously, arguing that human ecology "might well be regarded as the basic social science," because its central question of the adjustment of humans to the environment is an underlying assumption in other social sciences as well.

Another branch of urban studies that emerged from the Chicago School was community ethnography. These descriptive case studies of daily life in urban neighborhoods provided valuable insights into the subcultural norms and behaviors of poor and marginalized groups. Although earlier studies had tended to see life in poor areas as disorganized, later studies such as *The Urban Villagers* (Gans 1962) and *The Social Order of the Slum* (Suttles 1968) revealed the distinctive but obvious social organization of these urban neighborhoods.

The paradigm of urban ecology informed the vast majority of the urban studies that were undertaken between the 1920s and the 1960s. Even researchers working within its framework, however, sometimes questioned how far urban ecology could go in explaining urban form and urban social life. Some critics noted such problems as the failure to find a model of growth that would apply to all cities (Davie 1938) and the ecologists' inability to make a clear distinction between the biotic and the social levels of social organization (Alihan 1938).

Others thought that human ecology relied too heavily on economic competition among individuals to explain urban patterns, overlooking such shared cultural factors as social prestige and ethnic prejudices (Firey 1945; Hollingshead 1947). Another potential problem has been ecology's tendency toward determinism; that is, seeing social patterns as the outcome of impersonal social forces rather than of decisions made by human beings (Wilhelm 1964). As we shall see, determinism is not confined to human ecology but can be a problem for political economy theories as well.

One critique of human ecology was particularly fruitful in directing later research. In an article published in 1954, William Form argued that human ecologists had ignored the role of social structure, or organized groups, in shaping the city. He contended that real estate groups, big business, residents, and local governments all organize themselves in ways that permit or exclude land uses from locating in urban areas. The most highly institutionalized aspect of this organization is property zoning, through which local governments channel certain land uses to certain areas, regardless of their ability to pay for different locations. What Form questioned was the ecologists' adherence to the assumption of neoclassical economic theory that land use is the natural result of competition in a free market. Rather, Form (1954, 323) proposed that researchers study land use by "isolating the important and powerful land-interested groupings in the city."

By 1970, researchers working within the paradigm of urban ecology had run out of questions that they could answer using their theoretical framework. Several limitations of human ecology prevented researchers from adapting the paradigm to new questions. First, urban ecology's assumption that society followed natural laws, and that it was an outgrowth of the biotic level of life, tended to make researchers ignore the role of human action and decision making on urban patterns. Second, the ecologists' emphasis on describing urban patterns confined them to the superficial questions of *where* different activities took place and how those patterns changed rather than *why* they changed. Third, urban ecology's assumption that competition for land within the market determined the location of different land uses distracted researchers from the important impact that government officials and other powerful actors could have on the city through policy decisions.

As we will see, a new set of urban realities and a new set of questions challenged researchers to develop a new set of theories to explain urban patterns. In the next section, we will turn to the paradigm of political economy and see how and why researchers adopted this new framework.

POLITICAL ECONOMY PARADIGM

Antecedents: Marx, Engels, and Weber

Just as the Chicago School was influenced by the writings of Tönnies, Durkheim, and Simmel, the political economists were influenced by the theories of Karl Marx (1818–1883), Friedrich Engels (1820–1895), and Max Weber (1864–1920). These early writers observed and analyzed the same urban conditions that the classical theorists were examining: the growth of industrial cities, migration from rural to urban areas, physical patterns of urban land use, and social characteristics of urban life. The aspects of the cities they highlighted and their perspectives on them, however, were quite different from those of Tönnies, Durkheim, and Simmel. Both sets of theorists observing the same phenomena were developing different understandings and interpretations of their underlying causes.

In the *Grundrisse* (1971, originally published in 1939), Marx discussed the growth of cities and their connection with the development of industrial capitalism. In his view, trade between towns and the countryside disproportionately benefited the town dwellers, particularly capitalists. Marx identified a division of labor not among individuals (as Durkheim had discussed) but among places, with the towns specializing in producing goods and the rural areas specializing in producing food. In this division of labor, Marx argued, the towns were dominating and exploiting the rural areas. He thought that towns drew surrounding rural areas into their economic webs by encouraging rural dwellers to buy products. To get cash to buy goods, farmers had to produce additional food and sell it in the urban marketplace. In Marx's view, this process made rural dwellers dependent on urban markets to sell their products, and transformed rural life, making it more like town life and less self-sufficient than it had previously been.

Although Marx did not focus his studies directly on cities, some concepts that he introduced in other contexts were later used to analyze urban phenomena. One of these concepts is the distinction between the use value and exchange value of objects. To most people, their home represents a safe and comfortable place to live—it has **use value**. For some people, their home may also represent a financial investment—for them, it has **exchange value**. At times, one person or group gets the use value of a property while a different person gets the exchange value. This is the case with rental property—the person who owns the property lets someone else pay to use it—and it is also the case with property developers, who buy and sell property as their business.

Marx argued that capitalism was converting many material objects into **commodities**, or objects that could be bought and sold for a profit. As a result, possessions such as land and houses had acquired a dual nature: they derived some of their value to owners from the fact that owners could use them for their own needs, and some of their value from the fact that owners could exchange them for cash (Marx 1970).

Another important concept drawn from Marx's writings is the idea that economic systems have inherent **contradictions** that prevent their smooth and consistent functioning. Marx's view of societies is that they are always changing and that the social patterns of any given time are temporary arrangements or compromises among different groups and institutions struggling for gain. To use one of Marx's most famous examples, the growth of industrial capitalism in the eighteenth century created a new social class—namely, the urban industrial working class, or proletariat. The creation of this class benefited the employer class, or bourgeoisie, because the employers needed workers. Furthermore, employers were able to make profits by paying workers low wages. Marx pointed out the contradiction inherent in capitalist economic systems between the need for a working class, the need to pay its members low wages, and the possibility for political and economic upheaval as this class grew and as the members became aware of their exploitation. The contradiction in this example is that the "solution" to one problem (the need for cheap and plentiful labor) leads to another problem (the potential for the workers to get out of control), for which a new "solution" will be found, which will generate a new set of problems, and so on in a never-ending series of historical changes.

Friedrich Engels, who worked with Marx, studied and wrote about urban patterns. Engels took an empirical approach, mapping the spatial patterns and describing the social life of England's growing industrial cities, or as he called them, the "great towns." His most vivid discussion is of the relationship between work, social class, and living conditions in Manchester, described in *The Condition of the Working Class in England* (1958, originally published in 1848). He found that the workers' residences were confined to the smallest, least accessible streets in the unhealthiest and least desirable physical locations of the city; whereas the more substantial residences of the industrialists occupied the cleaner, more desirable, and more centrally located main streets.

Engels's analysis of this pattern was that the employer class had arranged the city in a way that permitted the workers to live near their places of employment but that also kept them hidden, off the main streets, so that the employers would not have to see their miserable living conditions. Employers could do this not simply because they had the ability to pay more for individual parcels of land (as the neoclassical economists would argue) but because as a group they held economic, political, and social domination over the town, and thus could control its spatial layout. Engels rejected the notion that urban land use was simply a matter of the process of bidding for land in an impersonal marketplace. Instead, he pointed us toward a more fundamental mechanism of the social, economic, and political domination of one social class over another. To Engels, the economic and social relations of the workplace, in which the employers dominated the workers, formed a foundation for all other aspects of life, including urban patterns.

The third important ancestor of contemporary political economy was Max Weber, whose theories made both direct and indirect contributions to research on cities. His most direct discussion of cities is found in the essay "Die Stadt" (The City) (1958). In it, Weber set out the idea that a city cannot be defined by a single dimension, such as population size. He argued that settlements recognized as cities have, throughout history, played both economic and political roles: They have served as markets for trade and as seats of government. Thus the essence of the city lies not in its size alone but also in its economic and political functions. Without these institutions, even sizeable communities would be socially insignificant and not truly cities.

Besides his essay on cities, Weber has had additional impacts on scholars' analyses of urban life. Weber's work on social inequality, for example, has contributed to significant research and theorizing about urban life. Weber agreed with Marx that modern societies were shot through with social and economic inequalities, but he disagreed about the relative importance of different aspects of social inequality. While Marx argued that workplace relations were fundamental in creating and maintaining inequality, Weber thought that multiple, somewhat independent sources of inequality existed. He pointed out that, although class (or economic position) significantly influenced people's lives, other factors such as social status and political power were also influential (1946). Later theorists used Weber's insights to examine urban patterns of inequality and conflict based on social divisions such as race, ethnicity, and religion as well as those based on class divisions.

In the United States the field of urban sociology developed from the 1920s to the 1960s without much reference to the works of Marx, Engels, and Weber (Abu-Lughod 1991). Not until the 1960s did a number of urbanists begin to recognize in these theorists' writings concepts that would help create a new paradigm for urban studies. An important reason for their discovery of these three theorists is that both the intellectual environment and the social environment had changed, encouraging scholars to ask different questions and to reexamine some fundamental assumptions about cities.

Emergence of Urban Political Economy

In the United States two sources contributed to the growth of the paradigm of political economy. The first was the limitations researchers had discovered on human ecology's ability to explain urban patterns. The second was the challenge presented to urbanists by the ever-changing conditions of urban life. During the 1960s and 1970s, new social and political developments arose that channeled sociological thinking in new directions. Some researchers found that they could not address new and significant questions through the paradigm of urban ecology, so they sought other approaches.

By 1960, the social and economic context of cities was different from the context of the 1920s, when the ecologists developed their theories. One difference was that suburban communities had grown steadily, relative to the central cities. After World War II, suburban growth accelerated while central city populations began to stabilize or decline. Resources that had long been identified with the city relocated to suburban areas. Many companies closed their urban facilities and built new plants in suburban locations. Housing construction crossed city boundaries into surrounding areas. With jobs and housing moving to the suburbs, large segments of the population followed, especially white middle-class homeowners. Some central cities experienced population declines, abandoned properties, and shrinking tax bases.

How to explain suburban growth? Human ecologists stressed the availability of automobile transportation, linking it to the process of adaptation to territory. In their view, new (suburban) territory became inhabitable because a new transportation technology had made it accessible. Political economists broadened the question of suburbanization to include related factors. They asked why and how automobiles had become dominant as a means of transportation. They asked how changes in the economy had encouraged companies to move to suburban locations. They asked how the federal government's highway policies and housing policies encouraged the growth of the suburbs. They argued that researchers had to look beyond the growth patterns themselves and examine the context that made it possible for suburban areas to grow (Jackson 2009; Mollenkopf 1983).

A second social trend that pointed the political economists in a new direction was the increasing racial polarization in urban areas. The Chicago School ecologists had more frequently studied immigrant neighborhoods than African-American neighborhoods, because the population of Chicago and other U.S. cities in the 1920s contained many more immigrants than African Americans. By the 1960s, however, the proportions were reversed, due to both drastic cutbacks in the numbers of immigrants and the migration of large numbers of African Americans from rural areas to cities. In addition, racial segregation had developed into more than just a matter of where people lived. The inner-city ghettos had become powerful symbols of the lack of social and economic opportunity for African Americans. One response of African Americans to this pervasive pattern of inequality was the nonviolent protests of the civil rights movement; another response was widespread urban social unrest. From 1964 to 1970, racial segregation and poor economic conditions precipitated rioting in the African-American neighborhoods of some forty North American cities.

The early human ecologists had thought that racial segregation, like ethnic segregation, would lessen with time, but later ecological studies showed that racial segregation had actually intensified (Taeuber and Taeuber 1965). Why had many white members of ethnic minority groups been able to move out of their inner-city neighborhoods while large numbers of African Americans were confined to racially segregated ghettos? Human ecology could not answer this question.

A third source of new thinking about the cities was the changing role of the government in urban affairs. In the 1920s the federal government had few if any policies oriented specifically toward cities. Local governments had just begun to develop some basic policies such as planning and zoning regulations. Over the next three decades, however, the federal government took on an increasingly active role, influencing such aspects of urban life as housing construction, highway location, and urban redevelopment. Some government actions seemed to exacerbate problems—for example, demolishing low-cost housing in the name of eliminating slums but replacing it with high-cost housing that was out of the reach of former residents. As government agencies became larger and government's role in urban life became more pervasive, the ecological assumption that urban patterns are the outcome of free market competition between different groups became questionable (Mollenkopf 1983).

A fourth trend that laid the groundwork for a political economy approach to urban issues was the changing nature of the economy and its impacts on cities. Beginning in 1973 with a recession and high rates of unemployment, the industrial jobs that had provided a livelihood for several generations of urban residents dramatically declined in number. Some of those jobs, as we have seen, moved from the cities to the suburbs; some moved from one region of the United States to another; some moved overseas or to Mexico; some simply disappeared due to changing technology and changing market demands. As researchers investigated urban social conditions such as poverty and inequality, they found that local conditions within neighborhoods and households were strongly influenced by the larger economic context. Thus, the ecologists' focus on individual cities and areas within cities was too narrow to take in the big picture (Cowie and Heathcott 2003; Bluestone and Harrison 1984).

A final set of influences on the emerging paradigm was the changing trajectory of cities around the world, particularly in the poor, nonindustrialized countries of the third world. Scholars had approached cities in other countries, looking for similarities and differences—but particularly for similarities—with cities of the United States. Yet by the 1960s it became apparent that many cities in the less industrialized countries were not only not similar to North American cities, they were becoming increasingly different from them. Researchers became dissatisfied with the assumption that less developed nations, including their cities, would become more like those of the industrialized world and instead asked why they were different. These and other changes in urban realities prompted scholars to ask the new questions and develop the new paradigm.

The new paradigm grew steadily throughout the 1980s and 1990s, and it was not until the late 1990s that a consensus about the name of the new approach seemed to develop. Although today most scholars use the term *political economy* to describe the paradigm (Walton 1993; Flanagan 1993), others have used *new urban sociology* (Smith 1995; Gottdiener and Hutchison 2000), others have viewed themselves simply as *neo-Marxist* or *neo-Weberian*, and others as *critical theorists*. These different labels, however, reflected different emphases within a single paradigm rather than the proliferation of competing paradigms.

Promise and Limitations of Political Economy

What defines the political economy paradigm? David Smith (1995) proposed five points of agreement among political economists. They include:

1. **Cities are situated in a hierarchical global system.** Much has been made of globalization as a fact of modern life, and at the "top" of the system are "global" cities such as New York, London, and Tokyo. These cities are home to many of the world's largest corporations and financial markets. Cities of national and regional importance are below them in the hierarchy, and are to a considerable extent dependent upon global cities for investment (Sassen 2001). Studies of smaller cities and towns have similarly shown dependence on the global system for investment and economic development (Tauxe 1993; Thomas 2003).

2. **The global system is one of competitive capitalism.** Cities are not only characterized by the benefits provided by a capitalist economy, but by the conflicts inherent in capitalism as well. Such conflicts between social classes are important for cities. Employer–employee issues such as the formation of labor unions, contract negotiations, strikes, wage levels, and numbers of jobs added or lost are reflections of conflicts between social classes and have serious economic consequences for communities. Conflicts among racial and ethnic groups can be expressed openly (as violence) or covertly

(as discrimination). They affect urban patterns because they channel people, housing, jobs, and other resources into certain geographic areas. People sometimes react to submerged conflicts or perceived inequalities by organizing for action in social movements. Urban social movements are the attempts of groups to increase their economic and political power—to shape the city and its resources in their favor. Cities have even been identified as the hub of such struggles over systemic resources (Castells 1983).

3. **Capital is easily moved, but cities are locationally fixed.** As economies have been restructured due to new transportation and communications technologies, cities have had to struggle with increased competition from other cities. Several shifts have been occurring simultaneously. A particularly important shift is the globalization of the economy, or an increase in the number of economic transactions taking place across national borders. Another is the consolidation of corporations within industries, with a shift from many medium-sized firms to a smaller number of large firms. In the United States, restructuring has also involved a decline in manufacturing industries and an increase in service industries. Economic restructuring has many implications for cities. It has affected the location of jobs, which has in turn affected the growth and decline of cities and regions. It has changed the types of jobs people have, thus contributing to a wider gap between the rich and poor and between whites and people of color. It has changed people's expectations of local government by adding the task of managing the community's economic base to the government's responsibilities.

4. **Politics and government matter.** Government (in the broadest sense, including laws, programs, spending priorities, and other actions) plays a role in where people live, where businesses locate, what type of housing is available, how racial and ethnic groups relate to each other, and many other urban phenomena. Local politics is a key arena for observing conflicts over resources. Even when a discussion seems to be about the common good, participants often define the common good in ways that are favorable to their own goals and interests. In complex societies like the United States, Canada, and European nations, federal or national governments have great power to influence what happens in cities. Because they spend a good deal of money and can establish rules for other investors, government agencies are significant shapers of urban life.

5. **People and circumstances differ according to time and place, and these differences matter.** Cities are shaped by decision making, especially the decisions made by powerful actors who control resources. These may be individual actors, such as investors, or they may be institutions, such as banks, schools, corporations, or government agencies. Decisions that involve investing money are particularly important in shaping cities. Cities have also taken different forms at different times, depending on the institutions prevalent at that time.

These basic items form a point of departure from which different scholars have gone in different directions. Although certain researchers have interpreted some of these points differently, they still agree with the overall paradigm. For example, let us see how scholars have investigated the proposition that cities are part of the political, economic, and social arrangements of their time. The following is one interpretation:

> Cities are influenced by the mode of production.

The mode of production, Marx's term for the economic system, includes the machinery, money, markets, and also the norms, laws, and social relations that accompany different economic systems. The mode of production currently operating in the United States and Europe is advanced capitalism, which is characterized by the dominance of large firms and the operation of a global economy.

British geographer David Harvey (1978) investigated why advanced capitalist cities have spurts of building construction. He argues that businesses normally reinvest their profits into machinery and raw materials, but that at certain times they make more profits than they can reinvest in equipment. As a response to this large profit, companies shift some of their investment out of the actual production of products and into building new buildings for offices or new facilities for production. When many companies make this decision simultaneously, motivated by their similar economic situations, urban building booms occur, as happened in the United States in the 1920s, 1960s, 1980s, and 2000–2005.

An alternative interpretation of the proposition that cities are part of the political, economic, and social arrangements of their time exists:

> In American society, cities are growth machines.

This interpretation emphasizes the way politics and the economy interact in shaping cities. John Logan and Harvey Molotch (2007; see also Molotch 1976) contend that cities are machines for economic growth and are built, shaped, and maintained by groups of people who stand to benefit from that growth. These pro-growth elites consist largely of business owners who need population growth to keep their businesses profitable, including the real estate, hotel, and restaurant industries, retail shops, newspapers, sports franchises, and banks. They support growth by becoming influential in local politics and using their influence to advance a pro-growth agenda for cities.

A third alternative interpretation is the following:

> Real estate development and government intervention
> are the most important influences in metropolitan areas.

This interpretation is part of the **sociospatial perspective**, associated with sociologists Mark Gottdiener (2000) and Joe Feagin (1988). The sociospatial perspective is similar to political economy in some ways, but it emphasizes physical space and how space can be manipulated to affect urban life. In contrast with the growth machine perspective, for example, the sociospatial perspective holds that real estate developers and local government officials are much more influential in changing the form and function of cities than are the many other businesses that might be included in a pro-growth elite. Further, in contrast with Harvey's emphasis on the mode of production as affecting urban change, the sociospatial perspective emphasizes people's understanding of space, including the ways in which local cultures differ in the symbolic meanings they attach to different spaces. Thus, rather than confining the analysis to political and economic factors causing the urban change, the sociospatial perspective adds cultural factors such as symbols and meanings to the analysis of urban life.

No single perspective has the answer to why cities grow, but all three have made significant contributions to understanding the issue of urban growth. Although their specific questions differ, each is consistent with the general assumption that cities are part of the political, economic, and social arrangements of their time.

The paradigm of urban political economy has grown in acceptance among researchers in recent years and has helped researchers address questions that were outside of ecology's scope. This paradigm, however, is far from perfect. It has two main problems that critics have noted. First, within political economy, it is easy to overemphasize the uniformity with which large-scale political and economic factors affect cities and neighborhoods, while ignoring local variations. As we will see, large-scale concepts such as the mode of production cannot explain fully the differences between different cities that are within the same mode of production. Second, within political economy it is easy to lose sight of the individual actor and the links between the macrolevel and microlevel of human existence. Just because sociologists categorize people as belonging to the same group (e.g., the working class), do these people think and act similarly? Although some political economists downplay questions of meaning and motive, others argue that we must explain why people take the actions they take. Critics within political economy as well as those outside it have pinpointed these problems, and researchers are increasingly trying to avoid them in their work (Pahl 1989; Flanagan 1993; Walton 1993).

POSTMODERNIST APPROACHES

One of the important developments in sociological theory since 1980 has been the growth of a paradigm referred to as "postmodernism." Grounded in an interdisciplinary approach and heavily influenced by the humanities, particularly literary criticism, postmodern approaches to architecture and urban form became prominent during the last quarter of the twentieth century. Fredric Jameson (1991) discussed at length a break between the logic of "culture" under "modernism" and how this differed from a new, "**postmodern**" reality. Similarly, Sharon Zukin (1991) extended such concerns to postmodern landscapes by noting how historical processes and modes of production under capitalism combined with new economic and social arrangements to create landscapes that reflected past and present relations of power. According to Zukin, for instance, a city that has lost its industrial base reflects not only an economic event, but a cultural and political event as well: economic relations make it possible for a company to move a plant from one city to another, and the culture and politics of a place influence how the city will respond.

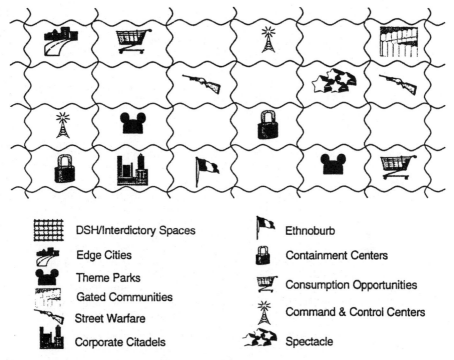

DSH/Interdictory Spaces		Ethnoburb	
Edge Cities		Containment Centers	
Theme Parks		Consumption Opportunities	
Gated Communities			
Street Warfare		Command & Control Centers	
Corporate Citadels		Spectacle	

F I G U R E 2.4 Cognitive Maps in Postmodern Urban Theory. Cognitive maps are an important feature of postmodern theories, such as this map representation of a multinucleated city. Dear (2002) Los Angeles and the Chicago School: Invitation to a Debate, *City and Community*, 1, pp. 5–32.

Postmodern approaches, sometimes collected under the name "Los Angeles School" because many of the studies were based in the city, are varied but tend to agree on five key aspects:

1. **Cognitive Maps.** Postmodernist approaches are often concerned with how spaces fit with one another and how they can be "mapped" by individuals navigating the city. In this regard, most theorists see the postmodern city as "fragmented" into discontinuous corporate spaces that have little relationship to one another (Dear & Flusty 1998; Soja and Scott 1996). Consider, for example, a suburban commercial district divided as it is into differing shopping centers, malls, office buildings, restaurants, and gas stations—a complex arrangement of places that do not relate to the surrounding landscape (Garreau 1991). For many postmodernists, it is ironic that such corporate-owned spaces as hotels, restaurants, and stores are designed to create a unique corporate identity but by doing so contribute to the sense that every suburban strip looks rather similar to every other strip. Consider a similar scene at a larger scale as residential areas are separated from one another because they are in different subdivisions or belong to gated communities (Davis 2006).
    A shown in Figure 2.4, the discontinuity of functions across space is stressed.

B o x 2.1 • Spotlight
Paradigms for Understanding Cities

This chapter outlines the differences between the human ecology, political economy, and postmodernist paradigms as ways of understanding cities. The following excerpts are examples of work in each perspective.

Human Ecology
A natural area is a geographical area characterized both by a physical individuality and by the cultural characteristics of the people who live in it. Studies in various cities have shown, to quote Robert E. Park, that "Every American city of a given size tends to reproduce all the typical areas of all the cities, and that the people in these cities exhibit, from city to city, the same cultural characteristics, the same types of institutions, the same social types, with the same opinions, interests, and outlook on life." That is, just as there is a plant ecology whereby, in the struggle for existence, like geographical regions become associated with like "communities" of plants, mutually adapted, and adapted to the area, so there is a human ecology whereby, in the competition of the city and according to definable processes, the population of the city is segregated over natural areas into natural groups. And these natural areas and natural groups are the "atoms" of city growth, the units we try to control in administering and planning for the city.

SOURCE: Harvey W. Zorbaugh, "The Natural Area of the City," *Publications of the American Sociological Society*, XX (1926) 188–97, reprinted in *Studies in Human Ecology*, ed. by G. Theodorson, (New York, Harper & Row, 1961), p. 47.

Political Economy
The reality of places is constructed through political action, with the term political encompassing both individual and collective efforts, through both informal associations and institutions of government and the economy. In explaining individual stratification and occupational hierarchy, scholars have offered a familiar wisdom that unequal occupational rewards inspire those with the most individual talent (brains, wit, persistence) to do the most difficult (and highest-paying) work, making the whole system more productive as a result. Systems of places have also been portrayed (by the ecologists) as differently endowed, some having such inherent advantages as centrality, mineral resources, or intersecting trade routes. Such qualities make them rise to the top among the places, becoming bigger and higher priced than their inferior competitors. . . .

We have a different way of explaining the two systems of hierarchy and how they are connected. Markets among individuals are socially structured (given oligopoly, racism, inheritance, and so forth). Rich people use their wealth to send their children to good schools, to provide themselves with excellent health care,

---

2. **Economic Restructuring and Globalization.** Postmodernism is very concerned with the dislocation—such as the movement of investment in factories and other corporate spaces—caused by economic and cultural changes collectively called "economic restructuring." These dislocations have been the result of new technologies in transportation and

and to keep others from usurping their privileges. This leads to longer lives, higher IQ scores, and happier days. As a result, they do better in the individual competition. The inequality among individuals thus not only results from differentiation but also causes it. Similarly, place inequality is both cause and consequence of differences among places. Those in control of the top places use place status to maintain privileges for their locations, often at the expense of the lesser locales. Often with the help of place-based organizations, they manipulate transportation routes, secure desired zoning, and keep out unwanted social groups.

The two systems of hierarchy are connected through the tendency for individual and place status to reinforce each other. Advantage in one can be used to develop advantage in the other. High status within the social hierarchy can bring access to the most desirable places (for residence or investment) and a guarantee of a rewarding future for whatever place one controls. At the same time a high status for one's geographical place means the availability of resources (rents, urban services, prestige) that enhance life chances generally.

SOURCE: John R. Logan and Harvey L. Molotch, *Urban Fortunes: The Political Economy of Place* (Berkeley, CA: University of California Press, 2007), pp. 48–49.

Postmodernism

The opposition between market and place is built into postmodernism. That is why no single landscape can control the difference between "outrageous" and "contextual" postmodern architecture, why one part of postmodern cultural style—that is, fragility, degradation, fragmentation—can refer to deindustrialization while another part—that is, the decentering of pluralism, the preeminence of visual over literal codes, and the freewheeling appropriation of different artistic modes—describes a postindustrial society. Postmodernism inspires two market cultures, each with its own practice, aesthetic, and political implications. Between "a postmodernism of resistance and a postmodernism of reaction" lies the unresolved ambiguity of market and place as loci of creative destruction. Perhaps postmodernism is best understood as the landscape of contemporary economic transformation: as both an uncertain social context and an ironic perspective on it.

This suggests an interior as well as a material landscape. Conveying a sense of rupture and discontinuity, and taking for granted that progress is fragile, the postmodern symbolic landscape represents the same destruction of longevity, of cultural layers, and of vested interests that opposes market to place.

SOURCE: Sharon Zukin. *Landscapes of Power: From Detroit to Disney World* (Berkeley, CA: University of California Press, 1993), p. 27.

communications that have made it easier for corporations to locate facilities in regions of the world where they can maximize their profits. For instance, a computer corporation may be headquartered in New York, maintain research facilities in Silicon Valley in California, manufacture the products in China, and rely on customer service agents in India. The restructuring of the economy has had an impact on many cities, particularly those heavily reliant on manufacturing, as plants close or move, disrupting employment and community life.

3. **Multiculturalism.** Postmodern theories are also concerned with the experience of diversity in cities, both in terms of segregation and in terms of how groups come together. This is particularly true of the experience of recent immigrants who have arrived because of dislocations in their home countries caused by the globalization of the economy. To the fundamental economic and political processes underlying urban form, postmodern theories add layers of cultural, religious, linguistic, and symbolic processes. They tend to see cities as less defined by economic differences among groups and more like a "prism" through which groups interact on multiple dimensions.

4. **Los Angeles as indicative of postmodern geography and future trends.** Not necessarily all postmodernists have accepted this claim, but those advocating a "Los Angeles" School of urbanism have been particularly vocal in such claims (Dear 2002, 2003; Soja 1996). Los Angeles is seen as a model of metropolitan fragmentation and spectacular places with little relationship of one place to another. Composed of multiple urban "cores" rather than one dominant downtown area, it is thought that future cities will also be "regional" rather than centered on one preeminent locality.

Criticisms of the Los Angeles School have focused on the use of Los Angeles to model urbanism (Beauregard 2003). Postmodernists have been critical of the Chicago School and urban ecology, yet have similarly been quite interested in urban form and the way in which residents perceive and live in the city. Postmodernism also tends to be rather flamboyant, and adherents to the Los Angeles School share this with other postmodern scholars. For instance, Dear & Flusty (1998) associate the following with postmodern urbanism: Global Latifundia, Holsteinization, Praedatorianism, Flexism, New World Bipolar Disorder, Memetic Contagion, Keno Capitalism, Citistat, Pollyanarchy, and the Disinformation Superhighway. This in part reflects an emphasis on avoiding former terms that carry unwanted cultural connotations and the desire to better specify observations, and is in part also related to an emphasis on rhetoric to critique social institutions (see Dear 2003). Postmodernist approaches also seem to repeat themes found in past research. For instance, Herbert Gans, in his 1962 classic *The Urban Villagers*, discussed how residents of Boston's West End perceived their neighborhood in a manner similar to cognitive maps, and political economists have long been interested in economic restructuring (Bluestone & Harrison 1984).

Postmodern urbanism, however, should not be understood as having the same goal as earlier paradigms in urban sociology. A trend can be intuited from the Chicago School to the Los Angeles School. In the early twentieth century, many sociologists perceived themselves as scientists concerned with general laws, and urban ecologists were therefore concerned with *explaining* how cities developed and functioned. Although their theories apply best only to capitalist cities, specifically fast-growing American cities, many sociologists at the time believed themselves to be working on more general propositions. Similarly, early political economists offered an alternative view on how cities grow and function that was by and large specific to capitalist cities, but nevertheless hoped to *explain* these processes. As a paradigm, postmodernism has been influenced more by the humanities than by the sciences, and as such the overarching goal has not been to *explain* urbanization but to *critique* postmodern society, cities and all. Seen in this light, the Los Angeles School offers invaluable insights into contemporary society, but its goals are not as ambitious as those of earlier urban ecologists and political economists.

CONCLUSION

Theories are useful for studying cities because they help us fit disparate ideas and pieces of information together into a larger picture. Urban sociology currently has two dominant paradigms—urban ecology and urban political economy—being used simultaneously to guide research. Increasingly, a postmodernist approach is also being developed and guiding research in cities around the world. The questions asked within all three paradigms overlap a great deal: Where do people live and work? How and why do cities change? How do different groups get along with each other?

This text is written with a political economy orientation uppermost in mind. The topics have been selected and the research reviewed with the goal of including the most significant advances in political economy. Nevertheless, the questions and contributions of the urban ecologists that have so greatly shaped the field are still important—partly as a foundation of valuable empirical research and partly as a pathway to address questions that are not within the realm of a political economy approach. Because of their important contributions to the field, the works of ecologists along with those of political economists are included in these pages.

DISCUSSION QUESTIONS

1. Examine the three ecological models of urban form: concentric zones, sectors, and multiple nuclei. What do you think is the benefit to analysts of identifying a model that describes the land use of a great number of cities? If you were to compare these models to a city with which you are familiar, which model do you think would most closely fit? Are there elements of the city's layout that would not fit?

2. Theories often contain a few basic assumptions about how the world works. What are the implications of assuming that cities are a part of the natural world, governed by natural forces? What are the implications of assuming that cities are the product of political and economic structures? What are the implications of assuming that cities are formed by human decisions?

3. Engels thought that the people with money and political power in a city determined the locations of residential neighborhoods, including poor and working-class neighborhoods. Do you see any evidence of this in urban areas today? Why or why not?

PART II

The Changing City:

Historical and Comparative Perspectives

3

Cities in World History

With the exception of a few isolated survivors, the rise
of the civilizations transformed the precivilized peoples.
We may think of civilization as a remaking of man in which
the basic type, the folk man, is altered into other types....
This remaking of man was the work of the city.
ROBERT REDFIELD
THE PRIMITIVE WORLD AND ITS TRANSFORMATIONS

Have you ever traveled to other countries? Have you seen movies that take place in different parts of the world? If so, you have probably noticed the striking differences among cities. One way cities differ is physically: different forms, locations, sizes. Another way they differ is socially: different ways of relating to other people, different ways of making a living, different forms of authority. Why do these differences exist? What causes the physical forms and urban cultures to develop along different paths? Why do these urban characteristics change over time?

Scholars have tried to answer these questions for centuries and are still finding new evidence about the origins, history, and development of cities. A few general principles are well known. First, economic, political, and cultural factors have interacted in shaping the location, layout, and lifestyles in cities. Second, each city must be seen in the context of its own society and within a worldwide system of cities. Third, cities have many different reasons for being, including trade, administration, defense, religious ceremonies, goods production, information coordination, or some combination of these purposes.

This chapter will provide a brief overview and history of cities from the earliest known settlements to the rapidly changing cities of today. It will focus on the following questions:

- When and where were cities first established?
- How are cities different from other types of communities?

- How have cities changed over time?
- What similarities and differences do we find in cities in different parts of the world?

ORIGINS OF CITIES

It is important to realize that although social scientists refer to the origins of cities as the "urban revolution," the evolution of cities was a process that took thousands of years to unfold. In fact, though we tend to see cities as a natural part of the human experience, the growth of cities has required considerable adaptation on our part (Massey 2005). This is evident in examining the periods in which major milestones on the path from a nomadic lifestyle to settled communities were reached. For instance, the first "sedentary" community, a small village in which people resided throughout the year, dates to 21,500 B.C. at Ohalo II in modern Israel (Nadel 2003). The first evidence of domesticated crops is from Abu Hureyra in modern Syria in about 10,500 B.C., although such crops did not become widespread for another thousand years (Moore, Gillman, and Legge 2000). The earliest domesticated agricultural animals, sheep and goats, appeared in the mountains of modern Iran about 8500 B.C. and gradually spread (Zeder and Hesse 2000).

Ohalo II was a site of perhaps 120 year-round residents living on the shores of the Sea of Galilee in what is now Israel. As agriculture was over ten thousand years in the future, these early villagers chose the location because of its benefits to their hunting and gathering lifestyle: Ohalo II was convenient for fishing, hunting thirsty game animals, trapping a variety of small animals, and hunting birds and their eggs. A number of ecological niches were within walking distance, and this meant that a real diversity of food and raw materials was nearby (Nadel 2003). After Ohalo II, however, there is no evidence of sedentary villages until after 12,500 B.C., a culture known as the Natufian. The Natufian economy was similar to that of Ohalo II, and Natufian villages were also found in places where a variety of ecological niches were available, often near water with access to more mountainous areas as well in what is now Israel and Jordan. It was during the Natufian, stretching from 12,500 B.C. to 9500 B.C., that the first evidence of cereal cultivation is found at a site called Abu Hureyra in modern Syria about 10,500 B.C. (Moore, Gillman, and Legge 2000). Even so, it was not until about a thousand years later that an economy based on plant agriculture became widespread, and another thousand years after that when animal husbandry became widespread.

It was during the Neolithic, specifically a period known as the Pre-Pottery Neolithic A (or PPNA) that lasted from 9500 B.C. to 8500 B.C., that the first large settlements appeared. Perhaps the most famous was Jericho, a village of approximately eight hundred residents that began as a Natufian encampment by a spring. Jericho of the PPNA sported a sizable plaza with storage silos at one side and a 30-foot tower and wall by the outer edge of the village. Although the wall was at one time thought to be defensive, later research has demonstrated it to be a barrier against floods (Bar Yosef 1986). Agriculture appears to have been a collective activity arranged through a highly variable power structure based on religion: such social organization was necessary not only in order to farm, but also to build the public structures discussed above. "Membership" in the villages appears to have been based on ancestry, as certain family members associated with a household were buried beneath the floor of the house, the skulls of ancestors coated with plaster or a natural asphalt called "bitumen" in order to "reanimate" the individual and be used in household rituals. By making such a claim on the house, a family could also claim the rights and responsibilities of community membership; in a sense, the house was the family's "stock" in the village (Cauvin 2000).

As some villages grew to nearly a thousand residents during the Neolithic, they were also home to new innovations. At Mureybet, a village of nearly one thousand residents around 8500 B.C., the world's first rectilinear architecture, rather than circular or oval huts, was used in storage silos and later in homes. At about the same time, at Mureybet and other related sites in modern Syria, Iraq, and Turkey, small clay tokens were used as accounting and mnemonic devices. Shortly after, the first "stamp seals," carvings in wood or clay that were impressed in clay to create a uniform design, were also in use (Cauvin 2000). By 6000 B.C., a handful of sites had as many as eight thousand residents. At Catal Hoyuk in what is today Turkey, for instance, trade in obsidian—a volcanic stone that even today is renowned for the sharpness of its blade—helped the village grow to nearly eight thousand residents at its peak (Hodder 2006). During the lifetime of this village, the use of pottery for tools and vessels became common, a major improvement for modern scientists seeking to identify differing cultures but a relatively minor advance for the people themselves.

The later phase of the Neolithic, from about 6000 B.C. to 5000 B.C., was a period in which small agricultural towns were the norm throughout the Fertile Crescent. The largest of these communities were home to as many as five thousand residents or more, but most villages contained perhaps a few hundred residents. Away from the villages were bands of nomadic herders who would drive their sheep and goats from pasture to pasture, occasionally stopping in villages along their route to trade. The region of northern Syria and Iraq was home to the Halaf culture, and to the east was the Samarra culture. It was the Samarra culture that used the elaborate trade system to gradually settle the desert areas further south between the Tigris and Euphrates Rivers, eventually developing a rudimentary irrigation system that enabled the culture to spread into the fertile but dry soils of southern Mesopotamia. As the Samarra culture spread south, it evolved into the Ubaid culture, which thrived during the fifth millennium B.C. and then spread back to the north and eventually supplanted the earlier Halaf and Samarra cultures (Akkermans & Schwartz 2003). With the Ubaid culture we see the expansion of a sophisticated irrigation network and agricultural fields arranged in long furrows to support it (Liverani 2006). The Ubaid also witnessed

F I G U R E 3.1   **The citadel of Erbil, Iraq, the capital of Iraqi Kurdistan.** The city was first settled as a small agricultural village in the seventh millennium B.C. and is thus one of the oldest cities in the world. The citadel sits atop a tell, a mound formed from the accumulation of debris formed from the settlement over thousands of years.

an expansion of the power of the temple as religion became more important in organizing community members to work in the fields; it is likely that the priesthood and even some artisans were, for the first time, freed from agricultural work in order to concentrate on their other responsibilities. As such, the earliest forms of social stratification can be dated to this period. Nevertheless, the largest Ubaid villages were no more populous than ten thousand residents, and the vast majority of villages contained no more than a few hundred people (Pollock 1999).

EARLY CITIES

The earliest cities arose during the fourth millennium B.C., during a time called the "Uruk Period" after its largest city, in Mesopotamia (see Figure 3.1). With about 50 thousand residents in 3100 B.C., the city of Uruk dominated the region, but numerous smaller cities also dotted the landscape. Most cities were in southern Mesopotamia, such as Ur, Lagash, and Eridu, where the fertile alluvial soil provided by the annual flooding of the Tigris and Euphrates Rivers combined with an extensive system of irrigation and transportation canals to provide an agricultural paradise (in good years) capable of sustaining a large urban population (Pollock 1999). Upstream, several cities have also been found in northern Mesopotamia, such as Leilan, Tell Brak, and Hamoukar, demonstrating that urbanization was not solely a southern phenomenon (Ur 2002). The earliest cities were not particularly larger than the largest Ubaid towns, so it is fair to say that what made them "cities" was more than just population. The archaeologist V. Gordon Childe (1950) constructed a list of attributes that made cities different. They include:

1. **Early cities were, in relation to neighboring communities, geographically and demographically larger.** This was true in ancient Mesopotamia, and is still true today (Fall et al. 1998). Urban sociologists today discuss this in terms of globalization (Sassen 1994, 2008; Abrahamson 2004), and the relationship between cities and the countryside also speak to the validity of this characteristic (e.g., Thomas 2003; Tauxe 1993).

2. **Early cities exhibited a division of labor that includes individuals who do not work the fields for their own sustenance, such as priests, artisans, and administrators.** This trait was in actuality found before the rise of cities in the mid-fourth millennium B.C. (Maisels 1990, 1999; Pollock 1999).

3. **Each producer granted the agricultural surplus to a ruling elite through tax or tithe.** In Uruk, in about 3500 B.C., the organization of agriculture had evolved into kinship-based urban syndicates. Members of these syndicates contributed to a central authority and then redistributed food with standardized rations bowls (called bevel-rimmed bowls).

4. **Early cities contained monumental buildings.** If one looks for "public" buildings prior to cities, there is an abundance of examples. The earliest examples of monumental architecture in Mesopotamia—the temples—were in many cases built atop older temples dating back to the preurban Ubaid Period (5000–4000 B.C.). In other words, monumental architecture is notable for the scale of building and the capital required to do so, but it was a continuation of practices predating cities by thousands of years.

5. **Cities were characterized by social stratification, including a ruling class.** There was certainly a ruling class in the earliest Mesopotamian cities, but defining a ruling class is difficult. The temple elites of the preurban Ubaid period seem to qualify, but Ubaid settlements were not as stratified as later Uruk period cities. We are again faced with a long evolution, and singling out Mesopotamian cities as having a ruling class might actually be a little late given the true origins of such stratification.

6. **The culture of cities included the use of writing and numbers.** Full-fledged writing is found at Uruk, but the precedents predate Uruk by thousands of years. As noted earlier, simple tokens for record keeping from which Cuneiform writing evolved are found as early as 8000 B.C. at the Neolithic settlement of Mureybet.

7. **Cities were home to the creation of Predictive Sciences.** The emergence of such sciences as astronomy, used for predicting planting seasons and certain festivals, and mathematics, has its roots in the Neolithic but comes together with the first cities.

8. **In early cities we see a developed artisan class.** There is a general flourishing and increasing sophistication in the arts. This is beyond dispute, but it again builds on innovations from the past. For instance, both stone-work and pottery are innovations inherited by urban societies, and in fact it is generally recognized that the "quality" of pottery production found at Uruk is often lower than in its precursors—a fact that comes from the mass production of such items.

9. **Cities were parts of a long-distance trade network.** As noted earlier, a sophisticated trading network predates Mesopotamian cities by thousands of years, and in fact was a prerequisite of cities.

10. **Cities had a complex division of labor resulting in the presence of organic solidarity.** A certain interdependency of networks of villages for certain goods might have existed before cities, such as during the Halaf period prior to 5000 B.C.

To summarize, Childe's list of urban attributes contains many practices that predated the emergence of true cities. The significance of his list is that it helps us define a city by the presence of all ten attributes.

Although the earliest cities were found in Mesopotamia, they are followed in short order by urban civilizations in Egypt (after 3000 B.C.), the Indus Valley of Pakistan (after 2800 B.C.), and in Greece (after 2000 B.C.) (Maisels 1999). In these and other civilizations, the political control of a city seldom stopped at its borders. From the earliest times, cities had a tendency to expand and incorporate other localities into their spheres of influence. Usually this involved nearby rural land, but beginning over four thousand years ago, political leaders began to conquer and control other cities, forming empires or networks of communities under the control of a single political entity. A succession of warrior-leaders conquered the cities of Mesopotamia, early predecessors of the later Assyrian and Persian empires. Early cities in Egypt, China, and what are now India and Mexico were also parts of empires.

The earliest evidence of territorial expansion is at the northern Mesopotamian site of Hamoukar, a city of about twenty-five thousand people that was destroyed around 3500 B.C. (Ur 2002). The archaeological record shows a local pottery style, indicative of a thriving local culture, ending with a large battle as evidenced by sling balls. Immediately after, Uruk-style pottery and other artifacts are found, indicating a takeover of the site by people from southern Mesopotamia. About one thousand years later, the first detailed account of a war details how the southern Mesopotamian cities of Umma and Lagash, about eighteen miles apart, fought over a complex of fields about midway between the two cities (Pollock 1999). Similarly, urbanization in Mesoamerica has also been tied to the development of warfare and eventually the building of empires (Flannery & Marcus 2003).

Early empires were fragile and had short lives, averaging one or two centuries. Imperial capitals were periodically attacked by outside competitors and sometimes overthrown by internal revolts. The reason that empires continued to exist, however, is that the urban leaders had an interest in expanding the amount of territory they controlled. By attacking a competing city, warrior-rulers could destroy the competitor's military technology and take over parts of its territory, as well as plundering whatever other wealth the competitor had accumulated. This emphasis on imperial expansion made warfare one of the primary activities of the ancient world.

ANCIENT CITIES, 1000 B.C. TO A.D. 300

During the height of what historians refer to as the ancient civilizations, cities served as nodes, or points, within well-defined political empires. Each empire had a central, command city, such as Babylon, Athens, Carthage, Rome, Cheng-Chou, or Harappa, but the other cities in the empire were linked to the center by either land or water routes. The command center, the imperial city, typically would continue to grow in population as long as the empire was expanding (Kotkin 2005). Despite their many differences, stemming from their various histories, cultures, and locations, the ancient imperial centers shared several important structural characteristics.

All major cities in the ancient world shared characteristics that over time came to be associated with civilization itself. Most major cities of the ancient world attempted to grow their staple foods within the local environment, although this became increasingly difficult in such major cities as Athens (Hall 2001) and Rome (Morley 1996). Even with access to luxury foods and other items through the expansive trade network, food production was considered vital to urban health and thus a primary function of the local government (Van de Mieroop 1999). Nearly all ancient cities also functioned as religious centers with each city home to a favored god thought to preside over the city. Often, the ascent of a given city within the hierarchy of cities was also considered to be the ascent of a given deity, and mythologies were rewritten to account for the change. For instance, the Babylonian creation myth, *Enuma Elish*, was an attempt to explain the dominance of Babylon over other cities by explaining the dominance of its patron god, Marduk, over the other gods. Because of the nearly perpetual war, cities also functioned as fortresses into which the local population, urban and rural, would seek safety in case of attack. This meant that ancient cities were centers of power, the largest cities often capitals of empires or provinces within empires.

Cities were also the repository of knowledge, power, wealth, and control in the ancient world. The Greek playwright Euripides is quoted as saying, "The first requisite to happiness is birth in a great city" (quoted in Spates and Macionis 1987, 191). It is easy to see why that was thought to be true. All of the considerable resources and influence of the ancient societies were concentrated in these urban centers. The notions of *government, religion, civilization, family*, and *country* (as in "my country") were closely intertwined for the ancients with the concept of "city." The word *polis*, for example, meant to the Greeks not only a physical city but also a type of government characterized by the domination of a city (Wallace-Hadrill 1991). In Latin the word *civis*, which refers to a city-dweller,

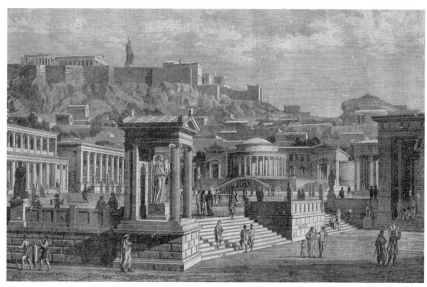

F I G U R E 3.2 The *Agora* of Ancient Athens. This central marketplace of Athens also served as the center of the city's social and political life. .

is also the root for civilization and civility. It is clear that to the ancients, the city was synonymous with the good life.

Physical Features of Ancient Cities

The built environment of the ancient cities was constructed with an eye toward public life. Many spaces and structures were explicitly designed for public use and social interaction: temples for worship, markets for commerce, theaters for entertainment, and fora (the plural of the Latin *forum*) for debate and discussion. Some spaces, such as the *agora* of Athens, shown in Figure 3.2, served multiple public functions. Political leaders frequently created impressive public works and gave citizens access to free goods and services.

The built environment was also a reflection of the nature of the government: highly centralized and militaristic. The cities of ancient Greece, for example, were partially planned, with main roads converging at a marketplace or at a temple. Every city was, by necessity, fortified, surrounded by walls and containing one or more extensive forts located in a high place (*acropolis*). During the frequent wars between rival city-states, the population took refuge within the walled city, living on food stored in the public storehouses. In an environment of centralized political power, the monumental scale and lavish embellishment of the public buildings and facilities not only represented great engineering achievements, but also symbolized the power and authority of the imperial system.

Rome, the largest of the ancient cities, with a peak population estimated at close to one million, undoubtedly had the most advanced physical infrastructure.

The level of Roman public works was the highest of all cities of the ancient world, with fresh water, sewers, public baths, roads, and other services provided by the public treasury. Like Athens, the center of Rome contained plazas, markets, and public buildings such as the Forum and the Coliseum. These majestic structures served as monuments to the power of the empire and also provided free entertainment for the population. Rome, as well as other cities in the empire, such as Ephesus, Carthage, and Alexandria, had population densities approaching that of Manhattan Island in New York City today. Many nonelite inner city residents, or the majority, lived in apartment complexes called *insulae* that grew to as many as seven stories, their residents crowded into small apartments (Stark 2006). Outside of the city center, residential districts were divided by social class, with the wealthy living on Palatine Hill and the less fortunate crowded into densely populated, unplanned, and unsanitary housing (Gates 2003; Goodman 2007).

The Romans were enthusiastic city builders, but rural areas of their empire did not fare as well as did the cities. The growth of the cities and the extensive public works meant that an increasing proportion of the resources of the rural countryside was siphoned off by the city. To supply water for household use and for the all-important public baths, Rome built a system of aqueducts that moved water from the countryside to the cities. To provide the growing urban population with free bread, more territory had to be incorporated into the empire and brought under cultivation. Rural residents did not benefit from this relationship because peasant farmers did not own the land they worked and had to pay rent to the urban property owners. In addition, historians have pointed out the considerable environmental degradation resulting from deforestation and from the cultivation of unsuitable soils, which caused desertification in some regions formerly under Roman control. Some evidence indicates that the resulting overuse of the land was a factor contributing to the vulnerability of the Roman civilization as well as the civilizations of Mesopotamia, China, and Greece (Wallace-Hadrill 1991; Boone & Modarres 2006).

Social Patterns in Ancient Cities

Another characteristic of the ancient cities is that their substantial wealth was available only to the elite. To gain access to the benefits of the society, one had to be a member, which in most cases meant being a citizen, but access to membership was severely restricted. We saw earlier that at ancient Jericho this was determined by ancestry—one's ancestors were literally buried beneath the floor. In later times, citizenship became even more limited. First, it was limited by gender; whereas men had full access to legal rights, women had limited or no access to citizenship and few property rights. Second, membership was limited by descent. The ancient civilizations used patrilineal descent systems, in which male children inherit their fathers' positions, including both property and social obligations. Because the *pater* (Latin for father) gives his *patrimony* (inheritance) to his sons, not only women but also unrelated males were excluded from these higher positions. The class of *patricians* who held power in Rome were thus a hereditary group whose fathers had also belonged to the privileged class. This group was closed both to non-Romans and to Roman residents who were not related to them, or *plebians* (Richard 2005; Mitchell 2005).

An examination of the political and economic institutions of the ancient cities helps to illuminate ancient class inequality. In this precapitalist economy, there was no wage labor, so there was no working class in the modern sense. Nevertheless, social inequality was still pervasive. A small artisan class produced necessary items for household consumption. The real engine of the economy, the means by which public goods and services were produced, however, was coerced slave labor. Slaves were by definition excluded from participation in the political and economic system, despite the fact that they constituted up to three-fourths of the population in Athens at its peak in the fifth century B.C. As in modern cities, social inequality was visible in the physical structure of the city. Many cities were segregated by occupation, and as certain occupations were dominated by certain ethnic groups, this translated into ethnic segregation as well (Van de Mieroop 1999). Similarly, in cities such as Rome, the wealthy lived in luxurious city homes called *villas*, while much of the population lived in high density *insulae*.

Some scholars, following Marx, consider the ancient imperial system to have been a unique mode of production based on the routine use of slavery as a means to increase economic production (Mann 1985). The empires survived by expanding their holdings. The continual wars of the ancient empires were devoted to subduing other peoples by military force and incorporating them into the empire for the purpose of acquiring both additional labor (slaves) and other resources (tribute payments from the colonies). The large number of cities that Rome controlled at its peak was connected by the famous Roman roads throughout Europe, North Africa, and the Middle East.

To summarize, the ancient cities were tied to empires, either as imperial centers or as nodes within the imperial network. They were frequently planned and invariably fortified. The cities, especially the imperial centers, were resource rich, containing high levels of public services and sophisticated, monumental public works. They were also culturally rich, containing the collected wisdom of the society. A strong emphasis was placed on public participation and social life, including the arts.

Notwithstanding the substantial achievements of the ancients, their cities had several characteristics that proved to be problematic over the long run. The high quality of life in the urban centers was supported by the extraction of resources from the countryside. The system relied on the military conquest of ever greater territories and the coercion of the colonies to provide slaves and tribute payments. Full participation in the society was limited to a small fraction of the population. Such a system could indeed build impressive cities, but the very characteristics that permitted the creation of the cities helped to make them vulnerable to decline. Some of the ancient cities vanished rapidly and rather mysteriously. Today, scholars think that famines or diseases may have struck the population. Most of the ancient cities in Europe fell by invasion; they were either plundered until not much remained or were converted into outposts of the conquering people. It is difficult to understand how a large and powerful empire like Rome could fall to invasion, but as many historians have pointed out, internal conflicts and problems had destabilized the system to the point where it was vulnerable to external attack.

When the Roman Empire fell in the fifth century A.D., it was divided into a Western region (Europe) and an Eastern region (Asia Minor and the Middle East). In the eastern part of the empire and around the Mediterranean Sea, urban life continued; but the cities of northern Europe shrank, and the vast majority of the population returned to the land, engaging in agriculture. Some towns still existed in northern Europe, to be sure, but their populations were miniscule compared to what they had been as cities of the Roman Empire, and their social and economic complexity was greatly reduced. Rome itself was reduced to a town of about twenty thousand (Gibbon 1879).

CITIES AROUND THE WORLD

Cities of the Middle East

The capital of the Eastern Roman Empire was Constantinople, named for the Christian emperor, Constantine, and situated in present-day Turkey. During the period after the fall of Rome, while nonurban, so-called barbarian tribes invaded much of the western part of the empire and destroyed its cities, Constantinople and other cities in the eastern part of the empire continued to flourish. They, too, were eventually invaded, but by tribes that maintained and built on existing cities. These eastern settlers were Arabic tribes that had become united into an empire based on the religion of Islam.

The center of the urban world from A.D. 500 to about A.D. 1000 clearly shifted back to the areas of North Africa, the Middle East, and Asia Minor. The Arab conquerors expanded existing cities and built new ones. As the Islamic empire grew, so did its cities. Some of the better-known urban centers were Baghdad, Cairo, Alexandria, and Damascus. The Arabs preserved more than the cities themselves. Advanced urban culture died in many parts of the West. In the East, however, it was kept alive by the Islamic civilization, whose scholars not only preserved the knowledge of the ancients but added many intellectual and artistic innovations of their own (Abu-Lughod 1991). (See Box 3.1.)

Islamic cities of Southwest Asia were dynamic and productive. The architecture of the time produced beautiful buildings arrayed in orderly cities with public amenities such as "mosques, palaces, gardens, fountains, libraries, bridges, and public baths" (Garraty and Gay 1972). Buildings were decorated with graceful arches, tiles, and carvings, and set off with quiet courtyards. Arts and crafts were very sophisticated, with masters producing fine works in materials such as leather, paper, glass, textiles, wood, and metals. The weaving of brocades, tapestries, and carpets was a particularly well-known craft of the time.

Islamic civilization represented a period of great creativity in the arts and sciences. Islamic writers, often basing their work on the Koran, produced many works of literature, particularly poetry and essays. Scientific pursuits included mathematics, medicine, geography, and astronomy. Theology and philosophy

B o x   3.1   •   Spotlight
Islamic Cities

By about A.D. 700, only a century or so after the birth of Muhammad, Islam had spread northward to encompass the Fertile Crescent and westward along the North African coast to reach the Atlantic. . . . As in earlier cases of imperial expansion, religion played an important role in unification. . . . But the Islamic Empire, while as vast in extent as the zone that had been politically unified under the Romans, was not as centralized. Instead of one major capital dominating the rest and drawing to itself the entire surplus of empire, many great cities coexisted, each center of a somewhat autonomous dynasty. Some of these cities reached impressive levels of size and sophistication. Cairo, for example, contained a population in excess of a half million at its height in the fourteenth century, when Egypt held the monopoly over the east-west spice route. Similar centers were sprinkled throughout the region—on the Indian subcontinent, in Persia, in the Fertile Crescent, in North Africa, and in Spain. With the rise to power of the Ottoman Turks, Istanbul (formerly Constantinople) became the prime empire city, containing almost a million inhabitants by the seventeenth century.

SOURCE: Janet Abu-Lughod, *Changing Cities* (New York: HarperCollins, 1991). p. 38.

gradually gave rise to legal thought that was codified in a complex system of jurisprudence. Because of its high level of learning, Islamic civilization had an indirect effect on the culture of Europe. Much of the knowledge, technology, and learning that vanished from Europe after the fall of Rome was reintroduced in later centuries with the Islamic conquest of southern Europe.

And what about city building in other parts of the world? A good deal of evidence shows that cities developed independently in far-flung parts of the globe, particularly in the Far East and the Americas. By examining these urban sites that developed independently of the Western European tradition, we can gain insight into the nature of urban life in general.

Cities of East Asia

In Eastern Asia, in present-day China, people began building cities as early as 2000 B.C. The earliest cities were found in the valley of the Huangho (Yellow) River. These cities were capitals of political dynasties, and each new dynastic leader built his own capital, so a single city such as Rome never became central to the entire system. Although the archaeological record is not complete, there seem to be certain regularities in the form of the Chinese cities (Maisels 1999).

Cheng-Chan, the capital of the Second Shang Dynasty, was probably typical of the cities of early China. It reached its peak about 1600 B.C. Like the ancient cities of Europe and the Middle East, it was walled and fortified. It had a somewhat different residential pattern, however: Within its walls were housed only the elite of the city, that is, its political and religious leaders. Artisans tended to live outside the walls. The peasantry did not live in the city at all; rather, they

---

B o x 3.2 • Case Study
Cities in China's Chou Dynasty 221 B.C.

Scores of new cities were built in eastern Chou times, usually rectangular or square and on a north-south axis. They had double walls, and occasionally also a moat. The residences of the nobles and the administrative buildings were within the inner wall, while the craftsmen lived and worked between the inner and outer walls, clustering in particular quarters according to their enterprises. The shops of the merchants were also located there. Commerce was not yet looked down upon, and nobles themselves engaged in it without disgrace. Barter probably remained the common form of trade, but copper coins were gradually coming into use.

SOURCE: J. Garraty and P. Gay, eds., *The Columbia History of the World* (New York: Harper and Row, 1972), p. 115.

---

lived in surrounding villages that were linked in a network. These village residents related to the city, providing its food and using it as their market and ceremonial center. Thus, most of the Chinese cities had a small central urban area, with a diffused, partially rural, edge. An exception was the Great City Shang, a much larger, planned city that incorporated all levels of the population within its boundaries while still retaining a special central section for its rulers (Cheng 1982). (See Box 3.2.)

Chinese cities were culturally highly developed; their arts and crafts included sophisticated bronze work, pottery, and bone carvings. Their residents left written records including accounts of battles and histories of the rulers' lives. Like early cities in other parts of the world, they had a highly stratified social structure, with a large social (and spatial) gap between the rulers and their subjects.

After the fall of the Roman Empire, while cities were dwindling in much of Europe, they were flourishing in China. The Ming Dynasty, which ruled a vast region after A.D. 1000, established Beijing as its capital. By about A.D. 1500, Beijing was the largest city in the world, with a population approaching two million.

Cities of the Americas

Another region that developed cities was the southern part of North America and the northern part of Central America, which has come to be known as Mesoamerica. This area, encompassing southern Mexico, Guatemala, and Honduras, was the site of the first cities in the Western Hemisphere. The first cities in Mesoamerica date from about 500 B.C., and are thought to have developed independently (Diehl 2004).

Several early Mesoamerican cities, such as Tikal, Copán, and Bonampak, were products of the Mayan civilization. The cities served primarily as ceremonial centers but also had other urban functions such as government and commerce. Mayan culture was highly developed, as seen in the evidence of its arts, sciences, and crafts: writing (hieroglyphics), astronomy, mathematics, painting, sculpture, pottery, and architecture.

B o x   3.3   •   Case Study
City Planning in Teotihuacán

Like Washington, D.C., Teotihuacán was laid out in quadrants on a precise gridwork pattern. Its master plan allowed for growth, and its ceremonial, official, and private buildings were linked by ruler-straight streets. . . . At its height, Teotihuacán had a minimum population of 75,000, a probable population of 125,000, and a possible population of 200,000. It was thus more populous than the Athens of Pericles and covered a larger area than the Rome of the Caesars. And then, having sprung seemingly from nowhere, Teotihuacán just as mysteriously collapsed, its buildings blackened by a conflagration that swept the city in about A.D. 750, nearly eight centuries before the arrival of Cortés.

The first American city was not only large, but, by contemporary standards, it was clearly a pleasant place to live. If the great ceremonial plazas were imposingly spacious, the city's dwelling compounds were on an intimate scale, most of them arrayed around an open patio in the style of the Mediterranean. The exterior of the single-story apartment compounds was generally white and windowless, but within, the walls blazed with color, for like modern Mexicans, the Teotihuacános were superlative muralists.

SOURCE: Karl E. Meyer, *Teotihuacán* (New York: Newsweek Books, 1973), p. 15.

From their remaining buildings, it is apparent that great pyramids and temples dominated Mayan cities, with residences for priests and rulers located nearby. The cities, however, did not have the walls characteristic of early cities in other parts of the world. Neither did they house the large and dense populations of other cities with equivalent levels of technological sophistication. Some scholars have hinted that these differences are based on their distinctive setting. Their subtropical environment did not readily support a form of agriculture characterized by large fields dedicated to a particular crop, and so they cultivated maize (corn), beans, and squash, probably producing less of a surplus food supply than did cities in other parts of the world (Bellwood 2005). By extension, this could mean that because the Mayan cities sustained a smaller population than did other cities, their food warehouses were not the target of constant attempts at invasions from outsiders, as was true in other cities.

The Mayan cities were abandoned after about eight hundred years of existence, probably due to a combination of political instability and an unstable food supply. Mayan civilization, however, influenced the development of the Aztec civilization. The Aztec cities shared several characteristics with the Mayan cities, including enormous ceremonial pyramids and a scarcity of walled defenses. Unlike Mayan cities, however, Aztec cities were rigorously planned and geometrically designed. Box 3.3 describes Teotihuacán, perhaps the greatest Mesoamerican city.

Although Mesoamerica was the earliest site for city-building activity in the Americas, it was not the only one. The west coast of South America later gave rise to the Inca and other civilizations, all of them based on urban centers.

MEDIEVAL CITIES IN EUROPE

As North Americans, we naturally focus on the history of Europe, because it is the home of the settlers who created our political nation and the source of our traditions. As we have seen, however, the path of civilizations and urban growth is not a straight line. Cities in other parts of the world arose independently of the cities that became European civilization's predecessors; although cities were dormant in much of Europe, they thrived elsewhere. Let us return to the thread of the European story that we left with the disintegration of the western part of the Roman Empire.

Feudalism and the Growth of Towns

The five centuries after the fall of Rome saw a new economic system gradually take root in Europe: the feudal system. Although **feudalism** was fundamentally an agrarian system, it also permitted the formation of new towns and the expansion of older ones. To form towns, groups of settlers bought charters, or rights to self-government, from feudal landlords. These charters allowed towns to become independent of the lord's control and to establish their own laws, money, and armies. Medieval towns grew by granting citizenship rights to their inhabitants after one year of residency. Peasant farmers, who were normally serfs bound to feudal lords, could be freed of their obligations by becoming residents and then citizens of the towns. This principle is embodied in a famous German saying of the time: *Stadtluft macht frei* (city air makes one free). As the rural population in Europe began to grow, an increasing number of people migrated from the countryside to towns, causing the urban population to swell and to turn some of these towns into true cities by the eleventh and twelfth centuries (Kotkin 2005).

In their physical structure, medieval cities of Europe shared many characteristics with ancient cities. Because warfare and invasion were still common, the cities continued to be walled and fortified. Life also centered around public spaces, such as a plaza and a marketplace. The presence of monumental buildings was another similarity; but rather than the ancient city's collection of temples, theaters, and so on, most medieval cities were typically dominated by a massive cathedral. Aside from that towering structure, the remainder of the city consisted of small-scale buildings, with tiny, densely built houses and streets just wide enough to permit the passage of a cart. Because of their small, terrain-hugging, energy-efficient buildings and pedestrian scale, Lewis Mumford (1938) called medieval cities "organic" and praised them for their efficient use of resources. Figure 3.3 shows the layout of a typical medieval city.

Social Institutions

The simple social structure of the medieval cities was based on the traditional feudal system of the nobility, the peasantry, and the clergy. In most parts of Europe, the Catholic church was the dominant institution and had numerous members of religious orders. Feudal lords and their retainers made up another

Adam Woolfitt/Terra/Corbis

F I G U R E 3.3   A Medieval City. The city of Carcassonne, France, contains the physical features characteristic of most medieval cities: fortified walls (in this case, a double wall), the lord's castle (center), and the cathedral (upper right).

social group. Two other important socioeconomic groups lived in medieval cities: artisans and merchants. Artisans were self-employed and economically self-governed, forming guilds to regulate the production of their crafts. Merchants, whose business was trade with other cities and other regions of the world, became an increasingly wealthy and powerful group during the Middle Ages. Peasants were at the bottom of the social structure (Ganshof 1996).

Life and social relations in medieval times were regulated by the church and the guilds, rather than by civil law as we know it. Social norms were far less likely to recognize or favor individualism than is true of contemporary life. The prevailing ethos put the welfare of groups, not of individuals, at the forefront, making even economic life more family- and community-oriented than individualistic. Although people valued material comfort, spiritual and social values took priority.

The wealth of the medieval cities was based on three elements: thriving trade, the increased production of handicrafts, and increasing agricultural output. The basis of the overall economy during this period was agricultural production, but the urban economy was closely tied to trade, particularly maritime trade. Most cities in what are now Italy, Spain, Portugal, France, England, and Scandinavia were located on the coast. During the Middle Ages, before the emergence of nations, the urban centers of Europe developed a strong network of economic ties with each other and with cities in other parts of the world through trading partnerships.

Pressures on the System

The medieval cities grew partly because of two contributions from their rural hinterlands: food and people. Increases in agricultural productivity by peasant farmers led to the production of sufficient food to support larger populations in the towns. As agriculture became more productive and the rural population grew larger, pressure grew for "surplus" serfs to escape to towns and take up other occupations.

As increases in agricultural production allowed medieval cities to support more people, however, the growth of the cities destabilized feudal agriculture and eventually helped cause its downfall. Two related factors contributed to this process. First, landlords periodically increased rents, encouraging an increasing number of serfs to abandon the countryside and move to the towns. In some places, this migration reduced the rural population to below the level needed to sustain agricultural production. Second, even though agriculture was highly productive, population pressures and the need for increased production led to some actions that ultimately hurt agriculture. In many parts of Europe, landlords brought unsuitable land under cultivation, leading to its gradual degeneration. In other areas, landowners converted croplands to pastureland to raise sheep for the more profitable wool business. It thus became more difficult to maintain the increases in food production that had been the cornerstone of the growth of the medieval cities. These environmental and economic changes, which were outcomes of the feudal system, prevented the feudal system from being able to sustain itself indefinitely (Anderson 1974; Ganshof 1996).

The feudal economic system also produced new social groups and social relations. With the growth of trade and craft production, along with related occupations such as money changing, a new social class, distinct from the traditional feudal groups of nobles, peasants, and clergy, began to emerge. This new social class, which was composed of the inhabitants of cities (in French, *bourgs*) was called the bourgeoisie. This group gradually gained influence, drawing it away from both the church and the feudal landlords. Over time the bourgeoisie became politically more powerful and acquired control over social institutions. Members of the bourgeoisie spearheaded movements to replace religious or baronial authority with civil law, to replace the traditional bonds of feudalism with the rights of individuals, and to raise the status of money over that of land as a form of property.

GROWTH OF CAPITALISM
AND THE INDUSTRIAL CITY

Changes in the nature of feudalism, increases in the production of handicrafts, and the rise of the bourgeoisie all contributed to the emergence of capitalism in Europe during the fifteenth and sixteenth centuries.

Cities Built on Trade

Between the eighth and sixteenth centuries, a prototypical "world" system (which included not the entire globe but most of what was the known world) had developed in the eastern part of the former Roman Empire. Constantinople and the other cities under Islamic control pursued vigorous trading relationships with each other and increasingly with parts of Europe. The city that became the most important link between the Middle East and Europe was Venice, a city built on trade. Although Venice had been geographically within the western part of the Roman Empire, it had gained its political autonomy and became affiliated with the eastern part of the empire. Venice's location on the Mediterranean made it the gateway to Europe for goods coming from the East. Like other trading cities, it also served as a melting pot for the ideas and information of a wide range of cultures. Venice was thus well situated to become a center of the rebirth of civilization in Europe, known as the Renaissance (Sjoberg 1960; Kotkin 2005).

During the Middle Ages, cities of the western part of Europe gradually began to establish more trade with each other. The early capitalist economy was built on trade as cities such as London, Antwerp, Hamburg, Cologne, Marseille, and Lisbon grew, because their locations made them strategic trade sites. A growing group of merchant capitalists invested in boats and established regular seagoing trade routes as well as the still-difficult overland routes. Initially, this group reinvested their profits in more and bigger trade routes. Eventually, however, their surplus became so large, they had to find other types of investments. Thus they began to invest in the production of handicrafts to increase the amount of goods available for trading. Over the course of two or three centuries, the percentage of profits gained from trade gradually diminished while the percentage of profits from the production of goods gradually increased, and the economy changed from one of **merchant capitalism** to one of industrial capitalism. The foundation of capitalism, however, was laid in the latest stages of what we think of as a different economic/social/political system, that of feudalism.

World-Economy

The rise of capitalism also occurred simultaneously with the integration of a large part of the Western world into a single economic system dominated by European cities. This system, the **world-economy**, has two key characteristics. First, it encompasses a global division of labor consisting of a core and a periphery. The **core countries** are those geographic areas that coordinate and control the world-economy, as a result becoming the wealthiest regions; the **peripheral countries** supply needed labor and raw materials and act as consumers for products, but retain few profits and thus are the poorer regions. Although this world-economy is most evident with the rise of capitalism, precursors to the global system have existed before; for instance, Algaze (1993) has argued that fourth millennium B.C. Mesopotamia was organized along these same principles, centered on the southern city of Uruk and extracting resources from northern Mesopotamia and western Iran.

The second characteristic of the world-economy is that it is internally divided into many competing nation-states. This political fragmentation perpetuates economic competition within the core and prevents any one nation from gaining permanent domination of the world-economy. The world-economy is similar to an empire in that it links many different places, but it is not an empire because it is not a political entity. Indeed, the world-economy of A.D. 1600 encompassed several empires, notably those being formed by Spain, Portugal, and later the Netherlands. Thus, the world-economy system differs from the economic systems of the ancient empires, in which economic ties were overlaid on the political ties that created the empire (Wallerstein 1976; Chase-Dunn 1985). Recognizing the existence of the world-economy—that is, the long-term economic ties among the different regions of the world, which began as early as 1400—will later help us to understand the differences among the cities in different parts of the contemporary world (Sassen 2008).

One of the characteristics of the world-economy today is *denationalization:* the decreasing importance of nation states to the overall functioned of the global system (Sassen 2008). Just as earlier cities built on the structures that came before, today's world-economy builds on institutions that came into existence as the nation-state evolved into the dominant political–economic form, such as the use of law to maintain order and the emphasis on private property that made capitalism possible.

Early Industrial Cities

Over the course of about three centuries, manufacturing gradually replaced commerce as the most profitable activity within capitalism. As that happened, European cities grew in population and also took on a different character from the old medieval towns. By 1850 the physical layout of the industrial city was markedly different from that of its predecessors in both size and organization. Whereas the medieval cities had been surrounded by walls, the emergence of nation-states had done away with the need for protection from invasion (on the scale of the city, that is); and in the intervening centuries, walls had been removed and city boundaries pushed out dramatically. Industrial workplaces, which were now large-scale factories rather than small craft shops, were located in their own districts, with separate housing for workers constructed close by. Rather than the earlier organic or star-shaped street layouts, a gridiron street pattern was frequently adopted to facilitate the buying and selling of property by making each lot uniform and predictable. The central marketplace remained in many industrial cities, but the central cathedral was replaced by stock exchanges and other commercial structures. In fact, when the city of London was reconstructed after the Great Fire of 1666, the architect Christopher Wren put the Royal Exchange building, rather than St. Paul's Cathedral, in the central square (Mumford 1961).

Industrial capitalism created new social classes and transformed the urban social structure into a pattern completely different from that of the Middle Ages. The feudal landed nobility, unless they had converted some of their property and become capitalists, had lost importance and power in the cities. The peasant class and many artisans had now been merged into an industrial working class, and the large-scale

T A B L E   3.1   Urban Growth in Europe, 1800 to 1890

City	Population	
	1800	1890
London	864,845	4,232,118
Paris	547,756	2,447,957
Berlin	201,138*	1,578,794
Vienna	232,000	798,719
Glasgow	81,048	782,445
Budapest	61,000	491,938
Madrid	156,670	470,283
Lisbon	350,000	370,661

*1820 population

SOURCE: Adna Weber, *The Growth of Cities in the Nineteenth Century: A Study in Statistics* (Ithaca, N.Y.: Cornell University Press, 1965), pp. 119–120.

capitalists, both commercial and industrial, rather than the landowners, had become the society's powerful elite. A smaller-scale (or petit) bourgeoisie of entrepreneurs and professionals, and a growing group of nonmanual workers, such as clerks and teachers, made their living essentially outside of the industrial structure.

Table 3.1 shows the rapid growth of cities in Europe during the nineteenth century. The Industrial Revolution was farthest along in England, and, not surprisingly, English cities provided the most striking case studies of the new form of industrial city. During the nineteenth century, the population of England tripled, due to dramatic decreases in the death rate and especially the infant mortality rate. During the same period, the urban population increased tenfold, and by 1891 more than half of the population of England lived in cities of over twenty thousand (Abu-Lughod 1991).

Urban population growth in England was the result of migration rather than natural increase. A combination of factors progressively displaced rural dwellers from farming. The rural population was growing much more rapidly than ever before, and the land available to support them was diminishing in size. As the economy gradually changed over to production of goods, land uses changed in rural areas. Common land that propertyless people traditionally used for farming was taken over for commercial agriculture or for grazing of market-bound sheep. The final blow to the rights of the rural population was the passage of the Enclosure Acts that formally allowed the common lands to be fenced and used by private owners.

Many of the industrial cities of England had begun as small towns, but they took on a whole new character as they expanded. The logic of capitalism guided both the physical layout of the city and its social life. The gridiron street pattern and the geographic centrality of the business district were reflections of capitalist economic reality. In addition, the discipline of wage work came to rule the lives of the working class. Huge numbers of workers in the industrial cities such as Manchester were recruited from the ranks of abandoned children, young unmarried women, and Irish immigrants fleeing pauperism at home. In his book *The Condition of the Working Class in England in 1844*, Friedrich Engels surveyed the working and living conditions common at the time. The findings were disturbing. With a common workweek of sixty-five or more hours, industrial workers were expected to work nearly every waking hour, six days a week. While imprisonment (for vagrancy) or starvation were the alternatives to joining the workforce, being in its ranks did not guarantee even a minimal quality of life. Wages in the late eighteenth- and early nineteenth-century factories barely paid for bread and the use of a mattress on a floor shared with dozens of other workers. The working-class districts were located in the least desirable areas of the city, where even rudimentary facilities such as water, sewers, and toilets were absent or rare.

Although the problem of the condition of the working class was most striking to Engels, other writers also decried the waste and misappropriation of natural resources and the general strain on the human spirit that was a by-product of early industrialism. In a critique of industrial urban life, Lewis Mumford took up Charles Dickens's descriptions from *Hard Times* of a fictionalized industrial city called Coketown. Mumford describes the industrial towns as "dark hives, busily puffing, clanking, screeching, smoking for twelve and fourteen hours a day, sometimes going around the clock" (1961, 446). The massing of many factories in the same district multiplied the effects of the resultant air and noise pollution. With the factory as the nucleus of the economy, all of the resources of the cities were diverted to the industrial sites. Factories typically occupied the best plots of land, often near a body of water, which the factory then typically used for disposing its raw sewage, thereby killing the aquatic life and making the water unsuitable for human use. Mumford (1961) argues that the dark, noisy, dirty, and highly congested environment became so much a part of urban life that it was taken for granted and endured by even the richer classes.

In sum, the cities of the early industrial period reflected many of the characteristics of the capitalist economy as it was then organized. The cities were laid out in a way that facilitated the production and transport of goods with little attention to public amenities. The lives of the growing class of industrial workers were subordinated to their machines, which had to be kept running long hours. The class structure, dominated by a working class and a capitalist class, became increasingly polarized as the latter became wealthier and the former, poorer. "Surplus" members of the rural peasantry were induced to migrate to cities, where they frequently joined the ranks of "surplus" workers. The great irony of the period was that, although industrial capitalism led to huge increases in economic production, the products were so unevenly distributed as to make life for the poor even more miserable than it had been in previous epochs. The transition to industrial capitalism made urban space into a commodity and people into laborers, and the urban face of early capitalism can be seen in its rawest form in the cities of England in 1850.

CONCLUSION

This overview of the prehistory and history of urban life has revealed several characteristics of cities. First, cities are social inventions. They were apparently invented in different parts of the world independently of each other. They rose, as far as we know, from the accumulation of knowledge and power based on local populations. Once founded, however, cities served as influences on other geographic areas, and urban life tended to become diffused or passed on to neighboring groups.

Second, cities have a distinctive set of physical and social characteristics that make them urban. They are not just big villages, and apparently they did not emerge from villages in a gradual process of population growth. Rather, it appears that leaders mobilized the people and the resources within the community to build these distinctive settlements.

Third, cities have not only economic functions but political and symbolic functions as well. Early cities were tied to political empires, and later cities retained many political and administrative functions. From early times, cities have been invested with symbolic meaning and have been the center for ceremonies that unify large numbers of people. Frequently, religious meaning and ritual have been intertwined with government.

Finally, cities are fragile. Early cities disappeared, were destroyed, were rebuilt over ruins, or were moved. Even huge cities like Rome did not endure continuously. This fragility is probably due to a combination of economic and political factors. The economy must be strong enough to support a large population without overtaxing its resource base, and the conditions that allow the city to thrive at one point may change to cause its demise at another point. The political leadership must be strong enough to build the city and then protect it from attack, either by conquerors from the outside or by new leaders with different goals.

DISCUSSION QUESTIONS

1. Scholars have not set a minimum number of residents as a way of deciding whether a settlement is or is not a city. Instead, they have tended to use social patterns as the main indicator of what constitutes urban life. If you discovered a new archaeological site, what physical and social features do you think you would look for to help you decide whether it was a city?

2. Why do you think government and political leadership have been so important in founding and maintaining cities?

3. Picture in your mind the different types of monumental buildings that have been the focal points for different types of cities. The ancients built religious temples in their city centers. Medieval cities were built around imposing cathedrals. What kinds of monumental buildings have been the focal points of cities since the Industrial Revolution? What kinds of monumental buildings do we build today? How do they differ from those of the past?

4

Urban Development in the United States

In Boston they ask, How much does he know? In New York,
How much is he worth? In Philadelphia, Who were his parents?
MARK TWAIN
WHAT PAUL BLOUET THINKS OF US

Mark Twain's preceding remarks reflect a fundamental fact about cities. Each is distinctive, not only in its landscape and buildings but also in its history, social patterns, and culture.

In the previous chapter, we examined historical patterns of urbanization in different time periods and in different parts of the world to identify some basic principles that affect the growth and character of cities. In this chapter, we move closer to home to examine cities in our own society. Although you are probably familiar with one or two regions of the United States, you may not know much about cities in other regions. For that matter, you may not know much about the past life of some cities with which you are very familiar now. We will take a brief tour of the history of American urbanization, concentrating on three questions:

- How have cities differed in various periods of U.S. history?

- How have economic and political actors shaped the growth of cities in the United States?

- Why do different regions of the country grow and develop differently?

A BRIEF HISTORY OF CITIES
OF THE UNITED STATES

Studying the history of cities of the United States is relatively easy, because all of our cities are new and recently built. Although the territory of North America was previously inhabited by people with, in some cases, very complex civilizations, the sites on which settlers from Europe built their towns seldom had any substantial buildings that had to be removed or incorporated into the new towns' structures. Additionally, the founding of the American cities was so late, compared to that of the cities of Europe or Asia, that most have had continuous settlement and have a stream of records, maps, and historical accounts that reveal exactly what the towns and cities were like throughout their existence. Thus, the historical record is relatively complete and quite detailed.

The major cities of the United States grew from towns in a more or less continuous process from their founding to the present time. If we take "stop action" snapshots of cities at certain historical periods, however, we find that cities of different eras had markedly different characteristics. Although, of course, a given city will have many differences with other cities that grow up at the same time, we stress the similarities to help isolate the important processes involved in urban development.

One common way of dividing up urban history is to use the categories of economic structure summarized in a prominent article by the economist David Gordon (1978). Gordon identified three time periods based on three stages through which the economy evolved:

1. The **commercial period**, from the beginning of the European settlement (1620) to about 1850
2. The **industrial period**, from about 1860 to 1920
3. The **corporate period**, from 1920 to the present

These dates, which are only approximations, indicate several major transformations through which the national economy progressed as it matured. Although the economy of the United States has been a capitalist economy throughout its history, different kinds of activities were central to the making of profit during different time periods. During the commercial period, trading dominated cities and towns; in the industrial period, the process of manufacturing dominated; and in the corporate period, mergers, stock sales, and the accumulation of paper wealth are the central activities.

In each time period, people who created the built environment in cities organized it to allow them to make profits, given the economic rules of the game. Because the very nature of the economy was changing, the social and physical organization of the city kept changing as well. Thus, over long periods—fifty years or more—new construction gradually produced a new pattern of spatial organization in the city, transforming commercial cities into industrial cities and industrial cities into corporate cities.

The Commercial City

From the time of the first colonial settlement to the eve of the Civil War, only a small proportion of residents of North America (from 5 percent to 15 percent of the total population) lived in towns or cities. Urban residents of North America engaged primarily in trade, crafts, and services, whereas most of the rest of the inhabitants made their living in agriculture. The most important, most rapidly growing, and most profitable segment of the economy was trade, especially with England. Raw or semi-processed materials, such as tobacco, salt fish, and lumber, were exchanged for manufactured goods. Trade drove the economy of the newly formed towns and provided many kinds of employment. Merchant-investors owned the trading companies and bankers financed them; shipbuilders made boats and seamen sailed them; dockhands loaded and unloaded the goods, which were packed in barrels made by coopers and brought to the docks in wagons pulled by horses shod by blacksmiths, and so on. Even the service providers such as cooks, ministers, police, and prostitutes indirectly depended on trade for their livelihoods.

During their early phase, **commercial cities** were actually quite small by today's standards; in 1742 the five largest cities in the country—Boston, Philadelphia, New York, Charles Town (Charleston), and Newport—ranged from thirteen thousand down to only six thousand residents, respectively (Green 1965). The amount of territory they covered was also minute compared to that of contemporary cities. It was usually possible to walk from one end of the city to the other in less than twenty minutes. Because walking was the primary mode of transportation, the compact layout of the city was a necessity, and the spaces occupied by both homes and workplaces were small. Despite their compact size, however, these cities contained, at least in rudimentary form, all the elements that were present in European cities: housing for different social classes, markets and shops, graded streets, public water supplies, churches, schools, newspapers, libraries, public meeting halls, postal services, and police.

During the early phase of commercial development, all cities were ocean ports, as seen in Figure 4.1. Because the English government tightly controlled colonial cities and decreed that all trade would be conducted with England, oceangoing vessels were the most common means of transport. The cities were physically organized around the waterfront, with nearly all significant economic activities and a huge proportion of residences located within about a quarter of a mile of the port. As Figure 4.2 shows, the early City Hall of New York City overlooked the docks. During the later phase of the commercial city—after 1800—trade and shipping routes spread beyond the Atlantic coast, as canals, rivers, and the Great Lakes became important trade routes. Newer commercial cities were established along these inland bodies of water, such as the Erie Canal (Buffalo), the Ohio River (Cincinnati), and the Mississippi (St. Louis). In these inland ports, urban life and employment continued to revolve around the waterfront.

The social life of the commercial cities was organized very differently from contemporary urban life. Cities were more heterogeneous and less differentiated than cities today. For example, work and home life were often conducted in the

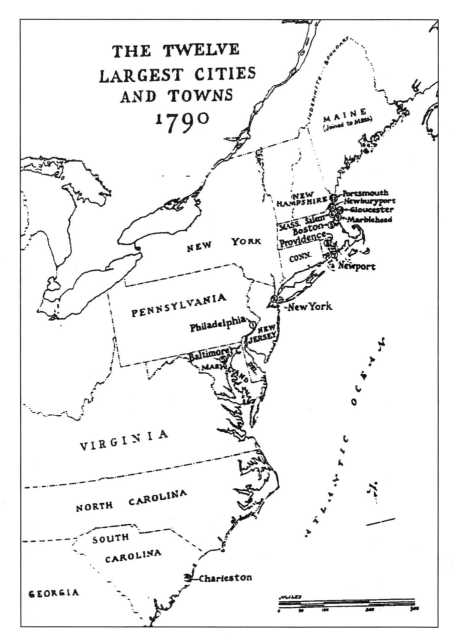

FIGURE 4.1 The Largest Cities in the United States, 1790. The largest cities in the United States during the early phase of commercial development were all ocean ports; their economies were built on trade with England. Later, as canals, rivers, and the Great Lakes became established trade routes, commercial cities were built inland, and many of the seacoast cities lost their importance for trade.

SOURCE: Adapted from Kenneth T. Jackson, *Atlas of American History*, 2nd ed. (New York: Scribner's, 1984), p. 97.

CITY HALL AND GREAT DOCK, 1679.

FIGURE 4.2 **New York as a Commercial City, 1679.** This lithograph shows New York's City Hall, originally built as a tavern and inn, which formed the early city's center of commerce.

same building. Craftspeople tended to use the front rooms of their homes as shops, and families ran hotels or taverns from their residences. Aside from a central market and perhaps one or two public buildings, these cities had no identifiable downtowns, and businesses, which were usually quite small, tended to be dispersed along the waterfronts and throughout the towns. As well, people of different social classes tended to live interspersed with each other rather than in separate neighborhoods, another example of the heterogeneity of the commercial cities. Although there were class distinctions along the lines of occupation and the amounts of property possessed by different social groups, these class differences were not expressed by spatial differentiation (or segregation) to the degree that they are today.

The commercial cities, then, had similar physical structures because they were small and organized around ports. Their land use patterns were relatively heterogeneous, both in terms of where different land uses (housing, shops, warehouses) were located and where different social classes lived. These urban characteristics were compatible with an economy based on trade.

The Industrial City

Over several decades the U.S. economy changed, and urban form changed as well. As had previously happened in Europe, trade gradually became less central to the national economy and manufacturing took its place as the activity that produced the greatest profits. This transformation did not take place all at once, nor was there a single moment when the nation became industrial. Many of the same firms and individuals who had been merchants and traders became manufacturers by investing ever-greater proportions of their capital in manufacturing operations. In the early days of industrialization, manufacturing establishments were generally located either in very small rural towns such as Rockdale, Pennsylvania (Wallace 1972) or in newly built company-owned cities such as Manchester, New Hampshire (Hareven and Langebach 1978). Gradually, however, manufacturing companies built factories in the established cities, changing the existing patterns of spatial and social organization to something very different from that of commercial cities.

How did these **industrial cities** differ from the earlier commercial cities? First, as the economy moved from commerce to increased manufacturing, the center of activity moved away from the port to a new center. Second, although cities continued to combine manufacturing, transportation, and commerce, these were now found in different locations. Third, the size and scale of cities grew tremendously during this period, from the small-town walking city of the 1700s to the giant industrial cities of 1900. All of these trends affected the existing cities and put their stamp on the newer cities.

Philadelphia's growth pattern is a good example of the transformation of a commercial city to an industrial city. Sam Bass Warner, Jr. (1968) shows that after 1860, the center of activity in Philadelphia moved west, away from the docks along the Delaware River. Rather than life centering on the port, new districts for manufacturing, working-class housing, shops, and offices were established. Although older districts continued to have a mix of homes and businesses, an increasing trend toward separating newer housing from business and industry arose. The central business district, known locally as Center City, was built up during this period. This densely packed area combined nationally known businesses such as banks and publishing companies, business-oriented services such as engineering firms and hotels, and mass consumer outlets such as department stores and theaters. Manufacturing districts expanded along rail lines to the northeast and the southwest of Center City.

New residential patterns also developed in Philadelphia as it became an industrial city. Whereas industrial workers and their families typically lived clustered within walking distance of the factories, new, strictly residential and homogeneous neighborhoods were built, either made-to-order for the wealthy as in Chestnut Hill, or on speculation for the middle class as in West Philadelphia. Residents of these outer neighborhoods could reach Center City via such new systems of mass transportation as the horse-drawn streetcar (1850s), the electric trolley (1880s), and the subway (1920s) (Warner 1968).

In other cities, too, the social patterns during the nineteenth century became increasingly differentiated. Cities were growing rapidly, and the new neighborhoods built to house people bore less resemblance to the heterogeneous towns of the eighteenth century. Entire districts of working-class flats or tiny houses were constructed near factories to serve as workers' housing. Middle-class and wealthy urban dwellers began to establish new residential districts, farther from the center of the city. The foundation for today's residential neighborhoods was laid during this period.

If industrialization was so important in shaping cities, why don't all of the industrial cities look alike? Some cities, like Philadelphia, Boston, and New York, were relatively well established as commercial cities and thus contained a street layout, buildings, and social patterns of commercial cities. These cities tend to have narrower streets, smaller buildings, and less open space in the commercial areas. Other cities, like Chicago and Detroit, had little in the way of a commercial heritage to overcome and grew up as purer examples of the industrial-type city. They have broader streets and larger-scale industry. But in all cities that existed during the industrial period—that is, most of the large cities of the United States—we find three characteristics: concentrated areas of industry, a large downtown, and different neighborhoods for people of different social classes.

The Corporate City

During the twentieth century, and especially after 1950, the urban economy was once more transformed. Continuing into the twenty-first century, although manufacturing is still important, the production of manufactured goods has taken a back seat to the production of paper profits. Firms that were once identified with a specific manufactured product, such as Kodak cameras or U.S. Steel, have become conglomerates producing a wide range of goods and services. Buying and selling other companies often proves to be more profitable than producing a better product or service. In David Gordon's terms, the economy has passed into the stage of advanced corporate accumulation.

These **corporate cities** have several characteristics that distinguish them from earlier types of cities. One striking difference is that economic activity, which was highly centralized in the industrial city, is decentralized in the corporate city. New manufacturing plants, office space, and retail establishments are much more likely to be built on the outer edges of cities than in the centers. Because of all this decentralized economic activity, urban areas have grown tremendously on the periphery. This growth often oversteps the city limits, producing suburban communities that are spatially continuous with but politically independent of the central cities.

Another characteristic of corporate cities is the changing role of the city center. Between the 1880s and the 1920s, the downtowns boomed and became true central business districts. Much of this growth was due to companies' increasing needs for office space. In more recent decades, downtowns have gradually been reorganized, with a decrease in the proportion of retail establishments and an increase in the proportion of corporate offices and business-oriented services such as law firms and advertising agencies.

Changes in the spatial patterns of residential neighborhoods, although less dramatic than the massive reorganization of the central business districts, have had profound consequences for urban social life. The trend toward differentiation of neighborhoods by social class, which began in the industrial city, continued in the corporate city. So did the trend for wealthier residents to move farther from the center. As more suburban housing was constructed, upper-income households were followed by the white middle and working classes, who purchased inexpensive, mass-produced housing in the suburbs, following the wealthier suburban pioneers out of the cities. More dispersed commuter suburbs gradually supplanted the close-knit residential neighborhoods of the industrial cities.

Los Angeles and Houston, the second and fourth largest cities in the country in population, are "late corporate" cities. Huge metropolitan areas with many suburbs and diffuse central business districts, they are products of highly decentralized industry. Because of political fragmentation, lack of land use controls, and an abundance of highways, development has leapfrogged over undeveloped areas, pushing out the functional boundaries of the city in a sprawling fashion. The communities, both urban and suburban, are highly segregated by social class and ethnicity, and homeowners' associations try to keep their neighborhoods homogeneous to protect their property values.

Houston, for example, was a small town in 1850, with only 2,400 inhabitants and an area of nine square miles. When it was founded, Houston's major industries were cotton, banking, and railroads. The oil industry was started in the early 1900s but was just another element in the economic mix until the 1950s, when it became the city's dominant industry. Since the 1950s Houston's growth has been based on the international oil trade, related petrochemicals, banking, and aerospace industries. As a corporate city, Houston's downtown is dominated by modern office space, more than 80 percent of it built after 1970. But the downtown is so diffuse that people joke about there not being one. Rather than geographic centralization, suburbanization of people and businesses has been the pattern in Houston for most of its history. The city has repeatedly annexed its sprawling suburbs, so that it has grown geographically as well as in population. Today, Houston is the fourth largest city in the country and covers over five hundred square miles of land (Feagin 1988).

Older cities, partly or mostly constructed during earlier periods, have adopted many of the characteristics of corporate cities. The unique geography and history of each city have created a set of conditions, such as rivers, hills, buildings, and roads, that cannot be totally undone in the future. Many aspects of cities that were settled during the commercial period, such as Boston, and cities that were settled during the industrial period, such as Chicago, are, however, becoming increasingly similar to those of the corporate-era cities, such as Los Angeles. The changes include decentralized manufacturing, corporate offices as the main activity of the central business districts, and tremendous growth of suburban communities.

EXPLAINING URBAN PATTERNS

What factors affect the growth, development, and changes of urban form? This question has provided material for many debates among scholars. The simplest answer, one on which there is widespread agreement, is that the potential for profit is the largest factor driving the shape of cities. But exactly what determines profitability, and how does it influence the shape of the city? Furthermore, why would these patterns change over time?

Ecological Explanations

One issue that ecological theorists have tried to explain is why and how cities came to be located where they are as well as why some grew to be much larger than others. An important factor that they cite is the set of advantages that each location has relative to other locations. In the development of cities in the United States, they argue that technology, particularly as it relates to transportation, is a key determinant of urban location and size.

Geographer John Borchert (1967), for example, argues that a city's location and size are the result of changes in the size and resource base of its **hinterland** and changes in the dominant technologies of transportation and energy. He examines the way that innovations such as the steam engine and cheap steel allowed cities to develop at inland sites, away from ocean ports, first on rivers served by steamboats and later in landlocked locations served by railroads. As new technologies developed, cities that had been built on the older technologies either adapted to the new ones or in some cases (such as small river ports) declined to the point of being "virtual museums" (Borchert 1967, 305). After steam and steel, he argues, the introduction of the internal combustion engine had three significant effects on urban growth and form. First, and best known, was the influence of the automobile and truck on the development of the suburbs. Second was the use of tractors in farming, which greatly expanded the size of the average farm and dramatically reduced the numbers of farmers needed, resulting in mass migration from rural areas to the cities. Third was the use of air transport, combined with the growth of the **service sector** of the economy, which gave an advantage to cities served by airports, turning many such cities into business centers containing many managerial functions.

In addition to the location and size of cities, another aspect the ecologists study is how cities are laid out internally. The traditional explanations of the changes in urban form and social structure that human ecologists and neoclassical economists use (for example, Burgess 1925, Hoyt 1933, Alonso 1964, and Kain 1967) stress two factors: centrality and technology. According to these explanations, the land at the center of a city is most desirable for the location of business, because it is accessible from more places than is land located anywhere else. This accessibility makes the land more valuable, as people who desire accessibility and are willing to pay the price will bid up the cost of the land. A nineteenth-century economist named von Thünen first put forth this principle, and it has influenced the thinking of most contemporary urban economists. According to von Thünen (1826), it is fairly easy to predict where any given type of land use will locate, based on three factors:

1. How much land is needed for the purpose at hand
2. How much "centrality" is needed (or the cost of transportation to a central market)
3. How much income the property could generate

These factors are combined in a graph called a **bid rent curve** which shows the theoretical trade-off between the cost of land and the cost of transportation at different distances from the town center. This theory assumes that people are acting on what is the optimal choice for them, and that they are competing for space within a free market for land, unstructured by government action, monopolies, or other impediments.

Although von Thünen originally advanced his theory to explain which plots of farmland would be most valuable for which crops, later economists adopted it to explain urban land use location. To modernize the theory, economists have considered the impact of changing technologies on the basic model. For example, the introduction of elevators allowed more intense use of land, increased the value of land at the center, and permitted a larger number of businesses to locate near the center. Thus, elevator technology had a centralizing impact on urban structure. The construction of superhighways, on the other hand, had a decentralizing impact, because it increased the accessibility of land on the outskirts and lowered the cost of transporting goods.

According to this view, residential property tends to be located at some equilibrium point between a need to be close to the center and the ability to pay for the land. The people in the household make a decision based on the location of their work, the amount of space they need, and the amount they can afford to pay for transportation. As these variables change, for example, as people change jobs or as new transportation routes become available, the overall pattern of who lives where also changes. The Burgess concentric zone model, discussed in Chapter 2, represents a snapshot of this process at work. Burgess hypothesized, based on the previous assumptions, that business and industry would be located at the center of the metropolitan area, that households would be arrayed by income in succeeding circles, and that growth would occur from the center outward as transportation technology permitted people to live farther from the center while still being able to get there within a reasonable amount of time.

Overall, human ecologists and neoclassical economists have tended to stress changes in transportation and other technologies as the major cause of changes in urban form. According to these theorists, as manufacturing, transportation, and communication technologies have changed, businesses have responded to their changing cost structures by reorganizing and relocating. They see these overall patterns as resulting from different actors responding to their self-interest within a free market.

Political Economic Explanations

Certainly, political economists would agree that changes in technology have been very important both in permitting businesses to move outward and in shifting the urban center from the ports to the new downtowns as cities industrialized. But to say that transportation and other technology *permit* certain types of locational decisions is not to say that they *cause* them. Political economists think that the causality has gone in the opposite direction, and that transportation and technology are consequences, rather than causes, of business decisions (Gottdiener 1983).

According to political economists, changes in the mode of production, or the basic economic structure, are responsible for changes in transportation and technology. Although the mode of production in the United States has always been capitalism, the specific forms of organization within the economy have changed greatly over the centuries. Larry Sawers (1975), for example, argues that the form of the corporate city directly reflects features of advanced capitalism. He notes two in particular. First, many firms moved from the old city centers in search of higher profits as economic conditions changed. Second, the auto industry became such a major economic force that it not only competed with but ultimately destroyed the mass transit system.

When the economy does change, political economists argue that those changes tend to come in bursts or cycles of activity. David Harvey (1978) pointed out that urban infrastructure, such as factories, office buildings, hotels, roads, bridges, parking garages, and so on, are not constructed on an ongoing basis. Instead, they are constructed in spurts, with many simultaneous construction projects taking place in a single city. Building booms are related to the cyclical nature of the economy. As the economy expands, investors expand their businesses by investing in equipment for producing goods. If they keep investing all of their capital in machinery, however, they will over time produce too many goods, creating a glutted market. Thus, periodically, investors transfer some of their profits into real estate investments, including new office buildings, retail shops, and other projects. Some of the construction, therefore, has the simple purpose of siphoning off investment capital.

Harvey (1978) argued that, besides being built in spurts, buildings are destroyed in spurts. Investors change the buildings to reflect current conditions because older buildings reflect what was profitable in the past and because what is profitable changes. Atlantic City, New Jersey, provides an example of this building and destruction. The city's first boom as a resort was in the 1880s, and many buildings were constructed on the famous Boardwalk through the 1920s (Funnell 1983). Then investment dwindled until casino gambling was legalized, resulting in another building boom in the 1980s. Figure 4.3(a) shows the demolition of one of the older luxury hotels as the Boardwalk-based amusements of Atlantic City were replaced by the new casinos, such as the one shown in Figure 4.3(b).

From this perspective, investors searching for more efficient means of making a profit are constantly changing transportation and other technologies, and these profit-driven decisions affect urban development. Harvey's theory relates to the impact of profits on the physical form and the built environment of cities. Now let us examine David Gordon's (1978) theory, which relates to the impact of profits on social relations within cities.

Gordon argues that in the commercial cities, people of all the different social classes lived near each other and knew each other. Thus, when disputes ensued between workers and employers, workers could gain support from friends and neighbors of different social classes. As industrial cities were constructed, however, employers built separate districts of workers' housing. This situation helped

(a)

(b)

FIGURE 4.3 Destruction and Reconstruction. Some theorists argue that both the construction and the destruction of buildings are parts of a typical real estate investment cycle. (a) Demolition of the Traymore Hotel, a remnant of Atlantic City's first tourist boom. (b) Casino gambling brought a new wave of hotel construction, much of it on the same sites as the older hotels.

to reduce the support workers received from the middle class, but by bringing workers into close proximity with each other, the new housing pattern helped increase the social ties among the workers themselves. In the early twentieth century, employers began to locate industrial plants outside of the cities, where workers were more isolated from each other. This spatial dispersal, Gordon argues, hampered workers' ability to organize, bargain, and strike, weakening their position relative to that of their employers.

Gordon concludes that employers' attempts to control their workforce affected the cities. This factor alone, however, cannot account for changing urban form. Although Gordon has direct evidence that some companies consciously strategized to control workers, little evidence shows that suburbs are simply the result of a conspiracy by employers to divide and conquer their workers.

In sum, it is fair to say that no single factor (such as transportation, technology, or labor control) is responsible for changing urban form. Rather, a complex of factors has shaped cities. In general, the quest for profit, or the accumulation process, is the driving force behind most urban activity. The accumulation process itself changes over time, though, and so does the way it affects cities. It also results in the constant building, destruction, and rebuilding of urban communities.

PROCESS OF URBAN GROWTH AND CHANGE

We have thus far seen several major historical patterns in urban history—how cities have changed. We have also identified some of the underlying processes that have changed them—particularly economic changes. How have these macrolevel patterns been created? These patterns do not just appear as a coincidence; nor are they the product of universal laws of urban development. They are the result of human actions, people who have motives, thoughts, and intentions of their own, apart from whatever force is behind the patterned outcome of their actions. We cannot attribute patterns or regularities in urban form to either some laws of nature or some laws of economic relations apart from understanding the actual people who take actual actions in actual cities. A shorthand way of summarizing this approach is the idea that structures do not act, people act. People cannot, however, act any way they wish; rather, they choose their actions from among a limited range of choices available to them, choices that are structured by the situation they are in.

The actions of individuals make up the totality of urban life, but the actions of some individuals and groups are more significant than those of others in forming the urban patterns we have been discussing. In this section, we will examine a few of the groups that have been most influential in shaping the cities of the United States. Although this is not an exclusive list, and more groups will be mentioned throughout the text, in this chapter we will examine three types of influential actors: people involved in the process of developing and building, people involved in local government, and people involved in managing major industries.

City Builders: Property Capitalists

Who decides to build office complexes, shopping malls, industrial warehouses, and residential subdivisions? Who matches available spaces with suitable occupants and who decides on the prices to be charged for occupying a given space? Who anticipates the future needs of a region for commercial and residential space, and who figures out how the future demands for space will differ from current demands? A segment of business called property capitalists, or **rentiers**, specializes in shaping space and reselling it as a commodity. The existence of these entrepreneurs relieves other business managers of the necessity to produce the spaces their businesses use. In other words, rentiers reduce the work, and thus the indirect expense, of other businesses (Lamarche 1976). Two of the most important types of property capitalists are developers and speculators.

Feagin and Parker (1990) show how real estate developers play a key role in the production of the built environment. Developers are catalysts, overseeing hundreds of activities from initially choosing a site to obtaining financing, to arranging for various permits and utilities, to coordinating the architects and contractors, and finally to renting or selling the finished space.

Some real estate developers start out as individual entrepreneurs, using borrowed funds as their investment capital. Although a few of these individuals, like Donald Trump, have become public figures, many of the largest developers, such as Trammel Crow, Robert Campeau, and the Reichmann brothers, are far less visible than their projects. In recent decades, large corporations have tended to replace individual entrepreneurs in the development business. Companies in other industries, including ExxonMobil and Gulf (oil), Aetna (insurance), Phillip Morris (tobacco), and DaimlerChrysler (automobiles), have tended to branch out into real estate as a profitable area for investment of their extra capital (Feagin and Parker 1990).

Understanding the financing of real estate ventures may help explain why entrepreneurs and large companies are attracted to real estate development. First, large non–real estate companies often want to diversify their investments. They may have excess profits to invest (for example, from a period during which oil prices are unusually high) or they may be responding to a decline in demand for their primary product (such as tobacco) and be looking for alternatives. When these large companies have profits to invest, they often invest a portion of them in real estate, to balance their investment strategy.

A second reason that real estate is attractive is that even small developers can and frequently do put together multimillion or billion dollar real estate deals. Banks and other financial institutions are rather liberal about lending large sums of money if the loans will be used for real estate investments. Through this process, called **leveraging**, developers with a relatively small down payment borrow the rest of the money for a project. Once that project is under way, they can use the first project as a partial down payment on their second project, and so on, thus multiplying many times the spending power of their modest initial investment. This practice is very risky; failed big projects have resulted in prominent bankruptcies for some of the largest real estate companies. Despite the substantial risk inherent in leveraged investments, the tremendous profits of a successful project entice developers to begin new projects. Developers with a good track record are often successful at borrowing for new projects even after a spectacular failure.

Another subset of property capitalists is people who speculate on land. **Speculators** buy and hold land that they think will be valuable in the future. A speculator identifies a parcel in a potentially good location (say, near a proposed road, adjacent to a university that might want to expand, or near an area where new apartments are being constructed), then buys the property and keeps it for a period of time, hoping that it will increase in value. Speculation usually does not involve building anything on vacant land, or improving any existing buildings. Rather, speculation involves strictly unearned increases in the value of the property. Speculators can have an enormous impact on where new development will be located by buying up relatively cheap land and assembling large tracts for resale. They can also choose to withhold and release land to the market at certain times, shaping when, where, and what kind of housing, industrial properties, or other land uses will be built (Lamarche 1976).

Since the 1940s the scale of real estate development has increased dramatically, from an industry dominated by small builders to one dominated by giant companies. With their increase in size, real estate developers have taken on a new role, from being simply builders of buildings to being builders of entire communities. This change has had many political as well as economic implications, because the large scope of newer projects has meant that developers work closely with government officials to get their projects built. In *The Rise of the Community Builders* (1987), Marc Weiss notes that many federal, state, and local laws and practices have been tailored to aid these large developers in building their projects.

The government encourages real estate investment and the public subsidizes it. Real estate investments often receive special tax treatment. It is not unusual for some of the wealthiest investors in the United States, the *Forbes* 400, to avoid paying income taxes on multimillion dollar incomes by declaring paper losses on their real estate holdings (McIntyre 1987). When real estate investments receive such favorable tax treatment, more people will invest in them, and consequently the industry can become saturated with investors. This set of conditions occurred during the 1990s, with investors rushing to invest in real estate deals, resulting in severe overbuilding of certain kinds of space, especially downtown office complexes and suburban shopping malls (Fainstein 2001).

Local Government Officials

As we have seen, private actors make many decisions that affect cities, but the public sector—government agencies—play an important role as well. Government shapes the market for property by passing regulations, offering incentives, and either aiding development or erecting barriers to it. Through planning and zoning regulations, government agencies attempt to channel certain land uses into certain areas. Although public agencies carry out these actions, they often reflect the interest of businesses. A good example is zoning laws. Businesses typically create and support **zoning** laws, even though the laws take away some freedom from individual businesses to locate anywhere they want. Why? Because in the wider scheme of things, most business owners prefer to prevent incompatible land uses from locating near them, endangering their business or property values. Although government establishes and administers zoning regulations, they do so to give established property owners some control over nearby land uses.

When analysts have examined cases of government involvement in the urban development process, they have consistently found an underlying commitment to a business agenda. This can be because businesses influence politics and can determine who gets elected, because business leaders are often better organized and can articulate their desires more directly than can other citizens, or because public officials fear that businesses might leave the city if they do not have the favorable business climate they seek.

In describing the growth and changes inherent in San Francisco since 1960, for example, Chester Hartman (1984, 320–321) says:

> San Francisco City government overall has been extremely supportive of what the corporate community wants to do in and to the city. The individuals elected and appointed to major positions in City government—at City Hall, the Board of Supervisors, the Redevelopment Agency, and Planning Commission—have come overwhelmingly from, or are closely linked, economically and socially, with the business community.… The business community has a collective sense of itself and its needs, and directly influences the plans prepared by government agencies. Should local government, pressed by popular protest movements, challenge business hegemony too greatly, threats of capital flight and abandonment, with attendant job and tax revenue loss, serve to discipline the public sector. It is not a contest of equals.

Hartman's insights help explain the fundamental strengths of the pro-growth elites that work for development in so many cities. As Logan and Molotch (2007) point out, economic growth is taken so much for granted as a desirable goal that local governments are often forced into either joining pro-growth coalitions as partners, helping to smooth the path for such coalitions' activities, or at the very least applying regulations to shape growth in ways beneficial to the community while not deterring it too greatly.

Government can play an important role in urban development even in those cities that are less obviously regulated than others. Let's look again at Houston, described by Joe Feagin (1988) as a Free Enterprise City. Houston is the only major American city lacking zoning regulations and has had very little planning in the public interest, although private groups have sometimes organized research and planning teams to address potential problems. Yet, Feagin points out, government at the federal, state, and local levels has subsidized, aided, and promoted Houston's development; and for most of its history, development-minded mayors and city councilors who were part of the business leadership of the city governed Houston.

Local government does not have to be closely tied to business interests, however. Many cities have elected reform governments pledged to the "little person" or to the public good. Policy actions in such cities favor less advantaged or grassroots groups rather than businesses. The systems of incentives, zoning, and subsidized construction may be changed to encourage low-income housing, small business development, or community services for those in need. In other words, the power and the resources of local governments can support private interests or the common good. But, given a basically capitalist economy, where are the limits of what government can do to shape private economic decisions or redistribute resources? We will explore this issue in more depth in Chapters 12 and 13.

Corporations

Corporations also affect the process of urban growth and change, particularly through their decisions about where to locate, increase, and decrease their operations. Companies must consider several factors when they decide where to build an office or plant. Among these factors are labor availability, wages, location of markets and suppliers, and access to relevant technology. A particular city or region of the country can be a good location for an industry when it can supply the factors the companies need to operate. When conditions are positive for industry growth in a geographic area, the region can grow with the industry; conversely, when conditions are negative for industry growth, the region can decline with the industry.

Beginning with the earliest cities in the United States, a clustering pattern of similar businesses, or **agglomeration**, was evident. Agglomeration has occurred on several levels. One is within an individual city; for example, banks frequently cluster together, creating financial districts within cities' central business districts. A second level of agglomeration occurs within metropolitan areas; for example, large factories often cluster near each other, as do warehouses and transportation companies. A third level is regional: many companies in the same industry have historically clustered in the same city or region, such as garment manufacturers in New York City, automakers in and around Detroit, and computer engineering in California's Silicon Valley.

When agglomeration occurs in a city or region, many companies within a single industry locate in a concentrated geographic area in a relatively short span of time. This concentration can produce an economic boom in an area that becomes the site of an emerging industry. Because companies in new industries typically have high rates of growth and profit, they create many jobs and spur population growth in the areas in which they locate. Conversely, communities or regions that contain large concentrations of mature industries are often vulnerable to companies' decisions to cease operations (Markusen 1987).

Economist Ann Markusen (1987) explains that understanding **profit cycles**, or the growth and contraction of profits in an industry, can tell us a good deal about why industries locate where they do and why companies agglomerate with similar companies. A profit cycle is the pattern of initial high profits in a new industry, followed by the leveling off and eventual decline of profits as the industry matures. Companies in new industries typically have high rates of profit and rapid rates of growth, as, for example, computer companies did in the 1980s. As the industry matures and more companies compete in the market, individual companies' profits begin to level off. Finally, as new products are introduced that replace the established products, company profits fall, putting pressure on them to cut back or close operations.

A prominent example of the impact of agglomeration and the profit cycle is the Detroit metropolitan area, home to the automobile industry. In the first half of the twentieth century, automakers grew rapidly and invested in plants in and around Detroit as area residents became increasingly dependent on the auto industry for jobs. Likewise, the city of Detroit and state of Michigan became increasingly dependent on the auto industry for tax revenue. For several decades, the auto industry's dominance provided a comfortable economic basis for the city and state. Beginning with the 1980s, however, foreign companies such as Honda, Toyota, and Nissan challenged the dominance of the U.S. automakers, and the share of vehicles sold by Detroit-based companies such as General Motors, Ford, and Chrysler declined. In Markusen's terms, U.S. auto companies could no longer reap the profits they had become used to because of increased competition. One response by the automakers was to cut expenses by moving some of their manufacturing facilities from Detroit to areas such as Tennessee where labor costs were lower, beginning the gradual decrease in automotive-related jobs in Detroit. Changes in the world economy also affected the auto industry. After 2005, dramatic increases in the price of gasoline and a global economic recession caused a precipitous drop in the sales of American-made vehicles, especially trucks and SUVs, as demand increased for smaller and more fuel-efficient vehicles. These changes in the global economy presented serious challenges to the American automakers and therefore to the city of Detroit.

Another important aspect of companies' decision-making processes is whether the management of a company is local or distant (as in the case of an absentee owner). With the increasing concentration and globalization of the economy, firms are frequently bought by others. These parent companies may not even be in the same industry. Indeed, with shrinking profits in established industries, a built-in incentive exists to diversify into other products. Thus, companies that were established in a particular community, often by an individual or partnership of people who were residents of that community, are more often bought out or merged into larger conglomerates whose headquarters are located elsewhere. In these cases, an owner or a manager may determine the economic stability of a community or other community consequences of a plant or business shutdown to be unimportant. The locally owned company does not base its decisions primarily on the good of the community either; but when managers and owners live in a community, they are more likely to take the health of the area into consideration, especially as it could affect them personally.

To summarize, corporate investors make decisions based on many different factors. Although the bottom line is "Where can I make money?" the answers to that question can be quite complex. Conditions change over time and so do investment decisions. Economic and political conditions influence investment decisions, and investment decisions in turn influence economic and political conditions (conditions>decisions>conditions).

REGIONAL DIFFERENCES IN GROWTH AND DEVELOPMENT

Different regions of the United States have grown at different rates throughout the country's history. The types of conditions we have already discussed have been important engines of economic growth. In this section we will compare the growth patterns of three regions to see how the chain of conditions> decisions>conditions has played out in those regions.

The South

In their book *The Rise of the Sunbelt Cities*, Albert Watkins and David Perry (1977) trace the development of the South. They show that the South did not develop its tremendous potential for exporting agricultural products during the commercial phase of American economic growth. Only one Southern port, New Orleans, shipped a substantial amount of freight, mostly European goods headed up the Mississippi to Ohio and processed meats going down the river from the Midwest. New Orleans lost a great deal of its shipping traffic when the construction of the Erie Canal made access to the inland cities cheaper and faster through New York.

Northern bankers controlled the money supply in the South. Southern farmers, the largest group of small business owners in the region, were forced to borrow from Northern bankers, rather than developing any large financial institutions of their own. In the period of industrialization, this lack of capital in the South slowed the formation of industry and made the region function more as a market for Northern goods than as a competitive producer. In addition, Northern-based companies often organized their industry to preserve their regional advantage. In the steel industry, for example, all steel was priced as though it came from Pittsburgh, with an additional freight charge being tacked on based on its distance from Pittsburgh. The steel companies headquartered in Pittsburgh controlled steel prices all over the country. This pricing policy inflated the price of Southern steel from plants in Alabama and Tennessee, preventing it from being priced competitively, even within the South. Thus, the South remained a relatively undeveloped region for about two centuries, through a combination of its own internal characteristics—such as a lack of capital—and its relationships with the North (Watkins and Perry 1977).

After World War II, however, a new pattern emerged. Watkins and Perry document substantial growth in manufacturing in the South in two economic sectors. One is in the low-growth, low-wage manufacturing industries, which, although declining nationally, are growing in the South. Textiles and furniture, for example, have matured in other regions, and companies have moved south for cheaper labor costs. But surprisingly, even more growth has occurred in the high-wage manufacturing industries. These companies, mainly high-tech manufacturers, are not relocating from other regions. Their growth in the South is partly due to the general expansion of high-tech industries in the economy, but it has also been spurred by government policies and actions. Government has aided the growth of the South in several ways:

1. Government programs installed the electricity and highways that the South had previously lacked.
2. The federal government's military and aerospace bases are located disproportionately in the South.
3. Government agencies grant contracts to Southern-based companies that produce technologies for military applications.

The key point that Watkins and Perry make about the growth pattern of the South is that we can understand the regional pattern only by looking at the big picture of the national and international political economy. Growing regions grow by capitalizing on some particular advantages that they have. Sometimes these have been preexisting conditions, such as location at an ocean port or deposits of coal; sometimes they have been new developments, such as the opening of a canal. The South benefited from the fact that the North industrialized first and leading eventually to its obsolete infrastructure and higher wage structure. In comparison, the South became more attractive to investment because of its compatibility with the needs of the growing industries. Thus, the region as a whole grew steadily in the last half of the twentieth century, although the growth was concentrated in certain Southern states and metropolitan areas.

New England

New England was the first region in the country to become a commercial power as well as the first region to become an industrial power, but its growth has been sporadic. In the early commercial period, up to about 1800, the New England cities of Boston and Newport dominated shipping. They were later eclipsed by the Mid-Atlantic ports of New York and Philadelphia, which had access to larger inland areas, more agricultural products, and more people than were available in the hinterlands of Boston and Newport. In the early industrial period, New England mill towns produced the majority of the textiles, shoes, machine tools, and armaments that were made in the United States. Again, over time, they were outdone by other regions: the Mid-Atlantic states, the Midwest, and finally the South, as conditions changed. Much of the movement to other regions resulted from changing technologies and patterns of corporate organization, but the desire of companies to avoid the highly skilled, highly paid, and predominantly unionized workforce that had become established in New England was another crucial motivating factor (Harrison 1984).

The decline of manufacturing, however, left New England open to the potential for the development of new high-tech industries in the post–World

War II period. Harrison (1984) argues that the cycles of growth and decline left New England with four characteristics that would make it viable for new industrial development. First, the region had a good supply of workers who badly needed jobs. Years of recession and plant closings had lowered workers' expectations for wages and greatly reduced the strength of the trade unions. Second, New England companies had a great deal of untapped capital to invest in new ventures. Mergers and selloffs of plants in the declining industries created this resource. Third, the federal government invested billions of dollars into high-technology research and development for new high-tech weapons systems, a large proportion of which went to universities such as the Massachusetts Institute of Technology and private firms associated with them. Finally, local governments supported new industrial development through favorable tax structures and industrial development support programs.

Growth in high-tech manufacturing led employment booms in the 1980s and 1990s, causing the Boston metropolitan area to become the fastest growing city of the United States in family income. After a sharp downturn in the late 1980s, an economic rebound, again led by high-tech industries, led to additional population growth and the lowest level of unemployment in the country by the late 1990s (Bluestone and Stevenson 2000). However, the demise of the "dot-com" businesses led to an actual decline in population after 2000. Besides high tech, other growing industries such as producer and business services (e.g., accounting, advertising, legal firms), finance, real estate, insurance, construction, health, and education provided employment. Bluestone and Stevenson have described a "triple revolution" in the Boston metropolitan area, from predominantly white to an ethnically diverse population, from a manufacturing economy to a "mind"-based economy, and from a city with a strong central hub to a decentralized metropolitan system.

Some of the economic growth of New England has spilled over from the Boston area to other parts of the region. Portions of Rhode Island, southern New Hampshire, and Maine have gained from their proximity to Boston, as well as their lower costs of living and doing business. Other sections of New England, however, are still suffering from the declines of the traditional farming and manufacturing economies and are losing population steadily as a consequence.

California

Large enough to constitute a region by itself, the state of California illustrates another aspect of the boom and bust cycle of regional development. The state has grown explosively since the 1880s but its growth, both in population and in employment, has not been steady. Rather, the pattern of growth has been a series of rapid surges punctuated by periods of slow growth.

The southern California area, centered on Los Angeles, the second-largest city in the United States, has experienced five growth surges, according to Soja and Scott (1996). The first growth surge, in the 1880s, was the result of a significant real estate boom caused by marketing of the pleasant climate for leisure and retirement living. The second, shortly after 1900, was based on the expansion of the port for international trade and the discovery of oil in the region. The third surge, in the 1920s, was the result of the rapid growth of two new industries: films and aircraft. The fourth growth period, in the 1950s, was due largely to the expansion of the aerospace industry. The fifth surge, in the 1980s, was based on a diversified manufacturing sector (including continued expansion of aerospace and defense industries) and financial services.

In the late 1980s, however, a series of national and international economic changes, coupled with some local political and economic decisions, led to the worst recession in sixty years and radically slowed growth in California. An important cause of the economic trauma was the end of the Cold War, accompanied by a precipitous drop in defense spending in the late 1980s. Because California contained one of the largest concentrations of the defense-related aerospace industry, the national cutbacks heavily affected the state. This job loss had a ripple effect, causing a general downturn in the economy, so that in the two-year period between 1990 and 1992, the state of California accounted for 38 percent of all jobs lost in the United States (*The Economist* 1993).

The state's famed Silicon Valley was the first home of the computer industry, but during the 1980s and 1990s, the computer and electronics industries began expanding in other western states, notably Washington, Utah, and Texas. Thus, when the "dot-com" bust of 2002 occurred, the job loss was not highly concentrated in California but spread across several states. Furthermore, as high-tech firms in California closed or moved, other types of companies gradually opened, helping diversify the economic base of the state. Some of these were low-tech firms such as clothing and furniture manufacturing and freight shipping. California currently has a diversified economy with opportunities for both high-skilled, educated workers and less skilled, often immigrant workers. This economic diversity helped both the state's population and its employment grow faster than the national average between 2000 and 2007 (U. S. Census Bureau, n. d.).

The up-and-down growth of industries that affected the South, New England, and California shows how investment can seesaw between regions. As investment flows into region A, costs of doing business (wages, property, taxes) increase. Investors then look for more profitable locations, say within region B, which has cheaper land, lower taxes, and a cheaper labor force. With additional investment going into region B and less into region A, however, region B over time becomes more expensive, and region A could begin attracting investment of a new kind. This fluctuation of investment capital can help explain regional ups and downs (Smith 1984). Because of our market economy for investment, a pattern of boom and bust is more typical than one of consistent and steady growth of metropolitan regions.

CONCLUSION

The growth and development of U.S. cities has followed broad patterns over time, including the changing of physical form. These changes involve not simply growth but also reorganization of where different tasks are performed and who lives near whom. In general these changes are reflections of changes in political and economic contexts within which the cities are located. People have continually built and rebuilt their communities to take advantage of economic opportunities available to them, but the exact nature of those opportunities has continually changed as well.

From this vantage point, we cannot predict what trends will be likely in the future. Current trends may not continue. The growth of a particular city or region can peak, level off, decline, and perhaps increase again. Why? When? No firm laws dictate these patterns, but several principles contribute to urban growth and change.

1. Because investors produce, either directly or indirectly, most of the built environment, the strategies companies use for making profits are highly influential in the growth and organization of cities.

2. Strategies for profit making continually change as conditions for profit making change. Changes in political and economic conditions, whether global, national, regional, or local, impact the size and organization of cities through their influence on companies' decisions.

3. The costs of doing business and the potential for profit are of major importance in making business decisions. In turn, the actions of government at all levels (such as taxes, labor laws, business subsidies, and investment in infrastructure) strongly influence these factors, all shaping the economic conditions within an area.

4. Some economic reasons for the growth and decline of particular cities and regions are the profit cycles in new versus older industries (that make agglomeration more or less useful) and the fluctuating effects of overinvestment in one region versus underinvestment in another.

DISCUSSION QUESTIONS

1. Think about a city you know well, and identify the older and newer sections. Has this city gone through the phases of a commercial city, an industrial city, and a corporate city? What buildings and other types of infrastructure give you the clues to determine how the city used to be? What has been changed, destroyed, or renovated to fit with the changing needs of businesses?

2. Can you name the largest real estate development firms in your area? How big are they? Do they specialize? For example, what kinds of projects do they produce: residential, commercial, office buildings? Is their focus urban, suburban, or both?

3. Who are the major employers in your area? Do they represent a concentrated sector of the economy or a highly diversified group? Which employers are growing, stable, or declining, and what impact do you think their employment patterns are having on the community?

5

Cities, Suburbs, and Metropolitan Areas

In this unpredictable world, nothing can be predicted quite so easily
as the continued proliferation of suburbia.
HERBERT GANS
THE NEW YORK TIMES MAGAZINE, JANUARY 7, 1968

In the previous chapter we examined some of the historical patterns and general principles behind urban growth and change in the United States. We saw that cities are continually changing, especially in response to shifting political and economic circumstances. How corporations and the government decide to invest money has a great deal of influence on which cities will grow, how rapidly, and when. In this chapter we will examine the contemporary metropolitan area to see the effects that recent political and economic trends have had on the nature of central cities and their surrounding suburban communities. We will focus on the following three questions:

- Why and how have the suburbs grown since World War II?

- During the same time period, how and why have central cities changed?

- How have changes in the national and international economy contributed to the changing shape of metropolitan areas in the United States?

CHANGES IN METROPOLITAN
AREAS SINCE 1950

As we saw in Chapter 4, the growth of suburban and metropolitan areas has been a characteristic of the North American city since at least the early 1900s. In recent decades this growth has accelerated and taken on different characteristics. In 1950, about 60 percent of the population of the United States lived in

TABLE 5.1   **Urban and Suburban Development Compared**

	Urban	Suburban
Transportation	walking	automobile
	mass transit	
Density	high	low
Settlement pattern	centralized	decentralized
Land use	mixed	homogeneous
Location of activities	outdoor/street	indoor
Control of space	public	private

metropolitan areas, that is, central cities and their surrounding suburban counties. The majority of this metropolitan population lived in the central cities. By 2000, 80 percent of the U.S. population lived in metropolitan areas, and the majority of those lived in the suburbs. So metropolitan growth means largely suburban growth. See Table 5.1 for a description of the characteristics of suburban as compared with urban settlement patterns.

In addition to continued growth, the recent past has brought a massive restructuring of the metropolitan areas. The central business districts, so much a part of the early corporate city, have retained their function as corporate centers but have lost many of their other functions, such as retail sales centers and mass entertainment outlets. Retailing and mass entertainment have tended to decentralize, locating in suburban shopping malls, cineplexes, and restaurant strips.

Restructuring has affected the demographic patterns of U.S. metropolitan areas. As a group, the central cities are home to far higher proportions of nonwhites or members of ethnic minority groups than the population as a whole. In contrast, suburban communities are home to far lower proportions of nonwhites or members of ethnic minority groups than the population as a whole. In addition, some minority groups are more highly concentrated in the central cities than others. For example, in 1990 African Americans made up 22 percent of the population of the central cities, but they represented only 7 percent of the population of the metropolitan areas outside of the central cities (U.S. Census Bureau 1990).

Although the metropolitanization of the United States is not a new trend, it has taken on new forms and has had important consequences for urban life in the past three decades. In this chapter we will examine the twin phenomena of suburban growth and central city restructuring to understand their causes and their consequences for the metropolis as a whole.

GROWTH OF SUBURBS AND
METROPOLITAN AREAS

The continual expansion of urban boundaries has been a feature of cities in the United States since they were first founded. As we have seen, the ecological explanations of this phenomenon stress the cost of land at different distances from

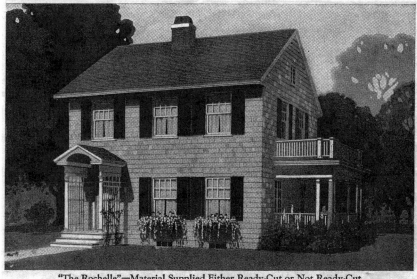

"The Rochelle"—Material Supplied Either Ready-Cut or Not Ready-Cut

F I G U R E 5.1 Plan for a suburban home, 1920. Even before the widespread use of automobiles, streetcars allowed families to move to outlying neighborhoods characterized by single-family homes, lawns, trees, and gardens. This model is one of fifteen designs that were marketed through the Montgomery Ward catalog, including blueprints and precut lumber shipped to the building site.

the center versus the costs and availability of transportation. In analyzing the growth of the suburbs in recent decades, many analysts argue that North Americans prefer to live as far from the city's center as they can afford to go, based on the costs of transportation available to them. They point out that the introduction of electric streetcars in the 1800s fostered the development of suburban neighborhoods even prior to the introduction of the automobile. Figure 5.1 shows an example of a typical house plan for one of these "streetcar suburbs." In this view the steady increase in the use of automobile transportation after 1920 fueled the intensification of suburban growth since the 1940s. This analysis assumes that most people have preferred decentralized residences since at least the mid-1800s (Hayden 2003). It further assumes that consumers' preferences are the most important force behind the changes that have occurred.

In the past two decades, other studies have questioned this model of suburban growth, arriving at a series of additional factors and causes to be considered. They have found that, although the general process of outward movement from the center has indeed been apparent for over a century, consumers' preferences have not been the only factor driving the growth of the suburbs. Rather, they argue that the formation of suburbs has been shaped by a variety of political and economic decisions by public officials, policymakers, voters, taxpayers, corporate investors, and managers. Let us examine a few of the major types of decisions that have shaped the contemporary metropolis.

Policy Choices by the Federal Government

From 1945 on, following the conclusion of World War II, Congress and government agencies adopted a set of policies and programs that increased the pace of suburbanization and gave suburban growth its particular character. Although these policies and programs were not consciously aimed at building suburban communities, they contributed greatly to the process.

The first such policy decision Congress made was to create a national system of highways, of which the federal government funded 90 percent and the states 10 percent. This system linked every major city and the rural areas of all forty-eight contiguous states, with connections to other roads. The high speed limits and limited access structure of this interstate highway system made it amenable to long-distance driving and freight shipment. Although passed by Congress as a "defense" bill (with the idea that troops and supplies would have to be moved in case of a future war), the interstate highway system was actually the nation's new transportation system. In a very short period of time, government subsidies to the highway system had the effect of supporting trucking rather than railroads, and private automobiles rather than public mass transit. In addition, these highways opened up otherwise inaccessible land to development and helped create the sprawl of the suburbs by moving development out from the cities to highway interchanges. The creation and use of the auto/truck technology by itself would not necessarily have had the decentralizing impact it had if it had not been for the political decision to build the roads in a decentralized pattern.

A second important policy that the federal government instituted after World War II was a set of programs to encourage homeownership. Up to the 1920s, it was difficult for ordinary working people to buy houses because mortgages were much more difficult to obtain than they are now and because the terms of the mortgages made them inordinately difficult to repay. Congress, fearing that an economic depression could follow the end of the war, decided that encouraging homeownership would be a good stimulus for the economy. It passed a number of bills intended to make it easier to buy a home. One set of programs was the Federal Housing Administration (FHA) and Veterans Administration (VA) mortgage guarantees, in which the federal government guaranteed the mortgages of qualified applicants. As a result, the private banks that actually loaned the mortgage money no longer had to assume any risk in the event that the borrowers defaulted on their loans. Bankers quickly took advantage of this new opportunity for practically risk-free lending and made millions of dollars available for home mortgages. The federal government also supported homeownership through the homeowner's tax deduction, which allowed taxpayers with mortgages to deduct the interest on their mortgage as well as their local property taxes from their income on their federal income tax returns. This policy allowed households that could not previously have afforded homes to buy them and allowed homeowners who already owned homes to move up to more expensive ones, because the federal government was helping to pay the mortgage. The combination of the mortgage guarantee program and the tax subsidy program was massive. These policy decisions greatly increased both the availability and ease of obtaining mortgages and the federal government's direct financial subsidy to homeowners, making homeownership, in some cases, cheaper than renting. In practical terms nearly any family that had a steady job and a small bank account could now get a mortgage, and other taxpayers generously subsidized the payments.

The combination of these homeownership programs, particularly the mortgage guarantee program, fostered the growth of the suburbs at the expense of the central cities. The guidelines on the FHA and VA mortgages provided that to qualify for the mortgage guarantee, the house should be a newly constructed, single-family detached house (in a racially homogeneous neighborhood, a condition that will be discussed in more detail later). In other words, it was much more difficult to obtain the mortgage guarantee for apartments, duplexes, or townhouses. Buying and renovating previously owned houses was also discouraged under this program. So, in effect, the FHA/VA mortgage guarantee encouraged the practice of constructing single-family detached housing on open land, much of which happened to be located on the peripheries of metropolitan areas (Aldana and Dymski 2004). Much of the reason the suburbs are designed as they are (low density, primarily single-family houses, homogeneously grouped) can be attributed to the guidelines of the programs that helped to construct them. After nearly two decades, those guidelines were changed, but the basic nature of most suburban communities had already been thoroughly established. (In Chapter 14 we will explore in more detail how these policy decisions are made.)

The third policy that was influential in shaping the nature of the suburbs was the federal government's support for and encouragement of large-scale builders who employed mass-production techniques. In mass production, hundreds of houses can be built at a low cost by completing each stage (for example, digging and pouring the foundation, framing the house with precut lumber, roofing, installing electrical and plumbing systems) one house after the other on a fixed schedule, similar to a manufacturer's assembly line. During and after World War II, builders such as Levitt and Sons received the financial support of the federal government to experiment with and introduce mass-production building into the private home market, again as a stimulus to homeownership and to the economy in general. Their mass-production techniques required immense plots of land, sometimes resulting in the construction of entire new communities, such as Levittown, New York, shown in Figure 5.2. Checkoway (1980) details this government support and the related lobbying efforts of the National Association of Real Estate Boards to reduce government subsidies for low-income public housing while increasing subsidies to middle-class homeowners. As a result, homeownership rapidly became the norm in American society rather than just one alternative among other living arrangements.

These three types of federal policies, highway construction, encouraging homeownership, and support for large-scale builders, helped to speed up and to shape the process of suburbanization and the growth of metropolitan areas over a period of twenty to thirty years. Some analysts have explained the growth of the suburbs by citing consumer preferences for increased space and the availability of

Levittown Public Library

F I G U R E 5.2 **Large-Scale Builders and Suburban Growth.** Levittown, New York, shown here, was one of the three Levittowns; the other two were in Pennsylvania and in New Jersey. The Levitt and Sons used mass-production techniques to build complete communities on a scale far larger than had previously been possible.

the automobile, but they have often missed the larger context. By focusing on what individual households did as consumers, these analysts neglected to ask why the choices that were available to consumers were limited in the ways they were. Wolch, Pastor, and Dreier (2004) argue that even Los Angeles, a city that supposedly "just grew," was highly influenced by public policies. (See Box 5.1.)

Local Political Choices: To Annex or Not to Annex?

One of the paradoxes of the contemporary metropolitan area is that even while the population of the entire metro area can be growing, the population of the central city can be shrinking. The central cities of Detroit and Philadelphia, for example, reached their peak population sizes in 1950 and have been losing population ever since. Their metropolitan areas, however, have been steadily increasing in size. Some central cities, however, have experienced population growth in parallel with their metro areas. The central cities of Los Angeles, Houston, Nashville, Columbus, Indianapolis, and Raleigh have continued to grow in population.

B o x 5.1 • Public Policy and the Development of Los Angeles

Although the notion that public policy influences the geography of opportunity is accepted in many metropolitan areas on the East Coast, Los Angeles is sometimes portrayed as the grand exception in American urbanism—the city that "breaks the rules." Diverse, fragmented, polarized, and ungovernable, a metropolis without a geographic center or unifying civic culture, Southern California is said to have grown without benefit of planning or policy. But in fact, federal, state, and local public policies have profoundly shaped the region and continue to do so today. Government policies have promoted the L.A. region's intertwined dilemmas of urban sprawl and the deterioration of older communities, undermining its sustainability by creating deep-seated and overlapping social, economic, and environmental problems.

In this way, L.A.'s story is similar to the tales that might be told of other major metropolitan regions in the United States. In fact, like much else in Southern California, it may be an exaggerated version of the broader American story. Not only has the region felt the impacts of the usual suspects—federal defense spending and transportation and housing policies—it has also been shaped by immigration policies, water and environmental policies, and even local and state tax policies...

SOURCE: Jennifer Wolch, Manuel Pastor, Jr., and Peter Dreier, "Making Southern California: Public Policy, Markets, and the Dynamics of Growth" in *Up Against the Sprawl: Public Policy and the Making of Southern California*, ed. Jennifer Wolch, Manuel Pastor, Jr. and Peter Dreier (Minneapolis: University of Minnesota Press, 2004), p. 3.

Different central cities have different growth rates for two reasons. One is simply that the growth rate of the metropolitan area can affect the growth of the central city. The second reason is that different political decisions about where urban boundaries are drawn can also affect the growth of the central city. Some historical perspective is necessary to understand this phenomenon.

Between 1700 and 1900, North American cities routinely grew by either annexing portions of the vacant land surrounding them or by consolidating smaller adjacent communities with the city. Indeed, this process was so much the norm that if cities had not grown this way, New York (with its original boundary of Manhattan Island) would now be the only city in the country with over a million population. Some cities, such as New York, Philadelphia, and Chicago, grew by giant consolidations, the largest being Philadelphia's incorporation of the entire county in 1854, and the most famous being New York's incorporation of Brooklyn, the Bronx, Queens, and Staten Island with Manhattan in 1898. Other cities grew by smaller steps, adding one village or town after the other, as Boston added Charlestown and Dorchester, and Detroit added Fairview and Delray (Jackson 1985).

The practice of geographic expansion through annexation and consolidation is no longer routine. Some cities practice it; others do not. Suburban annexation slowed around 1900, when the balance of power began to change within metropolitan areas. In the earlier decades of the nineteenth century, suburban areas almost always stood to gain by annexation because the large cities had superior schools and services (water, sewers, streetlights, and so on) than the smaller villages and rural areas. Residents usually approved proposals to consolidate with the city, and the formation of a village was the first step to becoming part of the larger city, thus gaining all of the advantages city residency offered as well as the disadvantage of higher taxes. Political decisions about annexation or consolidation were not problematic as long as the residents of the annexed areas did not forcefully protest. As more middle-class people moved to the suburbs and as the towns increased their provision of public services, however, much of the suburban support for annexation disappeared. Some state legislatures have upheld forced annexation laws; others have made it easier for suburban towns to resist annexation through legal means (Rusk 1993).

The resulting pattern has been uneven: some central cities have continued to grow through annexation and consolidation; others have not. Today, the consequences of the decisions to grow or not to grow geographically impact other aspects of life in the city. Those cities that have continued to expand their boundaries have continued to increase in overall population; those that have not grown geographically have shrunk in population. Some evidence shows that the cities that have kept expanding geographically have been better able to grow economically and to cope with or prevent the level of social problems that have come to be associated with big cities. One important example is racial segregation levels. Although, in general, central cities have higher proportions of minority populations than do suburban communities, those metropolitan areas that are characterized by expanding city boundaries (the so-called elastic cities, such as Phoenix, Indianapolis, and San Diego) have lower levels of racial and economic segregation than do the cities that have had stable boundaries, such as New York, San Francisco, and Milwaukee. Similarly, the distribution of services (for example, the quality of the schools) is more equal in those metro areas that have consolidated than in those characterized by a fixed central city and surrounded by independent suburbs (Rusk 1993).

Comparative studies of urban areas have shown that the growth patterns of the cities and the existence of separate suburbs is not preordained, is not part of the natural order of things, and is not inevitable. In the most general terms, the formation of political boundaries between communities is the result of conflicts among different groups. Kantor (1993) argues that political choices have produced the boundaries of the cities. He charges that the increasing social inequality between city and suburb reflects a strategy some political officials have consciously chosen to contain the problems resulting from social divisions of class and race. Kantor suggests that political leaders can choose to build new political forms (such as consolidated city-suburban governments or school districts) that can help ameliorate the results of those divisions.

Corporate Decisions: New Industrial Spaces

We have seen that federal and local government decisions have contributed to the growth of the suburbs. In addition, some corporate decisions have fostered suburban growth by concentrating manufacturing and other commercial businesses in the suburbs. Three major business trends have contributed to the suburbanization of industry: the separation of management and production, vertical integration of companies, and the rise of the information economy.

As we saw in Chapter 4, companies began to separate the management of the firm (the offices and administration) from its production functions (the plant itself) during the early twentieth century. In the previous historical period of the industrial city, a company's offices, including every function from the president to the bookkeeper, were located in the same building or cluster of buildings as the machinery that produced the products. We saw that as corporations grew, they began to move their headquarters into central business districts although their manufacturing plants remained in the industrial districts. This trend toward separating the functions of management and production is still occurring.

The second factor driving the suburbanization of industry has been vertical integration of companies. **Vertical integration** refers to a company's practice of producing most of the subsidiary products and processes needed to make the final product. During the early part of the twentieth century, many large-scale industries (for example, steel and auto companies) began to build new, vertically integrated plants that produced their component products as well as their final product. In other words, an auto manufacturer would also produce the batteries, window glass, tires, electronic systems, seat covers, and other components of the vehicle besides the engine and body. As you might imagine, these integrated plants were enormous—often large enough to be small cities in themselves. Because of the space they needed, companies increasingly chose to build new facilities on the edges of cities, spurring the pace of outward movement.

The third factor contributing to outward movement of industry is a change in the organization of industry since the 1970s, namely the transition to an informational economy, marked by the growth of high-technology companies. Manuel Castells (1989) followed the development of high-technology research, development, and manufacturing to investigate its effects on the pattern of urban growth. His study found that, throughout the country, in every region where high-tech production is occurring, it is disproportionately being located in suburban as opposed to urban communities. The particular characteristics of high tech that lend themselves to suburbanization are "large batch production facilities combined with automated subsidiary plants, in the vicinity of test sites and relatively close to the research and design centers. Access to a large resourceful [sic] area by means of the freeway system seems to be the main spatial requirement" (Castells 1989, 295). Companies in the high-tech sector need access to information as much as to raw materials, labor, and energy. High-tech industry, Castells points out, is not just a technological change but an organizational change. In the information economy, many companies choose locations near research universities and highly skilled labor forces, resulting in their concentration in certain geographic areas.

To summarize the types of industrial decisions that have fostered suburbanization, in the first wave of industrial decentralization (about 1900 to 1950), the key changes were the separation of control or management functions from production and the increased size of some manufacturing plants due to vertical integration. In more recent decades suburbanization has been driven by the growth of high-technology industries.

Consequences of Suburbanization

Clearly, the decisions of industry and government leaders were not the sole cause of suburbanization. Their actions, however, were decisive in permitting and encouraging suburban growth. Once the highways were in place, the new industrial spaces constructed, and the home mortgage plans in place, those conditions set the stage for individuals' decisions. Individual households did play a role in selecting locations for their dwellings. Given the pluses and minuses, the incentives and disincentives of urban versus suburban living, more people chose suburban communities. New housing was more likely to be constructed in suburbs than in the cities. Banks were more willing to provide money for mortgages in suburban than urban neighborhoods. Because of the new highways, commuting to work was no longer restricted to train or bus routes. Gradually the new standard package of household goods came to mean a single-family detached house with a large lawn and a car, for both the middle class and the working class.

The phenomenon of suburbanization, begun by industrial decentralization and carried along by households' movement to the suburbs, developed a momentum of its own. "The suburbanization of everything" has been an accompaniment to many of the changing trends in our society. The best example of this is retailing. With more people working and living in the suburbs, good opportunities for retailing in the suburbs became apparent. The downtown shopping districts formed in the early twentieth century contained a few large department stores and many specialty shops clustered around bus and trolley lines. Downtown retailers relied almost exclusively on weekday shoppers, housewives, workers shopping on their lunch hours, or people shopping on Saturdays. With suburbanization came an explosion in self-contained shopping centers and enclosed malls that were open not only during the day but also at night and on weekends. Retailers responded to a population that lived farther from the downtown, was not tied to public transit routes, and contained more women in the paid labor force. The same kinds of conditions that brought retailing establishments to the suburbs also brought restaurants, theaters, and other commercial leisure spots such as miniature golf courses.

An important but often overlooked consequence of "the suburbanization of everything" has been a decrease in public space and an increase in privatization. The public street has given way to the privately owned (and security-guard controlled) mall; the public park has been superseded by backyard pools and commercial theme parks; and the public cafeteria has been replaced by drive-up, fast-food establishments. Residents of the United States have traditionally had a more privatized approach to services and problems than residents of other industrialized countries, and the change from an urban to a metropolitan way of life has reinforced and even enhanced this general point of view (Popenoe 1985).

Although suburbs have a great deal of heterogeneity within them where ethnicity, education, and age of the population are concerned, they are much more homogeneous where race and income are concerned. This is partly because the law in most states gives communities the option to exercise stringent control over who and what can locate where. Many exclusive suburban communities have chosen to limit the types of housing and businesses that locate in their area through restrictive zoning. By requiring a certain size house lot, forbidding the construction of apartments, and setting certain standards for building materials or noise levels, officials can assure that certain kinds of households and businesses will not be able to move into the community (Keating 1994). Even nonexclusive suburban communities often adopt restrictions on the number of apartments, for example, or on the number and kind of subsidized housing units allowed.

Within metropolitan areas, then, a general trend has developed, more pronounced in some than in others, of growing class and racial inequality between the central city and its suburbs. Not all suburban communities are wealthy; some are populated by mostly working-class families. Not all suburban communities are white; some are racially integrated, and a few house mostly minority residents. But, in general, the pattern that first emerged, then solidified over the past forty years, has been one of increasing levels of differentiation by social class and race.

Another important consequence of suburbanization is suburban sprawl. Sprawl has been defined as "… a pattern of urban and metropolitan growth that reflects low-density, automobile-dependent, exclusionary new development on the fringe of settled areas often surrounding a deteriorating city" (Squires 2002, p. 2). Sprawl typically results from uncontrolled housing and commercial development at the edges of developed areas and "leapfrogging" over undeveloped areas to create a patchwork of different land uses. It is often associated with dramatic differences in income and resources in different communities within the same metropolitan area (Bullard et al. 2000).

Gregory Squires (2002) summarizes the problems associated with sprawl. First, sprawl is detrimental to the environment. Because a sprawling community is highly decentralized, its residents typically will not have mass transit available but will rely on automobile (and limited bus) transportation. This pattern not only encourages the greater use of fossil fuels but the resultant air pollution also contributes to a range of diseases, including asthma and lung cancer. Traffic congestion results in more people spending more time in their cars, often in traffic jams, adding yet more exhaust emissions. In addition, sprawling development harms water resources as aquifers are depleted for sprinkling lawns and lakes and streams are degraded by air pollution. Sprawling development also consumes farms and forests, replacing them with concrete and asphalt. Because it is always pushing development outward, sprawl results in duplication and inefficient use of existing infrastructure such as roads, water, and sewer systems, while encouraging the abandonment of older buildings such as shopping and office complexes from previous generations of development.

Besides the environmental impacts, Squires (2002) notes that the intensified economic inequality among communities associated with sprawl creates large disparities in the tax bases of different municipalities. Wealthier communities have fewer social services to fund and more to spend on schools, libraries, and recreation. Poorer communities within the same metropolitan area typically have higher rates of unemployment and social problems, but lower tax bases to fund public services. Finally, people's sense of community and connectedness can

---

B o x 5.2 • Responses to Sprawl

Contradictory forces, both public and private, have historically shaped urban and metropolitan development. In recent years, many communities have responded to the phenomena of sprawl and uneven development with a range of so-called "smart growth" proposals that embody many common themes and practices. In general, such proposals call for more metropolitan or regional planning that makes more efficient use of existing resources and provides a more equitable distribution of the costs and benefits of uneven development. Among the objectives of many proposals are:

1. More effective reuse of existing land and infrastructure resources
2. Restrictions on development in outlying suburban and exurban areas
3. Development of a range of transportation modes and less reliance on the automobile
4. Concentration of residential and commercial development in central locations and along the lines of mass transit arteries
5. Creation of area-wide revenue sharing and regional investment pools
6. More affordable housing construction and distribution of such housing throughout metropolitan areas
7. More vigorous enforcement of fair housing laws
8. Increased public and private investment in central cities to achieve more balanced development throughout the region

SOURCE: Gregory D. Squires, "Urban Sprawl and the Uneven Development of Metropolitan America," in *Urban Sprawl: Causes, Consequences, and Policy Responses*, ed. Gregory D. Squires (Washington, D.C.: The Urban Institute Press, 2002), pp. 15–16.

---

be undermined by living in a sprawled area because of the increased amount of time they spend commuting, their insularity from people who are different from themselves, and the lack of connection between home and work. In other words, sprawl exacerbates the social inequality that has been a characteristic of North American society over the past fifty years. Box 5.2 shows some policy recommendations that help alleviate the problems associated with suburban sprawl.

RESTRUCTURING THE CENTRAL CITIES

In addition to the growth of the suburbs, another striking trend in metropolitan areas, particularly since the 1970s, has been the economic, physical, and social restructuring of the central cities. The term *restructuring* can be used in several senses; it will be used here to mean the changes in the characteristic patterns of urban form and urban social institutions that had been apparent up to World War II. We will first examine those changes that have taken place in the central business districts and then move on to changes that have occurred in the central cities outside of the central business districts.

Transformation of the Central Business Districts

Central business districts, the downtowns of the corporate city, came into prominence in the early decades of the twentieth century. As we saw earlier, they typically contained some mix of offices (including corporate headquarters, business services, government offices, and professional offices), retail establishments, hotels, restaurants, and theaters or other cultural institutions. These were often located in clusters, such as a financial district, a court/legal district, a department store district, and a theater district. They might also be subdivided—for example, an area within the shopping district dedicated to the sale of specialized products such as musical instruments or fur coats. In addition, central business districts of most older cities, particularly in the Northeast and Midwest, also contained substantial remnants of manufacturing activity. Buildings that had been or in some cases still were used for manufacturing or storing goods, such as factory lofts, warehouses, and wholesale shippers, often ringed the more commercial streets and tended to be densely built, low-rise structures.

Economic Restructuring of the Central Business Districts.   The structure of the old central business district reflected the transition that was occurring from the manufacturing base of the urban economies to the corporate service base. Until the mid-1950s, most employed people worked at manufacturing jobs; although, as we have seen, a smaller proportion of those jobs were located in the central cities as more employers opened plants on the outskirts. By the mid-1970s, a clear-cut pattern of urban economic restructuring was occurring. Employment in manufacturing, although holding steady nationally, was rapidly decreasing in the central cities; employment in the retail and wholesale sectors was declining more slowly. Employment in the service sector, however, was increasing rapidly, even in those central cities that were experiencing overall job loss (Beauregard 1993).

This national pattern of the shift from manufacturing and retail activity to the service sector had different consequences in different cities. One reason for the differential impact had to do with the city size. The largest cities tended to gain the lion's share of the growth in services—especially the corporate-oriented producer services—in all regions of the country (Noyelle and Stanback 1984). A second factor in the shift's impact had to do with the age of the city and its past history. In general, older cities whose economies had been devoted to the older economic sectors, such as mining and manufacturing, had less growth. This pattern was not due to age alone. Some older cities, such as New York, Denver, and San Francisco, became prominent service-sector cities and took on new economic functions in the global or regional economy. Other older cities, such as New Haven and Detroit, failed to develop a large enough service sector to retain jobs in the central city (Fainstein and Fainstein 1983).

The growth of offices in the central business districts was only partly due to the growth of service work. The reorganization of manufacturing also contributed to the office boom. As manufacturing became increasingly located on the outskirts of cities or in suburbs, corporate offices were increasingly likely to be moved into locations separate from the plants. The management functions moved to downtown office buildings, linked to the manufacturing facilities through telephones and computers. Thus, employment in central business districts was changing both because of the increase in the service sector relative to manufacturing and because of the reorganization of the manufacturing sector.

What implication does the continuing growth of service employment have for the central cities? Some analysts have argued that services will ultimately become dispersed into the suburbs just as manufacturing has (Steinaker 1998). Some kinds of services, for example, consumer services such as medical offices and the more routine corporate services such as accounting, have already begun to decentralize. In general, however, the tendency of the major control functions of corporations, the decision-making functions, have remained centralized in major cities, as have the corporate-oriented producer services.

Smith (1986) argues that companies will, in all likelihood, continue to locate their top management in the central business districts even as they move clerical functions to the suburbs. Corporate managers work in a highly uncertain and changeable economic environment, affected by such volatile factors as the stock market, interest rates, suppliers' or customers' decisions, and government actions. Because they are constantly responding to change, the physical proximity of the company's decision makers, their clients, their consultants, their bankers, government agencies, and even their competitors' headquarters is valuable to businesses. Whether advanced communication technologies will gradually undercut the advantage of physical proximity remains to be seen. If e-mail and videoconferences can actually replace personal meetings, the corporate office function of the central cities could decline dramatically.

Restructuring trends are most apparent in those cities that play the largest role in the international economy. The cities in the United States with the strongest ties to the international economy, such as New York, Los Angeles, and Miami, have been transformed more rapidly than other cities. The growing financial and producer service sectors that have emerged nationally dominate their local economies. In addition, although the manufacturing sector is still present in these cities, it has become downgraded to minimum-wage or even piecework standards as a new labor force, largely composed of immigrants from poorer countries, provides cheap labor within those cities (Sassen 2001). Box 5.3 shows how this transformation in manufacturing took place in Los Angeles. We will explore this trend in more detail in the next chapter.

Physical Restructuring of the Central Business Districts.   Beginning in the 1960s, new buildings and other physical structures for work and living spaces gradually reflected the central cities' new economic foundations. More office space was needed; and fewer manufacturing, retail, and wholesale spaces were needed. Those cities that were experiencing a boom in the service sector typically saw huge increases in office space, particularly in the construction of new high-rise office towers. Corporations constructed some of the more prominent of these to house their headquarters and related businesses; speculators who relied on strong demand for new office space to sign tenants constructed others. During the 1980s corporate profits were at an all-time high, and companies began to

---

B o x 5.3 • Restructuring of Manufacturing in Los Angeles

Unlike Detroit or Youngstown [Ohio] ... L.A.'s derelict industrial core was not simply abandoned. Almost as fast as *Fortune* 500 corporations shut down their branch plants, local capitalists rushed in to take advantage of the Southeast's cheap leases, tax incentives, and burgeoning supply of immigrant Mexican labor. Minimum-wage apparel and furniture makers, fleeing from land inflation in Downtown L. A., were in the vanguard of the movement. Within the dead shell of heavy manufacturing, a new sweatshop economy emerged.

The old Firestone Rubber and American Can plants, for instance, have been converted into nonunion furniture factories, while the great Bethlehem Steel Works on Slauson Avenue has been replaced by a hot dog distributor, a Chinese food products company, and a maker of rattan patio furniture. Chrysler Maywood is now a bank "back office" while U.S. Steel has metamorphosed into a warehouse complex, and the "Assyrian" wall of Uniroyal Tire has become a façade for a designer-label outlet center. (On the other hand, the area's former largest employer, GM South Gate, remains a ninety-acre vacant lot.)

SOURCE: Mike Davis, *Dead Cities* (New York: New Press, 2002), pp. 193–194.

---

invest larger portions of their earnings in new buildings rather than in increasing production of their products. In the early 1990s the office explosion stalled, due to corporate downsizing and the glut of office space added during the 1980s, but construction continued again after 1995 (Fainstein 2001).

The building booms in service-sector cities such as New York and San Francisco had consequences for the style of new buildings as well as for the number built, and the search for the "right" office space took on symbolic as well as practical dimensions for corporations. When large companies decide to move their headquarters, location is normally their most important consideration; but over the period of the 1980s and 1990s, companies began increasingly to look for distinctive style and design in the architecture of their buildings. A handful of prominent architects whose signature design features became well known were in high demand as corporate designers, because the status of corporate headquarter buildings began to rival the actual use value of the buildings. This phenomenon flourished, because clients of firms engaged in corporate services such as banking, investments, law, and management consulting are sold as much by the symbolic aspects of a company's image as by the actual products they offer (Larson 1993).

As a consequence of the departure of manufacturing, many old industrial spaces were abandoned in central cities. Some were demolished; others were renovated to house service-sector businesses such as architectural firms, galleries, or restaurants; still others became housing. A combination of government policy, local economic conditions, the demographic characteristics of the city, and the level of demand for housing and other space decided the fates of individual buildings. Still other physical remnants of the older industrial cities were removed or remade to accommodate the new service economies of the central cities. In many cities, old streets were widened, railroad tracks and stations moved, parking facilities expanded, and old working-class neighborhoods removed to provide physical space more appropriate to the needs of modern corporations.

Social Transformation of the Cities

From a humanistic perspective, these changes in urban form over the past twenty to thirty years, although vivid, are far overshadowed by dramatic changes in the urban population. City residents today represent a different segment of the population than they did in the 1950s. We will examine three trends that have contributed to making cities different places in which to live: income polarization, gentrification, and racial and ethnic fragmentation.

Income Polarization: The Dual City?   With all of the changes taking place in the economic bases of cities, it should not come as a surprise that the social class structure of central cities has changed as well. Compared to the 1950s and 1960s, trends since the 1970s show a polarization of incomes. Thus, the proportion of central-city residents who could be classified as middle income decreased relatively, and the proportion of wealthy and poor residents increased.

Increased suburbanization of the middle class is partly responsible for income polarization in cities. As we saw earlier, middle-class homeowners have made up a huge proportion of the recent migrants to the suburbs. Another factor that has contributed to income polarization is the decline of manufacturing and the growth of the service sector, leading to income polarization in two ways. First, the decline in manufacturing jobs in the established manufacturing centers has reduced the number of stable, unionized, high-pay and high-benefit jobs, especially in the older industrial cities. Second, within the growing service sector, the new jobs being created fall into two sharply different categories. On the one hand, service-sector growth has meant an increase in the number of highly paid managerial, professional, and technical workers such as investment bankers, attorneys, and computer systems analysts. On the other hand, a substantial proportion of the service-sector growth is made up of low-skill, minimum-wage jobs such as cleaners, parking lot attendants, and food servers. The earnings gap between high-wage and low-wage employment is greatest in the cities with the fastest-growing service economies. This wage gap in new jobs is a major contributor to the urban income polarization of recent decades (Sassen 1990).

Some writers have dubbed the urban effects of income polarization "the dual city," noting that homelessness and luxury have both increased in urban areas. The problem with the term *dual city*, however, is that it singles out the division between wealth and poverty and understates the other divisions present in urban populations. As we will see in Part III, race, ethnicity, and gender cut across the divisions of social class or income. Thus, the pattern of inequality is less clear than a simple division into rich and poor; the *tendency* toward polarization does not mean that the urban population is divided into only two groups (Mollenkopf and Castells 1991).

Gentrification.   In recent years, geographic shifts in the preferred neighborhoods of residence for different social groups have accompanied changes in income and occupation. Increases in highly paid service-sector employees in cities such as New York, Boston, San Francisco, and Chicago have increased the demand for expensive housing in those cities. Some of these highly paid employees continue to live in established affluent neighborhoods, such as the Upper East Side of Manhattan, but the expansion of this group has pushed the boundaries of the fashionable neighborhoods outward to new neighborhoods.

In the 1960s, when affluent residents began moving into nonaffluent London neighborhoods in large enough numbers to make a change in the overall composition of the area, trend spotters called the movement **gentrification**, or the growth of the gentry. That name has taken hold and expanded to include an up-scaling of any urban area, whether it is a residential neighborhood or a business district.

Probably the most common form of gentrification is the gradual movement of middle-class households into poorer neighborhoods. Typically, the neighborhoods that are ripe for gentrification are those that are close to amenities such as a park, river, university, or hospital. Often the scenario is that an older neighborhood with large homes that were abandoned by the middle class and cut up into apartments for lower-income households is "rediscovered" as a potentially attractive place to live. The homes are then reconverted back to single-family homes and occupied by professional households. Once a neighborhood begins to gentrify, housing values soar, attracting more middle class people who see it as a good housing value and a more convenient location than a suburban neighborhood. The arrival of new residents of differing class and often racial and ethnic backgrounds can also lead to social conflict as the norms of one group is different from the other (Anderson 1990). For instance, middle-class homeowners may wish for more quiet at nighttime, or discourage residents from sitting on their stoops.

Gentrification has both positive and negative outcomes for cities. A positive result of gentrification is that the influx of middle-class population raises housing values and strengthens the city's tax base. In addition, gentrifying neighborhoods can support small businesses such as delis, boutiques, and bookstores, adding to the urban economy. On the negative side, rising home values can push out long-time residents. Frequently, landlords sell multiunit buildings, the new owners evict the tenants to renovate and improve the building, and the tenants, unable to afford rising prices in their own neighborhood, are forced to move to different areas. In *Harlem: Heaven or Hell,* Monique Taylor (2002) shows how the gentrification of Harlem in New York City is dependent upon both the past and the present. During the 1920s Harlem was home to the "Harlem Renaissance," a flourishing of African-American culture that endowed the neighborhood with great symbolic significance for many African Americans. By the 1970s, however, Harlem was faced with the problems of many inner-city neighborhoods: high crime, unemployment, and neglect. By the 1990s, middle and upper class African Americans began to return to the neighborhood, attracted by both the significance of the neighborhood's illustrious past and the relatively inexpensive property values. As in other gentrified neighborhoods (see, for example, Anderson 1992), there was conflict between some long-time residents and the new gentrifiers, and some newcomers even left the neighborhood to return to neighborhoods in lower Manhattan. As Taylor summarized:

> Dilemmas of difference, now based on class and home ownership, complicate residents' arrival in Harlem, where they ostensibly came for solidarity...What practices can overcome an outsider status that leaves the group of middle-class blacks still suspended between two worlds? (127)

Gentrification is not limited to residential neighborhoods. In the 1970s many old manufacturing and commercial spaces of the industrial era were converted, not only into housing but also into restaurants, exhibit spaces, retail shops, and offices. Creative reuse of space became an important criterion in location, and "character" increased a property's value. Property capitalists invested in gentrifying areas, building or renovating living spaces for buyers not interested in doing their own construction. Galleries and specialized shops, attracted by the combination of relatively inexpensive space and the proximity of a group of highly paid and well-educated consumers, often located in gentrifying areas. Some of these clusters, like the loft districts in lower Manhattan, became major cultural centers (Zukin 1982).

A good deal of the analysis of gentrification has emphasized the cultural and aesthetic characteristics of the new spaces created by a relatively young, highly educated urban elite. The stereotypical gentrifying household might consist of either a professional couple renovating a Victorian house in a "promising" neighborhood, or an artist living and working in a former factory loft on the edge of the central business district. These households, although different, would both represent a choice other than the suburban locations that dominated residential movement of their social class in the 1950s and 1960s. Gentrification, then, has often had some characteristics of a subculture characterized by a different set of lifestyle choices than the suburban norm, "a distancing from the traditional middle class and an aspiration to power" (Zukin 1991).

Gentrification has two causes. First, the restructuring of the economy provides additional jobs for professional workers, who need places to live. These well-paid house hunters can afford high rents and can bid up housing prices. Second, the relatively cheap real estate surrounding many older central business districts provides opportunities for existing housing or industrial buildings to be renovated and converted to upscale residences. These two factors (as well as the actions of government, which will be addressed shortly) combine to set the groundwork for an influx of affluent households into previously poor areas.

Racial and Ethnic Fragmentation.   Economic restructuring of the cities has affected the racial and ethnic makeup of the urban population. During the 1970s the proportion of whites in the larger central cities declined, and the proportion of African Americans increased sharply. During the 1980s and 1990s, the proportion of Latino and Asian residents also increased. (See Box 5.4.) These newcomers

B o x 5.4 • Case Study
Restructuring of the Metropolitan Los Angeles Economy

The economic vitality of the Los Angeles region after the turbulent late 1960s and early 1970s was accompanied by an intensified bifurcation of regional labor markets. On the one hand, there has been a growing high-wage, high-skill group of workers (managers, business executives, scientists, engineers, designers, celebrities, and many others in the entertainment industry); on the other hand, there has been an even more rapidly expanding mass of marginalized, low-wage, low-skill workers, the majority of whom are women and often undocumented Latino and Asian immigrants, who find employment throughout the service sector and in a widening pool of manufacturing sweatshops, from the garment industry to electronics assembly. Between these two strata is the traditional skilled and semiskilled blue collar working class, which has been shrinking with such rapidity that it is now commonly referred to as the disappearing middle stratum of Southern California society. Many industrial sectors have based their main competitive strategies over this period on labor cost reductions rather than on reskilling workers or on product and process quality improvements, thus capturing much of the labor force in a vicious circle of cost squeezing. This has been made easier by the dramatic decline of industrial unionization throughout the region. As a result, the wages of production workers have declined in real terms since the 1970s, even as the overall economy boomed.

... The restructuring of the regional economy of Los Angeles was associated with a dramatically changing demographic pattern. As in earlier surges of urban development, waves of new immigration provided abundant cheap labor to fuel economic expansion and control labor costs, typically at the expense of established working-class communities. After the late 1960s, however, the migration waves reached unprecedented heights, transforming Los Angeles into the country's major port of entry for immigrants and making it probably the world's most ethnically and racially diverse metropolis. This demographic and cultural transformation and diversification has been most pronounced in Los Angeles County. The county's population shifted from 70 percent Anglo to 60 percent non-Anglo between 1970 and 1990, as what was once the most white and Protestant of American cities changed into what some commentators now call America's leading Third World city.

SOURCE: Edward Soja and Allen Scott, "Introduction to Los Angeles: City and Region," in *The City: Los Angeles and Urban Theory at the End of the Twentieth Century*, ed. A. Scott and E. Soja (Berkeley: University of California Press, 1996), pp. 13–14.

to the newly restructured urban economies disproportionately work in low-paying positions, often within ethnic "niches" of one or two industries (Waldinger 1996). As the numbers of Asian, Latino, and African-American residents increase in metropolitan areas, we can observe significant clustering by race and ethnicity. As shown in Figure 5.3, Los Angeles County, one of the most diverse metropolitan areas in the world, is home to some two dozen identifiably "ethnic minority" communities.

The continued movement of white middle-class and working-class families to the suburbs has been accompanied by the more gradual outward movement of minority middle-class households. Overall, high levels of racial segregation, especially among African Americans, persist in major metropolitan areas. Within the central cities, particularly those in the Northeast and Midwest, levels of racial

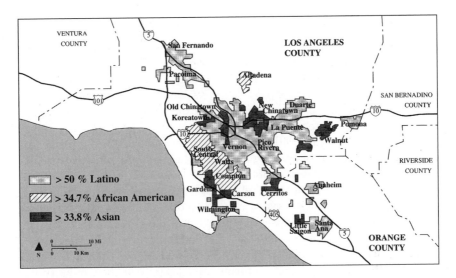

FIGURE 5.3 Racial and Ethnic Fragmentation. Despite its overall population diversity, the Los Angeles metropolitan area shows significant clustering of its three main racial and ethnic minorities into separate communities.

SOURCE: Edward Soja and Allen Scott, "Introduction to Los Angeles: City and Region," In *The City: Los Angeles and Urban Theory at the End of the Twentieth Century*, ed. A. Scott and E. Soja (Berkeley: University of California Press, 1996), p. 15.

segregation have hardly declined since the 1950s. In addition, racial divisions often overlap with class divisions to create a more extreme situation. Some central city neighborhoods that have very high proportions of African-American residents, for example, have very high rates of poverty as well, a spatial pattern that has become more pronounced because of the cities' economic restructuring. These extreme poverty neighborhoods are often older African-American neighborhoods, where the combination of a decrease in access to jobs and the departure of the employed middle class has left behind only those residents who are trapped economically (Wilson 1987).

To summarize, cities since the 1970s have undergone a fundamental restructuring, which involves the economic and physical restructuring of the central business districts as well as the social restructuring of the entire city and metropolitan area. Some social changes include income polarization, gentrification, and increased ethnic and racial fragmentation.

EXPLAINING URBAN TRANSFORMATIONS

Now that we have seen the various manifestations of urban restructuring, we must ask what has caused these transformations. Two factors are most important: the changing place of the United States economy within the world economy, and the policies that government bodies have implemented as a response to the changing economy.

The United States in the World Economy

In Chapter 4 we saw that the U.S. economy has gone through different stages of development in which different ways of making a profit have been prevalent. Since the 1920s the economy has been in a stage of corporate accumulation, characterized by the growth of very large corporations, often conglomerates, making more than one product. The growth of these large corporations has had many consequences for other aspects of life.

From the 1920s to the 1960s the United States had the fastest growing and most highly productive economy in the world. This rapid economic growth (except during the Great Depression of the 1930s) provided the conditions supporting both high profits for companies and high wages for workers at the same time. Many of the dominant industries such as autos, steel, airlines, and food processing were controlled by one or a few firms, which had similar contracts with their unions and paid similar wages. The economic domination of the U. S. increased during the period after World War II (1945–1960) because the other industrialized countries, such as England, Germany, and Japan, had their industry destroyed during the war. In the U.S., manufacturing rapidly shifted from ships, tanks, and guns to consumer goods.

One consequence of the period's high productivity and relatively high wages was the rapid growth of working people's incomes from the 1920s to the 1960s. This situation provided a continual boost for the national economy. The expansion of incomes gave working people a growing ability to consume, which, in turn, allowed the sale of more products. Suburbanization was an important part of this economic expansion in that it encouraged families to spend money at far greater levels than did urban living. In addition to a new house, furniture, appliances, and so on, the move to the suburbs came to imply the purchase of a standard package of household consumer goods: lawn and garden care equipment, a collection of power tools, sports and leisure items, and extra automobiles. The appeal of these items, and even the space to store them, was a new feature of postwar suburban life, one that encouraged a greater level of consumer spending than was previously seen. As the suburban way of life became the ideal at home, U.S. government and industry leaders mounted a campaign to export this way of life abroad. Under the Marshall Plan, the U.S. government lent money to the European nations so they could purchase American products and technology (Beauregard 2006).

To understand the changes that have taken place in the decades since 1970, it is important to recognize that the postwar economic stability of the United States from 1945 to 1970 was partly because the United States had the dominant position in the world economy during those years. Since 1970 the economy is increasingly globalized, with companies locating their plants and offices in many different nations. With the global economy, companies have spread out across national boundaries to take advantage of different cost structures in different countries. Thus, even the firms that have headquarters in the United States produce and sell products, components, and services in many different countries. So an increase in profits or sales of U.S. firms does not automatically translate into an expansion in employment for U.S. workers.

The globalization of the economy is related to the changes in community life and the restructuring of urban areas that have occurred since the 1970s. Large, stable firms, providing long-term employment for workers are on the decrease. The old industrial regions have been shaken by an overall decline in manufacturing jobs. In cities experiencing an increase in manufacturing jobs, such as New York and Los Angeles, expanding companies are paying low wages and recruiting many workers from the ranks of immigrants rather than native U.S. residents. Formerly, large firms operated primarily with capital and plants in a single nation; now, many industries are dominated by multinationals, which have operations in many locations. In short, much of the premise of the increasing standard of living for all and the stable geographic employment base on which the postwar suburban growth trend was based have eroded.

On the other hand, as parts of the United States become enmeshed in the global economy, a whole new set of opportunities for high profits and high pay has emerged. New high-technology production requires a more highly skilled labor force and in many cases pays better than did the older low-skill assembly line. Another area with opportunities for high pay is in the service sector. Within the global economy, some geographic locations have become international centers for certain high-level business operations. For example, from 1985 to 2007, New York City consolidated its position as one of a handful of global centers for banking and investment. As the stock market boomed and the investment climate thrived, thousands of people made substantial fortunes. The economic meltdown of 2007, however, resulted in a crash not only of the stock market but also of major banks, investment companies, and other industries. Because the economy is so globally interconnected, this crisis that began in the United States quickly spread around the world.

All of these disparate causes have added up to two important changes in the economic basis of community life. First, the overall standard of living, as measured by wages relative to inflation, grew steadily from 1950 to 1973 but has declined since that time. Within that general trend it is apparent that not everyone has been equally affected; rather, an increasing polarization has occurred between rich and poor in communities all over the United States. That polarization can be seen both within cities as well as between cities and suburban communities. The homeless person sleeping in the park, the highly paid professional eating in the chic urban restaurant, and the suburban homeowner struggling to pay the mortgage are all affected by these economic trends.

Second, local communities, which during the decades of the 1950s and 1960s tended to be relatively stable, have become more changeable. Business startups, movement, and closures are more frequent and pose a problem not only to the local employment base but also to the local tax base. Population movements have increased as the instability of local economies has increased; children who grow up in a certain community can no longer be confident that they will find jobs there when they are ready to enter the labor force. Greater mobility among the population creates more fluctuation in real estate values, levels of need for public services, and other aspects of community life. In both the communities that are growing and in those that are shrinking, instability can produce social problems to which government must devote resources.

Government Responses to Economic Changes

What has government done in response to the economic changes described here, and how have those policy responses affected cities? We will examine in some detail the complex role of government actions in Part IV, but at this point the most significant government action to consider is the role of government in attempting to foster economic growth.

After World War II, the federal government implemented a program of economic stimulus measures designed to prevent the economy from slipping into a postwar recession. The highway construction, mortgage guarantee, and the homeowners' tax deduction programs that we have discussed were major stimulus packages that fostered economic growth. The effect of these policies spurred suburban growth but unintentionally drained both human and economic resources from many central cities. By the 1960s, as these negative effects were becoming apparent in the cities, some federal programs such as Urban Renewal and Model Cities were instituted to rebuild cities and attract investment. Although these programs often managed to modernize the central business districts and to replace a certain number of older residences with housing for the more affluent, they had a minor impact compared to the huge support for decentralization.

The federal government has also fostered growth through government spending, which puts money into the economy by deficit spending of government funds. Tax cuts that give consumers more spending money are an example of this approach, as is direct government spending. The most significant direct government spending in the postwar period has, ironically, been military spending. The continuation of hostilities with the communist bloc through the Cold War of the 1950s and various hot wars with North Korea, North Vietnam, Afghanistan, and Iraq provided the motivation for trillions of dollars to be spent on armaments. This spending has been highly uneven in its geographic effects because the majority of defense contracts are geographically clustered, both in suburbs as opposed to cities and in certain regions of the country (Markusen 1987; Castells 1985).

Most recently, as a response to the 2007 economic crisis, the federal government has enacted a host of economic stimulus programs. It is too early to determine whether these will have any specific impacts on cities or suburbs.

CONCLUSION

Cities and metropolitan areas have experienced significant changes in the period since 1950. The first important trend was the growth of the suburbs and metropolitan areas due to decisions by large companies, government agencies, and consumers. Although the movement out from the centers of the cities had been a long-established trend, it took on a new intensity in the postwar period. In addition, in many areas the suburban communities have remained politically independent of the central cities, creating a more fragmented metropolis than in those areas that have remained politically unified. New patterns of racial and class division have emerged, both within the suburbs and between the suburbs and the central cities.

The second important trend of the postwar city has been the restructuring of the central cities. Changes in the national and global economy have caused changes in local economies. A new mix of businesses in the central business districts has necessitated rebuilding the downtown districts. Changes in local economies have often downgraded jobs for blue-collar workers while increasing jobs for educated professional workers. Thus, restructuring has changed both the physical form and the social class patterns in cities.

Many of the aspects of suburbanization and restructuring can be related to the general shift in the capitalist world economy over the past fifty years. U.S. industry, which was preeminent in the period immediately after World War II, is now more fragmented and internationalized, both competing and cooperating with multinational firms from all over the world. In addition to their direct impact on the income and job security of most working people, these economic changes have caused changes and dislocations in the previous patterns of life in many urban and suburban communities.

DISCUSSION QUESTIONS

1. What kinds of businesses are expanding or newly locating in the area surrounding you? What kinds have shut down or moved? What do you think the local impacts of these changes are on your community?

2. Think about the difference between the decision of where to locate a service station and the decision of where to locate a law firm. What kinds of questions would the owners ask in each case, and how would their needs differ?

3. Central business districts have changed considerably in the past few decades as cities have decentralized, but they still play an important role in the business world. As the economy continues to change, what do you think might be some alternative futures for central business districts?

6

Cities in Europe

When a man is tired of London, he is tired of life;
For there is in London all that life can afford.
SAMUEL JOHNSON (1709–1784)

Cities are a worldwide phenomenon, but the specific forms and lifestyles of cities vary according to the history, culture, economy, and politics of the country and region in which they are located. Having taken a close look at North American cities in the previous two chapters, we now turn to examine cities in another part of the world.

This chapter will focus on cities in the industrialized countries, chiefly in Europe, and the next chapter will focus on cities in the developing world. We will be looking for comparisons with North American cities, as well as for similarities and differences among the cities on other continents.

The main questions this chapter addresses are:

- What aspects of contemporary city life are inheritances from the past?

- What current political and economic changes are affecting cities?

- What kinds of problems are emerging in industrialized cities, and how are different governments addressing those problems?

- How has the process of globalization affected cities?

- What are *global cities*, and how are they different from other cities within the increasingly global economy?

As we saw in the previous two chapters, cities constantly change in response to the conditions of the time. Yet each change is "layered" over the previous set of changes. In the United States, a relatively young society, only a few layers of previous history lie beneath the built environment of contemporary cities. In Europe, on the other hand, cities have been constructed and reconstructed over centuries and even millennia. The heritage of the past gives inhabitants of cities a distinctive culture, a sense of tradition, and often significant architectural treasures.

The heritage of the past can also inhibit change and growth by making it difficult to find space to build something new.

In this chapter, we will examine patterns and trends in three groups of cities: cities of Western Europe, cities of Eastern Europe, and the emerging global cities.

CITIES IN WESTERN EUROPE

Western Europe includes the nations of Great Britain, France, the Netherlands, Belgium, Switzerland, Austria, and Germany, as well as northern Italy. It is the most highly industrialized and economically powerful portion of Europe. During the twentieth century, industrialization encouraged the growth of large agglomerations and metropolitan areas, creating what some have called an "urban crescent" from central Britain south to northern Italy (Mackensen 1999).

Comparisons with North American Cities

Western European cities are not uniform. They were constructed in different economic circumstances: during periods of industrialization, agrarian production, and trade. They had their origins in different political regimes: some in feudalism, others in monarchies. They have had different types of planning and land-use policies. Despite their differences, however, when we compare the cities of Western Europe to cities of the United States, certain characteristics of the European cities stand out. White (1984) notes the following traits that distinguish Western European cities from North American cities.

- The major landmarks in European cities are castles, churches, or palaces rather than banks, insurance companies, or hotels.

- Buildings, even in the city centers, tend to have multiple uses, combining businesses or offices with residential apartments.

- Compared to the United States, European cities have higher living densities but fewer skyscrapers. This is partly the legacy of the old fortified walls that prevented expansion and partly due to extensive government regulation of building and land use.

- Because city structures grew up over a long period of time, markedly different types of buildings can be found adjacent to each other.

- The center of the city is the most prestigious location, with a gradient of desirability dropping off according to the distance from the center.

Central Cities and Suburbs.   One of the striking differences between cities in Europe and those in the United States is the prestige and power associated with the historic cores of the European cities. The most prestigious locations are at the center, and the least prestigious are on the periphery. Thus, central cities are desirable locations; suburbs are undesirable locations. This cultural belief has an enormous impact on land use, housing prices, and the location of the different social classes (Kazepov 2005).

If one were to map the location of different social classes within Western European cities, the result would resemble an inside-out version of the concentric zone pattern that Burgess described for Chicago. (See Chapter 2.) A typical city layout would reveal that the wealthy and professional residents live in the center of the city and the poorer blue-collar workers live on the periphery (along with industry); the lower white-collar workers occupy the intermediate areas. Beyond the industrial belt, if the area has a major natural feature such as a lake, river, forest, or mountain, the nearby land might become a retreat for the wealthy (White 1984).

The process of suburbanization, as we saw in Chapter 5, has been almost a continuous feature of the growth of U.S. cities throughout their history. Suburbanization in Europe, however, did not take place on a large scale until the nineteenth century, when political stability allowed the removal of the old fortified walls that had limited growth in many cities. Typically, suburban expansion involved the construction of new factories and housing for industrial workers. Consequently, suburban housing densities are higher in Europe than in North America, and a greater proportion of suburban housing is in multifamily apartment buildings. Suburbs, then, have a much different meaning in Europe than in the United States. As White says (1984, 213), "the suburb has not been an area of positive residential choice by its inhabitants who have, instead, been 'sent' there by the exigencies of the housing market, especially in the publicly rented sector in recent years."

Besides the historical and cultural reasons for the differing patterns within cities and suburbs in Europe and the United States, government policy has also influenced the different growth patterns of suburbs on the two continents. As we saw in previous chapters, local governments in the United States have no jurisdiction outside of their own boundaries, and metropolitan areas are composed of many local jurisdictions, so no agency has power over land-use control in the metropolitan area as a whole. In Western Europe, however, regional planning bodies normally control development in an entire region. This difference has two major consequences for cities and suburbs. First, suburban towns in the United States often encourage the development of new shopping centers despite their negative impact on the central city's downtown. In Europe, planning bodies have deliberately discouraged such peripheral construction, thereby preserving the dominance of the cities' centers. Second, housing developers in the United States can "leapfrog" over undeveloped areas to buy cheap land on the outermost edges of a metropolitan area. This contributes to sprawl as well as to undermining the housing markets in central cities. In Europe, however, regional authorities have usually confined new development to the immediate edges of the city or to the practice of "infilling" vacant lots within the city. This policy has helped discourage urban sprawl and protect agricultural land from being sold for housing developments (Häussermann and Haila 2005).

Factors Affecting Western European Cities

Just as in the United States, the major factors affecting the cities of Western Europe over the past fifty years have been economic and political changes. Specifically, four types of factors have had major impacts on European cities: technological change, a reduction in government control of the economy, privatization of the housing markets, and the formation of a single European economy.

Technological Change. In the previous chapter, we saw how the change from an industrial to an informational economy has affected U.S. cities. This change has affected the cities in other industrialized nations as well, but not always in the same way as it has affected American cities.

Although, like the United States, the overall trend in manufacturing is downward, manufacturing is still strong in many parts of Europe. Germany is the manufacturing center of Europe, with France, Italy, and the United Kingdom tied for second place. Automobiles, electronics, and food processing are the sectors in which the largest European manufacturing firms are concentrated.

The overall decline in manufacturing employment has affected different areas differently. The traditionally heavily industrialized regions in Germany, for example, were the Ruhr, Aachen, and Saar districts in the north of the country, including the cities of Bonn, Cologne, and Düsseldorf. In recent years, the new growth areas for manufacturing have been in the southern areas around Frankfurt, Stuttgart, and Munich. This has been due partly to the location of newer firms, partly to the availability of a highly qualified labor force, and partly to government subsidies that have helped cities in certain areas (Mackensen 1999).

As some cities have declined with the decline in manufacturing, others have risen with the rise in the service and information economy. One of the fastest growing sectors of the economy in industrialized Europe is the advanced **producer services**. These are services that are purchased not directly by consumers, but by other companies. Many producer service companies act as consultants to other companies, providing services that the other company needs but does not want to provide itself. Examples are information technology, human resource planning, legal services, marketing, and tax accounting. Although such firms theoretically could be located anywhere, they tend to cluster in large cities. Because larger cities have more diversified workforces, the advanced producer services often are drawn to these large centers. Some evidence shows that medium-sized cities adjacent to large cities are attractive locations for producer services. Daniels (1998) characterizes the result as "concentrated decentralization" that has spurred the growth of parts of London, Paris, Milan, Amsterdam, and Vienna.

Changing Government Policies. Compared to the United States, governments in Europe have had more power and authority to manage the economy. Another way of looking at it is that Americans have been historically more willing than Europeans to let the private market shape social and economic realities for all citizens. After World War II, many countries in Western Europe adopted a set of government policies that led to the creation of what came to be called the "**welfare state**." This approach to public policy, associated with liberal and leftist political parties, assumed that governments should provide basic services to all citizens. Thus, countries such as Great Britain, France, Germany, Sweden, and the Netherlands introduced substantial old-age pensions, unemployment benefits, government-financed health care, subsidized housing, and free education from nursery school through university. Governments paid for these public services by instituting relatively high income taxes. Governments also took a strong hand in regulating and directing private businesses, often with the cooperation of business and labor leaders. Welfare state policies dominated European politics from about 1945 until about 1980.

The election of Margaret Thatcher's Conservative Party in Great Britain in 1979 ushered in a new free-market approach in that country that many analysts simply call "Thatcherism." The stated goal of the Thatcher administration was to dismantle the welfare state and to rely on the free market to promote economic growth and well-being. Because urban planning was one of the main policies of the welfare state, the Thatcher government made some dramatic changes in urban policy. These radical changes involved two elements: replacing planning with the market as a process for making decisions, and replacing local government control of urban development with strong central government control. Under Thatcher, urban planning was reoriented to maximize income for investors and downplay community objectives such as protection of the environment. Keystones of this market-based approach were enterprise zones, which reduced regulation in designated sections of cities, and urban development corporations, which bought up land for urban redevelopment by private investors (Newman and Thornley 1996).

In France, urban policy also underwent a dramatic change as a result of electoral politics. The change was different from the British case, however. Unlike Great Britain, urban planning and policy had traditionally been highly centralized in France. In 1981, a series of new laws decentralized planning power and put it in the hands of local communities. The impetus for the decentralization of power came from the large cities, particularly from left-leaning mayors, after the election of a socialist government. They advocated for legislation to create new regional bodies that would oversee economic development and planning. This decentralization of planning encouraged many mayors to become entrepreneurial in promoting their locales and to form partnerships with companies to invest in their cities (Newman and Thornley 1996).

In the cases of both Great Britain and France, the outcome was to encourage private and public development in real estate. This similar outcome occurred by different routes. In England a strong central government seized power from localities to prevent them from exerting control over developers. Thus, centralization of power was a step toward reducing local government regulation over land use and planning. In France, the localities pushed for decentralization of power, which freed them from previous strong centralized control. Thus, decentralization of power was one step toward reducing national government regulation over land use and planning.

Changes in the Housing Market. One of the most striking differences between urban life in Europe and in the United States is the nature of **housing tenure**. With the exception of the United Kingdom, homeownership rates are much lower in Europe than in the United States. Furthermore (again with the exception of the U.K.), homeownership often does not mean owning a detached house but owning an apartment (in an arrangement similar to a condominium). Rental property is also different in Europe. In the United States, we are used to thinking of rentals as privately owned, except for public housing developments operated by local housing authorities. In Europe, however, a much larger proportion of rental property is in the **social housing** sector, owned not by private individuals but by local governments, nonprofit housing associations, or cooperatives. Furthermore, rental properties often include single-family houses as well as apartments. Another complicating factor is that rents of privately owned dwellings are more often controlled by legislation than they are in the United States (Häussermann and Haila 2005).

Social housing has a longer and more glorious history in Western Europe than in the United States. (See Chapter 14 for a discussion of public housing in the United States.) In most of Western Europe, government-funded housing construction began between 1900 and 1920. Government-produced housing was particularly important in the years after World Wars I and II, as a way of compensating for the wartime destruction of European cities. In Western Europe, social housing is not provided exclusively for low-income tenants but also provides moderately priced alternatives for the middle classes. Although social housing developments, or "estates," range widely in price, maintenance, and appearance, social housing as a type of housing does not carry the association with poverty in Europe that it does in the United States. The main reason for this difference is that European governments chose to subsidize rental housing for all classes, whereas the United States chose to subsidize homeownership for the middle class and limit publicly subsidized rental housing to the poor and elderly (Harloe 1995).

Beginning in the 1980s, a similar shift toward privatization occurred in housing provision, as we saw above in planning policy. In several Western European countries, the government moved away from public investments in housing and instead encouraged private development of housing. In Great Britain, for example, local city councils built and operated social housing in the past, which has made the name "council housing" synonymous with social housing. Since 1980, however, the national government has shut off the flow of housing funds to the city councils, instead channeling a decreasing pool of housing development funds to nonprofit housing associations. At the same time, the government has encouraged city councils to sell existing council housing to private owners, thus greatly reducing the number of low-cost rentals available (Fainstein 2001). Figure 6.1 shows a social housing development in Amsterdam that is undergoing gentrification.

Although Great Britain was the leader and the most prominent example of the shift in housing policy, more European countries are beginning to follow the American pattern of reserving subsidized housing for the poor. Instead of a mass-housing policy that assumes that the role of government is to provide alternatives

Marcus Sloog, Kazepov (2004) Visual Paths through Urban Europe CD in AMSTERDAM/
Yuri Kazepov © 2004

F I G U R E   6.1   Changing housing patterns. This Amsterdam housing development, originally built as social housing, is now becoming gentrified.

to private housing, European nations are increasingly relying on the private market to provide housing for groups that can afford it and providing social housing only as a last resort for those too poor to pay for private rental housing. Despite this relatively recent policy shift, however, a much greater proportion of housing in Europe than in the United States remains in the social sector because of decades of support for social housing in the past (Harloe 1995).

The European Union.   Western Europe is composed of a number of relatively small nations, and over the course of history they have adopted different currencies, administrative systems, and laws. These different structures act as barriers to commerce among the European nations. Since World War II, several efforts have attempted to reduce barriers and increase cooperation among Western European countries. These efforts are aimed at making Europe more economically competitive with the United States and Japan. Beginning in the 1950s, organizations such as the European Economic Community and its successor, the European Community, worked to remove barriers to trade such as tariffs and customs regulations. The original members, Belgium, Luxembourg, the Netherlands, France, West Germany, and Italy, were later joined by the United Kingdom, the Republic of Ireland, and Denmark, then by Greece, Spain, and Portugal. In 1993, the European Community transformed itself into the **European Union (EU)**, with the goal of forming a seamlessly integrated European community, including a single market for goods, a common European bank, and a common currency (the euro). In addition to the EU members noted above, Austria, Finland, and Sweden joined the European Union in 1995 while Cyprus and Malta joined in 2004.

The collapse of the Soviet Union, beginning in 1989, also had a tremendous impact on European unification. The end of the East–West division from the Cold War made it possible to think about the potential for regional alliances between the countries of the former Soviet bloc and the Western European democracies. The European Union invited several Central European countries to become members, and the Czech Republic, Estonia, Hungary, Latvia, Lithuania, Poland, Slovakia, and Slovenia joined their Western neighbors in 2004; Bulgaria and Romania joined in 2007. In a later section we will explore in more detail the situation in the cities of Central and Eastern Europe.

The integration of Europe has had an important economic effect on cities in Western Europe. Although it has helped spur economic growth in some regions, it has removed the national policies that formerly protected weaker regions. In general, the largest cities, where the growing service sector is concentrated, have seen the most economic growth resulting from European unification. The older industrial cities, especially those dominated by the coal, steel, and shipping industries, have fared the worst (Cheshire 1999).

Emerging Problems in Western European Cities

Although the Western European economies are generally healthy, the impact of recent economic changes has been unequal. Economic restructuring has been disruptive for many people, and European unemployment rates have tended to be significantly higher than those of the United States. In this section, we will explore two emerging problems evident in Western European cities as the century begins—increases in immigration and the growth of excluded populations.

Immigration. The more industrialized and affluent countries of Western Europe (for example, England, Germany, France) are located in the northern section, while the poorer and less industrialized areas (such as Greece and Spain) are in the south. The years following World War II were a time of rebuilding in Europe, and rapid growth of industry created an abundance of jobs but a shortage of workers in the northern countries. As a solution, some more affluent countries encouraged immigration to supplement their industrial labor forces. Often, as in Germany, Switzerland, and France, laborers were permitted to enter as "guest workers," normally men who left their families to work for a supposedly limited period of time. Over the years, however, many of the guest workers, rather than returning home, had their families join them in their new countries. Thus, a temporary labor situation was transformed into a fairly steady stream of immigrants into the industrialized countries (Van Kempen 2005).

Many European countries attracted immigrants from their former colonies. Algerians went to France, people from Surinam and the Dutch Antilles went to the Netherlands, and migrants from India, Pakistan, and the West Indies went to England. In other countries, such as Germany, the majority of foreign workers came from poorer areas of southern Europe such as Greece, Yugoslavia, and Turkey. In fact, a new and long-lasting pattern of international flows of migrants across borders replaced the former pattern of rural-to-urban migration within

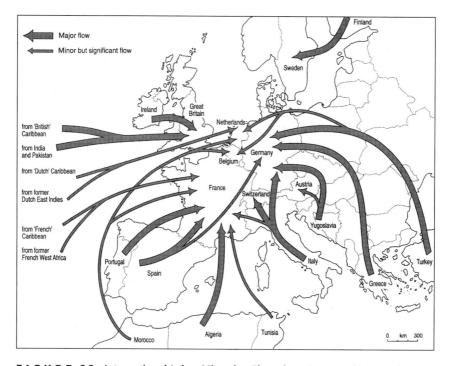

F I G U R E 6.2 **International Labor Migration Flows into Europe.** This map shows the direction and the relative size of the groups that have migrated to different European sites to seek work.

SOURCE: Russell King, "From Guestworkers to Immigrants," in *The New Europe*, ed. D. Pinder (Chichester, England: John Wiley and Sons 1998), p. 265.

nations. Figure 6.2 shows how the pattern of labor migration brought immigrants into northern Europe in the 1960s and 1970s.

North Americans often think of European populations as being homogeneous, at least in comparison to our own ethnic and racial mixing bowl. But Europe has always been affected by population flows into and out of different countries. Wars, religious persecutions, and economic upheavals have encouraged much migration within Europe and from other areas. So the postwar migrations were not unprecedented. What changed for European cities was the type and the concentration of the immigrants (Murie 1991).

As a large proportion of the "temporary" laborers have become permanent immigrants, their high birth rates relative to those of the native population in their adopted countries have increased their proportion in the population. In many cases their skin color, religion, and dress have made them an identifiable minority group in their adopted countries. Because of their differences, they are often marginalized in their adopted societies (Body-Gendrot and Martiniello 2000). Figure 6.3 shows Muslim women shopping in a market in Antwerp.

One example of immigrant **marginalization** is the housing situation for immigrants. In the early years, many companies that recruited guest workers provided minimal barracks-like housing for them, separate from regular neighborhoods.

Marcus Sloog, Kazepov (2004) Visual Paths through Urban Europe CD in AMSTERDAM/Yuri Kazepov © 2004

F I G U R E 6.3 Immigrants in Europe. Muslim women shop at an outdoor market in Antwerp.

Where company housing was not provided, guest workers sometimes lived in squatter settlements on the outskirts of cities. In the 1960s, governments generally did not see the housing situation of the immigrants as a problem because they expected them to leave when the "temporary" labor shortage was over. Since then, the worst abuses of the 1960s have abated, but a more routine pattern of housing deprivation and segregation for immigrants has emerged in many cities. Increasingly, in countries like Great Britain, France, and Germany, immigrants have been moving into the less popular social housing complexes, even as the conditions there worsen because of reduced government support for social housing (van Kempen 2005).

The poor housing situation of immigrants in Western Europe stems from three factors: the lower incomes of immigrants relative to the native population, their lack of political influence (especially among those who are not citizens), and some measure of direct discrimination. If we compare immigrant segregation in Europe to racial segregation in the United States, however, we find that the segregation levels are much lower in Europe (Musterd and Ostendorf 2005). Even cities such as Berlin and Amsterdam, which have high levels of ethnic segregation for Europe, contain neighborhoods of only about 50 percent minority population, whereas (as we will see in more detail in Chapter 9) many large cities of the United States contain neighborhoods with over 90 percent minority population.

A second example of marginalization of immigrants is politics. Immigrants vary in their legal status and therefore their ability to vote, own property, or receive social services. Guest workers are usually granted temporary visas, which must be renewed annually, and have no legal rights. Ex-colonials may have limited rights, but in most countries cannot become full citizens. Refugees who have been granted asylum for political reasons (often fleeing communist regimes in Eastern Europe) can often, after a lengthy period of residence, apply for citizenship in their new country. Because immigrants have little political power, they are in a weak position to gain government protections.

The years since World War II have been years of social and economic transformation in Europe. Changes have often been disruptive, for example, the shift
in employment from manufacturing into the service sector, and the decrease in
welfare state programs. Such disruptive changes can be exploited for political
gain, and immigrants have often been scapegoats for economic problems.
Because many of the new immigrant groups are dark-skinned, they provide an
obvious target for hatred and fear. In France, for example, a political party led by
Jean LePen has gained a following by criticizing North African Muslim immigrants. In Germany, a neo-Nazi movement has coalesced around the expulsion
of foreigners. In recent years, several neo-Nazi youth have attacked and killed
Turkish or African immigrants because of their race. Such political mobilization
is frightening to many of the older generation who remember how the Jews
became scapegoats in Hitler's quest for political power.

Socially Excluded Groups.   Immigrants are not the only group in European
cities who suffer from marginalization. Recent research has revealed several social
groups at the bottom of the economic and social hierarchy that have become
increasingly obvious in cities, especially noticeable in urban areas such as slums,
squatter settlements, and social housing developments. These groups include the
unemployed, disaffected youth, particular ethnic minorities, single parents,
and the homeless. Although they may have little else in common, they are all
socially excluded groups.

The exclusion of these groups comes from several sources. Some are excluded because they do not have full legal status. This is the case for most immigrants; in some countries (such as Germany) the children of immigrants born
in Germany are not eligible for citizenship but permanently remain "foreigners."
Other groups are excluded because of their need for a social good that is not
available to them, for example, homeless individuals who cannot receive state
housing because of cutbacks in social housing programs. Others are excluded
by being treated as social outcasts, for example, the Rom (or Gypsies), people
with AIDS, and unemployed youth. Finally, some groups are excluded simply
by virtue of being poor—excluded from the mainstream level of consumption
that others take for granted. More than just poverty, however, what socially excluded groups have in common is a lack of participation, integration, and power
(Murie 2005).

The existence of socially excluded groups is not a new phenomenon, but
their numbers are growing. This increase is due to a squeeze on the people
at the bottom rungs of European urban society. From one side, they are feeling
the pressure of economic competition, the reduced availability of manual jobs,
and high unemployment rates. From the other side, they are feeling the pressure
of a disappearing social safety net of government services. At the current time,
most major cities of Europe are home to significant portions of their population
who experience this type of exclusion from the good society. As Paul White
(1998, 305) states, "[I]n the new Europe the particular circumstances attendant
upon processes of economic restructuring, globalization, ideological shifts, the
crisis of welfare systems, and the opening of new market economies have created

Marcus Sloog. Kazepov (2004) Visual Paths through Urban Europe CD in AMSTERDAM/Yuri Kazepov © 2004

F I G U R E 6.4 **Excluded populations.** This Amsterdam neighborhood shows signs of distress.

a particularly profound combination of pressures on urban life." Figure 6.4 shows an excluded neighborhood in Amsterdam.

CITIES IN EASTERN AND CENTRAL EUROPE

For approximately forty-five years, from the end of World War II in 1945 until the dismantling of the Soviet Union in 1989, a political **iron curtain** divided Eastern and Western Europe. The dismantling of the Soviet Union and the rejection of communism by most of the countries of Europe provided the opportunity for the reintegration of Europe. The impact on both the East and the West, especially in the formerly divided nation of Germany, has been dramatic.

"Eastern" and "Central" Europe are the post–Cold War names for the former Soviet Union and its allied nations. In current terminology, *Eastern Europe* encompasses those nations within Europe that were formerly part of the Union of Soviet Socialist Republics: the Ukraine, Belorussia, Lithuania, Latvia, Estonia, and Moldova, as well as the western portion of Russia. (The western portion of Russia is in Europe but the majority of the nation is in Asia.) *Central Europe* encompasses the countries of Poland, the Czech Republic, Slovakia, Hungary, Romania, Bulgaria, Slovenia, Croatia, Yugoslavia, Macedonia, and Bosnia, all of which formerly had communist governments (Blacksell 1998).

Urban Planning

The philosophy of Soviet communism was to use the considerable power of the state to direct the economy from the top down. Thus, the economy and all related functions were subject to centralized planning rather than to the chance of the market. Cities were no exception. During the intense drive toward industrialization that characterized most of the history of the USSR, the government planned cities and produced housing. Industrialization encouraged a mass migration of rural residents to cities, with a corresponding need to build infrastructure and housing. Between 1917 and 1982, the population of the cities in the Soviet Union grew by some 142 million people (Yanitsky 1986). This urban construction program was layered over the historic cities of the czarist times, such as Moscow, Kiev, and St. Petersburg. What Westerners think of as the quintessential type of Soviet construction, the wide boulevards, superblock apartments, and large industrial plants, was not characteristic of all Soviet cities but only of the newer areas constructed during the 1930s and later.

The official philosophy of planning in the Soviet Union, according to urban analyst Oleg Yanitsky (1986), was one of integrated social and economic development. The vision for urban planning was guided by the attempted "obliteration of the social differences between town and country ... and development of the socialist type of settlement, overcoming rural desolation and the unnatural crowding in the large cities" (Yanitsky 1986, 277). He goes on to explain that the goals of planning were to equalize people's access to jobs, services, and housing; to balance industrial development among different regions; to restrict the growth of cities to save resources; and to improve the comfort and convenience of housing. This description reflects the socialist theory of planning, but it was not always carried out in the execution.

Another view of the philosophy of planning in the USSR is outlined by urbanist Yuri Bocharov (1997), who argues that urban planning in the Soviet Union had a number of political functions. He describes a series of different plans proposed for the city of Moscow after the Russian Revolution. According to Bocharov, the plans for Moscow kept changing because each time the political landscape changed, planners were urged to advance a different plan. He thinks that the plans upheld a series of "myths" that supported different political messages. In the first phase, under Lenin, Soviet foreign policy was oriented toward reassuring foreign nations that the communists were preserving the Russian heritage ("The Myth of the Legitimacy of the Bolshevik Regime"). So the 1918 plan for Moscow emphasized the preservation of historic churches and czarist monuments. Next, as Russia became a superpower, political strategy turned to creating enthusiasm for socialism at home ("The Myth of the Leading Role of the Industrial Proletariat"). The 1924 urban plan was changed to emphasize politics, replacing historic churches with political monuments such as Lenin's tomb.

B o x 6.1 • Case Study
Planning for Moscow as a Communist Mecca

[T]he "General Plan of Moscow 35" [1933–34] planned for a population of five million in an area of 232 square miles, a plan conceived as a supermodel for the building of a future communist society. The city's structure was subordinated to the quasi-religious Lenin Monument, the Palace of Soviets, symbolizing the "resurrection" of the prophet of world revolution. His mummy was "preserved forever" in the Lenin Mausoleum.

The plan of the city was worked out on the basis of a closed radial-concentric scheme. The new center of the capital was designed for public demonstrations by millions of people in the vicinity of monumental edifices, providing an ideal system of greenery, parks, and forest parks, and numerous pools of water and stadiums to be filled with exuberant athletes.

... [T]he architects endeavored to turn the city into a Mecca of the international proletariat and to surpass Paris, London, and Berlin by the number of radial avenues, to surpass Washington by the size of the public center (1730 acres) and to surpass all of the cities of the world by the height of the main monument (1362 feet) and the size of its crowning sculpture of Lenin.

The social utopia triumphed. Stalin approved the razing of the Cathedral of the Savior and the implementation of both the Palace of the Soviets and the General Plan. This was an attempt to embody in architecture the political myth of the twentieth century: The Myth of the Inevitable Victory of Communism.

SOURCE: Yuri Bocharov, "Political Myths and the Architecture of the Capital," in *The Architecture and Building of Moscow*, ed. A. Grushina (Moscow: Voznesenski Pereulok, 1997).

In the next phase, Stalin attempted to transform Moscow into the Mecca for world socialism ("The Myth of the Inevitable Victory of Communism"). Thus, the 1934 plan conceived of the city as a world-class monument to communist politics. (See the description in Box 6.1.) In the current phase, political leaders are projecting an image of democracy and economic freedom ("The Myth of Successful Economic Reform in Russia"). Planning in Moscow now emphasizes the demolition of the monuments to communism, the selective rebuilding of historic Russian churches and palaces, and the addition of Western-style amenities, such as a shopping mall next to the Kremlin.

In contrast to the USSR, which was in the process of building cities throughout much of the twentieth century, most of the cities of Central Europe are centuries old and were well established before communism. Cities such as Krakow, Budapest, Prague, and Belgrade have existed since medieval times and have long traditions of urban housing, public buildings, and public services. Several of these cities are now finding that their historic past has made them international tourist attractions.

Since the "Velvet Revolution" of 1989, Prague has become one of the most frequently visited cities in Europe and a magnet for tourists from all over the world. (Box 6.2 describes the youth culture of Prague.) The key to Prague's attractiveness is that it has consistently used historic preservation policies to retain and enhance the charm of the old city quarters. This preservationist impulse,

> **B o x 6.2 • Case Study**
> **The International Scene in Prague**
>
> Historically, the area that makes up contemporary tourist Prague has been the site of many urban functions. From the medieval period to the nineteenth century, it was a center for trade. Charles University, founded by Charles IV in the fourteenth century, is located here. One also finds national libraries, theaters, concert halls, museums, major schools for the applied arts, and numerous government buildings. Because of the abundance of educational institutions, this area has traditionally been known for its bookstores and served as the center of the printing industry.
>
> ... After 1989 a community of foreigners quickly established itself in Prague—touted as the Paris of the 1990s—replete with avant garde publications and coffee-houses. This represents an evolving cultural scene, existing alongside the Kafka T-shirts and Mozart posters of "tourist" Prague and drawing an international population of students, artists, and young professionals in search of alternative work and lifestyles at a time when the United States and Western European countries were laying off such people. During 1995–96, there were an estimated twenty thousand to thirty thousand Americans in Prague.... As of 1996 there were five English-language newspapers and two English literary journals, as well as German and French newspapers.... Two American bookstores function as meeting places for foreigners abroad as well as for the local expatriate community.
>
> SOURCE: Lily M. Hoffman and Jiri Musil, "Culture Meets Commerce: Tourism in Postcommunist Prague," in *The Tourist City*, ed. D. Judd and S. Fainstein (New Haven: Yale University Press, 1999).

which had been part of the culture since the late nineteenth century, was reinforced by the tendency during the socialist years to concentrate new construction in the outskirts of the city, ignoring and thus preserving the core. In the postsocialist period, market pressures are coming into conflict with historic preservation in some cases, but reinforcing it in other cases. For example, real estate development has led to the demolition of some older properties, but as tourism has increased interest in the historic heritage of the city, private investors have refurbished several older buildings to serve as shops, cafes, and tourist-oriented services (Hoffman and Musil 1999).

Housing

During the years of communism in Europe, the state assumed much of the role of financing and building housing. Different state governments created a number of different mechanisms for building and distributing housing. One model was for government agencies to build and operate rental housing, similar to public housing in the United States. Another was for large firms to build housing for their employees. Another model was for local authorities to build housing (normally apartments), which they then sold to individual households in the Western European manner. There were also other forms of private ownership. In addition, members of the middle class who lived in urban apartments often privately purchased small rural plots for summer residences.

In some cases, governments attempted to replace the private market for housing with a system of distribution based on need and merit. Ivan Szelenyi (1983) describes what happened in Hungary, where the postwar government attempted both to improve housing conditions overall and to rationalize the distribution of housing. Through the construction of social housing, the Hungarian government was successful in raising the housing standards of the majority of the population between 1950 and 1970. Although dwelling units might have been small and poor by Western standards, the availability of new apartments with hot water, bathrooms, and kitchens was a step forward for many families.

The Hungarian government was not successful, however, in meeting the goal of reducing inequalities in housing among the different social classes. According to Szelenyi (1983, 74), this failure was not due to corruption or to bureaucratic inertia but to the "logic of policies of equality applied in conditions of scarcity." To distribute housing based simply on need was ineffective, he argues, because the large number of needy households overwhelmed the supply. To distribute housing through a waiting list was ineffective because the waiting period could be ten to fifteen years long. So the Hungarian government, like those of other Eastern European countries, chose "merit" as a criterion for distributing housing. By doing so, they found a paradox, namely, the more "meritorious" citizens were already being rewarded with higher incomes. Thus, the housing allocation based on merit resulted in the wealthier residents getting the best housing and actually paying less for it than the poorer residents. In Hungary, then, as in other socialist countries, attempts to make housing more equal actually resulted in making it less equal. Szelenyi concludes that the reason people generally did not mind this inequality is that over the twenty-year period, the overall housing situation improved noticeably for all classes.

The dissolution of the Soviet Union and the transition to a market economy in Eastern and Central Europe has meant major changes for the housing market. Although the trend toward privatization of social housing is slower than in Western Europe, it definitely exists. Privatization of rental housing has pushed up rents across the board. Privatization of homeownership has also caused some hardships for middle-income people, as residents who purchase apartments find that the extra cost often strains their budgets. Housing privatization is one aspect of a widespread redefinition of the boundaries between the public and private sectors throughout Europe—both East and West. The retreat from the welfare state is a reality of life on both sides of the former iron curtain (White 1998).

Economic Restructuring

During the communist period, manufacturing and mining were the economic growth engines of Eastern Europe. Governments invested massive amounts of resources in mining and manufacturing, built new cities for manufacturing, and paid high wages to factory workers. Much of the manufacturing was defense related, with several "closed" cities created to develop and construct secret weapons. Whether for defense or other purposes, the production of energy and basic products such as steel and rubber were high priorities for the state. Consequently, the USSR became an international industrial leader in a few short decades, and the domestic economy relied on manufacturing production for growth. With the political and economic reforms of the 1990s, however, these "heavy" industries have lost their privileged positions in the economy. As a result, many workers have lost their positions or have taken huge pay cuts, necessitating supplementing their incomes with second jobs (Dawson 1998).

The economic restructuring that has affected the former Soviet Union has simultaneously hit all of Central Europe, including the Czech Republic, Poland, and the former German Democratic Republic (East Germany). The philosophical direction of the reforms is similar throughout Central Europe, namely, privatizing state-owned industries. The specific approaches that different countries have used, however, vary greatly. Germany established a commission to sell off former East German companies to private owners. The Czech Republic issued vouchers for shares in state-owned enterprises to private citizens. Some countries have sold their state enterprises to large international companies: Poland sold its food-processing enterprise to Nestlé; the Czech Republic sold its automobile plants to Volkswagen; Hungary sold its major lighting company to General Electric; and Romania sold its shipyard to Daewoo (Dawson 1998).

Environmental Challenges

Protecting the environment is a challenge that transcends national boundaries. Despite the political and economic differences between Eastern and Western Europe, the fact remains that the two regions are united by a common geography. As one analyst says, "Europe—east and west—is a single environmental complex with a diverse range of interdependent links" (Saiko 1998, 381). Air and water pollution travel across national boundaries irrespective of politics.

With the collapse of the Soviet Union, some analysts predicted that the newly emerging democracies of Central and Eastern European would be in a good position to protect the natural environment, given that they had not developed the wasteful patterns of consumption that characterized the Western democracies. Such expectations, however, have not been fulfilled for two reasons.

First, the values of a consumer society are rapidly spreading to the former communist societies. Automobile ownership is much in demand, creating additional congestion and air pollution in the larger cities. As consumption increases, the level of solid wastes from discarded goods is also increasing.

Second, the scope and magnitude of the inherited environmental abuses of the Soviet industrial system were much greater than Westerners realized previously. Rapid industrialization and the drive to find energy sources led to an official lack of concern about environmental consequences of economic growth. Probably the most significant environmental crisis was the 1986 nuclear reactor disaster at Chernobyl, which contaminated over 10,000 square miles of territory, mostly in Belorussia. Another devastated area is the so-called "Black Triangle," which overlays portions of Poland, the Czech Republic, and Germany. In this region, sulphur dioxide from massive coal-burning plants created so much air and water pollution that the natural vegetation and animal life disappeared.

Also, Europe's longest river, the Volga, has been drastically reduced in volume and heavily polluted with toxic material including agricultural, industrial, and radioactive wastes. In recent years, industrial air pollution has diminished; however, the reduction is due not to the adoption of cleaner production methods but to economic problems that have closed many industrial plants (Saiko 1998).

Transportation, particularly by automobiles and buses, is a major cause of environmental degradation in cities. European cities have an advantage over sprawling North American cities because they tend to be compact, so that large numbers of people can walk or cycle to work, to shop, and to other daily destinations. As a transportation policy, European countries have invested heavily in environmentally friendly mass transit systems such as subways, trolleys, light rail, and commuter trains. This investment in public transit continues today, although growing automobile ownership is bringing increased demand for highway construction. As of 2007, seventy-three European cities had subway or light rail systems and two additional cities were planning for light rail systems (UrbanRail.net > Europe).

For long-distance transportation, European countries are continuing to invest in rail systems as an alternative to the more fuel-intensive transportation methods of auto, bus, truck, and airplane favored in North America. Although European railroads are run by national agencies, they have been integrated into an international system for decades. In the 1980s, France introduced the TGV (French abbreviation for "very fast train"), which travels at speeds over 100 miles per hour. Other nations, such as Belgium, Germany, Italy, and Spain have developed similar high-speed systems to create an international system of high-speed rail lines. The Channel Tunnel linking England and France is an important piece of this emerging trans-European rail system (Pinder and Edwards 1998).

GLOBALIZATION AND GLOBAL CITIES

As we have seen, cities in the industrialized nations are changing in response to changes in economic and political conditions. These economic and political changes occur on both a national and a global scale. Many scholars argue that since the 1980s, the most significant factor affecting cities is the process of economic **globalization**.

The Process of Globalization

Globalization refers to the increasing interdependence of the world's economies. This process has created a new set of relationships between formerly distinct economies, nations, and societies. The most obvious manifestation of globalization is the massive flow of information, goods, money, and people across national boundaries. Less obvious, but still real, is a new set of social, political, and cultural realities that result from life in the global economy. Globalization has been encouraged by a number of factors, including the development of new technologies that permit rapid information exchange, the growth of international financial and trade partnerships, and the increased concentration of control over investment by a relatively small number of actors. Globalization is not a brand-new phenomenon; it has existed to some extent since the world-economy emerged in the sixteenth century. But it has accelerated so quickly since 1980 that scholars now recognize it as having a major impact on cities.

One of the most important influences on globalization is the revolution in information technology. The computer revolution of the 1970s and particularly the networking revolution of the 1980s made it possible to communicate instantaneously on a worldwide basis. Technological tools such as the Internet enable people to produce and consume products, manage enterprises, invest money, conduct research, and exchange information freely across national boundaries. Some scholars (for example, Castells 1996) argue that information technologies have created a new type of economy, an informational and global economy. In what he calls "the network society," information is the key to productivity, and production processes are organized on a global scale. Technology has allowed better and faster integration of economic activity so that the global economy has "the capacity to work as a unit in real time on a planetary scale" (Castells 1996, 92).

As global economic ties have gained importance, nations have reduced barriers to cross-national investment, production, and management. Governments in several regions have grouped together to reduce trade and investment barriers. As we saw, governments throughout Europe, including both East and West, are lowering trade barriers and moving toward a regional partnership in the European Union. The governments of the United States, Mexico, and Canada adopted the North American Free Trade Agreement to create regional synergy by permitting faster and freer movement of money, goods, and people on this continent. On a worldwide level, the General Agreement on Tariffs and Trade and the World Trade Organization have the mission of aligning national policies to promote easier global trade and cooperation.

Globalization and Politics

Some critics argue that "globalization" is a code word for "free enterprise." They argue that removal of "barriers to free trade" is actually removal of protections for workers and the environment. Christopher Chase-Dunn, for example, argues that the idea of the globalization of the economy has been used to "justify economic and political decisions such as deregulation and privatization of industries, downsizing and streamlining of work forces, and dismemberment of the welfare services provided by governments" (Chase-Dunn 2000, 6).

Some evidence shows that global economic institutions are contributing to the weakening of protective legislation as national governments deregulate their economies. The World Trade Organization, for example, supports reducing barriers to trade, including labor union contracts, health and safety regulations, and environmental standards. The International Monetary Fund, which gives loans to national governments, can dictate social and economic policy in poor countries by making their loans conditional on the nation adopting certain steps such as not raising the minimum wage, dropping interest rates, and cutting government services.

Another perspective is that the regulation of the economy is not disappearing but is moving from the national level to the international level with such developments as the General Agreement on Tariffs and Trade (Newman and Thornley 1996).

Because political institutions are normally organized on the national and local levels, they can have little influence on these global trends and global organizations. In response to corporate and economic globalization, some citizens' groups have begun to organize on a global basis as well. The growth of hundreds of **nongovernmental organizations**, or NGOs, is a response to the internationalization of socioeconomic issues. Some examples include the Beijing Women's Conference, which brought together women from all over the world; Amnesty International, which advocates for political prisoners in any country; an international movement against land mines; and *Médecins sans Frontières*, an organization of medical professionals who volunteer their services. Although these organizations are not "the equivalent in clout of AOL Time Warner or the IMF" (Barber 2000, 19), they provide a forum for mobilizing resources to address issues through national-level political processes.

The Spatial Impact of Globalization on Cities.   Has globalization created a new spatial order within cities? This is the intriguing question that a team of planners and geographers set out to answer. (See Marcuse and van Kempen 2000.) They began their inquiries with descriptions of how globalization might have an impact on city form and layout. Some possible trends they investigated included a reduction of the importance of the downtown, heightened spatial separation of different races and social classes, increasing gentrification, and the growth of ghettos of extreme poverty. After investigating cities on every continent except Antarctica, the scholars concluded that globalization has less of an impact on cities spatially than previous scholars thought. They found that many of the urban characteristics that have been previously linked to globalization, such as racial and class segregation, are longstanding trends.

The team of scholars did find, however, that certain spatial patterns have become more pronounced and more widespread as the result of globalization. One example is **citadels**, or high-tech, high-rise office projects such as Battery Park City in New York. A related spatial feature that globalization has accelerated is the trend toward **exclusionary enclaves**, whether in high-rise condominiums, gated developments, or other secure and isolated locations. A third trend they see is the intensification of isolated poverty in **excluded ghettos** stripped of services and removed from middle-class neighborhoods. A fourth is the development of **ethnic enclaves** where immigrants live and often work. Finally, they see the development of regionalization, including **edge cities**, as a relatively new development encouraged by globalization (Marcuse and van Kempen 2000).

Global Cities

During the twentieth century, social scientists generally recognized a handful of cities—all in Europe—as **world cities**. Their status as world cities was based on worldwide recognition of their pivotal historical, political, and cultural roles. National (or imperial) capitals such as London, Paris, Berlin, and Vienna were considered world cities throughout most of the twentieth century (Newman and Thornley 1996).

Within the globalized economy, economics has replaced politics as the defining characteristic of a significant city. The global economy has reduced the importance of the cities that serve as capitals of nations, while it has increased the importance of cities that serve as the command posts for international business. Because of their key economic functions in the global economy, Saskia Sassen (2001) has identified three cities, New York, London, and Tokyo, as the **global cities** of the current era.

Characteristics of Global Cities

The global cities have four characteristics, according to Sassen. First, they serve as command points of the global economy, coordinating the increasingly far-flung production of goods and services. Sassen argues that, as companies and industries have become more decentralized (in what has sometimes been called a global assembly line), command and control powers have become increasingly centralized so that some coherence over the whole can be maintained. These control functions—often found in the form of corporate headquarters—have clustered in a handful of global cities.

Second, the global cities have become the leading locations for financial services and other specialized producer services that corporations use. Financial and producer services include stock exchanges, investment banking, corporate law, advertising, accounting, management consulting, and other sophisticated corporate services or facilities. (Consumer services, on the other hand, are used by individuals and might include health care, dry cleaning, or home maintenance.) Producer services has been a rapidly growing sector of the economy since the 1970s, becoming more highly specialized as time passes. Such sophisticated producer services have tended to cluster within a few global cities, although their clientele is international in scope.

Third, in addition to their command functions, London, Tokyo, and New York are also sites for the production of goods and services (particularly services) in the evolving postindustrial economy. Thus, not only are the management decisions made in these cities, but, to a large extent, goods and services such as advertising copy or architectural plans are actually produced there. Moreover, these three cities have become leaders in research and innovation of new products for corporations.

Finally, the global cities have also provided markets for the products produced there. The close proximity of service providers to each other has created a critical mass for the consumption of each other's services. Sassen further emphasizes that the production of these services does not just happen to be in these cities. Rather, she argues, the types of producer services in the three cities represent key functions of the global economy that are of necessity located in cities.

B o x   6.3   •   Case Study
London's Docklands

A major cause of the spatial restructuring in world cities was the growth of the financial service industries and associated increase in the demand for office space. There was a commercial office boom in the world cities in the mid to late 1980s. Where the pressure cannot be met by intensification of existing spaces there is pressure for the extension of commercial space. The tight clustering of such industries means that extensions cannot be too far away; firms renting space that is too distant lose credibility and vital contacts....

Located just east of the capital's financial center, the 16 square miles of Docklands are the commercial water frontage of London. It was also the home of working-class communities, almost 40,000 people initially based on dockwork. By the 1960s the docks were being closed because they were unable to cope with the bigger container ships. The port functions moved east to Tilbury, and in Docklands registered dock employment fell from 25,000 to 4,100 between 1960 and 1981.

London Docklands was well placed for spatial restructuring. Proximity to the City gave opportunities to developers for the recommodification of derelict land into offices and residences. There was an alignment of investment-rich institutions, a demand from a buoyant City for office property, and housing requirements of the growing new middle class, which all led to the recommodification and yuppification of the area. ...

A barrage of publicity has changed the mental map of London. Previously the Docklands was "unknown" to the majority of middle-class Londoners. It was a spatially and socially self-contained segment of the capital. The London Docklands Development Corporation campaign gave Docklands a higher profile and more "positive" image. Publicity photographs were carefully taken to show only the glitzy areas, and color enhancement changed the murky Thames into a sun-kissed, bright blue river, pollution-free, just waiting for you to windsurf.

SOURCE: John Rennie Short, *The Urban Order* (Oxford, UK: Blackwell Publishers, 1996), pp. 159–164 *passim*.

Box 6.3 and Figure 6.5 show how the London waterfront was redeveloped to provide additional office space near the financial heart of the city in response to the growth of producer service firms.

Increasing Similarities Among Global Cities

An interesting phenomenon that Sassen has observed in her study of London, Tokyo, and New York is that, despite their disparate histories, cultures, and locations, the nature of life in these three cities has been converging since they have taken on their roles as global cities. This convergence is particularly evident in the type of work available and its implications for people's incomes and lifestyles. All of the global cities have experienced huge increases in the occupations related to producer services. These tend to be skewed toward high-skilled, highly paid jobs. But the growth of these good jobs, in all three cities, has occurred in the context of overall stagnation or even decline in the number of jobs generally. Because of the decrease in manufacturing jobs, many lower-skilled residents (those

F I G U R E 6.5 **London's Canary Wharf Development.** Part of the redevelopment of Docklands, the Canary Wharf project provided additional office space and housing close to the financial heart of the city.

with the equivalent of a high school education or below) have become unemployed or marginally employed. Without steady work, they turn to whatever way they can of making a living. Thus, the global cities are experiencing large increases in what economists call the **informal sector** of the economy: working "off the books" either in manufacturing (for example, home sewing on a piecework basis) or in services (such as gardening, cleaning, and child care).

As a result of these changes in the structure of jobs, the population of the global cities has become increasingly polarized into the rich and the poor. High wages in the growing producer services industries have helped create a visible class of affluent, consumption-oriented, educated residents; hence gentrification has occurred in all three cities. At the same time, job loss and rising rents have eliminated affordable housing for many residents, forcing them onto the streets or into public housing. The existence of the wealthy group has provided some job opportunities for poorer workers, for example housecleaning for two-executive households, or delivering take-out food. The low levels of pay, benefits, and opportunity for advancement, however, indicate that these jobs are only stopgap measures. Global cities have thus been called "divided cities" (Fainstein and Harloe 1992) or "dual cities" (Mollenkopf and Castells 1991) because of the tendency toward income polarization.

Another similarity Sassen notes among the global cities is that they have attracted many immigrants or members of racial and ethnic minority groups. London has drawn immigrants from the many arms of the former British Empire such as India and Jamaica; Tokyo has drawn Chinese and Korean workers; and

New York has attracted many Caribbean and Asian immigrants. These groups are highly concentrated in the lowest-paying rungs of service and manufacturing industries and in the informal sector. Their presence in the cities has become a visible symbol of the increased international flows not only of money and goods but also of people in the global economy.

One difference among the global cities is the degree to which they dominate, in size, in politics, and in the level of economic activity, the other cities in their own country. (This factor, called **primacy**, will be discussed in more detail in Chapter 7.) Whereas London and Tokyo dominate the other cities of their nations, New York has the competition of Los Angeles and Chicago as not only sizeable, but also economically influential, competitors (Abu-Lughod 1999).

Since the initial publication of *The Global City* in 1991, scholars have raised a number of questions that challenge Sassen's views about global cities. The questions the critics raise include the following: Are there only three global cities, or do other economically important cities share the role with New York, London, and Tokyo (Newman and Thornley 1996)? Are New York, London, and Tokyo as similar as Sassen thinks, or are there significant differences among them (Marcuse and van Kempen 2000)? Are global cities really a new phenomenon, or do they reflect a continuation of longstanding trends (Logan 2000)? Although these questions have helped sharpen the definition and identification of global cities, they have not undermined the basic premise of Sassen's argument: that a few cities now serve as the command posts of the global economy.

CONCLUSION

Because European cities are generally much older than North American cities, they have been influenced by more historic events and trends than have cities in the United States or Canada. Their characteristic differences include being more compact, more densely settled, more heterogeneous with regard to land use, and more oriented to the city center than to the suburbs.

In recent decades, several changes in the world's economic and political context have had major impacts on cities in Europe. These intertwined influences include changing technologies, the emergence of new industries, increasing immigration, the dismantling of welfare-state policies, the reduction in government regulation of the economy, the end of the Cold War, and the globalization of the economy. The results of these changes are mixed: some cities have prospered, but others have not. Even within the cities that have attracted investment as centers for the new information-based economy, all segments of the population have not benefited equally. Thus, observers can note substantial poverty and dislocation, even within generally prosperous cities.

Globalization of the economy is likely to continue and perhaps even accelerate in the future. Because of the process of globalization, a few cities have emerged as global cities, in which a large proportion of the control of the world economy is centralized. Although currently only three cities are generally recognized as global cities, it is possible that others will emerge in coming decades as globalization intensifies.

DISCUSSION QUESTIONS

1. Interview someone who was raised in a European city or who lived in one for a year or more. Ask your informant to describe life in the city and compare his or her recollections with your own experiences in an American city.

2. Watch one of the many movies that have portrayed the experiences of immigrants within European societies such as *Bread and Chocolate, My Beautiful Laundrette, East Is East,* and *My Son, the Fanatic.* What issues does the film raise about assimilation, social identity, and prejudice?

3. Discuss the section of this chapter on how political leaders in the former USSR planned to shape Moscow to make political statements. What do you think the "statements" are that cities can make to people? Give examples from your experiences of some different statements that cities make.

7

Cities in the Developing World

The pain in our shoulder comes
You say, from the damp; and this is also the reason
For the stain on the wall of our flat.
So tell us: Where does the damp come from?
—BERTOLT BRECHT

Thus far, our survey of cities has concentrated on cities in North America and Europe, the most highly industrialized and richest regions of the world. The nations of these regions are referred to as being part of the **developed world**. In this chapter we turn to cities in those parts of the world that are considerably less industrialized, and as a consequence, tend to be poorer than the industrialized nations. Despite their considerable differences due to history, geography, and culture, some theorists argue that characteristic differences exist between the cities of the poor countries and those of the wealthy countries. Thus, in this chapter we will explore several questions:

- What characteristics do cities of the developing world share?
- What accounts for similarities among these cities?
- Why have the rich and poor countries developed along different paths?
- What is the future likely to hold for cities of the developing world?

CHARACTERISTICS OF CITIES IN
THE DEVELOPING WORLD

What is the developing world? The term refers to those countries that have lower levels of industrialization and consequently poorer populations than the fully industrialized countries. The nations of the developing world were at one time referred to as the **third world**. The term originated from the idea that the Western nations had adopted the first route to a modern industrial society, namely, a gradual transition from feudalism to capitalism. The Soviet bloc had industrialized and modernized via a second route, namely, a rapid transition from feudalism to a state-dominated form of socialism. The remainder of the world, that is, the nonindustrialized nations, were thus called the third world (Horowitz 1966). Although this term sometimes has been used in its political sense to mean those countries in neither the Western nor the Eastern bloc, it was more generally used in its economic sense to mean the less than fully industrialized nations. After the dissolution of the Soviet Union in 1991, the term third world fell out of favor.

Scholars used and continue to use a variety of other terms as the name for this category of countries, including *less industrialized countries, postcolonial nations*, and *the periphery*. This text uses the name *developing world* not to presuppose a particular theoretical orientation but because it is in widespread public use and therefore understandable to readers.

URBAN POPULATION TRENDS

Cities in the developing world are growing very rapidly and several now rank among the largest cities in the world. Table 7.1 shows the ranking of the world's largest cities. Two-thirds of them are located in countries in the developing world.

When cities of the developing world are compared to those of the fully industrialized nations, several common population patterns appear. One characteristic common to many cities of the developing world is called urban primacy and has to do with the size of the largest city. A huge proportion of the population of the entire nation is typically concentrated in a single city. To understand why this is remarkable, it is important to grasp the usual distribution of city size within countries. As we saw in Chapter 1, the pattern of city size in the industrialized nations is for the largest city to be twice the size of the second largest, three times the size of the third largest, four times the size of the fourth largest, and so on. In cases of urban primacy, the largest city can be many times the size of the second largest; in the extreme case it may be the only city. Primate cities, which are usually the nation's political capital and cultural center as well as its largest city, represent intense concentrations of both the nation's political power and its economic resources. These cities grow because of migration from the countryside as peasants leave rural land for what they think are superior economic opportunities in the big city. Although not all developing nations are characterized by a primate pattern, fifty-five of the world's sixty-six primate cities are located in the developing world (Gilbert and Gugler 1992, 37).

A second characteristic of cities in the developing world, sometimes called **overurbanization**, is again linked to population size. In the past when cities in the industrialized nations of the world grew in population size, their growth was usually accompanied—or caused—by industrialization. This historic link has been broken in many of the developing world cities, where urban population growth is far outstripping the pace of industrialization. This pattern has been

TABLE 7.1   **The Twenty-Five Largest Cities in the World, 2008**

City	Country	Estimated Population in Millions*
1. Tokyo	Japan	33.8
2. Seoul	South Korea	23.9
3. Mexico City	Mexico	22.9
4. Delhi	India	22.4
5. Mumbai	India	22.3
6. New York	United States	21.9
7. Sao Paulo	Brazil	21.0
8. Manila	Philippines	19.2
9. Los Angeles	United States	18.0
10. Shanghai	China	17.9
11. Osaka	Japan	16.7
12. Calcutta	India	16.0
13. Karachi	Pakistan	15.7
14. Guangzhou	China	15.3
15. Jakarta	Indonesia	15.1
16. Cairo	Egypt	14.8
17. Buenos Aires	Argentina	13.8
18. Moscow	Russia	13.5
19. Beijing	China	13.2
20. Dhaka	Bangladesh	13.1
21. Istanbul	Turkey	12.5
22. Rio de Janeiro	Brazil	12.5
23. Tehran	Iran	12.5
24. London	Great Britain	12.3
25. Lagos	Nigeria	11.4

*Population figures include cities and surrounding agglomerations.

SOURCE: Thomas Brinkhoff, *Principal Agglomerations and Cities of the World* (http://www.citypopulation.de, June 1, 2009).

given the name of overurbanization, although the real issue is not the size of the city's population but the inability of the economy to provide jobs for the rural-to-urban migrants. The practical impact of overurbanization is that, where rural people are migrating to cities but are not being absorbed into manufacturing jobs, massive unemployment can result. To some extent, overurbanization contributes to the depressed wage levels in cities in developing nations and to the growth of the informal sector (Flanagan 1993) (See Figure 7.1).

A debate exists over what causes this massive, if "inappropriate," migration to cities and what the economic consequences would be if rural people stopped

Darrell Norris

F I G U R E 7.1   Squatter Settlement. The capital cities of third world countries often contain neighborhoods of squatters' settlements or informal housing. In Jakarta, hundreds of families live on boats with little access to services such as fresh water and electricity.

migrating to cities. Some scholars have argued that overurbanization is the result of a cultural bias that encourages rural people to move to the city, thus stripping the countryside of the population and resources that could potentially foster rural development. In this view, if the pro-urban bias were to be reduced or eliminated, economic development could be more balanced between the urban and rural areas of developing countries. Others (for example, Smith 1987), however, have emphasized the economic factors that make rural life increasingly difficult and therefore force peasants to leave rural areas. These factors include the reduction of opportunities for agricultural work caused by extreme concentration of land ownership in a few hands and the recent growth of large-scale, capital-intensive export agriculture, which substitutes machinery for human labor. In Smith's view, the urban-rural population balance is less a matter of voluntary migration than of where the demand for labor is greater; as bad as job opportunities are in the cities, they are worse in the countryside.

The extensive population migration to cities in the developing world and the shortage of adequate employment have contributed to the explosive growth of the informal sector of the economy. As we saw earlier, the informal sector, including work that is not formally recognized or is not recorded, is increasingly important in the economies of the industrialized countries. But it is much farther reaching and encompasses a greater proportion of the population and a wider range of activities in such cities. From housekeeping to manufacturing piecework to scavenging in refuse for recyclable materials, the informal sector not only provides an income to officially unemployed workers but also supplements and complements the regular economy by providing goods and services at cheaper than normal prices. Indeed, even housing construction, road building, and utility installation become part of the informal sector, when rural migrants living in shantytowns organize themselves to build infrastructure outside of regular channels. The common occurrence of these self-help activities explains how rural migrants with little or no money can afford to live on the fringes of cities, where the cost of living should be prohibitive to them (Drakakis-Smith 2000; Lynch 2005).

Developing Regions

Most developing nations and the cities within them typically share a common political background. Most of the developing world was at one time colonized by one or more of the Western powers: Spain, Portugal, the Netherlands, England, France, Belgium, and even the United States. As we saw in Chapter 3, the widespread empires that had existed in antiquity but had shrunk or disappeared during the Middle Ages were reestablished during the fifteenth century with the growth of overseas trade. For the next five hundred years, European nations gradually incorporated other regions, beginning with Central and South America, then North America, Asia Minor, and finally, Africa and a good part of Asia.

These empires exerted political as well as economic control over their subjects. Colonial powers typically controlled the governments in their colonies, either by appointing colonial administrators or by instituting puppet regimes of indigenous officials under colonial control. Colonial status, especially if it lasted for an extended period, thus undermined local forms of governance and the development of indigenous political leaders. Because of the long political domination of colonized people, the relatively recent termination of colonialism has sometimes left problems, such as leadership vacuums or sharp internal struggles for control between tribes, religious sects, ethnic groups, or other factions.

The economic system of the empires was very straightforward. Colonies existed for the enrichment of the colonial power. In many cases the chief reason for colonization was the extraction of natural resources, either through mining or agriculture. Another important economic resource was labor, sometimes obtained through slavery. The impact of colonization on the local economy was often devastating, especially in agriculture, where the variety of indigenous crops was usually wiped out and the greatest possible proportion of land turned over to the production of one or two cash crops for export.

An additional consequence of the colonial system was a marked increase in inequality and the frequent impoverishment of formerly self-sufficient peoples. Some local people could rise within the colonial system as managers, but the average colonial laborer was exploited far beyond the usual levels of exploitation experienced elsewhere. If not legally coerced by slavery or indentured servitude, local people were often economically coerced by the absence of other alternatives once the colonial power had rearranged the local economy. The historical incorporation of these countries into the colonial system has shaped their current situation, both politically and economically. Colonialism has left a heritage of economic and political problems in many areas of the developing world.

The legacy of colonization has been felt differently in differing parts of the world. Although there is much variation within them, four major developing regions have all experienced colonization and responded in a variety of ways during the postcolonial era. The first of these is Africa, especially but not exclusively south of the Sahara Desert. Asia has experienced colonization as well, and the two major developing regions—Southeast Asia and South Asia—have responded in differing ways. In the Western Hemisphere, the portion of the Americas known as Latin America has also responded to the postcolonial world in divergent ways (Ferro 1997).

The continent of Africa often comes to mind when one thinks of colonialism. Much of the continent was claimed by European nations during the twentieth century, and even after many colonies were given independence they remained heavily tied to their former occupiers (Murray & Myers 2007). There is considerable diversity in Africa. For instance, the north coast runs along the Mediterranean Sea and was home to such peoples as the Berbers and the Carthaginians. The Moors, for instance, had occupied large portions of what is today Spain until being forced out of the nation in the late fifteenth century. The most ancient North African society, dating to 3000 B.C., was spread along the Nile Valley in Egypt, and today is a major tourist attraction. To the south, Ethiopia maintained its independence from colonial rule for most of its modern history except for a period of Italian rule from 1936 to 1941. One of the oldest civilizations in the world, Ethiopia is also home to one of the oldest Christian churches in the world and reputedly the resting place of the famed Ark of the Covenant. Its capital city is Addis Ababa, one of Africa's largest cities. In the south, the nation of South Africa was the focus of international pressure to end the practice of Apartheid—the legal segregation and immiseration of native Africans in place from 1948 through 1994. The nation's power structure was dominated by white descendents of Dutch and British settlers called Afrikaners. Under apartheid, much of the nation's black population was forced to live in predominantly rural "homelands" that were defined as separate from the nation, with the result that many residents needed to commute great distances to the cities controlled by Afrikaners (Wilson 2001).

The peculiar legacy of European colonization in Africa (See Figure 7.2) can be seen in Nairobi, the capital of Kenya (Anderson 2005). Known as the "Green City in the Sun," Nairobi was founded in 1899 as a railroad town in what was then British East Africa. The city today is home to over three million residents, half of whom have moved to the city since 1990. As a former British colonial city and capital, Nairobi has a very Western architectural character. Like many American cities that grew quickly, Nairobi has a central business district, complete with a Western-style skyline, and is subject to many of the same problems found in the developed world, including transportation, traffic congestion, and crime. Centered on Kenyatta Avenue, downtown Nairobi is lined with high-rise office buildings and ample land dedicated to parking. To the southwest of downtown, the legacy of colonization can be seen in the names of two

---

B o x   7.1   •   Case Study
Finding Housing in Cairo

... Housing expert Ahmed Soliman discusses four basic shelter strategies for the poor in Cairo. First, if access to central job markets is paramount, the household can consider renting an apartment; the rental tenements offer centrality and security of tenure, but are expensive and hold out no hope of eventual ownership. The second option is centrally located but informal shelter: a situation described by Soliman as "a very small room or rooftop with a location with a poor quality environment and a cheap rent, or no rent at all, with good access to job opportunities but with no hope of secure tenure. Such illegal dwellers will eventually be forced to move to squatter camps or semi-informal housing."

The third and cheapest housing option is to squat on publicly owned land, usually on Cairo's desert outskirts and almost always downwind of pollution; negative tradeoffs include the very high cost of commuting to work and the government's neglect of infrastructure. "For example, the squatter area in El Dekhila district has been a settlement for 40 years with no public action or intervention from the local authority." The fourth solution, eventually preferred by most poor Cairenes, is to buy a house site in one of the vast semi-informal developments (often on land purchased from Bedouins or peasant villages) with legal tenure but without official building authorization. Although far from jobs, such sites are secure and, after considerable community mobilization and political negotiation, are usually provided with basic municipal services.

SOURCE: Mike Davis, *Planet of Slums* (New York: Verso, 2007), p. 29.

---

parks: Central Park and Uhuru Park. Such juxtapositions in place names are found in other parts of the city as well, including the suburbs of Eastleigh and Ngong. Although many important buildings are downtown, the central business district also faces competition from suburban locales such as the rapidly growing Westlands and Upper Hill, home to new office buildings for such companies as Citibank and Coca-Cola. As the largest city in Kenya and one of the largest in East Africa, Nairobi is home to numerous Western corporations, such as Goodyear and Toyota, that produce products and sell to an expanding African market. It is this Western investment and the promise of jobs that has driven much of Nairobi's population growth, and it is the relative lack of investment in the surrounding countryside that makes Nairobi a primate city. As one of the few places in which Western companies will invest, it is not surprising that it is to Nairobi that people move looking for employment. Unfortunately, population growth has outstripped economic growth, with the consequence that many migrants to the city are unable to find employment and live in a series of shanty towns in the city's suburbs. The slums continue for miles along the major highways leading out of Nairobi, densely populated communities with water and sewage conditions that are dangerously inadequate, leading to frequent outbreaks of diseases such as cholera and typhoid. Many of the migrants to the city come from Kenya's countryside, but there is also a substantial population of immigrants from other former British colonies, such as India and Pakistan (Anderson 2005).

Peter Macdiarmid/Getty Images

F I G U R E 7.2 Known as the "Green City in the Sun," the skyline of Nairobi, Kenya, looks similar to those found throughout the world.

SOURCE: http://www.kenyamission-un.ch/?About_Kenya:Kenya_Tourism

In much of East Asia the cities are booming, and several countries, such as Japan and South Korea, are classified as developed countries. Nevertheless, Western-style industrial development has occurred in this part of the world primarily during the past one hundred years, with the result that while the cities often feature fully modern technologies and infrastructure, in many countries the surrounding countryside often lags years behind the cities. Although the region as a whole is vital to the world economy, the two major economies are Japan and China.

The significance of Japan's role in the Cold War on other nations and cities in the region cannot be underestimated. Japan industrialized rapidly after the 1867 Meiji Restoration reasserted the authority of the Emperor. Japan was a credible military force in the Pacific by the outbreak of World War II, and remained a highly industrialized nation after the war. When in 1949 the Chinese Civil War ended in the assumption of power of the communist government of Mao Tse-tung, Japan was transformed from an American enemy to a critical strategic point. American foreign policy invested millions of dollars in the Japanese economy and favorable trade policy created an easy market for Japanese goods, helping to rebuild the economy and solidify the position of such industrial giants as Toyota, Fuji, and Seiko. As the Cold War resulted in "proxy wars" between Western and communist powers in Korea and Vietnam during the 1950s and 1960s, the role of strategic countries led to increased Western investment and favorable trade policies for friendly countries, such as South Korea, Singapore, and Taiwan. In the case of Japan and South Korea, by the end of the century both were considered developed nations with modern cities such as Seoul, Taipei, and Singapore itself. As a result of such favorable treatment by Western powers, numerous cities in the region have industrialized and in many ways re-semble cities in other parts of the world. In fact, some of the tallest buildings in the world are now located in Southeast Asia, such as Taipei 101 in Taiwan and the Petronas Twin Towers in Kuala Lumpur, Malaysia. As in Africa, however, residents of the countryside experience a considerable lack of development, and this encourages rural to urban migration and the rise of slums surrounding many Southeast Asian cities (Drakakis-Smith 2000).

In contrast, China was one of the communist powers against which Western investment was hoped to act as an obstacle. Unlike other communist regimes in the region, however, China's government pursued a Western-style development strategy. By introducing significant capitalistic reforms and aggressively entering international commerce, it has become an economic giant. Its population of over one billion residents also makes China the largest consumer market in the world by population. In fact, China has become one of the largest trading partners with the United States based in large part on the scale of manufacturing in China, particularly in Shanghai, Beijing, and other Chinese cities. Numerous Western corporations "outsource" manufacturing to Chinese firms, taking advantage of comparably low wages, labor protection laws, and environmental protection laws. In addition, low tariffs on imports to Western nations such as the United States have enhanced demand for Chinese manufactured goods and resulted in an economic boom for many cities. The example of Shanghai, China's largest city, shown in Figure 7.3, demonstrates the various phases of China's recent history (Friedman 2005).

On the Western shore of the Huangpu River runs a strip of buildings col-lectively referred to as the Bund. To the south was the original Chinese town of Shanghai, a village that had grown from the tenth through the nineteenth cen-turies as one of the major shipping ports in the Yangtze River Basin. At the conclusion of the first Opium War in 1842, China agreed to "concession areas," in which delegations from foreign nations, such as the British, French, and Americans, were granted territories to administer independent of the Chinese government. In 1863, the British and American zones merged to form the International Settlement. Although the existence of the concession zones led to increasing trade between China and other nations, they also amounted to forfei-ture of local government control. In effect, the concession zones were small col-onies amid a wider Chinese population. The independence of the International Settlement was not ended by the Chinese, however, but by the Japanese during the occupation of China during World War II. When in 1949 China became a communist country, Western capitalist influence waned but a number of Soviet-style buildings were built in the city. In response to the communist takeover of the city, most Western corporations moved their regional headquarters from Shanghai to Hong Kong. In 1991, the Chinese government reversed course and allowed free market reforms in Shanghai, leading to the creation of over twenty-five special economic and trade zones. As a result, Shanghai is the main competitor for being the financial capital of China (with Hong Kong), its stock exchange has become one of the most important in the world, and the once residential Pudong area across the river from the Bund is now home to a new

FIGURE 7.3 The Pudong district of Shanghai, an area of intense foreign investment.

SOURCE: http://upload.wikimedia.org/wikipedia/commons/9/92/Lujiazui_Skyline_from_Bund.jpg

modern skyline in the only economic development zone in China aimed at financial markets. The city and suburbs today are home to nearly twenty million residents—about the same size as New York. Behind the Port of Singapore, Shanghai is now the busiest port in the world as the city exports many of the manufactured goods that Americans and other Westerners buy.

The colonial past informs the urban present on the Indian Subcontinent as well. As in China, the colonization of India began as a series of European trading posts as early as the sixteenth century. By the nineteenth century much of the subcontinent was under the control of the British East India Company. When the Indian Rebellion of 1857 and 1858 in the northern part of the country ended in Indian defeat, the British government took over control of the entire country. Independence from Great Britain remained a goal for many, and in 1947 it came in a modified form when the subcontinent was divided into two countries: a Muslim-majority Pakistan split to the east and west of India, and the remainder of the subcontinent as India itself. In 1971, a civil war in Pakistan resulted in a formal division between Pakistan to the northwest of India and the former East Pakistan becoming Bangladesh. British colonialism in India, as in Nairobi and Shanghai, deeply affected the cities of India, particularly in Delhi and Mumbai. Indian cities were seats of power from which the British could rule, but also became sites of social conflict and protest to British rule. The economic fortunes of India were subject to events in other parts of the world. For instance, when the American Civil War disrupted cotton supplies to Europe, cotton growers in India profited, permanently altering the cotton industry. Similarly, the export of cotton to factories in Europe also weakened India's domestic textile industry.

About the same size as New York, Mumbai is not only the largest metropolitan area in India but one of the largest cities in the world. Located on Salsette Island, at the outlet of the Ulhas River, Mumbai is home to the busiest port in India, accounting for almost half of the country's maritime trade. It was this deep water port that first attracted Portuguese and later English traders, and from this point that British colonization of the western coast of India proceeded. The name Mumbai derives from the Hindu goddess Mumba-Devi, but was spelled Bombay until 1996. Although settlement in the area dates back to as early as 250 B.C. when it was known to the Greeks, a small fortified town was built at the site by the British East India Company in 1661 as the company's Indian headquarters and principal trading port. The city became the capital of the Bombay Presidency, a British administrative district that grew to encompass much of western India, Pakistan, and the Arabian Peninsula. As a result, the city grew in importance over the next three hundred years. British tutelage altered the city's environment in many ways. For instance, Mumbai was originally composed of seven islands, but in 1782 British Governor William Hornby initiated the Hornby Vellard, an engineering project to connect all seven islands by a causeway, thus creating the single island one encounters today. As a major center for colonization, Mumbai was also a principle center of resistance to the British presence. The city remains the capital city of the state of Maharashtra.

Mumbai is one of the most densely populated cities in the world, with a population density of over twenty-five thousand per square mile, about the same as Manhattan Island. However, although many well-to-do residents live in high rise apartment buildings, it is estimated that 55 percent of Mumbai's population lives in one of numerous slums (Megacities Project 2009). The largest of these, Dharavi, is home to over eight hundred thousand residents and is Asia's second largest slum (Davis 2006). In the midst of such poverty Mumbai is also home to the Indian film industry, referred to as Bollywood, as well as the Bombay Stock Exchange, important banks and other financial institutions, and numerous high-prestige shopping areas and world-class restaurants. As a result, the character of Mumbai is marked by modern skyscrapers and commercial districts interspersed with shanty towns. At the southern tip of the island, for instance, a military base called the Navy Nagar gives way to the stylish Cuffe Parade, home to the Mumbai World Trade Center, and Badhwar Park, an upscale residential development with its own sports fields and entertainment. Adjacent to these land-locked high-price areas are three slum neighborhoods inhabiting the coast: to the south of Cuffe Parade, to the north of Cuffe parade and due west of Badhwar park, and another to the east of Badhwar Park. Mumbai is a city of contrasts that can occur by simply crossing the street.

The effects of European colonization can also be seen in Latin America, that portion of the Americas stretching south from the American border to the Antarctic

(Ferro 1997). Primarily influenced by Spanish and, in Brazil, Portuguese, explorers arriving during the fifteenth and sixteenth centuries, Latin America was home to several important civilizations that were decimated by their contact with Europeans, party as a result of war and conquest but mostly as a result of the intrusion of new infectious diseases (Mann 2006). Several of these civilizations were home to large cities. For instance, the Inca capital of Cusco, still today the capital of its province in Peru, was reputed to have had buildings clad in gold. Not lost on the conquering Spanish, they stripped the city of its riches upon their arrival in 1533. The current city was built on the ruins of the Inca city and has Spanish colonial architecture amid the original Inca stonework. The city of three hundred fifty thousand residents today receives a million tourists per year. In Rio de Janeiro, Brazil, the influence of Portuguese imperialism is felt. Rio de Janeiro was the capital of Brazil until the building of the new capital of Brasília, a planned city of wide boulevards and large modern buildings, during the 1960s. With over seven million residents and a metropolitan area of twelve and a half million, the city also is home to a modern looking skyline and very affluent areas. As in Mumbai, areas of slums often adjoin wealthy neighborhoods. As in a number of Latin American cities, affluent residents often hire private security as a buffer against widespread violent crime.

In 1325, the city of Tenochtitlán was built on an island in the middle of Lake Texcoco, one of several lakes in the Valley of Mexico in the central part of the country (Mann 2006). The Valley of Mexico is surrounded by high mountains and home to several lakes into which water flows—there is no outlet to the sea. The citizens of Tenochtitlán became powerful, and by the fifteenth century the city was the capital of the Aztec Empire. In 1519 the Spanish Conquistador Hernán Cortés first saw Tenochtitlán, a well-planned city organized around a central plaza with high temples similar in construction to Mesopotamian ziggurats but commonly referred to as pyramids. The largest of these was the *Templo Mayor*, the tallest pyramid temple dedicated to both the god of war and the sun (Huitzilopochtli) and the god of rain and agriculture (Tlaloc). In 1521, Cortés conquered the city, and the Spanish dismantled the temples and built a new city center on their ruins. To this day, the *zócalo*, or main city square, is the social and political center of Mexico City, sided by the cathedral, federal offices and the old city market. Immediately to the northeast by the city's cathedral lie the ruins of the *Templo Mayor*, now an archaeological site and tourist attraction. After the Mexican War for Independence, Mexico City became the nation's capital (See Box 7.2).

Mexico City is arranged according to a gridiron pattern, with middle and upper income residents often living in or near central city neighborhoods. As a result, much of the city's poor live in outlying neighborhoods and suburban shantytowns. In Nezahualcoyotl, an industrial suburb with over a million residents to the city's east, the regular gridiron pattern gives way to shantytowns set amid hillsides and near garbage dumps (Drakakis-Smith 2000). In fact, a 2006 initiative to build a new waste disposal system became controversial due to the large number of the region's poor who depended upon the existing landfill system for food and employment (PlanetArk 2009). In addition, extensive rural to urban migration has pushed Mexico City's population to nearly nine million residents and created

---

B o x 7.2 • Spotlight
Mexico City

Worse than a planner's nightmare, Mexico City is a depressing testament to administrative chaos and the excesses of rapid and concentrated industrial development. Since initiating industrial development in the 1940s, Mexico's capital has been transformed from a charming city with wide boulevards, an almost leisurely lifestyle, and a population of around 1.8 million to a living hell with nearly 16 million residents in the metropolitan area. It is now neck and neck with Tokyo for the dubious honor of being the world's largest city, and it shows in the daily disorder of urban life. Clearly the capital city was not always this way. Yet because Mexico's ruling political party, the Partido Revolucionario Institucional (PRI), concentrated national investments and industrial infrastructure in this central locale, Mexico City grew by leaps and bounds. Between the 1940s and the 1960s, the capital city more than doubled in size as it proudly showcased the nation's economic growth. The capital came to be synonymous with seemingly unlimited employment opportunities, wealth, and urban economic development. By the early sixties, Mexico City boasted Latin America's first skyscraper, rising standards of living, a sophisticated cultural life, and some of the developing world's most modern urban amenities, including a gleaming new rapid transit system. The economy flowered and the capital city sparkled as the symbol of the country's successful confrontation with modernity; in turn, Mexico's citizens lent relatively solid political support to the PRI and its one-party rule.

Almost as rapidly as it came, however, this urban-based miracle turned around. By the late 1970s and early 1980s, Mexico's import-substitution industrialization strategy had reached a point of saturation, and so too had Mexico City. Local officials were hard-pressed to meet the administrative demands of the monstrous city. In the capital, where most industries were located, investment and productivity declined precipitously, spurred by an economic crisis associated with massive foreign debt obligations and skyrocketing urban infrastructure expenditures incurred in the process of rapid industrialization. Visible changes in the capital city's social, spatial, and political landscape, in short, chronicled both the nation's rapid ascent and its apparent decline. Near-lethal levels of pollution from industrial firms that had made the industrialization miracle possible were strangling the local population. By 1990, as ozone levels reached dangerous heights, the government was routinely closing schools and factories and systematically restricting automobile usage with an elaborate system of vehicle permits. The overconcentration of vehicles, population, and industry also produced severe scarcities in urban services. With high demand and limited fiscal resources, critical services like electricity, water, housing, and public transportation became almost too costly for the government to administer or provide, at least at the rate demanded by this ever-expanding metropolis and its impoverished residents.

SOURCE: Diane E. Davis, *Urban Leviathan: Mexico City in the Twentieth Century* (Philadelphia: Temple University Press, 1994), pp. 2–3.

---

a metropolitan area of about twenty-two million people. As in other cities in the developing world, the central business district and other wealthy areas are as modern as neighborhoods found in the developed world. Mexico City is a good example of a primate city: the metropolitan area contains five times the population of the next largest metropolitan area, Guadalajara, with about four million residents. Mexico City as a whole is considerably wealthier than most other regions of the country, and as a result has attracted numerous stores selling luxury items. Similar to Mumbai in this respect, Mexico City is also highly segregated by social class, with the poorest living in a number of slums ringing the city and many middle- to upper-class residents living in the southern and western areas of the city. Due to considerable pollution, federal environmental policies have sought to decentralize manufacturing to other regions of the country, such as other cities and to the *maquiladoras*, industrial areas near the American border which import raw materials from the United States and manufacture them into finished goods to sell back to the United States and other countries. As a result, population growth in the Mexico City metropolitan area has slowed, allowing the public and private sectors a chance to address environmental, social, and housing issues.

EXPLAINING THE DIVERGING PATHS OF URBAN DEVELOPMENT

Scholars have been grappling with the questions about the growth and development of different cities and regions for many decades. The most current theories and explanations can be divided into two groups. One group of theories takes the experience of the European and North American cities during their period of industrialization and urban growth as a probable path that other cities and regions will follow. It is referred to as the **development perspective**. The second group stresses the differences between what happened in Europe in the eighteenth and nineteenth centuries and what is happening in the developing world today. This latter group, which can be called the **uneven development perspective**, will be further subdivided into Marxist and world system theories. Although this classification by no means exhausts the explanations of the divergence between the industrialized, wealthy countries and the relatively nonindustrialized, poor countries, it will provide an understanding of the basic directions in which this theorizing has gone. These theories will help make sense of the different future scenarios for cities in developing nations.

Development Perspective

During the 1950s and 1960s, most economists assumed that the process of industrialization, which had begun in Europe and spread to North America, would continue to spread in more or less the same way throughout the globe. They understood industrialization to be linked to two other processes: (1) economic development, or the growth of the economy and rise in general standards of living, and (2) modernization, or the adoption of modern attitudes, such as belief in science, the pursuit of wealth, and individualistic approaches to life as opposed to religious, traditional, or kinship bonds.

Scholars such as Rostow (1960; 1978) proposed a theory that holds that the major obstacles to development in developing countries are cultural, based on the knowledge and attitudes of the population. This theory holds that a lack of scientific and technical knowledge often prevents people in the poorer countries from using resources well or taking advantage of opportunities for increasing their wealth. Development theorists also argue that traditional religious and cultural beliefs can deter people from making money, working at certain kinds of jobs, or limiting the number of children they have. Thus people in what they call underdeveloped countries are prone to behave in ways that hamper the economic development process. They contend that many urban dwellers retain aspects of their traditional, rural-based cultures.

An example is the relationship between urban migration and economic development. Within this perspective, overurbanization is seen as being caused by a cultural preference for urban life over rural life. When people migrate to the cities in large numbers, however, the cities become filled with economically marginal people who have no reasonable prospects of employment. When many people remain unemployed for long periods of time, their lack of productivity acts as a further drag on the economy. The process of promoting economic development, then, should begin with changing people's cultural preference for living in cities (Flanagan 1993).

According to the development perspective, nonindustrialized countries can industrialize and modernize if certain conditions hold. One condition is that a certain minimal level of natural resources—such as agricultural land, minerals, and water—and of money capital be available to the population. A second is that a group of indigenous people organize themselves to mobilize or take advantage of those resources. A third condition is that people, through formal education or through the process of cultural change, adopt modern attitudes about work, money, medicine, families, and so on. If these conditions are met, the economy of the country can reach the takeoff stage, after which industrialization, modernization, and economic development should be expected to follow. Urbanization is seen as being caused by industrialization, a consequence of people moving off the land to get industrial jobs in cities (Rostow 1960).

The development perspective assumes that one path of economic development exists and that the more industrialized nations simply traveled that path at an earlier time than the developing nations are doing. It also assumes that industrialization will produce improved living standards and the growth of a middle class in the developing world as it did in Europe. A third key assumption of the development perspective is that the richer, more developed countries can help the poorer countries by providing material aid such as loans, equipment, and technicians as well as teachers and experts to educate people.

Unfortunately, this optimistic scenario has not come to pass in most poor countries. The Western path of industrialization generally has not been repeated in the poorer countries, and much of the developing world remains simply a source of raw materials for the richer countries. Industrialization has also not always had the expected benefits. A number of developing countries have had significant manufacturing industry for decades without ever reaching the takeoff point on the road to economic development (Barr 1991). Industrialization in the developing world has not usually brought the expected increase in their standards of living or the growth of the middle class. A more typical pattern is for the vast majority of residents to remain impoverished while a small group reaps the economic gains of industrialization (Walton 1987).

Is the failure of the poor countries to follow the development path of the richer countries due to developing world residents' attitudes, values, and behaviors? Although it is true that individuals' attitudes could cause them to be poor, it is also true that individuals' poverty could cause them to adopt a particular set of attitudes. It seems highly unlikely that if people in poor countries simply thought and acted like people in rich countries, the poor countries would prosper. Rather, to understand different countries' development patterns, scholars have begun to analyze the relationships among countries that form a global economic system.

Uneven Development Perspectives

If the development perspective assumes that all countries will, or at least can, develop economically along the same path as that followed by the industrialized nations, uneven development perspectives assume that the world will stay more or less permanently divided into richer and poorer countries (even if the status of individual countries might change over time). These theorists argue that the operation of the capitalist world-economy, not the behavior of individuals, is the fundamental cause of the economic differences among nations. We will examine two uneven development perspectives, Marxism and world system theory.

Marxist Theories.   More than a century ago, Karl Marx noted the huge disparity in economic well-being among the different nations of the globe, but he thought that capitalism would spread around the world, reducing the economic differences between countries over time. Marx thought that capitalists would try to expand their markets indefinitely, leading to what he called the universalizing tendency of capital (1971). He anticipated that, as capital investments reached the nonindustrialized countries such as India, their economies would become more like those of the industrialized countries.

Marx's follower, Vladimir Ilyich Lenin, modified Marx's view. He argued that imperialism, the development of political empires based on military conquest, was a natural stage of capitalist development. He said that the capitalist economy's inherent need for expansion led the most powerful capitalist nations to dominate poorer nations politically so that they could use their raw materials and labor. Like Marx, Lenin thought that capitalism would continue to spread throughout the world; but, unlike Marx, he thought that the gap between the richer and poorer nations might increase rather than decrease as the poorer countries became colonies and were exploited by the wealthier and more politically powerful countries (Smith 1984).

Some contemporary Marxists, such as Szymanski (1981), argue that the gap between the rich and poor countries is only temporary. They predict that the gap will close as capitalism becomes evenly distributed around the world. Other theorists have taken Marx's writings in a different direction. Some scholars argue that capitalism has two contradictory uses for the poorer countries: they serve both as consumer markets and as sources of raw materials and labor (Smith 2008; Harvey 2006). If residents of developing countries are to be effective consumers, they must make decent incomes; but if they are to be profitable sources of labor and raw materials, they must be cheap. It is the latter characteristic that has proven to be more useful to the capitalist economy over the long run, in Smith's view.

Another issue on which some contemporary theorists differ from Marx's original position is on the concept of national boundaries and the relative distinctiveness of political-economic systems. Marx thought that as the capitalist system expanded, national boundaries would become less important, because they restrict the free circulation of capital. To an extent, this has happened, as the global economy has become a reality. Contemporary Marxists acknowledge, however, that a spatial division of labor has also emerged in which some countries remain for long periods of time in either a dominant or subsidiary role in the international economy. National boundaries are still very much enforced as governments limit and regulate the flow of goods, people, and information. In the end, Marx's "drive toward universality" does produce some equalization among nations, but we still see a strong spatial differentiation and a division of labor of places (Smith 2008).

World System Theory. In 1967 André Gunder Frank introduced a new way of thinking about the relationship between rich and poor countries. His research on Latin America showed that, contrary to what the development theorists believed, underdevelopment was not a starting point or natural state for developing world countries. Rather, Frank found that the Latin American countries had become poor through their association with the wealthier countries of Europe and North America.

Frank's phrase "the development of underdevelopment" summarizes his position: that the wealthier countries have made the poorer countries economically dependent by controlling the amount and uses of capital investment that flows over their borders. Although capital from the highly industrialized countries has, indeed, been invested in the less industrialized countries, the residents of the less industrialized countries have not received the benefits of the investment. They may have received jobs (or perhaps not, as witnessed by the overurbanization phenomenon) but at meager wages; and, although they have been able to sell their raw materials, the prices they have been paid are low. In addition, the profits from these transactions have not remained within the poorer countries but have been repatriated to the countries of the corporations' owners. Thus the poorer countries are stuck, dependent on the industrialized nations for jobs and markets; the exchange between the richer countries and the poorer ones tends to keep the poorer countries permanently dependent on the richer.

Frank's dependency theory laid the groundwork for the **world system theory**, which Immanuel Wallerstein initiated (1976). Rather than starting the analysis of the developing world on the basis of the characteristics of individual countries or people, world system proponents begin at the level of the world economic system and the relationships among nations. They argue that within the global division of labor, the **core nations** perform different functions from those of the **peripheral nations**. Core nations perform the functions of capital investment, economic management, and innovation. They also have the most powerful military forces, which can gain them political as well as economic

---

B o x 7.3 • Spotlight
Urban Peasants in China

China has become a prime location for low-wage production in the global economy. The communist government anticipated this development by establishing "special economic zones" in coastal regions in the 1980s to attract foreign investment. By the mid-1990s, when the East Asian Newly Industrializing Countries had emerged as "middle-income countries" with relatively high-skilled labor forces, China became the preferred site for foreign investors—especially Korean and Taiwanese investors, who were experiencing rising labor costs at home. In 1995, the ratio of factory wages in China to South Korea/Taiwan to Japan was approximately 1:30:80. In her investigations of shoe factories (producing Reebok and Nike products, among others), in Dongguan City, sociologist Anita Chan observes that vast concrete industrial estates have mushroomed on former rice paddies. Local farmers now live off the rents from the factories, while tens of thousands of migrants from China's poorer hinterland swell the low-wage workforce. Twelve-hour shifts (with enforced overtime) and seven-day work weeks are common, with Korean or Taiwanese managers using militaristic methods to break in and control the migrant labor force (in addition to requiring a deposit of two to four weeks' wages and confiscation of migrant ID cards). As the cash economy has expanded in China, a huge migrant labor force has gravitated toward coastal industrial regions, attracting foreign investment. Between 1985 and 1996, the portion of Chinese exports from foreign-owned plants grew from 1 to 40 per cent. China now produces about half of the world's shoes and a proliferating array of electronic items, toys, and garments for the global economy.

SOURCE: Philip McMichael, *Development and Social Change* (Thousand Oaks, CA: Pine Forge Press, 2000), pp. 87–88.

It is generally accepted that the bulk of rural migrants end up doing work that is dangerous, dirty, and difficult: the notorious "Three Ds." This is partly because migrants tend to be less educated than urban (natives) and generally lack the requisite skills for better paid work. Increasingly, too, certain kinds of work are "reserved" for the growing number of legal urban residents who are unemployed. Many migrant workers work in small to medium-sized family enterprises. Others find jobs in jointly financed, larger factories producing primarily for export. Many men work in construction. Young women typically find work in garment industries and electronic assembly plants, but also as nursemaids in newly rich, middle class households. Some of the more successful migrants succeed in opening up small businesses, such as hair dressing parlors or restaurants that cater mostly to other migrants, though a few may serve an upscale market. The less fortunate become rag pickers and scrap collectors.

SOURCE: John Friedman, *China's Urban Transition* (Minneapolis: U. Minnesota Press, 2005), p. 66.

---

hegemony, or dominance. The periphery, on the other hand, has a different role. Peripheral nations have typically specialized in the export of agricultural products and raw materials, such as minerals. They sometimes produce manufactured goods, especially those goods that require more input of human labor than of machinery. In these cases, their low-wage rates may draw considerable foreign investment. Box 7.3 describes how low wages in China have attracted many foreign manufacturing companies.

World system theorists stress the economic relationships among nation-states and the coherence of the world-economy. Unlike Lenin, they do not think that political imperialism is necessarily the only way for some countries to dominate others economically. World system theory holds that, from the seventeenth to the nineteenth centuries, imperialism was (as Marx argued) the main way in which the capitalist economy expanded. But even without political domination, the core countries have been able to dominate the periphery by simply monopolizing economic advantages such as capital, research facilities, and communication channels, thus preventing the peripheral countries from stepping out of their places in the global division of labor.

What of the intermediary countries that the development theorists call developing nations, those that are partially industrialized? World system theorists see them as having mixed economies and classify them as the semiperiphery. These nations, such as Brazil, Mexico, and Korea, perform some functions of the core, especially within their own region of the world, and some functions of the periphery, especially toward the core economies. Thus, Mexico is both a banking center for Central America (a core function) and a location for cheap labor and agricultural exports for the United States (a peripheral function). The implication is that semiperipheral states may stay in that position for the foreseeable future without becoming part of the core of the world-economy. Even though some countries in the periphery have some core functions, few possess sufficient local investment capital to free them from the need for foreign investment or loans from foreign governments (Chase-Dunn 1985; Denemark 2000).

What, then, are we to conclude about urbanization in the developing world? Our interpretation is that foreign investment from the core countries rather than people's culturally based attitudes is the main cause of urban growth in the developing world. Large-scale, capital-intensive, and export-oriented agriculture push rural peasants off the land. Their actions, moreover, are related to the well-being of the richer countries. Most rural-to-urban migrants who cannot find jobs in the regular economy participate in the rapidly growing informal sector. This sector has sometimes been seen as marginal to the regular economy, but the cheap labor of these unwaged workers can be a hidden subsidy to the remainder of the economy. Through activities such as hiring out for day labor, reselling castoffs, and doing chores for food, workers in the informal sector provide cheap goods and services for those who are part of the mainstream. This hidden work helps reduce the cost of that country's exported goods on the world market and acts as an indirect subsidy to corporations and consumers in the richer nations (Portes 1985).

FUTURE DEVELOPMENT
OF DEVELOPING WORLD CITIES

What will the future hold for the cities of the developing world? Will urban growth continue at the same breakneck pace we have seen in recent decades? Will poverty and inequality remain at the same high levels? Or will there be some convergence between cities in the developed and developing world? Will economic trade equalize, creating more widespread prosperity and the growth of a middle class?

The economic gap between the rich and poor countries as measured by their gross national products has not narrowed but widened over the past half century, even accounting for such fast-growing economies as China and India (UNCTAD 2009). All countries and regions within the developed and developing worlds have not been equally affected by this general trend, however. After World War II, the countries of Latin America fared best, followed by those of Southeast Asia, then the Middle East and North Africa, then sub-Saharan Africa, with South Asia faring worst. Rather than a convergence of wealth caused by a great spurt of developing world economic development, the current prospect seems to be "a rigid hierarchy of wealth in which the occasional ascent of a nation or two leaves all the others more firmly entrenched than ever where they were before" (Arrighi 1991, 52). Since the 1990s, however, the fastest growing countries have been located in Southeast Asia and Eastern Europe (UNCTAD 2009).

Another point of view is that of Manuel Castells, author of *The Rise of the Network Society* (1996). As we saw earlier, Castells argues that the global economy is entering a new stage, one in which the traditional sources of wealth (such as trade, agriculture, mining, and manufacturing) are becoming more subordinate to a single source of wealth: the creation and manipulation of information. This new mode of development, Castells argues, is reshaping the global map of the rich and poor countries in some ways not predicted by world system theory. Castells argues that the world will no longer be divided into a relatively stable core, periphery, and semiperiphery, as we have seen, but that some countries will leapfrog into better economic conditions and others will be left decisively behind. The regions he sees as poised to succeed are portions of Asia (including parts of China and India) and portions of Latin America (particularly Mexico and Argentina).

Although Castells's argument is not incompatible with world system theory, it adds three new dimensions to it. His first point, and the most different from world system theory, is that the new international division of labor is increasingly organized not along the lines of nations but rather in networks and flows of information. On a global scale, populations that can perform "informational labor" will be the best off, populations that can produce lower-cost labor will be next, followed by producers of raw materials (dependent on their natural location), and finally by the "redundant producers," whose labor is devalued in the informational economy. Thus, it follows that education and technology are increasingly important because the type of labor valued by the informational economy is intellectual labor rather than manual labor. This means that poor regions can increase their chances for future development by making concentrated investments in education and technology.

Finally, Castells believes that rather than all regions being incorporated into the world-economy, in the new global division of labor, some regions will become totally irrelevant and lose any chance of economic participation. In this sense, he argues, areas such as sub-Saharan Africa could emerge as a "fourth world," utterly cut off from global flows of capital. He argues that being structurally irrelevant to the world-economy is a more threatening position than being dependent on it. In general, Castells's viewpoint allows for more flux in the future than does the world system approach.

CONCLUSION

Cities of the developing world differ from each other because of their differing geographies, climates, histories, and cultures. Despite these differences, however, they share some similarities due to their similar economic and political contexts. Most developing world cities have experienced huge and sometimes unmanageable migration from the countryside to the cities, resulting in a good deal of displacement and urban poverty. Causes for this migration include being forced off the land and the possibility of making a better living in the cities.

Theorists who have tried to explain why the developing world countries stay poor have either stressed the characteristics of the local population and culture (development theory) or the position of the countries within the global economic system (uneven development theory). This text supports the position of world system theory, that there is a relatively stable stratification system of economies based on their degree of control over investment capital and world markets.

Regardless of the theoretical position one takes, it seems likely that the future will include continued inequality between rich and poor countries and continued rural-to-urban migration. It is possible, however, that the ongoing transformation from a primarily goods-producing economy to a primarily information-producing economy will result in some shifting of where individual economies rank in the global hierarchy, and may prompt the development of cities beyond the traditional primate cities in each nation.

DISCUSSION QUESTIONS

1. Many rapidly growing third world cities have sizeable squatters' settlements on their outskirts. What do you think are some similarities between living in a squatters' settlement in, say, Lima, Peru, and being homeless in New York City? What do you think the differences might be?

2. The United States and several international organizations administer foreign aid programs for poorer countries. What do you know about such programs? How much and what kinds of assistance do they provide? If you were to design a program to improve economic conditions in one or more poor countries, what steps would you take based on the development approach? On the world system approach?

3. Interview someone who has lived in a third world (preferably non–English-speaking) country. How did their experiences of urban life in that area compare to urban life in the United States. If you traveled there, what would you expect to find?

PART III

Change and Conflict
Urban Social Groups

8

Immigrants, Ethnic Groups, and the City

Immigration is the sincerest form of flattery.
ANONYMOUS

The following is a sampling of comments that one group of Philadelphia residents made about a group of their neighbors. See if you can guess who is talking about whom.

> "They are materialistic ... they think we owe them."
> "When I came, nobody helped me make my way. How do they get all this welfare and stuff when we Americans can't?"
> "When we came to America, you went to Ellis Island, and if you had one scab on your finger you were sent back."
> "They don't support or go to church; they worship the almighty buck."

What did you guess? Whites discussing African Americans, Asian immigrants, or Puerto Rican newcomers? Although you might expect some whites to have these attitudes about groups with which they are unfamiliar, the comments were actually made by Polish-American Catholics about recent Polish immigrants who joined the parish church over the previous decade (Goode and Schneider 1994, 124). Even though these two groups of immigrants from different generations share a common race, national origin, and religion, the different timing and circumstances of their respective immigrations have created different social realities for the two groups.

One thing the two groups share is that both chose a large city as their destination when they came from Poland. Most immigrants, regardless of their nation of origin, choose urban life. Since the early 1800s the vast majority of immigrants have settled in cities; 81 percent of all immigrants currently live in metropolitan areas (U.S. Census Bureau 2003). The rich mix of different cultures in close proximity to each other contributes to the feeling of diversity, urbanity, and cosmopolitanism so characteristic of cities.

This chapter will explore the link between immigration and cities, especially examining the following questions:

- When and why do people leave their country of origin?
- Why do they settle where they do? Why do they settle in cities?
- What is the experience of immigrants settling in the United States, and how has it changed over time?
- What is the impact of U.S. immigration policy on the numbers, nationalities, and characteristics of immigrants?

OLD AND NEW IMMIGRATION

It has often been said that the United States is a nation of immigrants. Immigration has been a long-term trend, but both the locations where immigrants settle and the places from which they come have changed over the years. Before 1800, equal proportions of immigrants lived in cities and rural areas, the former working in crafts and the latter as farmers. Since about 1800, however, immigrants have disproportionately settled in cities. The reason for this choice is not because most immigrants were used to city living in their home countries—indeed, large numbers of them were peasants from rural villages—but because of the availability of jobs in cities. The overall immigrant settlement pattern in the nineteenth century was that the largest proportions of immigrants arriving at a given time would move to the cities of the most rapidly industrializing region at the time of their arrival: first New England, then the Mid-Atlantic, then the North Central states (Ward 1971).

More recently, we also find most immigrants settling in urban areas, especially in the largest cities. As Table 8.1 shows, New York, Los Angeles, and Miami currently head the list of immigrant destinations. The most common route for immigrant groups has been to move directly to their chosen cities. Large numbers of Mexicans move to Los Angeles, Dominicans to New York, and Filipinos to San Francisco; just as many Irish immigrants moved to Boston, Eastern European Jews to New York, and Poles to Chicago in the early 1900s. Another route to the city is indirect; some immigrants who did not initially settle in urban areas migrated to them later. Many Chinese, for example, initially lived in rural settings (farming, mining, and working in construction) but gradually moved to cities to work either in factories or as small business owners. Also Cuban immigrants, who in the 1960s settled all over the eastern United States, later migrated internally to Miami (Perez 1992). As we will see, cities provide immigrants with two important advantages: jobs and a community of peers.

T A B L E   8.1   Gateway Cities: The Fifteen U.S. Metropolitan Areas Receiving the Largest Numbers of Immigrants, 2008

Metropolitan Area	2008 Immigration
1. New York, NY	179,981
2. Los Angeles, CA	96,492
3. Miami, FL	87,787
4. Washington, DC	42,827
5. Chicago, IL	39,826
6. San Francisco, CA	36,120
7. Houston, TX	30,514
8. Dallas, TX	26,451
9. Boston, MA	24,691
10. Atlanta, GA	22,329
11. San Jose, CA	21,022
12. San Diego, CA	20,491
13. Philadelphia, PA	18,914
14. Riverside, CA	17,792
15. Seattle, WA	17,090

SOURCE: U.S. Department of Homeland Security, *Yearbook of Immigration Statistics, 2008* (http://www.dhs.gov).

Three Waves of Immigration

Although immigration is ongoing, it peaked at certain times during the history of the United States. Most historians identify three large waves of immigration: the first from 1860 to 1890, the second from 1900 to 1924, and the third since 1965 (see Table 8.2). With some exceptions, the ebbs and flows of immigration have followed the ups and downs of the U.S. economy. In boom times more immigrants entered the country; during recessions and wars, the numbers decreased (McLemore 1994).

The countries from which immigrants come, or **sending countries**, have also varied dramatically. During the first large wave of immigration, prior to 1890, the countries that sent the largest numbers of immigrants were the Northern European nations of Germany and the United Kingdom, with Scandinavia providing smaller but still substantial numbers. These immigrant groups were white, came from Northern Europe, were mostly Protestant, and had national origins similar to those of the **native-born population**, who were predominantly English, Irish, Scottish, Dutch, and French. The main feature that distinguished these early immigrants from the native-born population was their language or dialect (for example, the English-speaking Irish accent).

T A B L E 8.2   Immigration to the United States, 1820–2007

Years	Number of Immigrants (000s)	Rate per 1,000 Population
1820–1830	152	1.2
1831–1840	599	3.9
1841–1850	1,713	8.4
1851–1860	2,598	9.3
1861–1870	2,314	6.4
1871–1880	2,812	6.2
1881–1890	5,247	9.2
1891–1900	3,687	5.3
1901–1910	8,795	10.4
1911–1920	5,736	5.7
1921–1930	4,107	3.5
1931–1940	528	.4
1941–1950	1,035	.7
1951–1960	2,515	1.5
1961–1970	3,322	1.7
1971–1980	4,399	2.0
1981–1990	7,256	3.0
1991–2000	9,081	3.4
2001–2007	7,220	3.5

SOURCE: U.S. Department of Homeland Security, *Yearbook of Immigration Statistics 2007*, Table 44.

During the second large immigrant wave, from 1900 to the 1920s, the dominant sending countries were in South and Central Europe, with the largest numbers of immigrants coming from Italy, Austria-Hungary, and Russia. Although these second-wave immigrants were still European in origin, they spoke a variety of languages, were mostly Catholic, Jewish, or Eastern Orthodox in religion, and had markedly different appearances and customs from those of the majority of the native-born population (Ward 1971).

The members of the current third wave of immigration are drawn mostly from Asia (34 percent) and Latin America (32 percent) with the largest numbers (as shown in Table 8.3) coming from Mexico, India, China, the Philippines, and Russia. See Figure 8.1, which depicts how the sending countries have changed over time. The current wave of immigrants is predominantly from countries of the developing world and consists in large part of non–English-speaking people of color. Thus, the visible differences of race and ethnicity are even more apparent for current immigrants than they were for earlier immigrants.

TABLE 8.3   Where Do Immigrants Come From? Immigration to the United States, by Ranked Countries, 1971–1980 and 2000–2008

Rank	1971–1980	2000–2008
1	Mexico	Mexico
2	Philippines	India
3	Cuba	China
4	Korea	Philippines
5	China	Russia
6	India	Viet Nam
7	Dominican Republic	Dominican Republic
8	Jamaica	Cuba
9	Italy	El Salvador
10	United Kingdom	Canada

SOURCE: Derived from U.S. Department of Homeland Security, *Yearbook of Immigration Statistics 2008* Table 1.

Reactions to Newcomers

Throughout the history of the United States, reactions of the native-born population to immigrant groups have varied. In times of economic expansion, immigrants have generally been welcomed as a valuable addition to the labor force, especially in selected industries. In times of economic stagnation and recession, U.S. citizens have often reacted negatively to immigrants. In the press and media, immigrants have sometimes been described not only as economic competitors with native-born workers but also as socially, morally, politically, or religiously questionable people (see Figure 8.2).

Dominant American cultural values and beliefs have over the centuries encompassed two contradictory impulses: on the one hand, the belief that the United States is a land of opportunity where immigrants are welcome and where they can seek their fortune while contributing to the growth of the national economy; on the other hand, the belief that the nation's cultural, economic, and political stability are threatened by the incorporation of large groups of people with different ways. The latter part of this contradiction has at times given rise to the cultural phenomenon of **xenophobia**, or fear of foreigners, and sometimes to the political phenomenon of **nativism**, or the organization of political institutions to benefit native-born citizens over immigrants. Xenophobia is expressed in popular culture through language, such as in the phrases "the foreign menace" and "the Yellow Peril," and through negative stereotypes of foreigners in which they are depicted as being clannish, dirty, manipulative, or dishonest. Probably the best-known and most influential example of nativism was the establishment, in 1850, of the Know-Nothing party, whose political slogan was "America for the

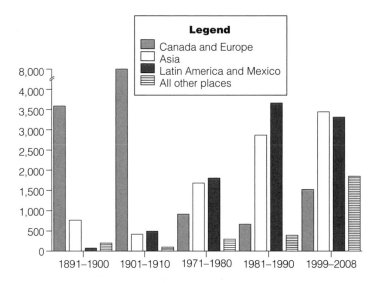

F I G U R E 8.1 Sources of Legal Immigration. Note the dramatic change in the countries sending immigrants to the United States, from mostly European countries to mostly Latin American and Asian countries.

SOURCE: Adapted from *A Field Guide to the U.S. Economy* (Amherst, MA: Center for Popular Economics, 1995), Graph 4.4, and U.S. Department of Homeland Security, *Yearbook of Immigration Statistics 2008*, Table 3.

Americans" and whose political platform included restricting immigration and preventing foreign-born people from holding political office (McLemore 1994). By examining the economic and political causes of immigration, we can more readily understand why immigration has ebbed and flowed, why the sending countries have changed over time, and why the response of the native-born population has varied.

Economics of Immigration

Why does immigration occur? To answer this question, we must examine factors at both the individual (micro) level and the social system (macro) level. When we examine the causes of immigration on the micro level, we find that people have three major reasons for **emigrating** from (or leaving) their native countries: to avoid political persecution, to join family members, and to look for work. Of the three reasons, looking for work is by far the most common motivation prompting individuals to move to another country.

When we examine the causes of international migration on the macro level, we find that, although wars and civil upheavals are a significant cause of movement from one country to another, work once again is the most important cause. Economists say that labor "flows" from place to place, both within national borders and across those borders. During times of labor shortages, the need for more workers sets off large immigration flows. For example, during the nineteenth century, U.S. employers in growing industries (such as coal and steel) faced

THE BALANCE OF TRADE WITH GREAT BRITAIN SEEMS TO BE STILL AGAINST US.
650 Paupers arrived at Boston in the Steamship *Nestoria*, April 15th, from Galway, Ireland, shipped by the British Government.

Culver Pictures

F I G U R E 8.2 **Stereotypes of Immigrants.** This cartoon, probably dating from the 1890s, depicts Irish immigrants as indigent.

a shortage of native-born workers who could do the heavy work they needed; thus, they actively recruited men from Southern and Eastern Europe to come to the United States and work in their factories.

Frequently, family members or friends who have already emigrated to another country recruit immigrants, writing back home offering job opportunities, loans, or even housing to their relatives. This informal network of contacts results in a common pattern known as **chain migration**, in which a number of relatives, friends, or neighbors from a single region or town within the sending country follow each other to a particular location in the host country. Box 8.1 shows an example of how chain migration occurs.

Immigrant workers do not always intend to stay in the country to which they move. In most other countries labor immigration is largely temporary (often in organized programs of "guest workers"), but in the United States, we find both

---

B o x 8.1 • Case Study
Chain Migration from Puerto Rico to Boston's South End
Neighborhood

Though most of the South End's early immigrants were Irish, they were followed, throughout the first half of the twentieth century, by Greek, Syrian, and Chinese immigrants, Eastern European Jews, African Americans, West Indians, and later, Puerto Ricans. They settled in the South End's roughly three hundred residential acres, in somewhat (although not completely) distinct sections of the neighborhood.

...The Puerto Ricans who migrated to the South End were among the most recent arrivals. Recruited by New England farm companies for seasonal employment, Puerto Ricans from the smallest towns in the island had been quietly settling in the northeast for decades. By the 1950s, hundreds of them had moved into the roomy, affordable apartments of the South End. They were, by and large, a rural people. As late as 1968, 77 percent of them had migrated from either the countryside or towns with populations of less than 25,000. Once in the city, they quickly found jobs—if often temporary and nonunion jobs—in the many factories in Boston at the time or set up small businesses to join the hundreds of such small businesses already existing in the South End.

Back in the towns of Aguadilla, Comerío, Ponce, and some neighborhoods in San Juan, among the kin and social networks of these immigrants, the South End developed a reputation as a place where cheap housing could be found in the center of one of the most vibrant industrial cities in the country. A brother, uncle, or even in-law was enough reason to pull north many islanders who had been perfectly content with their lives. One such islander was Ernesto, who told me he had lived happily if uneventfully as a construction worker and farmer in Ponce; he was married and had several sons and daughters. His older brother, Manuel, had migrated to Boston in the late 1950s and opened a bodega, a little grocery store in the South End. By the turn of the sixties, Manuel realized he desperately needed help to run the establishment. It was not as if Ernesto were a skilled businessman, but in those early years, Manuel simply could not afford the extra help, and if Ernesto moved up, they would both, he was sure, be better off. So Ernesto came north at age 50 with his oldest son; the rest of the family would migrate within a few years, as soon as it was affordable. The grocery store went out of business anyway, but Ernesto quickly found work at a foundry that paid him enough to afford the $60 monthly rent for a fully-furnished, three-bedroom apartment that had been carved out of the third floor of a brick row house in the neighborhood.

SOURCE: Mario Luis Small, *Villa Victoria: The Transformation of Social Capital in a Boston Barrio* (Chicago: University of Chicago Press, 2004), pp. 22–25 *passim*.

---

temporary and permanent immigrants. The latter are called **settlers**, who enter the country with the intention of staying for the rest of their lives, and the former are **sojourners**, entering the labor force with the intention of working long enough to amass a stake to use when they return to their native land. Besides sojourners, temporary immigrants may be contract workers, permitted to be in the United States only for the duration of a certain work project, or seasonal workers, permitted only during certain months of the year.

To understand immigration, we must examine economic conditions in both the host country and the sending countries. An example is the ways in which the relationship between the United States and China over a period of some 150 years affected Chinese immigration. North Americans first recruited Chinese laborers to work on sugar plantations in Hawaii in the 1830s. Once they had established the fact that China was a good source of labor, recruiters drew on it to build the Central Pacific Railroad in the 1860s, creating a highly homogeneous work force in which 90 percent of the thirteen thousand railroad construction workers were Chinese (Takaki 1989). After the completion of the railroad in 1869, Chinese laborers began to look for other jobs, putting them into direct competition with white workers. This competition aroused white workers to demand limitations on Chinese immigration and led eventually to the passage of a major piece of anti-immigration legislation, the Chinese Exclusion Act, in 1882. Thus, when North American employers needed workers, they sought out Chinese immigrants; when workers were not needed, however, the Chinese became "surplus" labor and were not welcome.

Between 1840 and 1920, two and a half million people left China, bound not only for the United States but also for Canada, Australia, New Zealand, Southeast Asia, the West Indies, South America, and Africa. Some of the Chinese who emigrated were refugees from political upheavals that had struck several regions of China during that period, and some were simply pursuing better economic opportunities than their own localities offered. The sojourners who left China were mostly young married men whose goal was to make enough money to support their families while saving for a stake with which eventually to return to China and buy land. As their opportunities for work in mines and on the railroad dwindled, however, many of these Chinese workers migrated to urban areas. Some acquired their economic stakes and returned home to buy land. Others remained in the United States and became settler-entrepreneurs, using their stakes to establish small businesses such as restaurants, grocery stores, and laundries in U.S. cities. Although they had not intended to become permanent residents of North American cities, events helped shape their futures differently than they had expected (Takaki 1989).

U.S. Immigration Policy

Economic factors were important in affecting the timing, origins, and length of stay of immigrants to the United States. But U.S. government policies that regulate flows of immigration also impacted the numbers, nationalities, and other characteristics of immigrants.

You have probably read or perhaps even seen at the base of the Statue of Liberty lines from the poem "The New Colossus" by Emma Lazarus (1944, originally published in 1883):

> Give me your tired, your poor,
>
> Your huddled masses yearning to breathe free,
>
> The wretched refuse of your teeming shore.
>
> Send these the homeless, tempest-tost to me,
>
> I lift my lamp beside the golden door!

Despite the welcoming (if unflattering) symbolism of the poem, the reality is that limitations on immigration have had a long history in the United States. The first anti-immigration law was the Alien and Sedition Act of 1798, which mandated a fourteen-year residency period for voting and allowed the president to expel aliens deemed to be dangerous. The repeal of that legislation led the federal government to establish an open-door immigration policy. Between 1800 and 1850, however, public sentiment became increasingly hostile toward Irish, Germans, and other Catholic immigrants. Nativist parties, such as the Know-Nothing and the Workingmen's parties, agitated for restrictive legislation and were finally successful in 1875, when a federal immigration act barred "undesirables" from entering the country. In 1882 this legislation was broadened and strengthened to prohibit the admission of lunatics, convicts, idiots, and people likely to become a public charge. That year also saw the passage of the Chinese Exclusion Act, the first legislation that barred individuals from entering the country not because of their individual characteristics (such as inability to work) but solely because of their ethnicity (Parrillo 1994).

During the second great wave of immigration, competition between native and immigrant labor for jobs led to protective legislation in 1921, 1924, and 1929. These laws sharply decreased the number of immigrants permitted to enter and restricted individuals according to personal characteristics and nationality. They established a quota system designed to allow immigrants into the country on the basis of the proportion of people of their national origin already living here. Thus, because the greatest proportion of the U.S. population was from the British Isles, that group had the largest quota. Conversely, because relatively few Hungarians (for example) lived in the United States, they received a very small quota. Under this legislation, the ban on immigration from China was continued and a ban on immigration from Japan was initiated (Johnson 2003). The overall impact of this series of laws was to cut immigration to less than 20 percent of its previous volume and to make the immigrant stream less discernibly different from that of the population already in the United States. These laws, as we have seen, were largely responses to the public's sense of economic competition and fear of social instability.

The legislation that set the stage for the current large wave of immigration was passed in 1965 and significantly raised the number of immigrants permitted into the country each year. This bill also abolished the national quota system and reestablished the preferences for certain types of individuals: people with family members in the United States, people with occupational skills needed in the United States, and certifiable political refugees. This law has dramatically changed the countries of origin and the occupational categories of the current stream of immigrants. Since 1965 we have seen increased numbers of immigrants from Asia and Africa, as well as a continued stream from Latin America. The proportion of immigrants with college or advanced degrees has greatly increased, although some unskilled workers are still admitted legally (Portes and Rumbaut 2006).

Why has immigration policy changed so dramatically over the course of U.S. history? On one level, legislation has been a response to public sentiment and attitudes about immigrants and immigration. As we have seen, native-born workers' fear of economic competition is one factor that has affected public sentiment, which has in turn affected legislators' priorities. Another is the political agitation by groups that believe they can gain by excluding newcomers. Such political action often consists of manipulating public opinion by promoting stereotypes and symbols that equate immigrants with undesirable characteristics or that blame (or **scapegoat**) immigrants for social problems that are not actually related to immigration.

Influential economic and political actors who lobby for specific policies have also steered the direction of immigration policy. Several exceptions in the law, for example, have allowed companies to import temporary workers into the United States without counting them as part of the regular allocation of immigrants admitted.

Another significant influence on immigration policy is foreign policy. The kind of treatment accorded to potential immigrants may have less to do with their individual characteristics than with political relations between their home nation and the United States. One instance of the politics of immigration is the question of who is granted status as a **refugee** rather than as an immigrant (or "economic immigrant" as immigration policy defines nonrefugees). Refugees have several advantages, including speed of entry and government financial assistance, such as housing, food, and medical allowances during the relocation period. Whether a person is labeled a refugee is often a function of the status of the government of their country of origin in the eyes of the United States government.

The terrorist attacks that destroyed New York City's World Trade Center and part of the Pentagon on September 11, 2001, also had a serious impact on the country's response to immigration. The federal government created the Department of Homeland Security and gave it authority over the agency that processes immigrants. Many new controls were set in place, including stricter scrutiny of international students and broader mandates for American citizens to use passports and visas when traveling out of the country. This is also discussed in Chapter 12.

In sum, the numbers of immigrants entering the United States as well as the types of countries from which they come and the types of characteristics they bring with them have changed greatly over the course of U.S. history. Economic conditions (both here and abroad) and U.S. immigration policy have influenced the levels of immigration and the types of immigrants accepted into the country.

CONTEMPORARY IMMIGRANT LIFESTYLES

Currently, more than thirty-seven million immigrants live in the United States (U.S. Census Bureau 2009a). They are profoundly impacting the economics, politics, and culture of the United States, primarily in major metropolitan areas. In this section we will explore the ways in which immigrants have adapted to life in the United States and the ways in which they are influencing urban institutions.

Ethnic Identification and Group Solidarity

Like earlier waves of immigrants, contemporary immigrants have created unique social institutions that serve their group. The persistence of immigrants' cultural institutions raises an important sociological question about the role of culture in forming individual identity. In the past all immigrants were expected to blend into the Anglo-American culture by learning English and by cooking, dressing, and in general acting like the native-born population. By taking on the cultural traits of the dominant population (that is, **acculturating**), immigrants were expected to blend in so thoroughly (be **assimilated**) that they would in effect disappear as separate ethnic groups. Until the 1960s most observers presumed that ethnicity was disappearing and that one Anglo-American culture would shortly dominate the society (Gordon 1964). Since that time, however, both an increase in newcomers and a resurgence of ethnic identification among some citizens whose ancestors arrived in previous immigration streams have heightened our society's appreciation for cultural differences. Some individuals are now questioning the desirability of adjusting to the Anglo-American standard, as they find that identification with a culturally distinct ethnic group is an important component of their personal identity and they can gain material advantages through ethnic group membership. (See Box 8.2.)

Ethnic **identification**, or the extent to which individuals identify themselves as members of a particular group, is not always simple. In answer to the question "What are you?" the same individual may have several answers.

An individual of Cuban ancestry may be a Latino vis-à-vis non–Spanish-speaking ethnic groups, a Cuban-American vis-à-vis other Spanish-speaking groups, a Marielito [person who arrived from Cuba in a particular wave of migration from the port of Mariel] vis-à-vis other Cubans, and white vis-à-vis African Americans (Nagel 1994, 155).

This statement shows that ethnic identification is constructed within particular contexts and with reference to particular audiences. The process of constructing ethnic identities has long occurred within immigrant groups. Immigrants from Italy, for example, became known as Italian only after they arrived in North America; in Italy, they identified with a region, a dialect, a village, or a family rather than with the nation.

Ethnic identification is an individual characteristic influenced by the existence of a group; **ethnic solidarity** is the extent to which a group thinks of itself as a whole, organizes itself, or acts in a unified way. Ethnic solidarity is sometimes fostered by discrimination against a group, encouraging the members to band together in a spirit of self-help.

Immigrants nurture ethnic identification and solidarity by maintaining ties with the home country. Telephone calls, letters, packages, videotapes, and cash help maintain ties, as does personal contact. Some immigrant groups have a pattern of very frequent travel back and forth from their homeland to the United States. In some parts of Mexico, for example, it is now considered not only routine but highly desirable for men to leave their families and become sojourners in the United States. Whether entering the United States legally or illegally, they

---

B o x   8.2   •   Spotlight
The Méndez Children

At school, children mingle with groups differentiated by their own self-perceptions and the perceptions of external observers. Especially when children equate success with power attained through conflict or physical force—as in the case of youth gangs—those groups can exert a downward pull on immigrant children. The paths that lead youngsters toward specific clusters are complex. However, one of the most effective antidotes against downward mobility is a sense of membership in a group with an undamaged collective identity. The Méndez children illustrate that proposition.

But for the fact that they are illegal aliens from Nicaragua, sixteen-year-old Omar Méndez and his younger sister Fátima could not be closer to the American Dream. They have grown up in Miami since they were five and three years old respectively. They are superb students full of spirit and ambition. They attend a school where discipline is strict and where teachers are able to communicate with parents in Spanish. Most decisively, they see themselves as immigrants, and that identity protects them from negative stereotypes and from incorporation into more popular but less motivated groups in school. In Fátima's words, "We're immigrants! We can't afford to just sit around and blow it like others who have been in this country longer and take everything for granted." To maintain her independence, she withdraws from her peers and endures being called a "nerd." She does not mind because her center of gravitation is within the family.

SOURCE: M. Patricia Fernández Kelly and Richard Schauffler, "Divided Fates: Immigrant Children and the New Assimilation," in *The New Second Generation*, ed. A. Portes (New York: Russell Sage, 1996), p. 49.

---

travel back and forth regularly and maintain social ties on both sides of the border (Durand and Massey 2004). Researchers have found similar patterns among immigrants from the Caribbean: Dominicans living in the United States now represent 14 percent of the total population of the Dominican Republic. Many Dominicans travel back and forth so much that they have become bicultural or "transnational" as sociologists now refer to this group. Levitt (2001) describes how these "transnational villagers" feel perfectly comfortable maintaining their kinship, friendship, and economic ties as they move between the Dominican Republic and the United States. More than with previous generations of immigrants, technology helps people stay in touch with their families. Foner (2000) describes Brazilian and Indian immigrants in New York City exchanging phone calls, faxes, e-mail, and videos with relatives "back home" to keep up with family events and even to run businesses from overseas.

Ethnic Neighborhoods and Ethnic Enclaves

We have seen that most present-day immigrants still choose to live in cities. Like the immigrants of previous generations, the contemporary newcomers often live in neighborhoods with a significant proportion of people of their own cultural background or national origin. In big cities these population clusters can be large enough to provide the basis for many businesses and organizations that cater to the needs of the group: shops, restaurants, churches, and even radio or television stations, where proprietors offer culturally specific goods or simply speak the group's language. Immigrant neighborhoods tend to be multiethnic, but a neighborhood can gain an association with a particular ethnic group if it has a large number of visible ethnic establishments.

In some cities immigrant settlements have become so large and dense that immigrants have established numerous businesses in which they employ other members of their ethnic group. These **enclave economies** can provide economic opportunities that may not be available to immigrants in the wider community. Some examples include Koreatown in Los Angeles, Little Havana in Miami, and Chinatown in San Francisco and New York. In enclave communities, several types of economic opportunities exist. Immigrants with skills and capital but little experience with English can open small businesses such as shops and restaurants serving members of their own ethnic group. Immigrants with English skills or their bilingual children can establish businesses such as manufacturing or construction that, while employing members of their own ethnic group, sell the finished goods or services to the larger public. Newly arrived immigrants without either language skills or capital can often find entry-level employment among their co-ethnic employers and use the initial job as a foothold into the U.S. economy. Although sociologists continue to debate about whether immigrants are likely to do better economically when they work in the enclave economy or in the general economy, it is certainly true that the formation of an enclave provides types of opportunities (especially entrepreneurial opportunities) that are not generally available in locations without enclaves.

Two studies of different groups of Chinese immigrants in New York provide a good illustration of the different ways in which newcomers from the same cultural group may adapt economically to the urban United States. Tellingly, the titles of the books are *Chinatown* by Min Zhou (1992) and *Chinatown No More* by Hsiang-Shui Chen (1992). Zhou traces the lives and fortunes of Chinese immigrants who live in the traditional Chinatown of lower Manhattan, an enclave that has existed for more than one hundred years, since the Chinese on the West Coast began facing discrimination and moving eastward. Chen examines the lifestyles of Chinese immigrants from Taiwan who have forsaken the traditional Chinatown for the multiethnic neighborhoods of the borough of Queens, still within the city of New York but farther from the commercial center. Zhou argues that immigrants who locate in Chinatown gain significant employment opportunities as well as access to cheap housing, which is very difficult to obtain in New York. In addition, she stresses that Chinatown residents and workers gain community connections that help them become upwardly mobile: opportunities for saving money, starting their own business, and sending their children to college. These valuable contacts are organized through work as well as through traditional Chinese kinship and regional associations, all located in the neighborhood. On the other hand, according to Chen, the Chinese immigrants who choose to live in Queens rather than in Chinatown are also able to find employment, but they obtain better housing because rents are lower in Queens than in Manhattan.

In Queens, Chinese immigrants have formed many Chinese social, cultural, religious, and political organizations that parallel those of other ethnic groups and, Chen argues, provide valuable contacts outside of the Chinese network. Thus, within a single city and a single ethnic group, we can find two different lifestyle patterns: that of the homogeneous enclave, and that of the multiethnic neighborhood. Which is better for the participants—and what "better" means—will undoubtedly remain the subject of discussion for some time.

Immigrants in the Workplace

We have already seen that most immigrants enter the United States to work and that most immigrants move to cities. How do the different immigrant groups fare in our changing urban economies, and in what ways does the presence of immigrants produce additional economic changes?

First, it is important to understand that immigrants enter the country with a very broad range of skills and educational backgrounds. Contrary to a widespread stereotype, immigrants as a group are not especially poor or unskilled, and immigrants who come from poor countries tend to be better off than most of their compatriots in terms of education, job skills, and savings. The main economic motivator for immigration is not an escape from poverty so much as the potential for a higher income from the skills and education people have already attained (Portes and Rumbaut 2006). Despite the wide range of immigrants' skills and education levels, a few typical workplaces and jobs recur among urban immigrant groups.

A large proportion of immigrants are self-employed entrepreneurs, or owners of small businesses. This has been true historically and is true of the current wave of immigration. Why do we find proportionately more immigrants than native-born individuals running small restaurants, shops, manufacturing companies, or construction companies? Waldinger and Lichter (2003) explain that the opportunity structure for small business can favor immigrants in several ways. First, a critical mass of newcomers from the same country can provide a market for culturally specific goods and services that are unavailable within the wider economy: foods, beauty products, music, newspapers, and so on. Immigrant entrepreneurs know what their co-ethnics need and may have connections for obtaining the desired products. Second, self-employment can be a defense against discrimination or blocked opportunity in the general labor market—for example, when poor English ability lessens employability. Third, because it is often difficult for them to find jobs with high hourly wages, immigrants sometimes choose self-employment because they can increase their income simply by working longer hours. Fourth, immigrant entrepreneurs can easily obtain stable and trustworthy employees by hiring relatives and friends within the ethnic community. All of these factors help steer a disproportionate number of immigrants into entrepreneurial activity. Box 8.3 shows how Korean immigrants use their ethnic ties to establish businesses.

Those immigrants who are not entrepreneurs but are wage-earning employees frequently find work in the less desirable jobs that native-born residents

---

B o x 8.3 • Spotlight
Korean Businesses in Inner-City Neighborhoods

In 1965, when the United States liberalized immigration laws, the Asian immigrant population grew exponentially. While the reforms favored immigrants with kinship ties to U.S. citizens, it also created opportunities for highly skilled immigrants, such as doctors, engineers, nurses, and pharmacists. This created the opening for the first wave of Korean newcomers to the United States. Although Koreans constitute a relatively small proportion of New York and Philadelphia's immigrant stream—rarely more than 3 percent of the legal immigrants who come to these cities each year— they play an important and visible role in the cities' economies.

Korean immigrants are largely middle class and were motivated to emigrate because of limited economic mobility in South Korea. Because the supply of college graduates in South Korea far exceeds the demand for such a highly educated workforce, the average rate of unemployment in Korea for male college graduates is 30 percent. Professionals who are fortunate enough to secure professional employment in the Korean economy must endure fierce competition, delayed promotion, underemployment, and job insecurity. In addition, favoritism in the workplace based on kinship, region of origin, and school ties make mobility nearly impossible for those who are not immersed in these networks. Given the limited prospects for advancement in South Korea, middle-class Koreans view immigration to the United States as a means to mobility in an open opportunity structure, not only for themselves but also for their children.

In the 1970s Korean immigrants began setting up shop in inner-city neighborhoods and soon created a profitable niche for themselves. Initially drawing on their import connections to Korea and capitalizing on the wig craze of the 1970s, Korean immigrants' first foray into the inner-city retail niche was through selling wigs made in Korea. Taking over retail businesses that Jews abandoned and African Americans could not sustain, Koreans began with wig shops and fruit and vegetable markets and then expanded to other retail niches, such as fish stores, liquor stores, handbag and accessory shops, and dry cleaning establishments. Today [in 2002], one-third of the Korean families in the United States are self-employed. African Americans, by contrast, are extremely underrepresented, exhibiting a self-employment rate of only 4.5 percent. Clearly, African Americans have not been able to take full advantage of the

---

avoid. As we saw in Chapter 5, the manufacturing sector in New York has become downgraded compared to its former conditions, and, in doing so, has provided jobs for immigrants that in previous decades native-born workers would have taken for higher pay and with better benefits. An example of a manufacturing industry based on immigrant labor is the garment (or apparel) industry (see Figure 8.3). Immigrants to New York City traditionally worked in garment manufacturing, but their nationalities have changed from Italian and Jewish to Chinese and Dominican. The Chinese were able to establish themselves in the garment industry because just when the older, established garment firms were leaving New York, vacating many factory buildings, the new immigration from China brought entrepreneurs who wanted to start factories and also brought large numbers of women who were willing to work in them. Chinese immigrant women are virtually a captive labor force, because they are not highly employable in the general labor market and because their community's traditions

retail self-employment opportunities in their communities, reflecting their divergent networks and resources. Even today the process of setting up shop reflects the differential resources available to Jews, Koreans, and African Americans.

Korean immigrants choose self-employment as a quick route to upward mobility. Their relatively poor English language skills, inability to transfer their educational credentials, and unfamiliarity with U.S. corporate culture and customs lead Koreans to choose self-employment as their most viable and lucrative option. Koreans use a variety of class and ethnic resources to set up shop, drawing upon loans from kin and coethnics and turning to Korean-language newspapers to locate businesses for sale. However, unlike the previous literature on ethnic entrepreneurship that stresses Koreans' reliance on rotating credit associations (*gae*), my research indicates that few Korean immigrant merchants use this resource at the start-up phase. In fact, only 7 percent of the Korean merchants in my sample acquired capital to open their business through a rotating credit association. Instead, the majority relied on a combination of other resources: personal savings, loans from family members, and credit from the previous coethnic storeowner. Seventeen percent bought their business from a family member—usually a brother, sister, or in-laws—who had immigrated to the United States several years before them.

... Koreans are not the only ethnic group to benefit from social capital. In fact, first-generation immigrants of many backgrounds—such as West Indians, Asian Indians, and the Vietnamese—draw upon their own versions of rotating credit associations. Dense coethnic ties, based on a shared immigrant experience, a common language and lifestyle, and involvement in coethnic institutions, provide a firm basis for intraethnic cooperation. But as these groups acculturate into the American social structure, they utilize this resource far less frequently. For example, whereas first-generation Jewish immigrant entrepreneurs formerly used mutual loan associations, later generations have long since discarded the tradition. Second-generation Koreans, like the second- and third-generation Jews before them, have also abandoned the practice.

SOURCE: Jennifer Lee, *Civility in the City: Blacks, Jews, and Koreans in Urban America* (Harvard University Press, 2002), pp. 33–36 *passim*.

socially restrict their lives. Because of these limitations, they have been willing to work long hours for low pay, providing the foundation for a profitable industry (Zhou 1992).

Another industry that has hired many newcomers is meatpacking, a labor-intensive industry that historically has employed large numbers of immigrants such as the Lithuanians Upton Sinclair (1984, originally published in 1920) portrayed in *The Jungle*. In the 1970s and 1980s, meatpacking profits were declining due to a decrease in the public's meat consumption, stagnating prices, and rising labor costs. Several meat producers disappeared; the remaining few closed their old plants and built new ones in locations where they could hire nonunionized, cheaper labor forces. This decision often meant leaving large cities such as Chicago and St. Louis and opening new plants in smaller midwestern cities where unemployment rates were high. Plant expansion, however, created a larger demand for labor, which could not be met by the native-born populations at the new sites.

(a)

Photo by Lewis Hine, Courtesy of George Eastman House

(b)

Edward Keating/The New York Times/Redux Pictures

F I G U R E 8.3 Sweatshops in New York City, 1900 and 2000. Like (a) earlier generations of immigrants, (b) contemporary newcomers frequently find jobs in the garment industry. Although child labor is now illegal, many women continue to take their children to work because of a lack of child-care opportunities.

Consequently, large numbers of immigrants from Southeast Asia and Mexico have entered the industry in recent years (Kandel and Parrado 2005).

How does the economy provide jobs for immigrants when it is sometimes difficult for native-born workers to find jobs? First, recent immigrants often follow previous immigrant groups into jobs that the previous immigrants have left. As we have seen, Chinese immigrants followed Jews and Italians into New York's garment industry and Mexicans followed Eastern Europeans into meatpacking as the previous immigrant groups found better jobs. This pattern also holds for entrepreneurs, as the children and grandchildren of the second-wave (Italian, Jewish, Polish) immigrant entrepreneurs are likely to attend college and go into other professions rather than take over the family store or restaurant (Waldinger 1990). Thus, one group of immigrants sometimes vacates economic spaces for the next group to fill.

A second factor contributing to jobs for immigrants is that growing or restructuring industries have increased the number of low-paying jobs that native-born workers do not want. Large firms restructuring their workforces create many new jobs in cities. The firms often lay off permanent employees and hire temporary workers or contract with agencies to provide services that their regular employees formerly performed. This trend is clearly illustrated by Mexican immigrants who have found employment predominantly in this lower-level service sector, working through employment services as housekeepers, security guards, and janitors (Zlolniski 2006). These are industries that would not have outsourced their employment nor used immigrant labor a generation ago.

Third, the existence of the ethnic community itself can provide job opportunities for immigrants. Roger Waldinger (1990, 416) describes this process as an interaction between the "opportunity structure of the society and the social structure of a particular immigrant group." An ethnic community accumulates advantages simply by attracting a large group of workers for employers to hire. Employment in an ethnic business provides a source of information, skills, and role models for other co-ethnics. Money earned in immigrant businesses is frequently reinvested within the ethnic community, providing profits to other businesses in a ripple effect throughout the community's economy. Thus, the growth of an immigrant group can provide opportunities for local economic expansion that would not otherwise have been available. To quote one study of the Miami economy, "Had it not been for immigrants, and specifically the low wages they have been willing to accept, Miami's apparel industry would be like that of Tampa—that is, nonexistent. ... Miami's restructuring ... has also transformed the ethnic structure of ownership and management" (Grenier et al. 1992, 89).

Ethnic solidarity and ethnic enterprises can play a complicated role in the urban economy. The example of Korean immigrants in Los Angeles is one of a close-knit community in which family and friends help each other establish small businesses. Although the workers in these Korean enterprises are often family members, they are typically paid low wages and expected to work long hours. This has two consequences. The fact that entrepreneurs are willing to exploit themselves and their relatives means that they can eke out a living in situations (for example, convenience stores in inner-city neighborhoods) that other merchants have abandoned. Their very ability to make money in these neighborhoods, however, generates resentment among the non-Korean inner-city residents, typically Latinos and African Americans, who feel they are being "ripped off" by the Koreans (Light and Bonacich 1988).

Ethnic Groups and Politics

Ethnicity and politics have long been associated with each other in U.S. cities. Some groups, such as the Irish, have historically used political office as a strategy for upward mobility. As different immigrant groups entered the country, they provided new voting blocs for candidates to court. They also aroused opposition from nativist political movements. Many of the political processes that were in effect a century ago are still found in today's urban ethnic communities.

The new immigration provides the basis for new voting blocs in most gateway cities. As with earlier immigrant waves, not all groups are equally active politically, but a few provide vivid examples of political realignment and influence. Caribbean immigrants in New York City, for example, have had a long history of participation in local politics. In previous generations they tended to blend into the regular political establishment, first cooperating with a white Republican-led regime and later cooperating with native-born African Americans in the Democratic Party. With the growth of the third wave of immigration since 1970, however, Caribbean politicians and voters have formed their own organizations to run their own candidates or to endorse other candidates in exchange for some promised benefits to the Caribbean community—that is, a Caribbean vote and presence has emerged as a visible factor in the politics of New York City (Kasinitz 1992).

In Miami as well, large numbers of immigrants, particularly Cuban immigrants, have changed the city's politics. Although Cuban immigrants have been settling in Miami since about 1960, the earlier generation had little interest in local politics. Their political interests were still tied to Cuba, because as exiles they expected to return home. This orientation discouraged them from applying for citizenship or voting. The children of these immigrants, however, have spent their entire lives in the United States, and many are U.S. citizens by virtue of having been born in the country. The younger generation's rates of voting and other forms of political participation are significantly higher than those of their parents, and Cuban Americans have proportionally more representatives in Congress than the population at large. The political ideology of the new citizens, however, is still affected by their experiences in the ethnic community, For example, although nearly half of Cuban Americans favor lifting the embargo on trade and travel to Cuba, the most influential Cuban-American political leaders have been successful in maintaining a hard line against the Cuban government (Castro 2007). The homeland issue dominates political discourse over the more traditional economic issues, on which most immigrants find themselves in agreement with the Democratic Party (Perez 1992).

The visibility of immigrants has roused political debates in many parts of the United States. In some high-immigration areas we have seen a resurgence of nativism; in others debates continue about managing or further limiting immigration. Another way these conflicts have been expressed politically is through attempts to impose English as the official language in some communities.

Do Cities Gain or Lose from Immigration?

As the number of immigrants in the United States has increased over the past ten years, controversies have arisen regarding the impact that immigrants have on our society and our cities. The areas of the United States receiving the highest proportion of immigrants are those in which the controversies have been most prominent. California, the state receiving the largest number of immigrants annually, was the first state to challenge U.S. immigration policy by attempting to restrict the services available to immigrants. The 1994 California ballot measure, Proposition 187, sought to cut off illegal immigrants' access to state benefits such as education, welfare, and health services.

One controversial issue is whether immigrants—particularly undocumented immigrants—take jobs away from native-born workers. The argument is that if both groups are competing for similar jobs and the immigrants have a lower unemployment rate than the native-born Americans, they must be taking jobs away from these native-born workers. Labor market research provides evidence that immigrant workers do not largely compete for the same jobs as the native-born. Rather, each group is highly concentrated in a particular niche, with undocumented immigrant workers concentrated in low-paid service and manufacturing jobs and native-born workers in higher-paid clerical and administrative jobs. Furthermore, a good many of the jobs that attract illegal immigrants are seasonal jobs (e.g., in agriculture) that native-born workers avoid (Portes 2007).

Another concern is that immigrants, particularly undocumented immigrants, may be using public services such as schools, hospitals, and welfare benefits far in excess of the amount of taxes they pay. Much of this controversy stems from confusing three different groups: legally admitted immigrants, undocumented immigrants, and refugees. Whereas refugees are automatically entitled to receive welfare benefits (for a time) as part of the federal government's relocation program, other immigrants have very low rates of public assistance usage (Bean and Stevens 2003). Furthermore, immigrants as a group are more likely to be working and less likely to be on welfare than the general population. This situation reflects the fact that the majority of immigrants, here legally or not, come to the United States to find work; and if they cannot, most return to their native country. Immigrant workers, whether or not they are working legally, also pay the same taxes as other U.S. residents, including income tax, property tax, and sales tax. In fact, the Social Security system receives a huge subsidy from undocumented workers who pay an estimated $7 billion in Social Security taxes annually (Porter 2005).

The final controversy is over just how many immigrants are entering the country, how many are undocumented, and what kinds of controls the Department of Homeland Security has on the flow of immigration. Although growing, the proportion of immigrants in the population today is about 12.5 percent, still lower than the 15 percent foreign-born population of the United States in 1920

(U.S. Census Bureau 2009b). The current estimate of the total number of undocumented immigrants is eleven and one-half million, with between three hundred thousand and four hundred thousand entering each year (Hoefer et al. 2009). Due to a lagging economy and stepped up enforcement of visas, the U.S. Border Patrol has seen the number of illegal entrants apprehended at the borders fall from 1.2 million in 2005 to 724,000 in 2008, the lowest number since 1976 (Rytina and Simanski 2009).

Are immigrants a problem? Perhaps not as large a problem as a small number of vocal critics would have us believe. Some scholars go even farther and argue that immigrants are contributing to the revitalization of the national economy and particularly to the economies of the gateway cities. One economist argues, for example, that without immigration, the U.S. economy would be facing a massive labor shortage (Muller 1993). He also points out that many of the immigrants revitalize stagnant urban economies by investing their capital and rebuilding residential neighborhoods abandoned by the suburban migration of the middle classes.

Portes and Rumbaut (2006) point out that much of the public's concern over immigration is based on a fundamental misunderstanding of the nature of the pushes and pulls that drive the process. Many people believe that immigration is fueled by the migrants' own initiative and a certain laxness or tolerance by the United States government and population. According to this line of reasoning, if the government cracked down on illegal immigrants and tightened control on legal immigrants, immigration would stop. However, this reasoning is erroneous, according to Portes and Rumbaut. They say:

> Immigrant flows are initiated not solely by the desires and dreams of people in other lands but by the designs and interests of well-organized groups in the receiving country, primarily employers. Up to a point, public opposition to immigration can play into the hands of these groups by maintaining the newcomers in a vulnerable and dependent position. Similarly, governments are not omnipotent in their regulation of immigration. In particular, governmental attempts at reversing well-established immigrant flows do not generally have the intended effect because of the resistance of social networks linking places of origin and destination (Portes and Rumbaut 2006, 345).

CONCLUSION

Cities have long been the favored sites for immigrant settlements in the United States. To understand the likely impact of future immigration on our cities, we must examine more than the motivations and characteristics of the individuals who enter the United States. We must examine the context within which individuals make their decisions to come, stay, return, or reimmigrate. That context involves the ties between the United States (or any other receiving country) and the countries from which immigrants enter.

The United States has, throughout its history, had close relationships with many other nations. Much of the Southwest of the United States, for example, was at one time part of Mexico, and the people who lived there did not lose their Spanish language or Native American heritage simply by virtue of becoming citizens. Alaska, Hawaii, and Puerto Rico are in the same category, with people of different language and cultural groups being incorporated politically and economically, if not always culturally, into U.S. society. Some ties with other countries have been established through military action: the Philippines, as a result of the Spanish-American War; and Vietnam, Laos, and Cambodia, through long-term military intervention. Other ties have been established on an economic basis, for example, trade relationships between U.S. companies and the islands of the Caribbean. As an influential work on immigration puts it:

> Individuals do not simply sit at home and ponder the costs and benefits of going to Country X versus Country Y. Instead, they are guided by precedent, by the experience of friends and relatives, and by the alternative courses of action held to be acceptable and realistic in their own societies. ... The social environment of migration is molded, in turn, by the history of prior relationships between the country of origin and those of potential destination. ... Algerians go to France; Indians, Pakistanis and West Indians move to Britain; South Americans frequently migrate to Spain; and Koreans go to Japan. (Portes and Stepick 1993, 206)

It should be no surprise that as the economy becomes more highly internationalized, the international flows of people as well as goods, services, and information will continue or even increase in volume. Furthermore, once the immigration flows have become established, they can frequently become self-perpetuating. Even after the initial economic or political conditions in the sending country may have changed, migration flows tend to develop their own momentum through the operation of networks of families and neighbors. Immigrants send back home for family members or brides; they send money, which stimulates interest in economic possibilities in the new country; and they often set up a trade system, sending foreign goods back and forth between two countries. As migration across borders occurs, it alters both the sending and receiving countries so that people on both sides of the border come to expect and sustain it (Durand and Massey 2004).

That is not to say that the flow of immigrants never changes. Since the 1990s, researchers have noted a pronounced lessening of immigration into the five states that had previously received the most immigrants: California, New York, Texas, Florida, and Illinois. Instead, states such as Colorado, Arizona, Pennsylvania, Michigan, and North Carolina began receiving a larger share of new immigrants. Massey and Capoferro (2008) attribute this change of destination, which was most pronounced among Mexican immigrants, to four factors: the Immigration Reform and Control Act (which legalized long-term undocumented workers, thus freeing them to move), Proposition 187 (which made California a less desirable place for Mexican immigrants), surging demand for labor in other parts of the country (which made other states more attractive), and selective "hardening of the border" that deterred undocumented immigrants from entering California and Texas from Mexico.

Despite longstanding patterns of international immigration flows, public policy can influence (although not totally control) the volume of immigration and the characteristics of the immigrants: educational background, occupation, family status, and nation of origin. Scholars are researching and debating some policy proposals that have surfaced in the press. One issue is changing the skill levels of immigrants legally admitted. Some argue for greatly increasing the numbers of highly skilled and professional workers, especially during periods of economic expansion; others object that this policy would worsen the brain drain of educated professionals from the sending countries. A second issue is how to deal with undocumented workers. Some experts say the borders should be tightened and penalties strengthened (including jail sentences for captured undocumented workers); others say that keeping the border relatively permeable is the best solution to meet labor demands in the United States. A third issue is wage levels of workers. If U.S. companies were to raise wages so that certain jobs are more attractive to native-born workers, it might lessen the demand for low-waged, undocumented workers. Finally, the debates raise the question of cultural integration and cultural pluralism. Some scholars advocate pluralism; others argue that current immigration levels are stretching the limits of what the nation's culture can endure without fragmenting (Portes and Rumbaut 2006).

Whether the numbers and types of immigrants admitted to the United States will continue to remain as they have in the recent past will be the result of a series of political decisions in which many different interests will be advanced. Although the future of immigration is uncertain, the likelihood is that countries with strong ties to the United States will continue to send immigrants to the country. What is absolutely certain, however, is that each wave of immigration has had a profound influence on the economics, politics, and cultures of our cities, for cities have been overwhelmingly the places where immigrants have chosen to live.

DISCUSSION QUESTIONS

1. A Swiss citizen has said, "We asked for workers but people came." What obstacles do you think immigrants face in relating to native-born residents of the countries to which they move?

2. Use the U.S. Bureau of the Census population figures to answer the following questions: How many foreign-born people live in your community? In your state? From which countries did they come?

3. *If you are native-born:* Trace your own ancestry back to those relatives who immigrated to the United States or Canada from another country. When they arrived, where did they live and what work did they do? *If you are from another country:* What prompted you to leave your home? Were you part of a migration chain of others before or after you? Did other relatives or neighbors go to different countries?

9

African Americans in Cities

A ghetto can be improved in one way only—out of existence.
JAMES BALDWIN
NOBODY KNOWS MY NAME

Today most African Americans living in the United States live in cities and
metropolitan areas. Yet the traditional home for the majority of African
Americans until recently was in the rural communities of the South. From
1870 to 1970, the proportions of African Americans living in rural areas and in
urban areas completely reversed: in 1870, 80 percent lived in the rural South,
and in 1970, 80 percent lived in cities, half outside of the South (Massey and
Denton 1993). The movement of African Americans from the rural South to
the cities of the North shaped our cities and established the patterns of race relations that exist in urban areas today.

This chapter will address the following questions:

- When and how did African-American neighborhoods develop in cities?
- Where do African Americans currently live compared to whites, and why do
  residential patterns differ for the two groups?
- How is race related to social class?
- What are some current issues and policies regarding racial segregation in
  urban and metropolitan areas?

DEVELOPMENT OF AFRICAN-AMERICAN
NEIGHBORHOODS

African-American neighborhoods are a recent invention. Up to the 1920s urban-
dwelling African Americans were not highly segregated from their white
neighbors, and only a small proportion of urban African Americans lived in

neighborhoods that were identified as black neighborhoods. The term *ghetto* referred to Jewish neighborhoods and was not widely applied to African-American neighborhoods until the 1950s. The racially distinctive neighborhoods we see today did not develop until the period between 1916 and 1930, during the Great Migration that brought more than a million African Americans to the cities.

Urban Race Relations Before the Great Migration

Historians such as Spear (1967), Kusmer (1976), Zunz (1982), and Osofsky (1963) have shown that, up to the early 1900s, African Americans lived in all sections of major cities. New York's Harlem and Chicago's South Side were the only neighborhoods with sufficiently large concentrations of African Americans to support a sizeable group of specialized black institutions and businesses. Many workplaces, churches, and residential neighborhoods were racially integrated. In fact, in 1910 some of the European immigrant groups were more highly segregated from native whites than were African Americans (Lieberson 1980).

In his book *The Philadelphia Negro,* originally published in 1899, W. E. B. DuBois describes the lives of African Americans in the City of Brotherly Love. Because slavery was abolished in Pennsylvania some sixty years before the Emancipation Proclamation, Philadelphia attracted both free blacks and fugitive slaves. Their rapid increase between 1800 and 1830, however, caused some violent backlash and rioting among Philadelphia's whites. The African-American population stabilized between 1840 and 1880, then grew again after 1880. During the slow-growth periods, DuBois notes, African Americans had an easier time getting jobs and establishing businesses, but during the times of more rapid population increase, they were squeezed out of good jobs, particularly by immigrant workers. Peak migration periods also brought large numbers of poorer, less educated African Americans to cities, thus encouraging whites to stereotype the entire racial group as poor and unskilled (DuBois 1967).

Box 9.1 depicts life among the working classes of Philadelphia between 1860 and 1890. Although a certain amount of racism and prejudice is evident, so is a degree of toleration and mutual accommodation that would later evaporate.

The Great Migration

The Great Migration of blacks from the South to the North began in 1916 when the Pennsylvania Railroad sent recruiters to the South to hire workers. This migration, in which recruiters literally put African-American workers on trains, soon developed its own momentum. Once some migrants moved to cities, family members and friends followed in the same chain migration patterns that we saw in Chapter 8 for foreign immigrants. In addition, many Southern blacks learned of Northern job opportunities through widely read African-American newspapers, particularly the *Chicago Defender* (Marks 1989). Figure 9.1 shows some of the African Americans hired as factory workers.

B o x 9.1 • Case Study
Race Relations in Philadelphia Before 1900

Philadelphia's first public baths were built in the summer of 1870 and were operated by the Alaska Street Mission in an effort to provide the masses with the benefits of soap and towels. The water itself was provided by the Delaware, which flowed through the wooden slats of two enclosures—one sixteen feet square for whites, the other twelve feet square for blacks—which were open to men and women on alternate days. In time the city took over and expanded this modest operation, adding enough new baths at different locations so that people of either sex could use them on any summer's day. At the same time it lifted the color bar and added another: after six o'clock, at the workday's end, the men's baths were reserved for adults only. The formal rules were informally sabotaged during the daytime by picket lines of white boys, "themselves far from ordinarily clean," who organized to drive off any black youngsters who tried to approach. Once the evening hour was reached, the workingmen, black and white, soaped down in company and normally without incident.

These workingmen shared a good deal more than the river. Most of the popular masculine pastimes were sometimes enjoyed by both races together. Of the team sports that were becoming widely popular in the postwar era, only baseball was played by workingmen or professionals. Afro-American ballplayers were officially excluded from the National League shortly after its founding, and local teams, both amateur and professional, were organized along racial lines. Yet there were often games between black and white ballclubs, and the best local amateurs shared fields and other facilities, especially in the earlier years. Carl Bolivar, a local black historian, observed that "baseball did wonders in the way of levelling prejudice."

SOURCE: Roger Lane, *Roots of Violence in Black Philadelphia 1860–1900* (Cambridge, Mass.: Harvard University Press, 1986), p. 29.

The Great Migration occurred when it did because of conditions in the South as well as those in the North. The South's loss of the Civil War had kept it an economically underdeveloped region with few prospects for industrialization. Its major industry, cotton, was devastated by a boll weevil infestation. In addition to these economic problems, African Americans had to face the Jim Crow laws and legal color bar that the Southern states had adopted in the previous few decades. The future for African Americans in the South looked bleak. At the same time, the manufacturing industries that were flourishing in the North faced a labor shortage. The coming of World War I had added to the demand for products but had also virtually halted the flow of European immigration that had been feeding industry to that point. The combination of these "push" and "pull" factors resulted in some 400,000 African Americans leaving the South just in the years of 1916, 1917, and 1918 and over a million migrating between 1916 and 1930 (Marks 1989).

The Great Migration had two effects on Northern cities. First, the African-American populations of the industrial cities, such as Philadelphia, Newark, Cleveland, Detroit, and Chicago, grew substantially. Second, as their populations grew, African Americans began to be spatially concentrated in cities.

F I G U R E 9.1 **The Great Migration.** The shortage of immigrant labor during World War I opened up opportunities for African Americans from the South to work in industrial jobs. This photo from 1918 shows workers in Detroit's Packard automobile plant.

African-American neighborhoods with high proportions of black residents and with specialized institutions and businesses became the norm for cities rather than the exception.

Whites and Segregation

Why did segregation increase so sharply? Sociologists agree that the change was primarily the result of actions of the white population in the Northern cities in response to African-American population growth. White residents adopted and institutionalized several social and legal practices during this period to keep the races as separate as possible.

First, many city governments passed racial zoning ordinances that defined the boundaries of the "black belts," similar to the Chinatown zoning they had adopted in the 1880s and 1890s. However, the U.S. Supreme Court ruled this type of legislation unconstitutional in 1917 (Forman 1971). After that decision many areas adopted the practice of placing racially restrictive covenants on real estate transactions. People wrote legally binding provisions into deeds of properties, specifying the ethnic and racial groups whose members could and could not own the property. These covenants excluded African Americans, and some also named Jews, Arabs, Mexicans, Italians, or Poles. If property owners broke the covenant and sold to an "undesirable" group, their neighbors could take legal action to have the sale of the property cancelled (Philpott 1991). Racially restrictive covenants were commonly written into the deeds for entire subdivisions beginning in the 1920s and were common until 1948, when the Supreme Court invalidated them (Massey and Denton 1993).

Zoning regulations and racially restrictive covenants were polite compared to some of the other practices whites adopted to control the integration of the races. Philpott (1991) describes the formation in 1918 of Chicago's Hyde Park–Kenwood Property Owners Association, an organization with the stated purpose of making Hyde Park white and keeping "undesirables" out. In addition to tactics such as publishing inflammatory literature, holding whites-only rallies, and boycotting realtors and merchants who dealt with African Americans, the association eventually turned to violence to prevent blacks from crossing the color line. Arson, bombings, and mob raids became commonplace on the homes of African Americans who moved into white areas and on the real estate agents who served them; fifty-eight bombings of blacks' homes occurred within a three-year period (Forman 1971).

The actions whites took to avoid living with African Americans were not confined to the big cities. Historian James Loewen (2005) documented the creation of thousands of all-white towns and suburbs that both legally and informally drove out or kept out African Americans and sometimes other nonwhite groups between 1890 and 1968. He calls these places "sundown towns" because while African Americans were permitted to work or do business there, they had to be out by sundown. Box 9.2 explains when and how sundown towns were created.

Whites' agitation for racial segregation culminated in a major race riot in 1919. The riot began when an African-American child swam across the invisible line that separated the white and black sections of the beach on the Lake Michigan shore. The minor event at the beach unleashed several days' worth of firebombings, stonings, beatings, and house bombings aimed at African Americans. Based on his study of the history of race relations, historian Allen Spear (1967) concluded that whites instituted racial segregation in Chicago because of their desire to keep African Americans from competing with them for housing and jobs.

Public officials also took some actions to keep the races separate. With the introduction of federal funds for public housing, local officials had to decide where they would construct public housing units. In most cities they decided to keep the public housing racially segregated and to locate the units for African Americans in the heart of the developing ghettos. Nicholas Lemann recounts the decisions of the Chicago City Council to construct public housing in the heart of the black belt. He states, "The Chicago Housing Authority's role in responding to the great migration from the South would be to try to keep as many of the migrants as possible apart from white Chicago" (Lemann 1991, 73).

B o x 9.2 • Spotlight
Sundown Towns

A sundown town is any organized jurisdiction that for decades kept African Americans or other groups from living in it and was thus "all white" on purpose....
Beginning in about 1890 and continuing until 1968, white Americans established thousands of towns across the United States for whites only. Many towns drove out their black populations by posting sundown signs. [For example, "WHITES ONLY WITHIN CITY LIMITS AFTER DARK."] Other towns passed ordinances barring African Americans after dark or prohibiting them from owning or renting property; still others established such policies by informal means, harassing and even killing those who violated the rule. Some sundown towns similarly kept out Jews, Chinese, Mexicans, Native Americans, or other groups.

Most Americans have no idea such towns or counties exist, or they think such things happened mainly in the Deep South. Ironically, the traditional South had almost no sundown towns. Mississippi, for instance, has no more than 6, mostly mere hamlets, while Illinois has no fewer than 456.

Sundown towns arose during a crucial era of American history, 1890–1940, when, after the gains of the Civil War and Reconstruction eras, race relations systematically grew worse. Since the 1955 publication of C. Van Woodward's famous book, *The Strange Career of Jim Crow,* historians of the South have recognized that segregation became much stricter after 1890. No longer could African Americans vote; no longer could they use the restaurants and public parks that whites used; even streetcars and railroad waiting rooms put up screens or signs to isolate blacks in separate sections. African Americans were also beset by violence, as lynchings rose to their highest point.... This backlash against African Americans was not limited to the South but was national. Neither the public nor most historians realize that the same earthquake struck the North, too.

Sundown towns are not only widespread, but also relatively recent. Except for a handful of places ... most towns did not go sundown during slavery, before the Civil War, or during Reconstruction. On the contrary, blacks moved everywhere in America between 1865 and 1890. African Americans reached every county of Montana. More than 400 lived in Michigan's Upper Peninsula. City neighborhoods across the country were fairly integrated, too, even if black inhabitants worked as servants or gardeners for their white neighbors.

Between 1890 and the 1930s, however, all this changed. By 1930, although its white population had increased by 75%, the Upper Peninsula was home to only 331 African Americans, and 180 of them were inmates of the Marquette State Prison. Eleven Montana counties had no blacks at all. Across the country, city neighborhoods grew more and more segregated. Most astonishing, from California to Minnesota to Long Island to Florida, whites mounted little race riots against African Americans, expelling entire black communities or intimidating and keeping out would-be newcomers.

SOURCE: James W. Loewen, *Sundown Towns: A Hidden Dimension of American Racism* (New York: The New Press, 2005).

Enclave or Ghetto?

Early sociologists identified a number of similarities between the neighborhoods of African-American migrants and those of European immigrants. For example, both groups established their own churches, newspapers, businesses, and mutual aid groups. Some analysts hypothesized that as time went on, African Americans would become assimilated into the society's mainstream, losing their distinctiveness. They thought that the racially separate ghetto would be a temporary phenomenon as the ethnic enclaves of European immigrants had been. Their predictions, however, were wrong. As the segregation of white ethnic groups decreased with the passage of time, the segregation of African Americans increased. In the end, sociologists were forced to accept the fact that black-white racial segregation and discrimination were going to be a longer-lasting phenomenon than could have been predicted by the experiences of the European immigrants (Taeuber and Taeuber 1965; Hershberg et al. 1979; Lieberson 1980).

Massey and Denton (1993) summed up the differences between the experiences of the European immigrants who arrived prior to 1920 and those of African Americans. They found three fundamental differences between the immigrant enclaves and the black ghettos. First, immigrant enclaves were never as ethnically homogeneous as today's African-American areas are. In immigrant neighborhoods, a single ethnic group typically made up between one-quarter and one-half of the population, whereas in many African-American neighborhoods, blacks constitute over three-quarters of the population. Second, only a small proportion of members of a given ethnic group lived in ethnic enclaves, whereas the vast majority of African Americans in large cities live in them. Third, ethnic enclaves were temporary adjustments to American society and aided the groups' economic mobility; black ghettos, in contrast, have become permanent features of cities and do not foster upward mobility (Massey and Denton 1993).

In Chapter 8 we saw that "true" enclaves have a specialized ethnic economy made up almost exclusively of ethnic workers in a few industries. Only a few immigrant groups have such enclave economies, and almost no African-American neighborhoods have them. In addition, the difference between an enclave and a ghetto is also partly the difference between voluntary and involuntary clustering (Gans 2008). To the extent that a group sticks together for mutual aid and to participate in familiar institutions, their community can be thought of as an enclave. To the extent that they stay together because they are not welcome elsewhere, their clustering becomes more involuntary, and their community resembles a ghetto. As we will see, African-American communities in large cities have some characteristics of both voluntary and involuntary clustering.

CURRENT RACIAL PATTERNS IN
METROPOLITAN AREAS

At the beginning of the twenty-first century, we find that, although racial segregation is no longer increasing, neither is it noticeably decreasing. Rather, it appears that racial residential segregation has become part of the normal operation of our society—an institutional pattern. Recent research shows that segregation has declined only slightly since 1980 and that those declines are concentrated in the Southern and Western states (Logan et al. 2004). Most urban African

T A B L E 9.1   **U.S. Metropolitan Areas with the Largest African-American Populations, 2007**

City	African-American Population	African Americans in MSA (%)
1. New York	3,683,044	20
2. Chicago	1,724,505	18
3. Atlanta	1,661,986	32
4. Washington, D.C.	1,412,729	27
5. Philadelphia	1,224,434	21
6. Miami	1,127,643	21
7. Detroit	1,032,358	23
8. Los Angeles	1,000,987	8
9. Houston	974,730	17
10. Dallas	887,487	14

SOURCE: Derived from U. S. Census Bureau, *Statistical Abstract of the U.S. 2009,* Table 21.

Americans live in neighborhoods that could be classified as highly segregated ghettos (Massey 2001).

Racial patterns in residential areas are far from uniform throughout the country. They vary by region and by the size of the African-American population. The cities of the Midwest are the most segregated, the cities of the West are the least segregated, and those of the Northeast and the South fall in between. In addition, some evidence indicates that the proportion of African-American residents in the population has an impact on the level of racial segregation. Racial segregation is lowest in cities where African Americans make up a small proportion of the population (Charles 2003).

Table 9.1 shows the ten metropolitan areas with the largest African-American populations. Note that, with the exception of Los Angeles, this group constitutes a substantial proportion of each area's population. Despite the rapid growth of Asian and Hispanic groups that we saw in the previous chapter, in most cities, African Americans are much more segregated from whites than other racial groups are.

Institutional Barriers to Housing Choice

Many researchers have investigated the housing market and how people of different incomes and ethnic groups get access to housing. We will explore the housing market in greater detail in Chapter 10, but for now we can ask about the relative importance of people's income compared to the importance of their race in looking for and obtaining housing.

Let's begin with income. We can ask how much racial segregation is due to the fact that African Americans, on the average, have lower incomes than whites and simply cannot afford to live in white neighborhoods. This is often the first explanation that comes to mind, and it holds a great deal of intuitive appeal because it is true that African Americans on the average earn less than whites. But the income distribution between African Americans and whites overlaps much more than do their residential patterns. When researchers control for income, they find that whites and African Americans with similar incomes still mostly live apart from each other.

In his study of race and income, John Kain (1987, 71) summarizes the research on the relationship between income and residential segregation as follows:

> A large number of empirical studies have considered whether existing patterns of racial residential segregation can be explained by income and other socioeconomic differences between black and white households. While these studies have consistently shown that the intense segregation of black households cannot be explained by these factors, the myth that income differences are a major, if not the principal, explanation of racial residential segregation persists.

Some compelling evidence that income does not explain racial segregation was compiled by the National Fair Housing Alliance (2005). Its study examined sixty-nine metropolitan areas that have a majority of African Americans in the population. They found that two-thirds of the whites in those majority African-American cities lived in areas containing fewer than 5 percent African Americans. They found that even poor whites live in overwhelmingly white neighborhoods. A host of recent studies (summarized in Charles 2003) demonstrate that only a small proportion of racial residential segregation is due to income differentials between African-American and white households.

To what degree are racially separate neighborhoods the result of discriminatory and preferential treatment that people of different races experience when dealing with the institutions that distribute housing? Survey research reveals that a large proportion of African Americans believe that real estate agents and mortgage lenders, as well as individual homeowners and landlords, discriminate on the basis of race. Whites, on the other hand, believe that individuals may discriminate but tend not to think that established institutions or groups discriminate on the basis of race. Instead, they express the belief that the fair housing movements and the antidiscrimination laws passed in the 1960s and 1970s largely erased institutional discrimination (Farley et al. 1993).

Whose perception is correct? Social scientists have collected substantial evidence to show that institutional discrimination, although more subtle than in the past, is still widespread. Research on the real estate industry, for example, details the role of realtors as the gatekeepers of neighborhoods. Numerous studies, called housing audits, have sent pairs of white and African-American couples with similar jobs, incomes, and family sizes to real estate offices to see if the agents treat them the same or differently. They show that African Americans are consistently "steered" away from white neighborhoods and vice-versa (Turner et al. 2002; Pager et al. 2008).

Why would realtors discriminate, particularly when such actions are clearly illegal? Prior to the passage of open housing and civil rights laws in the 1960s and 1970s, real estate professionals were trained to discriminate actively in their role as gatekeeper of the neighborhoods. The real estate code of ethics actually prohibited licensed realtors from selling homes to buyers who did not share the racial and ethnic characteristics of the other neighbors. They believed that they should protect property values by screening out "inharmonious" neighbors. Until the 1970s realtors were obligated to steer homeseekers to neighborhoods whose residents shared their race or nationality. Realtors could actually lose their licenses for selling homes to people of the "wrong" race for the neighborhood (Helper 1969).

Today, the code of ethics has been rewritten, and most realtors subscribe to the ideal of open housing. But as the housing audit evidence shows, some agents do not follow the new code all of the time. One reason is that realtors must maintain good relations with their clients and may be influenced by the wishes of homeowners who are opposed to selling their home to members of minority groups. Or they may fear generating hostility from neighbors if they sell a house to someone not welcome in the neighborhood. Despite their individual beliefs and values, realtors can serve as institutional gatekeepers because they have control over the information about whether housing is for sale, and can grant or withhold access to that information (Turner et al. 2002).

This subtle, institutional type of discrimination is what maintains racial segregation for the most part. At times, however, we see a more active form of racism emerge. Episodes of organized violence and intimidation by whites directed at African Americans (or sometimes Latinos and Asians) are still common in many metropolitan areas. One of the more highly publicized instances of such activity occurred in 1989 in the Bensonhurst section of New York City, when a young African-American man was killed simply for walking down the street in a white neighborhood, where, according to residents, he did not belong. Often, such incidents do not make national news. On Election Day, November 4, 2008, four men in Staten Island, New York, reportedly harassed and attacked several African-American men because of the support for Barack Obama, sending one victim into a coma for several weeks (civilrights.org). Many African Americans who do move to predominantly white neighborhoods experience harassment, expressed verbally or through actions such as vandalism of their property (Roscigno et al. 2009).

The combination of institutional barriers and individual preferences has in many cities produced a racially divided **housing market**, sometimes called a dual housing market. A dual housing market exists where housing is differentially available to white and African-American households. A given home, because of its location, is socially labeled as either "white" or "nonwhite" by neighbors, real estate agents, and potential homeseekers. Integrated neighborhoods are presumed to be in the process of changing from white to black. In a dual market, a given home may not cost the same to potential buyers or tenants of different races, particularly in a neighborhood that is undergoing racial transition. If an African-American family wants a certain type of house, location, school, and other features that accompany the home itself, and if they do not have many choices of good housing (often the case), they may be willing to pay a higher price than a white family would pay for the same house (Downs 1981; Kain 2004).

Being able to buy or rent a particular home, then, is not simply a question of how much money a family has to spend and how many bedrooms they need. The process of looking for, buying, and financing a house or of renting an apartment is socially structured, and the experience differs depending on the race of the person seeking housing. In turn, the relative lack of access to good housing lessens the opportunities of many African-American households to accumulate wealth by investing in homeownership.

Correlates and Consequences of Racial Segregation

Does a separate housing market have an impact on the quality of housing or access to neighborhood resources? It does seem to have a negative impact for African Americans. Researcher Philip Clay (1992) conducted a long-term study of housing quality for African Americans over a span of forty years. He examined the availability of housing according to its adequacy (condition and presence of basic characteristics such as heat and plumbing), affordability (cost relative to income), neighborhood characteristics (safety, proximity to schools, level of public services), and other housing characteristics. Clay found that it is more difficult for African Americans to obtain adequate housing than it is for whites. In addition, Clay found that it is more difficult for African Americans to find affordable housing—a unit that meets both their needs and their budget.

Clay's research (1992) also shows that economic disinvestment is a major problem in neighborhoods with large African-American populations. Disinvestment takes many forms, from businesses avoiding or moving out of African-American neighborhoods, to investors withholding resources that residents need to maintain their property.

One form of urban disinvestment is mortgage **disinvestment**, or the unwillingness of lenders to grant mortgages in certain neighborhoods. Mortgage disinvestment is sometimes called **redlining** after the practice of lenders drawing different colored lines around "safe" (green), "questionable" (yellow), and "unsafe" (red) areas in which to make loans. Nearly two decades of research on mortgage lending patterns has shown that mortgage disinvestment is most likely to occur in African-American neighborhoods (Squires 1994). These patterns of mortgage lending apply to *entire neighborhoods*, regardless of the credit worthiness of the loan applicant or the condition of the individual property.

After decades of redlining, a number of changes in the law and in banking regulations during the 1990s resulted in increased availability of mortgages in minority neighborhoods. Unfortunately, most of those mortgages were high-interest or adjustable-interest loans—so-called "**subprime**" loans. According to Williams and colleagues (2005), 78 percent of the new loans that went to African-American neighborhoods between 1990 and 2000 were subprime. When housing values started to plummet after their peak in 2005, many residents found that they owed more on the house than it was worth. Unable to continue paying the high interest rate, and unable to refinance to get a lower interest rate, they were forced into foreclosure and had to abandon their houses. Box 9.3 explains how subprime lending hurt African-American inner-city neighborhoods.

Box 9.3 • The Subprime Mortgage and Foreclosure Crisis

This year, we commemorate the fortieth anniversary of the Fair Housing Act and the twentieth anniversary of the Fair Housing Amendments Act. We commemorate, not celebrate, because we are still so far from achieving the balanced and integrated living patterns envisioned by the original Act's authors. While we have made some progress in reducing levels of residential segregation, most Americans live in communities largely divided by race and ethnicity. There are at least four million acts of housing discrimination every year. And we are on the brink of an economic crisis fueled by a failed subprime lending market, a market built primarily on borrowers and neighborhoods of color.

In addition to residential segregation, Americans still experience differential access to mainstream financial institutions on the basis of race. Housing experts Kathleen C. Engel and Patricia A. McCoy write that "When people of color are in the market for home loans, they often do not look beyond subprime lenders and mortgage brokers." One reason for this, they argue, is a "lingering mistrust of banks" that developed as members of that community experienced past discrimination by banks when anti-discrimination laws were not adequately promulgated or enforced.

In fact, discriminatory treatment of people of color and members of other protected classes continued even after such actions became illegal under the federal Fair Housing Act. For example, at the request of civil rights groups, in the early 1970s federal banking regulators surveyed the industry about its underwriting practices; a surprising number of institutions acknowledged using prohibited bases in their mortgage lending decisions. Another factor contributing to minorities' patronage of subprime lenders is the failure of regulated depository institutions (banks and thrifts) to develop appropriate lending products and market them effectively and aggressively in communities of color. Additionally, many banks and thrifts simply did not open branches in Black neighborhoods. In recent years this has left a vacuum that has been filled by subprime and payday lending.

This period [since the mid-1990s] also saw tremendous concentration within the mortgage lending business and a shift away from retail lending. In 1990, the top 25 mortgage originators nationwide accounted for less than 30 percent of the $500 billion of mortgage loans made that year. By 2002, the top 25 originators accounted for 78 percent of $2.5 trillion worth of loans. Such consolidation was made possible by a change in the way the business was conducted. Lenders discovered that, in many cases, it was much cheaper to rely on third parties to find potential customers and gather their information than to maintain a large staff for this purpose. Thus began the rise of the mortgage broker.

There were 7,000 mortgage brokerage firms operating in 1987. That number rose to more than 20,000 by 1995, and by 2002, 44,000 brokerage firms were in operation, with some 240,000 employees. By recent accounts, brokers now originate more than 45 percent of the nation's mortgages.

The use of brokers, who originate 70 percent of subprime loans, represents a radical change from the previous era in which banks and thrifts dominated the mortgage business and made loans on a retail basis, using their own employees who were located in the lenders' branch offices and had direct contact with prospective borrowers.

Brokers, in contrast, are independent agents who shop loan applications around among a number of different lenders. They offer borrowers convenience, because they generally go to the borrower, rather than vice versa. Many brokers market their services very aggressively in target communities, putting flyers in mailboxes, knocking on doors, and running ads on late night television. They tend to emphasize low monthly payments and easy qualification standards, rather than the type of loan and its long term costs. Brokers' lower overhead, aggressive marketing, and flexibility and convenience are allegedly difficult for banks to compete with. Many banks have decided, instead, to work with brokers.

In recent years the predominant loan-type marketed by subprime lenders has been the hybrid adjustable-rate mortgage (ARM). These mortgage loans have a fixed interest rate for the first two (or three) years, at which point the rate adjusts, followed by serial rate adjustments (usually upward) every six months for the remaining years of the loan. Of the total subprime mortgage loans originated in 2005, more than 72 percent were ARMS. The periodic rate increases associated with these loans can increase the borrower's interest rate by 1.5 to 3 percentage points, and the monthly payment can go up by as much as 30 to 40 percent. This leads the borrower to suffer significant payment shock after the honeymoon of low fixed rates has ended. In some cases, there is no "honeymoon" as borrowers start out with unwarranted high interest rates that then adjust ever upward.

This type of loan was never designed to be sustainable over the long term. It was predicated on the idea that the borrower could refinance at the point of the initial rate increase. Many borrowers report that this is just what their mortgage broker told them: "Don't worry, when the rate adjusts, you can refinance." And while it was true that housing prices in general were rising at unprecedented rates, it was also true that repeated refinancings stripped homeowners of their home equity, with no guarantee of providing an affordable or sustainable loan payment.

In sum, what developed was a mortgage lending system in which brokers were paid to put borrowers into excessively expensive loans, loan originators immediately sold off their loans and had little interest in their long-term performance, and investors (until the current rash of foreclosures) earned huge profits but bore no liability for the actions of the brokers and lenders. It is hard to imagine a better recipe for fraud and abuse.

Several recent studies document the existence of severe racial discrimination in the subprime market. For example, according to one study that analyzed more than 177,000 subprime loans, borrowers of color are more than 30 percent more likely to receive a higher-rate loan than White borrowers, even after accounting for differences in creditworthiness.

Another analysis shows that borrowers residing in zip codes whose population is at least 50 percent minority are 35 percent more likely to receive loans with "prepayment penalties" than financially similar borrowers in zip codes where minorities make up less than 10 percent of the population. More than 70 percent of all subprime loans come with such penalties, which box borrowers into high-rate loans even after they've bettered their credit and wish to refinance. For example, for a family with a $150,000 mortgage at an interest rate of 10 percent, a typical prepayment penalty imposes a fee of $6,000 for an early payoff—an amount greater than the wealth owned by the median African-American family.

Another striking study of discriminatory lending practices has found that high-income African-Americans in predominantly Black neighborhoods are three times more likely to receive a subprime purchase loan than low-income White borrowers. African-American and Latino borrowers are disproportionately represented in the high cost loan market, with 55 and 46 percent of African-American and Latino borrowers, respectively, receiving high-cost loans. In contrast, only 19 percent of White borrowers are given high-cost loans.

(continued)

B o x 9.3 •   The Subprime Mortgage and Foreclosure Crisis (*continued*)

The nation is now finding that the house price increases that masked the problems in the subprime market have ended: the bubble has burst. Nearly 30 percent of homeowners reported that they saw the value of their house decrease during 2007. And according to Reuters, home prices fell 8.9% in 2007, while Baker calculates that prices dropped at a 16% annual rate in the final quarter of 2007.

Falling house prices have led to record foreclosures in recent months. A recent study by an online marketplace for foreclosed properties reports that more than one million properties went into some stage of foreclosure in 2007, a 75 percent increase from 2006. More than half of these foreclosure starts were on subprime mortgages. The *Wall Street Journal* reports that, just as the number of homes entering foreclosure in the last quarter of 2007 rose to the highest level on record, last year was also the first time that "American homeowners, in the aggregate, owned less than half the value of their houses," at 47.9%. This number stood at higher than 80% in 1945.

SOURCE: National Fair Housing Alliance, *2008 Fair Housing Trends Report* (Washington, D.C.: National Fair Housing Alliance, 2008), *passim*.

Besides discriminating against entire neighborhoods, lenders also frequently discriminate against African Americans as *individuals*. Data that the Federal Reserve Bank has collected since 1990 indicate that African Americans are two and one-half to three times as likely to be rejected when applying for home mortgage loans than are whites. A substantial racial discrepancy in rejection rates for mortgage loans exists, even when the income of African-American applicants is the same as that of white applicants (Munnell et al. 1996). So African Americans trying to buy properties in black neighborhoods in many cases receive a double discrimination in applying for loans—discrimination based on their own race and on the racial composition of the neighborhood.

Mortgage disinvestment is not the only type of disinvestment found in African-American neighborhoods. Most insurance companies refuse to insure properties in inner-city areas, particularly those with high minority populations (Squires 2003).

Understanding disinvestment helps explain why neighborhood decline is often linked to racial segregation. In many African-American neighborhoods, the resources are simply not available for individuals to own and maintain their property. In some neighborhoods, large investors buy up a good deal of housing and convert it to rental units. The absentee owners of such rental properties have little stake in the future of the neighborhood or even of their own properties. They too often invest minimal capital in their buildings, a practice called "milking" the property, as they try to squeeze every dollar of income possible from the properties. When African-American neighborhoods are deprived of the mortgage loans, insurance policies, and other resources that would help maintain the neighborhood properly, the overall impact can be severe property deterioration. That deterioration is, however, less often due to racial transition itself than to the withdrawal of resources that has accompanied or followed the process of racial segregation (Squires 2003).

One final correlate of high minority population neighborhoods is that they are often located in the least desirable parts of the metropolitan area and/or have fewer amenities than do white neighborhoods. This situation occurs not only in African-American neighborhoods but, in some parts of the country, in Native American, Latino, and other ethnic minority areas. One reason for this is that whites are more willing to relinquish areas that are lacking in aesthetic qualities (such as attractive housing) or practical advantages (such as good transportation). Another is that members of ethnic and racial minority groups may not have the political influence to protect their areas from intrusion by undesirable land uses. Environmentally detrimental projects such as landfills, incinerators, and garbage dumps tend to be located disproportionately near minority districts, leading many observers to conclude, as we saw in Chapter 1, that environmental racism is at work (Fitzpatrick and LaGory 2000). Lesser political clout may also influence the level of public investment in African-American neighborhoods. A great deal of research has shown that public services, for example schools, sanitation, street condition, and recreation facilities, are often inferior in minority neighborhoods (Massey and Denton 1993).

In theory, residential segregation can possibly produce separate but equal outcomes for blacks and whites. In practice, however, institutional disinvestment and negative labeling of African-American neighborhoods means that separate neighborhoods too often become unequal. The preponderance of research shows that neighborhood decline is not an inevitable outcome of racial integration, as some whites fear. Yet neighborhoods with high proportions of African-American residents often experience withdrawals of economic and political resources that prevent residents from maintaining their neighborhoods as they would prefer. Because of this dilemma, when middle-class African Americans have the opportunity to move to less segregated neighborhoods, some choose to do so, moving either into predominantly white urban neighborhoods or into suburban areas.

Suburban Movement

Growing numbers of African Americans are moving to suburban communities. What proportion of African Americans live in the suburbs? For the United States as a whole, about 40 percent of African Americans are suburban residents compared with 71 percent of whites (Charles 2003). Metropolitan areas do vary substantially: for example, in 1980 over 40 percent of the African Americans in the Los Angeles metro area lived in suburbs, 27 percent of African Americans in the Cleveland metro area lived in suburbs, and only 8 percent of African Americans in the New York City area lived in suburbs (Massey and Denton 1993).

For African Americans, living in the suburbs does not necessarily mean living in an integrated neighborhood. In the past, many African Americans counted as suburban dwellers actually lived in predominantly minority (and often poor) inner-city communities, such as Camden, New Jersey, and East St. Louis, Illinois, which bear little resemblance to the typical suburb. These communities are suburban only in relation to the major cities next to them—Philadelphia and St. Louis. Such ghettoized minority suburbs are home to a large proportion of suburban African Americans, but many others are moving to newer, racially integrated residential communities. Young, college-educated black families are most likely to choose the suburbs, for the same reasons that many whites do: good schools, newer housing, and an improved quality of life (Palen 1995).

Middle-class African Americans now have a wider range of suburban communities open to them, and different families make different choices about the optimal degree of racial integration. Lacy (2007) describes a study of middle- and upper-middle class African-American families living in three different suburbs of Washington, D.C. The three communities have vastly different levels of integration, from 4 percent black to 85 percent black. But of the three communities, the one with the highest percent black population is an upscale, exclusive development in which the vast majority of the residents is college educated or hold advanced degrees and work in professional jobs. These "blue-chip blacks" choose to live in a suburban community surrounded by families like them—other affluent, professional African-American families. One of their chief motivations is to provide their children with all of the advantages available to the middle class, including a middle-class identity, and to have them be in the company of other young people with the same identities and aspirations.

What impact has the African-American migration to the suburbs had on residential segregation? Overall, levels of racial segregation are lower in the suburbs than they are in the cities, but the majority of African Americans moving to the suburbs are moving to communities that already have substantial African-American populations. They are also moving to less affluent suburban communities than the suburbs to which Asian and Hispanic groups are moving (Alba et al. 2000; Charles 2003). As African Americans have moved to the suburbs, however, increasing proportions of the total African-American population have ended up in less segregated neighborhoods (Farley 1987). The trend toward African-American suburbanization may eventually lead to substantial overall decreases in residential segregation, or it may lead to a more mosaiclike pattern of pockets of whites and African Americans clustered by social class as well as by race.

SOCIAL CLASS PATTERNS IN AFRICAN-AMERICAN NEIGHBORHOODS

Ever since highly segregated African-American ghettos came into existence in the early part of the twentieth century, they have contained African Americans of all social class backgrounds. Prior to ghetto formation, however, educated and professional African Americans frequently lived nearer and interacted more with educated and professional whites than with the poor and uneducated members of their own race. As segregation intensified in the 1910s and 1920s, the color line became a more significant barrier in urban society than was the class line. The educated African-American elite became less able to distinguish themselves socially or distance themselves geographically from low-income African Americans (Zunz 1982; Frazier 1932). Although the social class differences within African-American communities were nearly as broad as those within white communities, African-American neighborhoods tended to contain a heterogeneous mix of social classes simply because so few neighborhoods existed where blacks were allowed to live.

Over time, significant changes have occurred in the social class composition of majority African-American neighborhoods. These changes are partly based on ideology or beliefs about the importance of racial solidarity versus integration with whites. They are also partly based on the possibilities for residential choice that were available to blacks in the metropolitan area in different time periods.

Changing Class Structure

Since the formation of the African-American neighborhoods, several trends have converged to change the nature of many urban African-American communities. One important trend is deindustrialization and the loss of jobs in manufacturing. As Adams et al. (1991) have shown for Philadelphia and Squires (1994) has shown on a national level, the decline in industrial employment in the United States since the 1970s has had a severe and disproportionate effect on African Americans. Between the 1940s and the 1970s, blacks made employment gains in manufacturing. After several decades of a narrowing black-white income gap, the gap widened between 1970 and 1990. Because industrial restructuring devastatingly impacted cities, the relative decline in black incomes compared to those of whites was sharper in cities than it was overall (Squires 1994). To phrase it differently, deindustrialization hurt African Americans more than whites and it hurt urban African Americans most of all.

A sizeable working class still exists in African-American neighborhoods, but some studies indicate that its members feel invisible compared to the growing underclass in their cities or to the *buppies*—the black professionals who have "made it." In a study of Chicago's South Side, Duneier (1992) argues that the majority of African Americans in ghetto neighborhoods are poor but respectable people working at stable but low-paying jobs. They are neither the tough drug dealers nor the flashy high rollers portrayed in the media. Duneier's subjects are a man named Slim and his friends who eat at the Valois Cafeteria. They work hard, help their friends, try to keep their families together, and hold to a standard of quiet respectability in dress and behavior. But they have watched their neighborhood slide into poverty, and they are shocked by the crime, drugs, and disrespect for authority that they see around them. As we see continued deindustrialization, we may expect to see a decrease in the size of the African-American working class parallel to that of the white working class.

A second large-scale trend, suburbanization, also changed the class structure of many African-American neighborhoods. The movement of large numbers of white families from cities to suburbs between 19660 and 1990 opened up new housing opportunities for African Americans in cities outside of the borders of the old ghetto areas. Middle-class African-American households began to move out of segregated neighborhoods and into racially mixed neighborhoods. The upshot of this increased housing opportunity was that the African-American

---

Box 9.4 • Case Study
Black Gentrification

Amid significant income flux, [Chicago's] North Kenwood-Oakland remains predominantly black. It has been so since the 1950s, and it is for the most part experiencing "black gentrification." Black professionals are moving in from other Chicago neighborhoods, from other cities, and back to the city from the suburbs. For some African Americans, the move is motivated by what legal scholar Sheryll Cashin calls "integration exhaustion," the sociopsychological fatigue experienced especially by blacks who work in integrated environments or have been pioneers in white neighborhoods. Respondents in North Kenwood-Oakland, though, talked more about factors that pulled them toward a black neighborhood than factors that pushed them away from whites.

...It is more than just names and symbols (and relatively inexpensive real estate) that attract black middle- and upper-income newcomers to the neighborhood. They come, or come back, to North Kenwood-Oakland out of a sense of racial pride and duty, to be conduits of resources, to model "respectability." In this milieu, disputes between black residents with professional jobs and those with no jobs, between black families who have been in the neighborhood for generations and those who moved in last year, and between blacks who don fraternity colors and those who sport gang colors, are simultaneously debates over what it means to be black.

SOURCE: Mary Pattillo, *Black on the Block: The Politics of Race and Class in the City* (Chicago: University of Chicago Press, 2007), pp. 10 and 3.

---

neighborhoods of many cities became increasingly differentiated by social class (Wilson et al. 1988). This trend has been countered somewhat since 1990 by the phenomenon of increasing numbers of middle-class African-American households choosing to remain in or move to traditionally black neighborhoods. Mary Pattillo (2007) calls this trend "black gentrification" and shows how Chicago's North Kenwood-Oakland neighborhood is experiencing an influx of prosperous African-American households. (See Box 9.4.) Figure 9.2 shows a gentrifying African-American neighborhood in New York City.

A third trend, immigration, may have an impact on the experience of African Americans in cities. As cities become more multicultural, does that affect the African Americans who already live there? A major study of inequality in the Los Angeles metropolitan area (Bobo et al. 2000) investigated that question. The authors describe Los Angeles as a "prism" in which many different groups are reflected, including large numbers of Mexicans, Chinese, Koreans, and many other immigrants. In commenting on this research, Portes (2003) draws two important conclusions. First, he holds that we cannot discuss race relations in the United States today without taking immigration into account; the old "black–white" divide of race is now blurred. Second, the evidence in the study shows that the influx of immigrants into the Los Angeles region has not helped push African Americans up the economic and social ladder as some had anticipated. Rather, African Americans continue to be disproportionately disadvantaged in

FIGURE 9.2 Black gentrification. The population of this New York City neighborhood is becoming more affluent while remaining largely African American. Professional households are attracted by the high quality and relatively low prices of the housing stock.

housing choices, employment, and discrimination. Although they have a long history in the United States, speak English, and understand the social structure, African Americans are being in many ways relegated to the bottom of the social and economic hierarchy in Los Angeles. Is this true of other cities? Research is ongoing on this topic.

CURRENT ISSUES AROUND RACE AND RESIDENTIAL PATTERNS

Will racial separation in cities continue? Among other factors, two will have a significant impact on this issue: government policy and social attitudes. To end the chapter, we will explore two questions:

- What has the government done and what is it planning to do to address racial segregation?

- What do people feel are the advantages and disadvantages of racially homogeneous and racially mixed neighborhoods?

Government Policy

Until the 1960s government policy was designed to support racial segregation. We have already seen that for decades, local governments fostered racial segregation through racial zoning ordinances and restrictive covenants. Until quite recently the federal government also actively discriminated against African Americans in several ways. One prominent example is the operation of the Federal Housing Administration (FHA) home loan program that resulted in the massive growth of suburban communities after World War II. For twenty years after the inception of the program in the late 1940s, it was nearly impossible for African Americans to obtain an FHA-backed loan. In addition, the FHA underwriting manual specifically prohibited granting loans to persons of races that were "incompatible" with the neighborhood (Citizens' Commission on Civil Rights 1983).

In the 1960s political support for segregation lessened sufficiently for government bodies to change long-standing discriminatory policies. Some examples were the desegregation of public housing (an executive order that President John F. Kennedy issued), the passage of the 1964 Civil Rights Act, which prohibited the federal government from discriminating in any of its programs, and a true fair housing bill, the Civil Rights Act of 1968, which barred racial discrimination in the sale or rental of private or public housing. Since then, the legal context has changed from one that was supportive of racial discrimination to one that opposes it, and antidiscrimination activists have successfully used court actions to punish and deter discrimination in housing (Herbers 1986).

Segregation is no longer the law, but racial integration has been difficult to achieve through government policies. Some local governments work with community organizations to manage the racial composition of their neighborhoods. Their aim is to stem white flight and maintain stably integrated neighborhoods. Some neighborhood associations and local governments use affirmative marketing techniques (actively recruiting whites to buy homes) and financial incentives such as low-interest mortgages to try to attract white residents and stabilize their populations at a manageable level of integration (Ellen 2000). Some pro-integration groups have also tried to make the suburbs more accessible to moderate-income African-American households by challenging exclusionary zoning in the courts. To date, the most significant challenge to exclusionary zoning has been in the state of New Jersey, where the state Supreme Court, in the *Mount Laurel* decisions, ruled that each suburban community must allow a proportion of its new housing to be affordable (Keating 1994).

Not only are the courts making it more difficult for government bodies to maintain segregation, in some cases they are forcing government agencies to integrate residential neighborhoods. A landmark 1976 court decision found that the Chicago Housing Authority had operated its public housing projects in a racially discriminatory manner. The so-called *Gautreaux* decision laid the groundwork for public housing tenants to be placed in privately owned rental housing units in mostly white neighborhoods, both within the city and in the suburbs. A number of studies of the program have shown high rates of satisfaction for the public housing tenants in their new neighborhoods, and minimal impact on the neighborhoods (Clampett-Lundquist and Massey 2008).

The success of the *Gautreaux* program and the increasing problem of poverty in inner-city African-American neighborhoods have influenced the federal government to adopt a policy that is called Moving to Opportunity. Since 1991 this program has provided housing vouchers for low-income households to move out of the neighborhoods in which they live, often public housing projects or other concentrated poverty areas. Such programs, designed to increase housing choices for low-income households of all races, have resulted in low-income residents leaving low-income neighborhoods in some instances. But the vast majority of African American voucher recipients who move still end up in racially segregated neighborhoods (Clampett-Lundquist and Massey 2008).

Attitudes About Racial Homogeneity

Ironically, as the federal government has slowly begun to endorse racial integration and has changed its policies to foster racial and economic heterogeneity in neighborhoods, some African Americans have begun to question the value of racial integration as a social goal. To conclude the chapter, then, we will consider what we know about people's attitudes toward racial integration and how changing public attitudes may impact the future of our communities.

The research on attitudes about race reveals that whites and African Americans overall have different attitudes toward racially integrated neighborhoods. A number of studies (e.g., Krysan and Farley 2002; Charles 2001) have shown that most whites prefer to live in all-white or almost all-white neighborhoods. One national study compared whites' interest in moving to neighborhoods with different characteristics, including different racial groups in the area. It found that when educational quality, crime rates, and housing values were the same in two neighborhoods, the proportion of Asian or Hispanic residents had no impact on the whites' interest in moving to that neighborhood. But with the same level of educational quality, crime rate, and housing value, the proportion of African-American population had a significant negative impact on whites' interest in moving there (Emerson et al. 2001). In the same studies, the majority of African Americans expressed preferences for neighborhoods that are about half black and half white. Almost all African Americans queried would feel comfortable moving to a predominantly white neighborhood if there was a visible African-American presence, but the vast majority of whites expressed reluctance to move to a neighborhood with "more than a few" African Americans living there (Krysan and Farley 2002). Dawkins (2004) summarizes the research on racial attitudes by saying there is an "asymmetry" between what whites want (all or almost all white neighborhoods) and what African Americans want (racially integrated neighborhoods).

Sociologist Joe Darden (1987) describes the attitude of the majority of urban African-American households as follows: "They indicate a black preference for mixed or half-black half-white neighborhoods and the rejection of all black and all white ones." He explains that people reject all-black neighborhoods because they perceive that they have a lower quality of life: housing, schools, police protection, and recreational facilities. But they also reject all-white neighborhoods because they fear social isolation or outright hostility of whites toward new African-American neighbors. Racially balanced neighborhoods, on the other hand, offer the possibility of a decent quality of life, coupled with a receptiveness to interracial social interaction. He concludes that only a small proportion of racial segregation is voluntary self-segregation by African Americans and that most segregation is due to perceived or real limitations on their geographic mobility, a finding that has been echoed in numerous studies (Charles 2001).

Some researchers find more ambivalence about integration among African Americans. Wiese (1995) finds that many members of the black middle class feel that it is "selling out" to move to white neighborhoods and that they wish to retain a sense of national identity and community available only in predominantly African-American neighborhoods. Many of his informants express the desire to move into a better *class* of neighborhood, for example, one with many black professional families. Wiese's research confirms other studies that show that that the most desirable neighborhoods for the majority of African Americans continue to be integrated neighborhoods, and that only a small proportion of African Americans are interested in being pioneers in white areas. A related concern is the dilution of political power for African Americans that could occur if they were more dispersed in metropolitan areas. Especially in the larger cities, many African-American candidates can be elected because of the numerical strength of black voters in certain election districts. Some political leaders charge that attempts to disperse African Americans to white neighborhoods will weaken their growing political influence.

Despite the overall persistence of black–white segregation in cities, there are urban neighborhoods around the country that maintain a pattern of stable racial integration over time. Often these communities are located near universities or hospitals, with good amenities such as interesting housing, parks, shopping, and public transportation. These stably integrated neighborhoods tend to be intentionally created and maintained by both African Americans and whites who value multicultural diversity (Ellen 2000).

CONCLUSION

With the migration of African Americans to cities and the subsequent migration of whites to the suburbs, the central cities of many metropolitan areas gained significant proportions of African-American residents. A combination of white people's resistance to integration and black people's struggles to provide homes and social institutions for themselves creates and maintains urban African-American neighborhoods. Institutional gatekeepers as well as families' incomes and needs influence where people choose to live. Institutional actors also frequently withhold resources from neighborhoods with high proportions of African-American populations.

Given the society's treatment of African-American neighborhoods, it is perhaps not surprising that more affluent African Americans have frequently chosen to live outside of ghetto areas. A relatively small proportion of urban neighborhoods combine characteristics of a half-black population and good housing and schools that many African-American households seek.

What does the future hold for urban African Americans? Two current trends that affect them seem likely to continue: the polarization of incomes and the suburbanization of the population. Income polarization implies that the opportunities for the impoverished African-American underclass will probably not improve substantially, whereas opportunities for educated African Americans to move into professional positions will probably continue to expand modestly. More working-class blacks will likely be pushed into poverty as the shortage of urban jobs continues. Suburbanization of the population means that the middle class, regardless of race, will probably continue to leave central cities in steady numbers. As in the past, this situation will probably permit African Americans to move into new city neighborhoods. If banks and other institutional gatekeepers continue to withdraw resources from racially integrated areas, however, African Americans will not be able to maintain the quality of life they sought by moving to those areas. Finally, when African Americans move to integrated suburbs, their white neighbors' actions can decide whether their communities will become resegregated.

As many commentators on American cities have noted, our society is deeply permeated with racial distinctions and preferences. The attitudes and actions of African Americans and whites, both as individuals and as part of social institutions, have shaped and will continue to shape where and how people live.

DISCUSSION QUESTIONS

1. Many middle-aged and older African Americans migrated from the rural South to cities. If you know such a person, interview him or her about what it was like to move. Who moved, why, when, where? What were the results?

2. What is the current law regarding fair housing and racial discrimination, including steering by real estate agents? How is it enforced in your area?

3. What is the racial mix in your community? Are there identifiably African-American neighborhoods? If so, what proportion of the population (according to the 2000 census) was African American in the entire community? In the African-American neighborhoods?

10

Social Class and Neighborhoods

Any city, however small, is in fact divided into two, one
the city of the poor, the other of the rich; these are at war
with one another; and in either there are many smaller
divisions, and you would be altogether beside the mark if you
treated them all as a single state.

PLATO

THE REPUBLIC

Plato's quote (above) shows that urban social inequality has existed for thousands of years. It also shows that class conflict was evident long before Marx and Engels wrote their theories. Although social inequality has been a feature of all complex societies, the forms of social inequality and the structure of social classes have changed over time. Despite some similarities with Plato's city of two thousand years ago, the cities of advanced industrial societies have unique patterns of social inequality and mechanisms for sorting different groups into different spaces.

In this chapter, we will investigate the relationship between social classes and urban life, focusing on four questions:

- How do social classes appear as spatially separate urban communities with distinctive ways of life?

- Why do social classes sort themselves into different neighborhoods, and what mechanisms facilitate the sorting process?

- How have social class patterns in cities changed in recent years?

- How is the changing class structure reflected in housing trends?

SOCIAL CLASS AND COMMUNITIES

All complex societies are stratified, or unequal, societies. The forms of stratification and the degrees of inequality, however, vary from one society to another. Like other industrialized societies, the United States is a **class society**—that is, the United States has large and persistent differences in wealth among different segments of the population (called social classes) and these class differences have consequences for people's quality of life. The term also means that an individual's social class membership is not, strictly speaking, inherited, even though there is a strong relationship between parents' and children's class membership. Class societies allow individuals to change positions (a feature known as **social mobility**) rather than assigning group membership at birth.

Different theorists have defined the term *social class* differently, but for our purposes the two most important definitions come from Karl Marx and Max Weber. Marx defined social class membership by an individual's relationship to the means of production—either working for someone else or being an investor. In other words, for Marx, the crucial aspect of people's social class position was *how they made* their money. Weber took a broader view, including issues of **status** (or social prestige) as well as class in his definition. For Weber, how people made their money was less important than how much they made and *how they spent* it. Even groups of people who are either all employees or all investors, Weber argued, contain internal status distinctions based on the tastes and preferences they have defined as prestigious. Finally, an additional dimension that Weber incorporated into his definition of social class was **power**, that is, control over other people or resources.

How do these definitions of social class relate to cities and urban patterns? Both help us see the sources of urban spatial patterns. Marx's definition is valuable chiefly in distinguishing a class of people who make their money from investing in property, the rentiers who buy and develop property for other people to use, as we saw in Chapter 4. Weber's definition of social class has been valuable in explaining where people choose to live and why.

Urbanists have studied social class patterns in cities and metropolitan areas for more than a century using different research methods in their studies. One set of studies, called **social geography** because it examines the interaction between space and social structure, chiefly maps out where different groups live and how that pattern changes over time. A second approach, called **ethnography**, describes how people live in the different class-based subcommunities. Ethnographic studies closely examine individual communities rather than broadly examining overall patterns. Because these two types of research are complementary, we can learn different lessons from exploring some of each type.

Mapping Studies: Pictures of the Whole City

The project of mapping out the locations of different social classes is usually identified with the Chicago School of human ecology. Although they did not invent the technique, the Chicago School researchers raised it to an art form by systematically mapping different areas and by searching for patterns among the maps. As we saw in Chapter 2, Ernest Burgess (1925) began the project of identifying patterns in the location of different residential areas. The main dividing principles he identified were social class and race. In his concentric zone model, all zones other than the central business district contained residences: the zone in transition (Zone II) contained slum housing, Zone III contained workingmen's homes, Zone IV was the more restricted zone of single-family homes and expensive apartments, and Zone V, the most distant from the center, was the commuter zone. Although Burgess wrote about *housing type* more frequently than *social class*, there is no doubt that he was in fact describing the social class structure of the city as it expressed itself in the type of housing occupied by different classes and the spatial divisions between the classes.

Urban mapping projects became more sophisticated with the development of statistical techniques that permitted researchers to find similarities and differences among neighborhoods. With the methods of social area analysis, or factorial ecology (see Chapter 2), researchers could statistically sort dozens of mapped variables into a few underlying factors. They found that they could often predict the type of neighborhood a household would choose by knowing how the household scored on just three factors: its rank, or social class; its ethnicity, including racial background; and its degree of "familism," that is, the number of children present and whether any adult women worked outside of the home. They also found that the social status of the neighborhood influenced residents' behavior. For example, researchers found that, regardless of an individual's social standing, people living in higher-status neighborhoods tended to participate in organizations more frequently than people living in lower-status neighborhoods (Bell and Force 1956).

A recent approach to mapping the city goes beyond the demographic characteristics of the households living in different neighborhoods to investigate their behaviors and lifestyles (Weiss 2000). Analysts can now combine basic demographic information from the census with data from voting records, consumer surveys, and sales reports for different neighborhoods (defined by census block groups and the Post Office's zip + 4 codes). Through a technique called *cluster analysis*, similar to factor analysis, it is possible to identify forty different types of local residential zones, each with characteristic patterns not only of social class, ethnicity, and family style but also of political, recreational, and consumer behavior. Cluster analysis demonstrates that although certain social groups may be *associated* with particularly urban locations (for example, young *urban* professionals), they are not *confined* to those areas but may be located in suburbs and smaller towns as well as in cities. Cluster research implies that, although social class and community are clearly related, the social definition of neighborhoods is more complex than simply a combination of class, ethnicity, and familism.

What is the significance of these mapping projects? To some researchers working within the ecological paradigm, they reveal the existence of natural areas, unplanned subcommunities within cities. They support the position that there is a natural fit between certain social groups and certain types of neighborhoods. Other researchers interpret grouping by social class not as evidence of natural processes but of a social order that gives wealthier groups greater choice of location than the less wealthy. Still others have identified institutional actors and processes that channel the choices of individual households in certain directions. The maps may be able to show us overall patterns, but they cannot explain why those patterns exist.

We will return later in the chapter to the issue of the processes involved in sorting out the different social class groups. Now we turn to some descriptive studies that have shown us the small picture of local communities within the big picture of the city as a whole.

Descriptions of Urban Life: Community and Neighborhood Studies

Sociologists have long investigated the lives of people in cities and towns, describing them in vivid prose as well as in tables and maps. They have frequently borrowed the ethnographic method that anthropologists use: the systematic observation and description of the social life of the community. Early research focused on the community as a whole, noting social and geographic cleavages based on social class and ethnicity. One of the early studies, *Middletown*, by Robert and Helen Lynd (1929), observed a Midwestern city in the 1920s, noting changes that had occurred in the previous thirty-five years. They found a relatively homogeneous community but with overtones of anti-Catholic, Jewish, and immigrant sentiment and a sizeable branch of the Ku Klux Klan. When the Lynds returned to Middletown a decade later, they found that the Depression and population growth had resulted in the emergence of a wealthy and influential circle dominated by one prominent family. This tightly knit group ran the city's major industries and had a controlling interest in the banks, law firms, school board, local newspaper, charities, YMCA, fraternal organizations, and even the churches. Although the group was perceived as public-spirited and philanthropic, it was decidedly the most powerful in town and dominated decision making. On the other hand, the situation of the poor had worsened during the Depression and the amount of racial prejudice had grown (Lynd and Lynd 1937).

Community studies repeatedly found that local institutions both reflected and reinforced social class structure of the town. A. B. Hollingshead's well-known study of a Midwestern community he called "Elmtown" showed how the schools and other institutions sorted the students based on the social class position of their parents. He followed several hundred teenagers over time and found that the class position of the teens' families was closely related to the length of time they stayed in school, whether they enrolled in the college prep curriculum, their grades, whom they dated, their choice of friends, and their leisure activities. The higher-status students played golf and bowled, while the lower-class students frequented the skating rink and pool hall. In the lowest social class group, 75 percent of the young people dropped out of high school before their sixteenth birthday (Hollingshead 1949).

Some community studies such as Warner's *Yankee City* (1963) mapped out the residential locations of the different social groups. In this old New England city, social class had a pervasive influence on the community, and people judged each other's status not only on wealth and occupation but also on family background and social connections. Warner's team found that the prestige of different neighborhoods was so apparent that address became a proxy for class standing. People routinely used the term "Hill Streeter" as synonymous with "high-mucky-muck" and "Riverbrooker" as interchangeable with "low class" (1963, p. 38–39).

Beginning with Robert Park and his students in the Chicago School, urban ethnographers have typically confined themselves to the investigation of a single neighborhood at a time. Because people cluster by social class, these studies of particular neighborhoods also turn out to be studies of particular social class groups within the city.

Elite Neighborhoods.   Of all the social classes, the wealthy have been studied the least. Perhaps because it is difficult to gain entrance into the homes and social circles of the elite, outsiders have had limited opportunities for such research. The works of insider E. Digby Baltzell have given us insights into the world of the elite. Born into the upper class, Baltzell wrote about the families and social institutions in which he had been raised. *Philadelphia Gentlemen* (1958) describes in detail the neighborhoods in which Philadelphia's elite families live as well as the churches and clubs to which they belong and the schools to which they send their children. Baltzell's study emphasizes that it is crucial for group solidarity that they live near each other and see each other frequently. The geographic clustering of the elite and their memberships in the same organizations help to make Philadelphia's upper class a **primary group**, or a cohesive group with very close, family-like ties. This tight social organization has allowed the group to develop a strong self-consciousness of their distinctive goals and responsibilities in society.

How are elite neighborhoods formed? How do particular neighborhoods become identified as the "correct" places to live? Evidence suggests that elite neighborhoods are not simply the product of the individual decisions of a number of affluent households but that economic, social, and political planning are involved in defining neighborhoods as "proper." Box 10.1 shows how Boston's upper class developed Beacon Hill as their neighborhood and reclaimed it after incursions from other groups. The case of Beacon Hill reveals that in addition to wealth alone, prestige and political clout help elite groups gain and maintain the use of desirable spots (see Figure 10.1).

A more recent study of an upper-class neighborhood (Maher 1990) describes an elite enclave within a Midwestern city. The residents have the usual upper-class characteristics: professional jobs, degrees from elite colleges, children in private prep schools, memberships in exclusive clubs. The setting is park-like and secluded from the rest of the city; a private security force ensures that nonresidents, except for servants, stay out. The powerful neighborhood association has worked diligently for over fifty years to maintain the exclusive nature of the community. Some of its initiatives include adopting an agreement with every home owner to give the "right of first refusal" to purchase homes to the association; working behind the scenes with the city to move a planned highway to a location that would buffer the area from a low-income, minority neighborhood; and persuading an art museum and theater to move to the enclave from a

---

B o x   10.1   •   Case Study
Creation of an Elite Neighborhood

Just before the turn of the nineteenth century, an elite group of Boston Brahmins began to develop [Beacon] Hill into a residential area for their clan. Working in concert, they bought up land and built stately mansions with servants' quarters and decorative gardens along tree-lined streets. Long and narrow private parks with grass, flowers, and trees also ran down the center of some of the streets, where the houses, set back from the roads on both sides, all faced the park....

The power of the Brahmins to influence political decisions in Boston was clearly reflected in the way they developed Beacon Hill. Encountering only token opposition along the way, the Brahmins were able to establish conditions that facilitated the development. Relying on connections they had made in other Boston land speculations, they were able to obtain building permits quickly and easily. When road improvements were needed to continue Beacon Hill's development, the projects were given priority and paid for by the City of Boston. With the increase in construction, land values on the hill were rising, but property on the hill was kept undervalued on tax rolls. Beacon Hill's location near the center of Boston made it attractive to people outside of the elite enclave who wanted to commercially develop the area, but the City of Boston enacted new zoning laws and reinterpreted old ones to protect Beacon Hill from unwanted commercial enterprises that would have detracted from its residential desirability....

In Boston in the early 1900s, a new area called Back Bay was developed. An elegant community adjacent to Beacon Hill, it came to be identified as "Boston's most fashionable," and a number of old families left the hill. As they left, the profile of Beacon Hill changed. Mansions were converted into rooming houses, and a new class of people moved in, along with a plethora of commercial shops. Property values began to fall, permitting still further invasions, pushing more families off the hill, and so on in a continuing cycle....

However, Beacon Hill still had a rich, long-standing symbolic value for Boston's elite, and when they banded together, their wealth and power were substantial. They outbid the competition for available mansions which they collectively purchased, modernizing the interiors and then selling them to families. Apartment-hotels and various specialty shops were then denied access to locations on the hill. Further attrition of elite families from the hill was reduced, and there was a return flow....

In the late 1950s, the Beacon Hill Association was able to get the hill designated as a historical district, and a board was established to review all restoration and renovation plans. Zoning ordinances were also passed to promote the hill's use as a distinguished residential area.... Their wealth, contacts, and prestige and their ability to appeal to preservationist values furnished the elite the power to institutionally structure arrangements....

SOURCE: Copyright © 1996 from *Urban Enclaves: Identity and Place in America* by Mark Abrahamson, pp. 23, 28–29. Reprinted with permission of St. Martin's Press, Inc.

---

different location within the city. It is clear that this traditional and privileged group acts collectively to maintain the exclusive nature of the neighborhood.

Middle-Class Neighborhoods.   Studies of middle-class urban neighborhoods are not much more numerous than studies of wealthy areas. Perhaps just as the sociologists' lack of membership in the upper class has denied them entree into

Courtesy of the Boston Public Library, Print Department

F I G U R E 10.1 An Elite Neighborhood. Boston's Beacon Hill was constructed and maintained by the elite "Brahmin" class of Boston residents.

its circles, their tendency to come from middle-class backgrounds has made that group less interesting as an object of study. The available sociological studies of middle-class neighborhoods tend to be investigations of suburban rather than urban communities. Two prominent early studies were *Crestwood Heights* by Seeley, Sim, and Loosley (1956) and *The Organization Man* by William H. Whyte (1956). Their findings are similar in that both show how life in the middle class revolves around work and family, especially children. The managerial middle-class families in these studies devote a great deal of money and time to their homes and possessions, using them for frequent entertaining. Although their corporate jobs make them highly mobile, these middle-class families are active participants in each neighborhood in which they live, joining many organizations and forming close social ties with other residents.

To what extent does the phrase *middle-class community* coincide with the phrase *suburban community*? In the 1960s some social scientists and a greater number of social critics commonly portrayed the suburbs as being demographically homogeneous and socially conformist. A kind of stereotype of the middle-class way of life developed: a giant revolving dinner party (in the winter) and barbecue (in the summer) where people socialized with others of the same age, race, income, religion, political party, education, occupation, number of children, and even the identical house style.

Herbert Gans (1967) confronted this picture of the suburban middle class by living in Levittown, New Jersey, for two years immediately after it was constructed as a new community. He found, contrary to the stereotype, that the people of Levittown were less homogeneous ethnically and religiously than those of most urban neighborhoods, although at the time, they were virtually all white. The social class backgrounds of the residents also varied considerably, because, as Gans points out, all they had in common economically was their ability to pay for a certain price of house. Households in similar economic circumstances still had widely varying backgrounds in education and occupation, not to mention future earnings potential.

Working-Class Neighborhoods.   Sociologists have studied more working-class neighborhoods than middle-class neighborhoods, perhaps because they perceived this group as more interesting than the middle class. Indeed, some classics of urban sociology have been studies of working-class neighborhoods, including *The Urban Villagers* by Herbert Gans (1962) and *Family and Kinship in East London* by Michael Young and Peter Willmott (1957). Their findings reveal an interesting twist on the studies of middle-class communities: if the middle class is focused on work and family, with leisure in the background, the working class is focused on family and leisure, with work in the background. Studies of working-class families show a great emphasis on maintaining family ties and on interacting with friends and relatives. Working-class communities take work for granted as a normal part of life, but work is not a subject that occupies people's attention. It simply provides the necessary income to support the family and to carry out social obligations. To working-class households in cities, family means the extended, multigenerational family, not the nuclear family of the middle-class community. In working-class city neighborhoods, relatives typically live in close proximity to each other, often in different apartments in the same house. Such traditional working-class neighborhoods tend to have very stable populations and tight social networks.

These urban working-class neighborhoods are slowly disappearing. The overall deindustrialization of the national economy and the movement of industry to the suburbs have had two consequences for working-class communities. First, the deindustrialized areas of cities that were home to working-class communities are being transformed. In some cases they are becoming home to the poor, in other cases they are being abandoned, and in still others they are being gentrified. (See Box 10.2 for a description of the effect of deindustrialization on Elizabeth, New Jersey.) Second, the movement of industry to the suburbs has drawn many working-class families to the suburbs, where their communities have taken a somewhat different form from those in the older urban neighborhoods.

Studies of working-class neighborhoods such as William Kornblum's *Blue Collar Community* (1974) and David Halle's *America's Working Man* (1984) portray the lives of families in industrial suburbs. Unlike the more traditional urban working-class neighborhoods, these communities place more emphasis on work and on mass consumption (such as shopping and watching television) than on family social activities. The suburban working-class families also feel less attached to the community and move more frequently than families in the older urban neighborhoods. Another complicating factor is that suburban working-class populations are often located in or near neighborhoods that are undergoing racial and ethnic integration. This pattern creates complicated political and social

---

B o x   10.2   •   Case Study
Dismantling of a Working-Class Community

Elizabeth, New Jersey, is, in many ways, typical of industrial America. It has seen periods of tremendous prosperity, presided over by the nineteenth-century captains of industry, and periods of sharp decline, occasioned by the abandonment of the area by manufacturers bent on lowering their labor costs by relocating to areas where unionism is weak and wages are low....

In 1873, the Singer Sewing Machine Company found Elizabeth an attractive place to establish a flagship factory, moving there from cramped quarters in lower Manhattan. For the next 100 years, the Singer company, a major multinational corporation since the mid-nineteenth century, dominated the city of Elizabeth. The plant produced consumer and industrial sewing machines that were sold all over the world, pausing only during the years of World War I, World War II, and the Korean War to produce munitions. Singer became the spine of the local economy, providing jobs and a secure life for generations of townspeople....

The Elizabeth factory was one of the largest industrial facilities in the United States up until World War II, but the postwar period was one of steady decline.... [L]osses spurred Singer to diversify, and to search for ways of lowering its production costs. Like many other firms, it began to move its American manufacturing operations overseas—to Italy, Taiwan, and Brazil. Eventually, the company initiated a slow but relentless dismantling of its sewing machine business. Today Singer is one of the largest independent aerospace electronics firms in the United States. The company that was synonymous with the sewing machine no longer produces it at all....

Like many other northeastern cities, Elizabeth had been a boomtown during the World Wars and the Korean conflict. Thereafter, however, a familiar pattern of industrial decline began to take its toll both in terms of factory flight and increased poverty in urban areas. The neighborhood around the Singer plant, which had once thrived with single-family homes and facilities that catered to the workers (e.g., diners), hit a steep decline.... Today [it] has a reputation as an eyesore and an enclave of danger.

SOURCE: Katherine S. Newman, *Falling from Grace* (New York: Vintage Press, 1991), pp. 176–177, 196.

---

relations, because the many different racial and ethnic groups who live in working-class communities have different reactions to ethnic and racial changes.

Low-Income Neighborhoods.   From the number of studies done, it is clear that social scientists have focused most of their attention on low-income neighborhoods. From the days of the earliest work of the Chicago School, urban community studies have often focused on slums (areas of run-down housing) or ghettos (areas of heavily ethnic or racial minority populations). Over the years and regardless of which ethnic groups happened to be living in these poor neighborhoods, the researchers' findings have been remarkably consistent. One common pattern they find is the separate social worlds of men and women (Liebow 1967; MacLeod 1995). A second pattern is the devastating impact of unemployment on family life in poor neighborhoods (Stack 1974; Wilson 1997. A third theme is the low level of control that poor people have over their own turf (Susser 1982; Jargowsky 1997).

One seemingly paradoxical characteristic of low-income neighborhoods is that many goods and services actually cost more in poor neighborhoods than in nonpoor areas. This pattern, which was first identified in the 1960s, still holds today. In a study of Gary, Indiana, Barnes (2005) investigated where low-income people shopped for food, clothing, and other services, what they purchased, and how much they paid. She found that the stores located in the poorer neighborhoods had higher prices, less variety, fewer services, and generally miserable amenities compared to their suburban counterparts. To overcome the high prices locally, many of the residents would periodically take a forty-five-minute bus ride to a shopping center and try to avoid shopping at the stores within walking distance of their homes.

A good deal of recent research has investigated neighborhoods that have extreme concentrations of poverty and their potential impacts on the residents. First identified by Wilson (1987), these neighborhoods contain over 40 percent of residents with incomes below the poverty line and are frequently located within the African-American ghettos of large cities. Based on data from Chicago neighborhoods in the 1970s and early 1980s, Wilson posited that the experience of living in neighborhoods of **concentrated poverty** had negative consequences on residents—especially young people—because of their isolation from the economic and social mainstream of the society. Several large studies (e.g., Brooks-Gunn et al. 1997) confirmed Wilson's initial finding that growing up in the conditions of an inner-city high-poverty neighborhood had detrimental effects on young people's cognitive development, school performance, employment chances, and criminal behavior. Researchers agreed on the negative impacts of living in extremely poor and highly segregated neighborhoods.

To complement these studies of concentrated poverty in African-American neighborhoods, researchers set out to disentangle the impacts of concentrated poverty from those of racial segregation. By examining low-income neighborhoods of all ethnicities, Jargowsky (1997) identified two main causes of concentrated poverty: decreasing job opportunities and increasing "sorting" of residential neighborhoods by income. As employment and population increasingly moved out of the cities after 1970, the poor and unemployed were increasingly left behind. More recent research shows that after steadily increasing from 1970 to 1990, however, concentrated poverty decreased dramatically during the 1990s, a "precipitous" drop of 24 percent between 1990 and 2000 (Jargowsky 2003). This decline occurred throughout the nation, especially in the Midwest and South, and for all racial groups, especially African Americans. Furthermore, these decreases in concentrated poverty were accompanied by dramatic declines in many of the problematic behaviors associated with poor neighborhoods, including the proportions of out-of wedlock births, high school dropouts, male unemployment, and public welfare usage. The declines in problematic behaviors in poor areas were even greater than the declines in concentrated poverty itself (Jargowsky 2006).

What accounts for the increase and then decrease in the extent of concentrated poverty? Jargowsky (2006) cites the sustained economic growth of the 1990s, increasing wages even for unskilled workers, and policies that discouraged welfare and rewarded work (welfare reform and the Earned Income Tax Credit). He points out that the gains of the 1990s are fragile and that concentrated poverty may well increase again due to a lagging economy and the spread of poverty to inner-ring suburbs.

Summary

To summarize what we know about neighborhoods and social class, the mapping studies and the ethnographic studies provide complementary pictures. Mapping studies reveal the big picture, namely, that the different social classes consistently sort themselves out in space. Ethnographic studies show in many smaller pictures how the different social classes live and how their neighborhoods impact their lives.

MECHANISMS FOR SORTING
THE SOCIAL CLASSES

We have seen that social classes sort themselves out in space. How do these spatially distinctive neighborhoods get established, and how do people get sorted into certain areas? We will look at three factors that help create these patterns: the housing market, institutional gatekeepers, and the labor market.

Housing Market

Let us begin with the most obvious fact about social class: people with more money have more choices of where to live. But even the most traditional economist will admit that money alone does not sort the population into neighborhoods. Instead, similar to social area analysts, housing market researchers divide the population of a metropolitan area into groups of different incomes, races, ages, and family types, yielding up to ninety different combinations. This is the *demand* side of the market: what kinds of space, location, and amenities does a household want, and how much can it afford to purchase (Anas and Arnott 1993)? On the *supply* side of the market, some sites are more expensive to build on than others, some have characteristics that make them more valuable (such as a good view) or less valuable (such as pollution), and some sites are more accessible, whereas others are more remote. These conditions in part determine the price that different properties can command (Vandell 1995).

Researchers of the early Chicago School were acute students of the housing market. They believed that the housing market played the key role in defining the status of different neighborhoods and in changing the big picture of neighborhood patterns over time. Homer Hoyt (1939), for example, mapped the location of high-rent districts in one hundred forty-two U.S. cities over a period of thirty-six years to see how they had changed. Hoyt found that the expensive residential neighborhoods tended to be newly constructed and tended to be located on the outskirts of the cities. He found that this expensive housing pulled fashion-conscious affluent households away from the older, more central neighborhoods. Hoyt's work concluded that, as part of the operation of the real estate market, high-status neighborhoods regularly change location and this change encourages the high-status population to move.

In addition to high-status neighborhoods, Hoyt examined poor and transitional neighborhoods. He found that some housing occupied by the poor had originally been built for the wealthy but had been converted to apartment or rooming houses as the wealthy moved on to more fashionable areas. Often single-family homes were passed down from wealthy households to middle-class households. The low-income neighborhoods, Hoyt found, had many nonresidential properties, high rates of vacancy, and wholesale property abandonment. Hoyt concluded that neighborhoods changed from high status to middle or lower status as the housing styles became outdated, new population groups moved into the neighborhood, or the proportion of rental properties increased (Hoyt 1939).

Institutional Actors

An alternative reading of why social classes live apart from each other relies less on the simple workings of a housing market and more on social practices and institutions that people have created to keep the classes apart. Remember that until about one hundred years ago, cities were much more varied than they are today, with more mixed land uses and populations. It was not until after the Civil War that land uses and social classes were sorted into different districts as we see today. At the same time that industrialists were constructing central business districts and manufacturing districts, the nation's new upper class was building fashionable neighborhoods such as Fifth Avenue in New York, and the upwardly mobile professional classes were constructing comfortable "streetcar suburbs," as Sam Bass Warner, Jr., (1962) called them.

During this period, property values emerged as a great concern. Social homogeneity—particularly the homogeneous single-family neighborhood—became a protection against encroaching land uses. By the 1920s most communities in the United States had adopted zoning plans to separate single-family homes from other land uses. Communities later expanded zoning regulations to differentiate one type of residential neighborhood from another. By laying out different zoning subsections, each mandating different lot sizes, square footage of houses, and other construction requirements, they were able to determine the income levels of the households that could buy the properties (Babcock 1966).

The institutions of planning and zoning boards have taken on even more power in suburban communities than in cities. Because suburban communities are politically autonomous, in many areas each town has the power to define its own guidelines for land use. Although this may be desirable from a local perspective, the overall results can be quite exclusionary for the metropolitan area as a whole. Some towns rule out apartment houses, mobile homes, and subsidized housing, thereby setting income limits for residents of the towns. Thus, the central city often remains the only community in the region with any sizeable stock of low-cost housing (Judd and Swanstrom 2008).

Another institutional mechanism that has maintained the separation of social class groups in cities is the formation of homeowners' associations. Logan and Molotch (2007) point out that residents of affluent areas are more likely to join community organizations, and their organizations are more likely to be effective, than residents of other areas. In surveying studies of neighborhood organizations, Logan and Molotch find that a primary purpose of such organizations is to defend their turf (2007). In Houston, a city that up to now has rejected zoning as a mechanism for regulating land use, neighborhood-based civic associations work to prevent commercial development in residential areas and to maintain racial and class homogeneity of the neighborhoods (Shelton et al. 1989).

In addition to defending turf, homeowners' associations can lobby to get their neighborhoods defined in favorable ways. Mike Davis (1990, 153) describes the near-religious fervor with which homeowners' associations in Los Angeles pursue special designation from the City Council. He says:

> *fact one:* Los Angeles Homeowners, like the Sicilians in *Prizzi's Honor*, love their children, but they love their property values more.
>
> *fact two:* "Community" in Los Angeles means homogeneity of race, class, and, especially, home values. Community designations—i.e., the street signs across the city identifying areas as "Canoga Park," "Holmby Hills," "Silverlake," and so on—have no legal status. In the last analysis, they are merely favors granted by city councilmembers to well-organized neighborhoods or businessmen's groups seeking to have their areas identified.
>
> *fact three:* The most powerful "social movement" in contemporary Southern California is that of affluent homeowners, organized by notional community designations or tract names, engaged in the defense of home values and neighborhood exclusivity.

These are not the only institutional actors that affect the neighborhood sorting that is so much a part of urban life. Other influential groups include realtors and lenders, whose impact we discussed in Chapter 9. But the existence of institutional mechanisms for sorting people and neighborhoods makes it apparent that social patterns in cities are not simply the result of the sum of individual households' housing choices in the housing market.

Labor Market

A final sorting mechanism that helps explain class segregation, and particularly the creation of the extreme poverty areas in recent years, is the labor market. Studying the labor market involves investigating what kinds of jobs are available for people and what kinds of skills and education people need to get jobs. The labor market in cities has changed dramatically and has influenced the types of class-based neighborhoods we see today.

As we saw in Chapters 4 and 5, global and national economic changes have resulted in deindustrialization and a downgrading of manufacturing jobs, a shift to service employment, and a polarization of the rich and poor. At the most fundamental level, two labor market trends have appeared in the central cities. The first is that economic opportunities have expanded more slowly than the workforce in the past twenty years, and the second is that the number of well-paying jobs has decreased while the number of low-paying, dead-end jobs has increased. These trends have resulted in increased competition for employment in which unskilled or uneducated workers are at a greater disadvantage than ever before—that is, the opportunity structure has closed for workers who rank low in education and skill levels (Wilson 2009b).

Why would large-scale economic changes produce localized poverty neighborhoods? One reason is that the residents of these districts represent large concentrations of people who, as a group, are on the lowest rung of the hiring ladder, the employers' last choice. Second, the impacts of economic change, such as plant closings and downsizing, have not been spread evenly but have been concentrated in specific geographic areas, particularly those areas with large proportions of residents of color. Third, when new jobs are created, they are being located disproportionately in suburban rather than urban areas. These changes have contributed to a spatial mismatch between the location of the jobs and the location of the workers who need them (Kain 2004; Wilson 2009). Overall, poverty is caused by a lack of economic opportunity, and the difference between a poverty area and a concentrated poverty area is partly a matter of the degree of economic distress. To use an old metaphor, when the nation's economy catches a cold, these neighborhoods' economies catch pneumonia.

From our consideration of several factors that affect the sorting process, it should be clear that in addition to simple market features (how much money a household makes and how much housing costs), other political, social, and economic factors influence how neighborhoods get to be defined as belonging to one social class or another.

THE CHANGING ECONOMY AND THE SHRINKING MIDDLE CLASS

Social class segregation in different urban neighborhoods is a long-standing feature of cities, but the picture has become more complicated in recent decades. In Chapter 5 we saw that the income distribution in U.S. cities has become polarized, with greater proportions of wealthy people and poor people living in cities. It is tempting to think that the middle class has simply moved to the suburbs, and indeed, that is part of the story. But economic changes have also contributed to the shrinking of the middle class. Some of these changes are changes in the cities' economies, and some are changes in the national economy. In fact, the middle class is shrinking in the country as a whole, but it is shrinking even more in the cities.

How do we know that the middle class is shrinking? The U. S. Bureau of the Census collects data on households' incomes, adds them to form aggregate income for all households, and compares the shares that different groups receive. The census breaks down the entire population into fifths (quintiles) and tracks

T A B L E   10.1   Growing Inequality in Incomes, 1970–2008

	Shares of the Total Income Received by Each Fifth			
Fifths of the Population	1970	1980	1990	2008
Top fifth	43.3	44.1	46.6	50.0
Second fifth	24.5	24.8	24.0	23.3
Third fifth	17.4	16.8	15.9	14.7
Fourth fifth	10.8	10.2	9.6	8.6
Bottom fifth	4.1	4.2	3.9	3.4

SOURCE: DeNavas-Walt, Carmen, Bernadette Proctor, and Jessica Smith. 2009. *Income, Poverty, and Health Insurance Coverage in the United States, 2008*. U. S. Census Bureau Current Population Reports P60-236. Washington, DC: U. S. Government Printing Office.

what percent of total income each one-fifth receives annually. As we can see in Table 10.1, between 1970 and 2008, the top quintile of the population increased its share of all income from 43.3 percent to 50.0 percent. All of the other groups experienced declines in their share of the national earnings, with the third and fourth quintiles experiencing the largest declines. Thus, income was, in effect, transferred from the groups at the bottom and especially the middle of the income distribution to the top group.

What does this mean for the middle class? As the top income group pulled ahead in the distribution of income, the other groups earned less. For more than three decades, the middle class has seen its income stagnate or even decline relative to the cost of living. A small proportion of the middle class has been upwardly mobile into the "fortunate fifth," but a larger proportion of the middle class has become downwardly mobile (Mishel et al. 2008). Income inequality increased both during periods of rapid economic growth (the 1980s and 1990s) and during periods of slow growth (since 2005).

A good deal of the change in income distribution has been due to an increasing wage gap between the "good" jobs and the "bad" jobs. While wages and salaries for the average person have stagnated and declined since the mid-1970s, the salaries for the highest paid workers have increased rapidly. Compensation to corporate leaders provides a dramatic example. In 1973 the average corporate chief executive officer earned $27 for every $1 that the average worker earned. But by 2007 the average CEO earned $275 for every dollar the average worker earned (Mishel et al. 2008, Fig. 3AE).

Why have these changes in the class structure occurred? First, because of basic economic changes: slow growth in wages overall, the decline of manufacturing jobs, the growth of services, and the increased differentiation between high- and low-paying jobs within both the manufacturing and the service sector. Second, a noneconomic reason for increasing inequality is the growing number of single-parent families. Two-earner households have gained a significant advantage over single-earner households, and single heads of households are at a particular disadvantage in competition for income (McLanahan and Percheski 2008).

As we saw in Chapter 5, cities are not completely devoid of a middle class. Yes, poverty is growing in cities, as is wealth; but the middle class, although shrinking as a proportion of the population, is still very much in evidence in cities. Although income polarization is increased, the class structure of cities is still a complex mosaic of different groups. In the next section, we will turn to some consequences of the changing class structure of the cities. We will examine the changes in housing conditions that have occurred as a result of the changing urban social class structure.

HOUSING PATTERNS

Housing is the most visible sign of the social class structure of a city. From mansion to brownstone to bungalow to tenement, the type of structure and its location within the city speak volumes about the resources of the inhabitants. As the social class composition and the economies of cities have changed in recent years, some changes in traditional housing patterns have appeared. In this section, we will explore several housing trends that are consequences of growing social inequality in cities.

Affluent Enclaves

The affluent population is growing as a proportion of central city residents; but even though they are living in the central cities, are the affluent participating in the city's life and institutions? We saw that the very wealthy elite have often created their enclaves, such as Beacon Hill in Boston. Now, the professional upper middle class may be following in their footsteps.

Take a neighborhood such as New York's East Side, home to large numbers of highly paid professionals. Such neighborhoods have become cities within the city, supporting private schools, private police forces, special sanitation districts, and other localized services. In one twenty-block area of the East Side in a single year, the residents assessed themselves $4.7 million for special services to their neighborhood alone. They spent over $1 million just on a private police force for the district (Reich 1991). Instead of their tax money going into the city coffers where it would be used for the entire city, they chose to maintain the funds for their exclusive benefit.

In addition, many affluent families have literally withdrawn behind walls. Particularly in the South and West, but also in other areas of the United States, many new upscale housing developments are being walled off from the surrounding community. It has been estimated that one-third of all new housing developments in California are such gated communities. (Figure 10.2 shows a gated community in San Francisco.) Originally designed to calm people's fear of crime, in many areas these homes have become status symbols. Some part of the attraction is also that the walls may increase property values; for this reason, some existing developments have added walls and gates in the hopes that they

David Butow/Corbis News/CORBIS SABA/Corbis

F I G U R E 10.2 **Withdrawal of the Wealthy: A gated community in San Francisco.**

will add to the value of the existing homes. Gating can be interpreted as a search for community (Low 2003), but it can also stem from a fear of social heterogeneity—i.e., exposure to differences (Vesselinov 2008).

How far can the withdrawal of the affluent and the privatization of space go? Some communities are virtually off limits to the public. For example, the resort community of Hilton Head, South Carolina, contains only ninety-three public streets of its total of more than one thousand streets (Dillon 1994). In contrast, when residents of a Los Angeles neighborhood erected gates on a city street, they were successfully sued on the grounds that the streets should be maintained as public spaces. If income polarization continues, we will likely see even greater use of spatial, financial, and symbolic barriers between the affluent and the rest of the population.

Displacement

Displacement is the process of people losing their homes against their will (Hartman, Keating, and LeGates 1982). It may be caused by a number of different factors: government action, actions of property owners, economic forces, accidents, and other reasons. As the urban economy has changed, changes in both the housing market and in government policies have resulted in people with fewer resources being displaced from their homes and neighborhoods.

We saw in Chapter 5 that certain neighborhoods in the central cities have become gentrified as well-paid professionals find jobs nearby. Gentrification can lead to displacement as wealthier buyers move in and bid up neighborhood properties. Over a surprisingly short period of time, a neighborhood can become a trendy or "hot" real estate market, with prices increasing rapidly. This situation might have some positive consequences for people who already own property (especially if they are interested in selling and moving elsewhere), but it can also have negative consequences. One is that, as property values increase, taxes frequently increase as well, putting a burden on those homeowners (for example, retired persons) whose income has not risen at the same pace as their property assessment. Second, as the overall price structure of the neighborhood changes, the type of people who live there changes. When working-class neighborhoods become gentrified, the children of the people who previously lived there can no longer afford the housing. In this way, the dynamics of the housing market cause the displacement not just of individual households but of a whole class or ethnic group (LeGates and Hartman 1986).

Renters are especially vulnerable to displacement. Investors frequently buy rental properties in gentrifying neighborhoods to renovate the units or to convert them to condominiums. They may evict all of the tenants during the rehabilitation process, at most with the understanding that if they can afford the new rent, they are welcome to apply to move back into their old building! Alternatively, in cities without rent control laws, new owners can simply raise the rents above the ability of the current tenants to pay, resulting in instant displacement.

Displacement also occurs through the processes of speculation. The changing urban economy and the process of neighborhood change have made it possible for some investors to buy rundown properties, hold onto them, and resell them for a good profit when the neighborhood begins to "heat up." Speculation can result in displacement when the owners think they will make less profit by running the building as an ongoing business than by selling it to be demolished or rehabilitated by a future owner. In such cases owners may neglect maintenance to the point at which tenants feel forced to leave. Some older neighborhoods with low property values but good locations become more valuable after they have been essentially abandoned because the land is worth more than the actual building. The changing urban economy makes low-income neighborhoods near the central business district ripe for speculation (Smith 1979).

Government redevelopment programs in response to deindustrialization have also displaced some vulnerable communities. Local governments can use the power of **eminent domain**, a legal process that permits the government to buy private property for the common good. Local authorities are required to pay for the properties they take, at the fair market value. This seemingly fair process results in much hardship, however, for low-income homeowners who receive too little to allow them to purchase a replacement home in another neighborhood, or for renters who are evicted and forced to move to more expensive housing (Kleniewski 1981). A public controversy arose in Detroit when a city agency seized land that was occupied by some fifteen hundred households to sell it to General Motors Corporation as part of a site for a new plant—a site that opponents of the land seizure argued could have been made smaller and still have accommodated the planned buildings (Fasenfest 1986). As in the case of the displacements from urban renewal, the households displaced in Detroit were mainly lower-income families that had too little political influence to prevent their properties from being seized.

Displacement is not an entirely new phenomenon. But with large-scale changes in the cities, including both deindustrialization and the growth of the service sector, the uses of property and the values of different areas have changed rapidly. A common pattern has appeared: The changing property market, perhaps in combination with government programs to redevelop land or retain businesses, has resulted in housing displacement. The most likely households to be displaced have been the most economically vulnerable: low-income households, members of ethnic minorities, renters, and elderly homeowners on fixed incomes.

The Homeless

It is an undeniable fact that the number of homeless people in our cities has increased dramatically since the 1970s. But analysts disagree over how much the economy has contributed to homelessness and how much other factors have contributed. We will start with the proposition that homeless people are virtually all low income and then proceed to examine changes in the housing market and government policy that have contributed to the growth of the homeless population.

Elliot Liebow (1993, 224) studied homeless people in Washington, D.C. He states, "Homelessness is rooted hard and deep in poverty. Homeless people are poor people, and they come, overwhelmingly, from poor families." Joel Blau (1992) calls the homeless "the visible poor." Homeless people are a heterogeneous group, encompassing old and young, men and women, whites and racial minorities, people with and without psychological problems or addictions, and many other different characteristics. Despite their differences, however, homeless people share (in addition to their lack of housing) one overriding trait: they are all low income.

We saw that incomes for most of the population have been stagnating and that the number of poor people has been increasing. Although people's real incomes have decreased since 1975, housing prices have increased. Because of this squeeze between rising housing costs and stagnant earnings, many people experience **shelter poverty**—that is, they are forced to pay so much for housing that not enough is left to meet their other needs. Although households in every income group have been forced to pay more for housing, households at the bottom of the economic barrel are faced with the grisly choice of paying for either housing or other necessities such as food and medical care. During the 1980s, we began to see what we now recognize as **incipient homelessness**—the existence of a sizeable group of people on the verge of homelessness if either their incomes or their living situations change. Given the fact that 40 percent of all tenants and 20 percent of all homeowners experience shelter poverty, what is surprising is not that the amount of homelessness has increased, but that it is not even greater (Stone 1993).

Government policies have also contributed both directly and indirectly to homelessness. Beginning in the 1970s, the amount of public housing that the government constructed was drastically reduced and replaced by a rent subsidy system (called housing vouchers). Although this new system gives low-income households increased choices, enabling them to live in private housing rather than in public projects, the low funding level permits only a small fraction of the eligible households to participate in the program. This policy change has made it more difficult for the poorest households to obtain housing (Dolbeare 1986).

Cutbacks in government health and human service programs have also contributed to homelessness, particularly as they relate to the care of the mentally ill. Beginning in the 1960s, states began closing or downsizing residential psychiatric hospitals in favor of short-term treatment and community-based care. The policy of deinstitutionalization was considered a more humane way of treating clients, but it was frequently adopted as a way for states to save money. Expensive long-term stays in the state hospital were replaced by short-term stays combined with the administration of psychoactive drugs for outpatients. The system of independent living may have worked for many patients, but some have fallen through the cracks. Studies of the homeless have found that between 20 and 25 percent of homeless people suffer from mental illness (Koegel 1996). Little evidence shows that closing the state hospitals led directly to an increase in the homeless population; but in the current system, mentally disabled people may not receive the care they need and may end up homeless as a result of their inability to cope with life. In many cities homeless people drift into what Dear and Wolch (1987) call "service-dependent ghettos."

Besides the housing market, the changing economy, and government policies, individual problems such as chronic illness, domestic abuse, and alcohol or drug dependency contribute to homelessness. People with severe individual problems —even if put in housing—may revert to being homeless if their fundamental personal problems are not addressed. An understanding of both the macrostructural causes of homeless and the individual contributions can help analysts and policy makers develop more complete approaches to homelessness.

One of the more thoughtful studies that has carefully traced the interplay between the macrostructural context and the individual's behavior is Snow and Anderson's (1993, 268) *Down on Their Luck*. They begin with the structural factors that caused homelessness to grow, noting the "increasing gap between the costs of subsistence needs, particularly housing, and the availability of economic resources to meet those needs." They note, however, that not everyone affected by those trends becomes homeless. Snow and Anderson find that three biographical factors are related to many cases of homelessness: the absence of family ties, the presence of individual disabilities such as mental illness or alcoholism, and unpredictable instances of bad luck. Furthermore, the risk factors are cumulative; often, one event touches off another, resulting in a kind of downward spiral culminating in homelessness.

Awareness of both structural factors and individual responses can inform the wide variety of policy initiatives that must be taken to deal with homelessness. Public officials and social service providers need to pursue three types of strategies to deal effectively with homelessness: helping people who are already homeless to regain housing, preventing people who are on the verge of homelessness from becoming homeless, and reducing homelessness in the future. Families and individuals who are *already homeless* need shelter and food to be sure, but they also need access to services that will help them make the transition to independent housing. Such services include education, job placement, psychological counseling, medical and dental care, substance abuse treatment, and financial planning. People who are *on the verge of homelessness* can often be kept in housing through measures such as eviction intervention and emergency housing loans. Such individual measures can help forestall or correct individuals' bouts of homelessness, but they cannot address the big picture of reducing homelessness overall. To *reduce homelessness in the future* will require public policies such as increasing affordable housing, increasing jobs and wages, and providing public services (such as health care and child care) for low-income families. Because poverty and inequality are at the root of the homeless problem, only a concerted effort to address the economic conditions that create poverty will have any chance of solving the problem.

What can we conclude? The structural factors of employment opportunities, income, housing costs, and government policies have provided the overall conditions leading to the recent increase in homelessness. Some proportion of low-income individuals with particular problems, disabilities, and family structures are more likely to be affected by these structural upheavals in ways that will result in their becoming homeless, at least for a short time. An even smaller subgroup will become chronically homeless. To explain the increase in homelessness overall, we should concentrate on the big picture of social inequality, rather than the individual experiences.

CONCLUSION

From the earliest studies of cities up to the present, we see social class patterns carved into the social geography of the city. Neighborhood differences can include not just differences in the income of households and in the amenities available, but also different ways of life in the community. Patterns of social class sorting and change are the result of both individual choices and the actions of organized institutions such as zoning boards and neighborhood associations. The distribution of the social classes throughout the city and the metropolitan area is not random or natural; it is created and maintained by economic and political actors making decisions.

In recent decades, the polarization of incomes has led to an increase in the number of wealthy and poor households and a decrease in middle-class ones. This trend is somewhat more pronounced in central cities than in the nation as a whole. In addition, urban social class groups have become more segregated and isolated from each other, a pattern that is reinforced and exacerbated by the effects of racial segregation and isolation.

Housing trends are visible manifestations of our growing social class inequality. In recent years we have seen the withdrawal of the affluent from public space, the vulnerability of low- and middle-income groups to housing displacement, and the growth of a homeless population. Both economic changes and public policy decisions have contributed to the changes in housing and social class structure.

DISCUSSION QUESTIONS

1. Read Box 10.2 about how Beacon Hill was created and renewed as an upper-class neighborhood. What evidence could you draw from this description that Beacon Hill's history has been affected by the operation of the housing market? What evidence could you find that institutional actors have affected the fate of the Hill?

2. Draw a rough map of your hometown from memory, noting major geographic features such as rivers, hills, and commercial centers. Then sketch in the residential neighborhoods, naming them if they have names. Where do the wealthy live? The poor? Different ethnic groups? Compare your map with that of a hometown friend or family member. Are your perceptions of your community's class structure similar or different?

3. Read the classified advertisements for housing in a daily newspaper. What clues do the ads give about the social class composition of the neighborhoods in which different houses or apartments are located? Make a list of the descriptive terms that are used as social class cues.

11

Women in Cities

> Never before in civilization have such numbers of young girls
> been suddenly released from the protection of the home and
> permitted to walk unattended upon city streets and to work
> under alien roofs; for the first time they are being prized more
> for their labor power than for their innocence, their tender
> beauty, their ephemeral gaiety.
>
> JANE ADDAMS
> "THE SPIRIT OF YOUTH AND THE CITY STREETS"

In our everyday observations of life in the city, when we see women and men
we may see them as individuals rather than as two distinct groups of people.
Yet researchers find pervasive differences between women and men in cities,
from the proportions of each group that live in cities to the locations and conditions under which they live and work. Sociologists have only recently begun
to establish how gender (or the social differentiation of men and women) is fundamental to many social institutions and processes (Acker 1992). In this chapter
we will examine the ways in which gender helps structure people's experiences
in urban and metropolitan areas.

We will explore the following questions:

- How do women and men experience the city differently? How do their
  spatial locations differ? Their activities? Their preferences and needs for
  facilities and space?

- How do different groups of women experience the city differently? What
  differences exist among women from different ethnic or racial groups? From
  different social classes?

- How can cities serve women better? How can the physical design of cities,
  neighborhoods, and buildings accommodate women's activities? What services and facilities can better accommodate the variety of women and families in contemporary metropolitan areas?

WOMEN'S SPACES, MEN'S SPACES

All societies differentiate their members according to gender (masculine or feminine) in some way. Usually this differentiation takes the form of defining the appropriate roles for women and men, including appearance, behaviors, and obligations. Sometimes men and women are spatially separated from each other, although the degree to which this is done and the occasions for separation vary from one society to another.

In present-day United States and other modern industrial societies, the distinction between *masculine* and *feminine* space overlaps with distinctions between *work* and *home* and between *public* and *private life*. Prior to industrialization, few spaces were designated exclusively as places for work because work and life were so closely intertwined. With industrialization came a distinction between paid and unpaid work as well as the development of new spaces specifically created as workplaces. As work moved into workplaces, home took on a new meaning as "not a workplace" (Oakley 1974). A second change with industrialization was the distinction between men's and women's jobs. Early textile workers included men, women, and children, but because women workers tended to be clustered in specific jobs within factories or even in completely separate industries, the genders were frequently spatially separated from each other at work (Kessler-Harris 1982) (see Figure 11.1).

Women's roles changed rapidly with industrialization. From 1800 to about 1850, large numbers of unmarried women entered the manufacturing workforce; and after 1850 many married women joined them. But between 1850 and 1900, even though large numbers of women were working outside of the home, a new definition of women's roles gradually emerged, raising the care of the home, children, and husband to women's highest priority (Kessler-Harris 1982). Instead of a routine necessity, paid work became a "misfortune and disgrace" for married women (Oakley 1974, 50), and women were pushed out of the paid workforce. A married woman was supposed to be a housewife, and the home was her place. Home was redefined in juxtaposition to work, as the realm of private life, a refuge or haven from the public issues and the economic demands of the outside world, and the place reserved for the family (Kessler-Harris 1976).

As domesticity became the primary role for women in the United States, people built living spaces that separated women and men. In the colonial era, houses typically consisted of one large all-purpose room and one or two small bedrooms, all shared by the household. In the nineteenth century, however, middle-class households built larger houses and divided them into more rooms. In these larger houses, both sexes used the dining room, but the kitchen and parlor were the women's spaces and the library was the men's space. Among members of higher social classes with even larger houses, the floor plans were still more elaborate and more highly sex segregated. Some Southern plantation mansions, for example, included separate wings and separate staircases for the male and female members of the household. The practice of

238   PART III CHANGE AND CONFLICT

American Textile History Museum, Lowell, MA

F I G U R E 11.1 Woman Factory Worker, c. 1910. Many factories in the nineteenth and early twentieth centuries hired women and teenage girls. Here, a young woman tends a spinning machine in a textile factory.

separating men's and women's spaces in middle-class houses reached its apex in the late nineteenth-century Victorian homes (see Figure 11.2); after that, the use of a single living room began to replace the separate parlor and library (Spain 1992).

Throughout the nineteenth century and into the early twentieth century, industrialization brought with it a number of changes in the roles and the spatial locations thought to be appropriate for women in our society. Even as our cities were growing, women were struggling over where they belonged in them. Women's reactions to industrialization and to the definition of their place as "in the home" varied, and not all women were ready to accept the newly constructed notion that men and women belonged in separate spheres of activity.

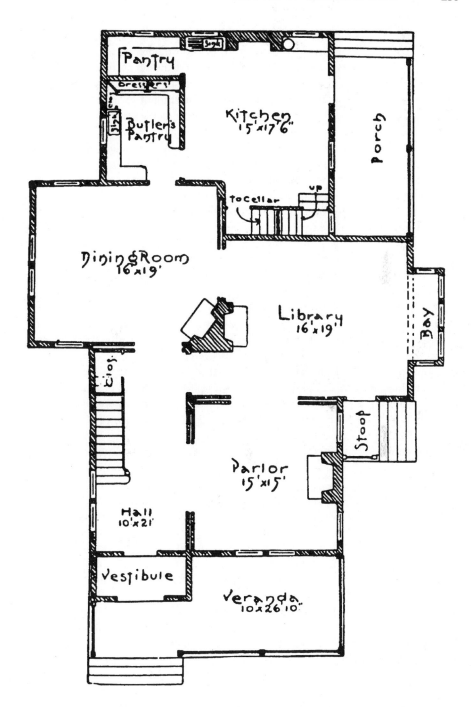

FIGURE 11.2 The Parlor and the Library. Victorian homes typically had separate rooms for men's and women's activities.

The first widespread feminist movement of modern times emerged at the end of the nineteenth century, in reaction to the constraints women were facing. The movement's leaders were women who resisted the social roles assigned to them and proposed ways of restructuring the society to promote greater equality between women and men. Some early feminists attempted to improve the lives of women in the paid labor force, advocating for higher wages, better working conditions, and better treatment of women workers. Jane Addams, social worker, organizer, and founder of the Chicago settlement house called Hull House, championed women workers. She encouraged women's trade union groups to organize at Hull House and helped women form cooperative housing groups to free them from paying board to private landlords (Wilson 1992).

Some women went beyond trying to make work life compatible with women's needs. They challenged the organization of the home itself. From the 1870s to about 1930, groups of women organized to create a "grand domestic revolution" that would end the society's reliance on women's unpaid work. Historian Dolores Hayden (1981) calls these women **material feminists** because their focus was on women's material—or economic—contributions and rewards. They were critical of the isolation and drudgery as well as the lack of recognition accorded to domestic work; thus, their reforms and proposals shared the underlying principles of reducing women's isolation and increasing their rewards for domestic tasks. The material feminists created collective organizations for housework and child care, in which they cleaned each others' houses and watched each others' children in groups. They designed houses without kitchens, clustering several homes around a collective kitchen in which all of the adjoining households participated, dining together and sharing cooking and cleanup duties.

Contemporary feminists have continued to challenge the perpetuation of the notion of the separate spheres for men and women and to promote women's full inclusion in the society. In the last generation, the proportion of *married* women working outside the home doubled, from 30 percent in 1960 to just under 60 percent in 2007 (U.S. Bureau of Labor Statistics 2008). Although women may have gained access to the workplace, few have found their way into top management. Employers still provide minimal support for employees who take their roles as parents seriously. In addition, although more married women work outside the home, their responsibilities inside the home have not diminished proportionally.

The current challenge to the separate spheres involves redefining some of our most basic concepts. Geographer Doreen Massey (1994) argues against dichotomous thinking that implies not only difference but also opposition. Massey and others argue that, in rethinking the dualities of not only the terms masculine/feminine but also public/private, work/leisure, rational/emotional, and so on, people can get beyond constricting social definitions and create new futures. In other words our greatest current challenge is to move beyond categorizing people by gender to recognizing and fulfilling individuals' needs—as *they* define them.

GENDER, ETHNICITY, AND SOCIAL
CLASS IN THE CITY

This chapter is about women and the city, but all women do not have the same experiences of urban life. Instead, their experiences are influenced by other aspects of their lives, such as social class, race, and ethnicity. Recent community research provides insights into how people of different groups experience and use the city differently—men and women within different class, ethnic, and racial communities. We will examine gender and ethnicity, by looking at Hispanic women's political activity; gender and social class, by looking at poverty among women; and gender, class, and race, by examining poor single mothers, both African American and white.

Ethnicity has long been recognized as a factor in people's political activity, but recent studies have shown that political activity varies between men and women within ethnic groups. As a group, people with Latino (Spanish-speaking) heritage have low rates of political activity, such as voting and holding office. When researcher Carol Hardy-Fanta (1993) studied the political activities of the Latino (primarily Puerto Rican, Dominican, and Central American) population in Boston, she found that people's political activity varied by gender and that even the meaning of the term *political activity* differs greatly between Latino men and Latina women in that community. To the men, politics centers on running for office or supporting candidates. To the women, it involves organizing other people to address issues of common concern. The women's broader definition of political action includes but is not limited to electoral politics, encompassing such issues as health care, immigration policy, and housing.

Hardy-Fanta pointed out that these Latina women contributed to their communities through the organizing they did among family, neighbors, and coworkers on a broad range of issues. She found, however, that they rarely participated in the broader (Anglo) women's movement, even though many of the issues they addressed were similar. Their reluctance to participate stemmed from two causes. Compared to the Anglo women, the Latina women were more concerned with social justice issues, such as jobs, and less interested in individual rights issues, such as sexuality. Also the Latina women were more likely to want to work with men for the overall good of the entire community (Hardy-Fanta 1993). Thus we see that being a woman *in the context of a particular ethnic community* can affect people's political activity and interests. The political worldview and style of participation differs between Latino men and Latina women, but it also differs between Latina women and Anglo women.

Social class is another important influence on women's lives in urban communities. We saw in the previous chapter that social class affects where and how people in general live in urban and metropolitan areas. What happens when we add gender to the equation? As one instance, we can focus on poor women, because we have a wealth of research on their lives.

Since the late 1970s, researchers have noticed a trend toward a growing proportion of women—especially mothers—among people with low incomes. They call this trend "the feminization of poverty" (Pearce 1978). The most recent census statistics reveal that the poverty rate, or percent of the population with incomes below the poverty level, for all families is 13.2 percent. It is higher for families headed by a single parent, with a dramatic difference between single-parent families headed by a single father and those headed by a single mother. In father-only families, the poverty rate is 13.8 percent, and in mother-only families, it is 28.7 percent (DeNavas-Walt, et al., 2009, Table 4).

Low-income women who head households have tough lives in urban areas. They face bleak job prospects at minimum wage or slightly better and must subtract the cost of child care from their wages. As an alternative—or a supplement—to low-paying jobs, they may receive public assistance, but even combining work and welfare payments usually keeps their incomes below the poverty level (Edin and Lein 1997).

Part of the reason for the feminization of poverty is the increased rate of family breakup and childbearing outside of marriage since about 1970. More than one quarter of the country's children now live in households headed by a single parent (Kreider 2007). But poverty is much more likely to be part of a single mother's experience than a single father's experience for three reasons. First, women have less access to high-paying jobs than men have; second, women are more likely to need to rely on welfare benefits than men are; and third, divorced or separated women are more likely to be awarded—but not receive—child support payments from their ex-spouses (Ellwood 1988). Thus, poverty is a more prominent experience for women than for men, and it is particularly a problem for women with children.

Studies of the lives of low-income urban women have raised several questions. How do women heads of households cope with poverty, and do the communities in which they live affect the coping strategies they choose? Also, do women of different racial or ethnic groups choose different strategies for coping with their less-than-adequate incomes?

First, a number of studies find that community membership can have consequences, both positive and negative, for low-income mothers. Carol Stack (1974) has described how low-income African-American mothers in a Midwestern city cope with poverty by using their family networks for assistance. In this particular community, women form close ties with their female relatives—mothers, sisters, and cousins—as well as with close female friends. Within these networks members freely give and receive assistance in the form of money, goods (clothing, household items), and services (cooking, babysitting). Because the community has developed norms of reciprocity or mutual obligation, members are bound to help each other, and people feel free to call on their kin for both routine and emergency help.

Stack points out that this type of women's community network is a positive adaptation to poverty because it spreads resources throughout the entire network. Everything is available to be shared—not only food, clothing, and furniture but also money, a place to sleep, and even children. Under the philosophy of "what goes round comes round," women give to others in need, knowing that they can count on others to help them later. This community sharing, however, negatively impacts the women's individual potential for upward mobility. The network's reciprocal obligations mean that every time a member of the network gets ahead financially, she has a moral obligation to help her kin. Her resources belong not to her as an individual but to the network as a whole. Because in such a poor community the need for help is virtually unlimited, it becomes difficult if not impossible for a woman to save enough money to work her way out of poverty (Stack 1974).

The kinship network also has a dampening effect on marriage in this community. Women in the kinship network frequently discourage each other from getting married because they fear that their married relatives will have less loyalty to the kin network than to their husbands. Similarly, when women consider getting married, they must balance the possibility of losing the help and support of kin against the gains they might make by having a husband. Husbands might not stay around long; and even if they do, they might not be good providers, given the scarcity of good jobs in the surrounding community. Within this setting, many women feel more economically secure relying on their female kin network than going it alone as an individual or a nuclear family (Stack 1974).

The second finding of this research is that the coping strategy of woman-based networks is not unique to African-American communities. Early research, such as Stack's, uncovered the phenomenon among African Americans, but subsequent research has shown that low-income women of other ethnic and racial groups practice it as well. Ida Susser (1982) described the complex sharing and household network in a low-income Brooklyn neighborhood. The core of the network consisted of three sisters and their daughters whose household arrangements were so fluid that at times it was difficult to tell who was living where. Within a multiethnic and multiracial neighborhood, this predominantly white Anglo family relied not only on each other but also on their white, Puerto Rican, and African-American neighbors to share food, sleeping space, and other necessities. Public assistance (welfare) and other forms of government aid (such as free food) intermittently supplemented their unstable jobs and incomes. The similarities between this network of white women and the African-American one Stack found show that poverty, not race or ethnicity, was the key factor motivating the women's strategies for economic survival.

In a study of an unnamed Midwestern city, Harvey (1993) identified three types of family structure that typically exist in poor communities: family networks centered around a man, family networks centered around a woman, and family networks centered around groups of sisters. In the community Harvey studied, he found that the availability of employment for men was the key to whether the men would or would not be a central part of the household. Harvey argued that proportionally more families organize themselves around women in poor communities than in middle-class communities because the lack of work in poor communities makes it difficult for men to contribute to the household. In communities where there are stable jobs for men—jobs that permit them to develop some financial standing—there are more families that include men and fewer that are organized around women. This research shows that the argument that Wilson and Neckerman (1986) made for African Americans applies also to a poor white community. Both researchers found that mother-only families are a response to poverty and to a shortage of "marriageable" men—that is, men capable of earning enough to contribute to a family's support.

In virtually every community, public housing projects are highly feminized neighborhoods: more than three-quarters of the families living in U.S. public housing units are mother-headed (Spain 1993), and virtually all have incomes below the poverty line. With the continued polarization of the rich and poor in the economy, we can expect that the demand for low-cost, subsidized housing for women and their children will continue to grow rapidly. Unfortunately, public policy since the 1970s has been to dismantle the public housing sector—despite the high level of need—based in part on the argument that public housing is an unfit environment for families. Field studies, such as those Feldman and Stall conducted in Chicago (2004), provide contrary evidence that shows that the creation of deep family and community bonds that women in public housing projects made and maintained helps ameliorate some of the worst aspects of poverty.

To summarize, not only gender but also social class and racial or ethnic group membership shape women's lives and experiences. Poverty is becoming an increasing problem for women in general but is even more acute for women living in areas of concentrated poverty—areas that happen to be located largely in inner-city neighborhoods. Women living in poor neighborhoods often cope with poverty by using their family networks. These coping strategies can help the group deal with and survive poverty, but they are not very useful for people trying to escape poverty. The importance of the community context is that the economic resources in the community, particularly the presence or absence of good jobs, provides the underpinnings for family and neighborhood stability.

GENDERED URBAN SPACES

What do we mean by *gendered institutions?* According to Acker (1992, 567), this phrase means that "gender is present in the processes, practices, images and ide-ologies, and distributions of power in the various sectors of social life." Gender is in our institutions not because men and women are necessarily so different from each other but because our society has built its institutions on the assumption that women and men are very different. We have already seen how the separate spheres of the masculine realm of work and the feminine realm of the home were created during the process of industrialization. Today, the trend toward gender segregation may not be increasing, but neither is it rapidly receding. Gen-dered spaces are still very much a feature of our society. In this section, we will review some ways in which gender currently shapes people's use of urban spaces.

Contemporary Workplaces

Women continue to be segregated from men at work, largely because they tend to work at specific jobs. Even though a significant proportion of women have entered a few formerly "male" jobs, such as attorney and bus driver, few men have entered the three largest "female" jobs: secretary, teacher, and nurse. The job at which the largest number of women work is secretary, and 98 percent of secretaries are female (Spain 1992). Spatial segregation often accompanies gender segregation in secretarial jobs. Secretaries, for example, do not typically share the offices with the executives or managers whom they serve, but are normally located in group offices, cubicles, or a public area outside of the boss's closed office. We see similar usage of space in other traditionally women's jobs: people holding these jobs are less likely than workers in traditionally male positions to have an enclosed space of their own and more likely to have to share space or be on public view (Spain 1992; Weisman 1992).

Besides being differentiated and segregated, women workers have less power to design and manage their workspaces. Clerical workers and nurses, in particular, have little space of their own. Typically working in open, shared, areas, they have only partial walls (if any) for privacy, visual screening, and sound control. They frequently have no access to light switches, windows, or air conditioning controls. The spaces in which they work are not only separate from men's but often smaller, of lesser quality, and less flexible for their individual needs (Feldman 1995).

Job segregation by gender also has impacted women's incomes, because job segregation allows employers to pay women lower wages than men. Employers routinely classify jobs as women's jobs or men's jobs based on stereotyped assumptions rather than on the actual skills and abilities needed to perform the work, and they consistently undervalue the women's jobs relative to the skill level necessary to perform the task. The ideology that women "don't need to work" supports employers paying them less than men are paid. Surveys show that even educated segments of the population such as women college students tend to think that a job done primarily by men *should* command a higher salary than a job done primarily by women (Reskin and Padovic 1994). Even in the same occupation, women and men are often segregated, making it easier to pay them differentially. Spain (1992) exemplifes this, showing that waiters earn more than waitresses, primarily because male waiters are employed in the more expensive restaurants. In sales, men are far more likely to sell high-priced items on commission, and women are more likely to be paid a flat rate, often the minimum wage. For an extreme example of a gender-segregated occupation, see Box 11.1 on women sex workers in third world cities.

The contemporary workplace, although not excluding women, still categorizes, differentiates, and spatially segregates people on the basis of the job they do, which more often than not, aligns closely with their gender. As a result, most workplaces still consist of gendered spaces.

Transportation

Women and men have different patterns of mobility and transportation in urban areas. Many studies within North America have established the fact that men travel substantially farther to work than do women. The reasons for this are related to the different work and family responsibilities of women and men as well

---

B o x 11.1 • Spotlight
Sex and the City: The Global Sex Industry

Exploitation of migrant labor, lacking legal status and language skills, is easy and widespread. This is particularly so for women, who constitute the majority of migrant labor from Asia today. In Thailand, female emigration took off in the 1980s as the East Asian boom consolidated, disrupting cultural traditions and family livelihoods. It drew on the young women fleeing into Bangkok from the Thai countryside, looking for income to remit to their villages. Many of these women would end up in Europe, Southeast Asia, the United States, Australia, South Africa, or the Arabian Gulf, in the burgeoning sex industry by deceit or by choice (being a relatively high-income trade open to uneducated women). Evidence suggests that sex tourism to Thailand contributed to the demand for Thai women overseas, and trafficking in women is more profitable than either illegal gambling or drugs and arms trafficking. By 1993 there were almost 100,000 Thai women working in the Japanese sex industry, and 5,000 in Berlin alone. Research in Northern Thailand has shown that about 28 percent of household income was remitted by absent daughters. A common motive is relieving poverty and debt (especially in the wake of the Asian financial crisis), and often parents sell their daughters to agents for a cash advance to be paid off by work in the global sex industry. Alternatively, individual women pay an agent's fee of around $500. From then on, women are devoid of human rights: they work as bonded labor, are subject to arrest for illicit work and illegal residence, have no rights to medical or social services overseas, are forced to sell sex with no power to choose their customers or service, remain at high risk of contracting HIV, and are targets of racial discrimination and public humiliation if arrested. Action against trafficking is difficult because of the collusion between families who benefit materially from absent daughters and agents of the trade; because of the underground lifestyle of the women, trapped by underground employers; and because of governments interested in suppressing information about the sex trade to avoid adverse publicity.

SOURCE: Philip McMichael, *Development and Social Change*, 2nd edition (Thousand Oaks, CA: Pine Forge Press, 2000), pp. 204–205.

---

as to the different types of jobs they are likely to take. It is more common for women than for men to combine their commute to work with other errands, such as taking children to school or day care, doing the grocery shopping, or picking up the dry cleaning. Several studies have found that significant numbers of women workers restrict their employment options to those that are located near the home to facilitate making family-related detours on their way to and from work. In many metropolitan areas it is easy for women to find work near their homes because "women's" jobs such as clerical and service work are more widely distributed throughout metropolitan areas than are executive or manufacturing jobs. Also, because women-dominated jobs tend to pay relatively poorly, women workers often shorten their journey to work to minimize transportation costs. Studies of the journey to work show that the commutes of African-American women are, on the average, longer than those of white women and close in length to men's commutes. Whether this finding is due to African-American women's residential location, work location, or some combination of the two is unclear (Hanson et al. 1994; Johnston-Anumonwo, McLafferty, and Preston 1995).

The gender gap in commuting distances is related to another gendered difference in transportation: access to different modes of transportation. Research on transportation in several industrialized societies shows that women are less likely than men to have access to an automobile, although the differences are much greater in Britain than in the United States or Canada. As a result, women use public transportation more frequently than men. Transit-use studies for different cities show that two to three times as many women workers as men workers commute by public transit, a great resource for people employed in central business districts. Because transit lines are commonly laid out to carry commuters from the outskirts to the center, however, it can be difficult for women who live in one suburb but are employed in another to get to work by public transportation (Pickup 1988).

Examining transportation patterns by gender shows that women are more restricted than men in where they go and how they get there. This transportation gender gap is related to other gendered institutions such as work opportunities, incomes, and family responsibilities.

Community Organizations

Women often play a significant public role within their neighborhoods. A disproportionate number of women have traditionally served as activists and even as leaders within community organizations. One of the reasons that women form or join community organizations is that their lives and activities are strongly rooted in the community; as we saw above, if they work in a paid job, it tends to be located close to home. If women do not work outside of the home, their activities may bring them into contact with each other at playgrounds, laundromats, and so on, enabling them to talk over issues of concern. Also, to the extent that women have primary responsibility for the care of children, they may be drawn into issues of education, safety, public services, and other factors that directly affect their children (Haywoode 1999).

Community organizations are thus an interesting example of the intersection of the public and private spheres of life. Rabrenovic (1995), for example, shows how Latina women in a low-income suburb of Boston were able to use their extensive family and friendship networks to organize for school reform. Although they lacked all of the traditional resources that contribute to political effectiveness, such as money, jobs, advanced educations, and recognition from or connections with powerful figures, they were able to use their strong social ties in forging their own organizations. Nancy Naples (1992) coined the term "activist mothering" to describe the extension of the role of mother to forces in the community that affect families.

Social class and race interact with gender to produce some interesting patterns in community organizations. The types of communities that have produced active community organizations are often of the type that sociologists call *defended* neighborhoods (Suttles 1972)—that is, they are neighborhoods that the residents believe are facing one or more threats to their stability. The threat may be the actions of some subgroup within the neighborhood itself, as when a few local residents begin to sell drugs and are challenged by others who want to uphold the law in the community (Rabrenovic 1995). Neighborhood threats may be external, such as a city bureaucracy that reduces or terminates services to a neighborhood by, for example, closing a fire station or ending a subsidized summer lunch program for children (Susser 1982). Sometimes the interplay of threats is complex. Many neighborhood organizations, for example, have been formed by white residents as a response to the possibility of racial integration. In some cases white residents group together very tightly and react violently to people of color entering the neighborhood (Rieder 1985). In others they strive by informal means to keep the neighborhood as white as possible while treating residents of color whom they know as part of the neighborhood (DeSena 1994). Some neighborhood organizations minimize racial and ethnic tensions in the community by focusing on problems that are common to all population groups or by joining with other organizations to address issues that transcend neighborhood lines (Luttrell 1988).

Why is gender related to community leadership? Students of neighborhood life tell us that women engage in more neighboring interaction than men do. Whether it is a matter of greeting neighbors on the street, chatting over the fence, lending needed items, or watching the house when neighbors go away, women tend to interact with their neighbors more frequently than do men. One study that investigated the reasons for this gender differential found that it was not because of differences in leisure time between men and women; regardless of women's hours spent at work or minding children, they still kept up the neighboring ties more than the men in their households. The researchers concluded that the gender gap in neighborhood activity is more a result of women's role expectations than of any extra free time they had (Campbell and Lee 1990).

One question raised by women's involvement in neighborhood and community organizations is whether the experience may provide the motivation and opportunity for women to seek political office. Nationally, we have seen an increase in women office holders, capped by the 2008 presidential election in which women were serious candidates for the two highest elective offices in the United States. The number of women in Congress has increased to 17 percent of both houses, and at the time of this writing, the posts of Speaker of the House and secretary of state are both held by women. Yet the "pipeline" for women candidates at the national level—the number of female elected officials at the local level—is deficient. The office that more women hold than any other is school board member, but few women view running for school board as a stepping stone to higher office (Deckman 2007). Although many other countries have surpassed the United States in the proportion of women in office, women in the United States are far less likely than men to run for office (Lawless and Fox 2008).

Recreation

Differences in the ways in which men and women use space are sufficiently far-reaching to include gendered differences in spaces for recreation. Traditionally, women's recreation has occurred in the private spaces of the kitchen and the porch; few public recreations have been created for women in the way that, for example, men's bars have been. But we do see patterns in how women use recreational spaces.

Ewen (1980) recounts the rise of movie theaters in the early decades of the twentieth century as related to women's growing freedom in public places. Movie theaters were not defined as exclusively feminine spaces, but they were places where women, either singly or in groups, could and did go without men. Ewen reminds us that this was a time when millions of immigrants had come to the United States, people often drawn from traditional, patriarchal societies in which women had little personal freedom. As their children became teenagers and then young women, immigrant parents had to confront their daughters' Americanization and loss of traditional ways. Yet because they relied on their children's earnings, immigrant parents had an economic incentive to prevent their unmarried daughters from moving out of their family households. As a kind of social compromise within the family, going to the movies provided safe recreation for young women but also a bit of titillation and a challenge to the parents' old-fashioned European norms.

Since the advent of television and videos, movie theaters have declined somewhat in popularity, at least for adults. Dixey (1988) describes the institution that has replaced them in much of Britain: the bingo hall. Bingo was legalized in Britain in 1960, just as television was beginning to challenge the movie business and erode the audiences in small-town theaters. As theaters closed, many were converted to bingo halls, featuring several forms of low-stakes gambling. By the 1970s bingo halls had become the most common place for a night out for working-class women in British towns, a place for married women to go on a regular basis with other women or when their husbands went to the pub. Dixey reports that bingo halls are the only regular social contact for a significant minority of senior citizens, particularly widows. They have become second homes complete with surrogate family members, the other bingo regulars.

In the past three decades the number of gyms and fitness centers has increased noticeably across the United States. Working out has become one of the common forms of recreation for both men and women, and increasingly people of all ages. Gyms and fitness centers vary substantially in their degree of gender segregation or integration. At one end of the spectrum are the predominantly masculine spaces that focus on boxing and bodybuilding. In the middle are the family-oriented centers (e.g., the YMCA) that cater to all ages and both genders. Some gyms are oriented toward young single adults, with juice bars and social activities providing social benefits in addition to the health benefits of exercise. And at the other end of the spectrum are the women-only fitness centers (e.g., Curves) that provide a nonthreatening environment for women who want to exercise but may feel self-conscious about their physical shape. The fact that these women's fitness centers have grown rapidly and spread to all areas of the country since 1992 shows that many women value the opportunity to work out in their own space and to establish camaraderie with other women.

When we think of gendered recreation areas, fewer exclusively female spaces come to mind as readily as the male spaces of bars, basketball courts, and corner hangouts. If we widen our definition of recreation to include consumer behavior, however, we find many women's spaces in shopping areas

Consumption

Shopping is both a necessity for the household and—sometimes—a form of recreation. With the emergence of the central business districts in the late 1800s came the giant department stores such as Macy's, Gimbel's, John Wanamaker's, Marshall Field's, and Filene's. Built as palaces of consumption, these stores included sculptures, tapestries, chandeliers, stained glass, fountains, and other elaborate decorations to attract women to the store as an experience in itself. Department stores were truly gendered spaces, however, because store designers treated men's and women's shopping activities quite differently. Assuming that men were not interested in the experience of shopping but simply wanted merchandise, designers positioned men's departments near street entrances so that men could quickly enter, make a purchase, and depart without going through the main part of the store. Many department stores added food and entertainment, such as concerts or fashion shows, to allow women to spend more time there and to socialize with friends. For a woman of the middle class, shopping and dining in a department store's fancy restaurant could serve as the equivalent of a man's lunch at his club (Weisman 1992).

The downtown department stores, with their elaborate window displays and tony dining rooms, have now been replaced by shopping malls, with their interior gardens and food courts. As many observers have noted, shopping malls are the downtowns of our suburban communities. Malls are not as carefully designed to separate the genders as were the old department stores, although the men's departments still tend to be located near an entrance and are decorated in darker, quieter tones than the remainder of the store. Still, these shopping spaces are disproportionately used by women. Mothers of young children take trips to the mall during weekdays, as do senior citizens. Weekends are family times, and, although sizeable numbers of teenagers and preteens frequent malls without their parents, overall, nearly two-thirds of visitors to malls are women (Weisman 1992).

Shopping for food is another female-dominated form of consumption that has changed greatly over time. Sophie Bowlby (1988) points out a pattern in Britain that also existed in the United States: the nineteenth-century separation of work from home occurred at the same time as the separation of food production and consumption. Industrialization and urbanization meant that large numbers of households were buying nearly all of their food instead of growing or raising some of it themselves. Shopping for food became part of women's work as an extension of the tasks of cooking food and feeding family members. In working-class neighborhoods during the nineteenth century, small take-out shops and street vendors sold ready-to-eat food to working women who had little time to cook. In middle-class neighborhoods, permanent food shops where housewives or their servants could buy uncooked foods on a regular basis appeared. By 1900 the large grocery chains such as A&P had developed, but small markets remained in virtually every urban neighborhood because the lack of transport and refrigeration necessitated daily shopping trips (Bowlby 1988).

With the increase in women workers, single mothers, and two-earner families since the 1960s, grocery stores have added more items and services to reduce the number of stops women must make on their rounds (and not incidentally because many of the nonfood items are more profitable than the food itself). These "superstores" are actually an amalgamation of specialty shops, with pharmacies, dry cleaners, photo shops, video rentals, florists, stationers, hardware stores, appliance stores, and banks, not to mention the food specialties such as delicatessens, pizzerias, fish markets, bakeries, and liquor stores, all under one roof. Like the mall, the superstores have placed in a single building the complex of small establishments that characterized the urban neighborhood of fifty years ago.

To summarize, the research on gendered spaces shows that although both women and men work in offices, drive cars, take trains, play bingo, shop, care for their families, and take part in community organizations, a discernable pattern of "male" and "female" spaces and activities is evident in cities. We can conclude from the research on gendered spaces that, regardless of an increasing flexibility in the social roles of men and women, their social expectations, pressures, constraints, choices, and activities still differ. If women and men experience and use the community differently, what implications does this information have for how we build and operate cities?

RUNNING CITIES AS IF
WOMEN MATTERED

Cities and suburbs as we know them were planned and constructed within a framework that assumed a certain kind of family and community life. From the location of workplaces and schools to the layout of homes and neighborhoods, urban design and urban policy have been based on the assumption of traditional family and gender roles. This so-called masculine bias in urban design includes the assumption that men will be the primary wage earners, that women will be responsible for unpaid family work, and that the environment will be organized primarily to support paid work (Saegert 1988). In a time of changing economic structures, changing family structures, and changing social roles of men, women, and children, researchers have begun to ask, "How appropriate are existing community structures for contemporary residents?"

What Do Women Want?

Choice of Community Type.   One question we can explore is whether women as a group have particular needs and preferences for their environments. Let us begin with where women and men live. Women in cities outnumber men by significant margins. In the entire population of the United States, there are only 93.4 men for every 100 women over 18 years old. In the central cities, women outnumber men by even more—only 91.5 men per 100 women— whereas in suburban areas, the ratio is 96.4 men per 100 women. In rural areas, the number of men and women is about equal (U. S. Census Bureau 2003). Does this mean that, on the whole, cities are the most attractive places for women to live?

Research examining women's housing preferences shows several contradictory elements. Some of the research is consistent with the notion that, everything else being equal, women prefer urban to suburban or rural locations, but other findings contradict or complicate that notion. For example, women have consistently reported greater preferences for living in close proximity to services than have men. They explain that it is easier to get around and perform their multiple roles when schools, public offices, and businesses are close to each other and close to home. Furthermore, women are more likely than men to prefer the cultural and social activities available in the city as opposed to those associated with suburban living. Women have reported preferences for good public transportation, because they rely on it more than do men. They have also more frequently reported a preference for living in racially homogeneous areas than have men. Finally, personal safety and a preference for safe neighborhoods is typically a greater concern among women than among men. (See Box 11.2 on our society's views of women as potential victims of crime.)

What can we conclude from this research? It seems that the most desirable type of neighborhood *in theory* for the majority of women is one that combines the urban characteristics of population density, availability of services, rich cultural life, and good public transportation with the suburban characteristics of social homogeneity and low crime rates. *Actual* choice of housing involves compromises. Some women who have moved to the suburbs report that they have compromised their own preferences to meet the needs of other household members. Some women, particularly single women, low-income women with children, and elderly women, choose to live in cities because they cannot afford to live elsewhere or they cannot get around without public transit. Also, these patterns may change in the future, as the generation of women who grew up in the suburbs—an increasing proportion of the population—are somewhat less likely to choose urban locations than are older women (Fava 1988; Saegert 1988).

Reducing the Burden of Household Work.   You might have expected that women's changing role at work might have changed how they organize their homes. More than a century ago, Catherine Beecher (Beecher and Stowe 1869) proposed that technological advances would provide women with relief

> **B o x 11.2 • Spotlight**
> **"Good Girls," "Bad Girls," and Crime Victims**
>
> For women, the fear of crime has the unique ability to organize consent or unify
> views about "proper" gender roles: women cannot engage in certain activities
> because it is dangerous for them to do so, whereas men have no such limitations.
> Although people may claim to support equal opportunities for women in the work-
> place or in the use of public space, their real opinions are usually shocked out of
> them when they are confronted with the possibility of crime. The same person who
> emphatically states, "Women and men have the same right to walk the streets of
> America," may well say, in the next breath, "Well, doesn't she know better? She
> should not walk by herself at night. What does she expect?" Fear of crime touches
> deep-seated beliefs and evokes many assumptions not only about crime, criminals,
> and victims, but also about "responsible" behavior for men and women....
>
> The fear of crime, and specifically the fear of male violence, not only perpetu-
> ates the image that women are powerless, weak, and more vulnerable than men but
> also feeds into the notion that women and men are not entitled to the same rights:
> women should not and cannot go places where men can go; women cannot engage
> in activities which are open to men; women should wear "proper" attire so that they
> are not molested by men; and since women must protect themselves and their chil-
> dren from criminal victimization, they had better stay home and be "good girls."
> Further, the fear of crime reinforces the subordinate role of women: if a woman
> wants to be safe and protected, she had better be accompanied by a man.
>
> SOURCE: Esther Madriz, *Nothing Bad Happens to Good Girls: Fear of Crime in Women's Lives* (Berkeley: University
> of California Press, 1997), pp. 2, 15–16.

from the burden of physical labor involved in keeping house. She designed sophisticated machines and systems for cooking, washing, cleaning, and child care
on the assumption that technology could make housework and family duties
more efficient and pleasant. Sure enough, we have lived through an explosion
of household technologies and inventions, but they have not released women
from household labor to the degree that Beecher expected. In fact, Cowan
(1983) argues that, by raising expectations of what is *possible*—for example, by
changing the standard for a clean shirt or a clean floor—mechanization of household tasks has over the long run helped create "more work for mother."

Household divisions of labor have changed gradually as more married
women have entered the labor force. Surveys now show that men report spending more time on household chores and child care than in previous decades. The
same surveys, however, show that the main impact of married women's work
outside the home is a reduction of the total amount of time devoted to activities
such as cleaning and cooking (Spain and Bianchi 1996). In North America new
service industries are providing many of the domestic chores women formerly
did for no pay, thus commodifying household work by converting it into products available for sale. The growth of commercial child-care centers, housecleaning services, and a plethora of frozen microwavable meals, fast-food
outlets, and pizza delivery services are a few examples of this commodification
of domestic labor.

Social change has also affected women's roles and family organization, but we must remember that there never was a single model of the family. A picture of the family of the past as a solid, home-owning, church-going, dad-working, mom-homemaking, and two-kids-living-at-home unit is as unrealistic as is a picture of the contemporary family consisting of a single working mother with two children by different fathers. Women's paid employment, family breakup, and single parents are not new phenomena. As we have seen, married women have always worked, and they have moved in and out of the paid labor force depending on their families' needs, industries' demand for workers, and social expectations. Families have always been broken up, whether by divorce, desertion, or death. Single parenthood has also been a longstanding phenomenon, even if the society's ways of defining it and coping with it (fewer adoptions and orphanages, more single parenting) may have changed somewhat over time (Coontz 1992).

User-Friendly Communities

Precisely because families and households are so varied and fluid, it is necessary to plan for a wide variety of family/household styles and needs within our communities. As we saw, the majority of our homes and communities were designed to fit the needs of a single type of household: the nuclear family with a male breadwinner and a female homemaker. Feminist planners and architects have explored how new principles of design and social organization could facilitate a wide range of residents' uses of the built environment. They have developed alternatives to the narrow range of housing styles dominant in the marketplace: the single-family detached house in the suburban subdivision, the garden apartment or townhouse complex, and the central-city high-rise apartment house.

Architects and urban planners have proposed designs to correct the "current misfit between old houses and new households" (Weisman 1992, 125). One of the most celebrated is Jacqueline Leavitt and Troy West's award-winning New American House (see Figure 11.3). They designed a flexible, easily maintained home that breaks down the rigid barriers of public and private space, indoor and outdoor space, and living and work space that exist in traditional homes. Rather than having a private front- and backyard, each house has a private courtyard and also opens onto a block-long outdoor recreational space shared by the other residents. The home contains a living room, two bedrooms, a bath, and a kitchen-dining area in one wing and a home office in the other wing, spaces "designed for active families with little time for housework and little need for a large space for formal entertainment" (West 1989, 17). Many different types of households can live here, from an adult who works at home while watching the children, to housemates who need both shared and private spaces. The design is particularly appropriate for single parents (Leavitt 1989).

Some households find ordinary housing developments isolating and desire more contact with neighbors, especially for their children. An alternative type of housing development that addresses this desire for community contact is called **cohousing**. A cohousing community consists of a number of households

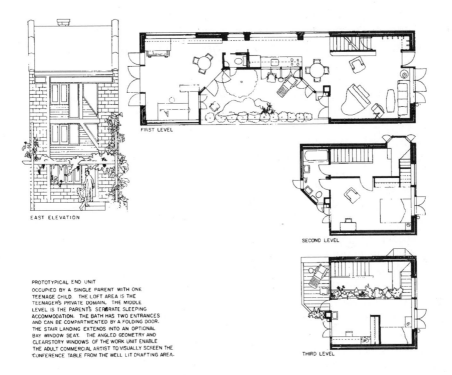

EAST ELEVATION

FIRST LEVEL

SECOND LEVEL

THIRD LEVEL

PROTOTYPICAL END UNIT
OCCUPIED BY A SINGLE PARENT WITH ONE
TEENAGE CHILD. THE LOFT AREA IS THE
TEENAGER'S PRIVATE DOMAIN. THE MIDDLE
LEVEL IS THE PARENT'S SEPARATE SLEEPING
ACCOMMODATION. THE BATH HAS TWO ENTRANCES
AND CAN BE COMPARTMENTED BY A FOLDING DOOR.
THE STAIR LANDING EXTENDS INTO AN OPTIONAL
BAY WINDOW SEAT. THE ANGLED GEOMETRY AND
CLEARSTORY WINDOWS OF THE WORK UNIT ENABLE
THE ADULT COMMERCIAL ARTIST TO VISUALLY SCREEN THE
CONFERENCE TABLE FROM THE WELL LIT DRAFTING AREA.

F I G U R E 11.3 The New American House. This townhouse is designed for a single-parent family. It provides space for a home office and a side yard where playing children can be seen from every room.

Designed by Troy West and Jacqueline Leavitt, based on a competition directed by Harvey Sherman.

(ranging from about a dozen to nearly a hundred) that live in separate units clustered around a community building. Each home is smaller than the usual single-family house, because many of the activities that necessitate their own rooms (a storage room, a guest room, a workshop, a rec room) are located in the community building. Cohousing allows the community to use its resources jointly, for example, by building a single large swimming pool instead of small backyard pools or by maintaining a nature preserve on its property. In addition to sharing common facilities and encouraging social contact, residents normally design, develop, and manage cohousing developments (McCamant and Durrett 1989).

Although our society has moved beyond the separate spheres of women and men, our buildings have not changed as rapidly as have our families. Home can be a workplace, both women and men can have a public as well as a private role, and families can take many forms other than the stereotypical patriarchal arrangement. In designing urban space that would better meet the needs of today's families, planners need to provide more facilities for child care, especially publicly funded centers and informal neighborhood-based co-ops, which will help parents better integrate their work and family responsibilities. Planners could rethink the designs of housing, workplaces, and public facilities to include children—not only in the private sphere of the home but also in the public sphere—by providing spaces for children in workplaces and shopping centers. New principles of organization and design can challenge the rigidly gendered assumptions of the past and give people more flexibility and options (Greed 1994).

These changes toward user-friendly communities require planning, imagination, and support in the arena of public policy. Zoning regulations that strictly limit the number of unrelated individuals, types of land uses, and permissible housing styles can be modified to provide for options such as cohousing, accessory apartments, community gardens, and home-based workplaces (Ritzdorf 1994). By recognizing the many varieties and differing needs of today's varied families and households, we can move toward what Saegert (1988, 36) has called the "androgynous city"—a city that "provides places and supports for the full range of human activities without biasing access on the basis of gender."

In addition to the need for different spaces and buildings, the research cited in this chapter points to women's particular economic and social needs. Women's needs include the following: pay that accurately values their work; assistance with raising children, whether from fathers, employers, or government agencies; safety and security in their homes, workplaces, and streets; and public services that support rather than stigmatize their clients. These are needs that all *humans*, not just women, possess; but in our communities as they are currently organized, women find it more difficult than men to attain these desired goals. If we ran cities as if women mattered, we would be running them as if people mattered.

DISCUSSION QUESTIONS

1. Are public spaces becoming less rigidly gendered? What evidence do you have for your answer?

2. Why do you think that women are more likely than men to live in cities and less likely than men to live in rural areas? What factors might be related to this difference?

3. What kinds of supports do you suppose employers in your area provide for women in the workplace (for example, maternity leave, emergency leave to care for family members, or on-site day care)? Make some notes on what you think a reasonable policy would be. Then ask two employed friends to describe their employers' policies, or obtain policy information from the human resources offices of two local companies. How do the actual policies compare with your expectations?

PART IV

Change and Conflict
Urban Social Institutions

12

The Urban Economy

Hog butcher for the World
Tool Maker, Stacker of Wheat,
Player with Railroads and the Nation's
Freight Handler
CARL SANDBURG
"CHICAGO"

As we saw in previous chapters, one of the most important reasons for the existence of cities is that they provide economic opportunities for the people who live in them. Cities are giant human resource marketplaces, bringing together employers who need workers and workers who need jobs. What attracts employers and workers to cities? Cities are sufficiently large and concentrated so that employers expect to find plentiful skilled workers and workers expect to find plentiful jobs.

In the United States the growth of cities was closely linked with the growth of manufacturing during the nineteenth and early twentieth centuries. Since then, as the industrial economy has changed its form, so has the form of our cities. In Chapters 4 and 5, we examined the historical changes cities have experienced and the implications of these changes for city dwellers. In this chapter we will first explore how economic changes have impacted cities and especially jobs. Then we will examine the types of policies that city governments use to maintain and improve their local economies.

The chapter will focus on the following questions:

- How have changes in the global and national economies affected cities?
- How have economic changes impacted people's way of life?
- What are cities doing to foster economic development?
- What options do cities have in trying to build healthy local economies?

THE ECONOMIC BASE

The economy of a metropolitan area can have a great impact on a variety of social indicators, including the racial composition and segregation of a city and the education level of its residents. The dominant economic base of a metropolitan area is referred to as functional specialization. As discussed by Logan et al. (2004: 13):

> The economic base or functional specialization that creates and sustains a metropolis influences who lives there, its housing stock, and neighborhood patterns. A metropolis in which there is a large university, a military base, or a state capital will differ in important ways from one in which manufacturing plants, with their blue-collar workers, sustain the economy.

One particular way functional specialization impacts cities is in terms of racial segregation. For instance, Logan et al. (2004) found that black–white segregation was highest in metropolitan areas specializing in manufacturing and, to a lesser degree, in those with a high proportion of retirees. In contrast, metropolitan areas with a high concentration of government workers (such as state capitals) and the military had lower levels of segregation. The reasons for such impacts are often quite complex. For instance, examining the effect of the military on racial segregation, Smith (2007) found that the military has been able to influence metropolitan-level segregation because it is a total institution that exerts considerable control over its members. This impacts the attitudes and the choices available to those employed by the military. The impact on segregation was most evident in cities that developed around the military itself, newer cities such as Colorado Springs and Fayetteville, North Carolina. Since functional specialization had the greatest impact as the cities grew, the implication is that segregation can be explained in part by the actions of the dominant institutions while a city developed. In contrast, cities where the dominant institutions fostered racist attitudes among residents during the city's initial development, such as manufacturing firms using race as a means to divide workers against each other (see Pula and Dziedzic 1991), exhibit higher levels of segregation.

In Chapters 4, 5, and 6 we noted several economic trends that have affected the U.S. economy during the past fifty years. Four trends are especially important for the economic well-being of cities. The first trend is the shift from manufacturing as the engine of the economy to the service sector and technology as the basis of the new economy. The second trend, suburbanization, is especially important as businesses move out of central cities and into surrounding suburban communities. The third trend is globalization of the economy, in which companies increasingly buy and sell materials, labor, and products across national boundaries. Finally, the fourth trend is corporate concentration: the tendency for larger companies to buy smaller companies, resulting in a shrinking number of firms in many industries. These four trends are interrelated, and as a whole they have had a striking impact on the urban economy.

Impact on Local Economic Bases

How have these four economic changes affected cities? First, let's look at the decline of manufacturing. Most of the large cities of the United States were constructed during the industrial era, and their economies were based in large part on manufacturing. Since 1970, the overall number of manufacturing jobs in the United States has declined and the types of manufacturing jobs have changed, as the high-technology sector has outstripped more traditional kinds of manufacturing. The decline of the manufacturing sector has most heavily impacted cities in the "industrial heartland" of the upper Midwest where employment was often concentrated in a single industry such as steel or automobiles. Many older industrial cities have lost jobs because they have not attracted either new high-tech investments or a sufficient number of good service-sector jobs to replace the old manufacturing jobs they lost.

Second, we can see that suburbanization has significantly impacted cities' economies. As businesses have moved to the suburbs, many central cities have suffered a loss not only of manufacturing jobs but also jobs in the service sector such as retail stores, offices, restaurants, theatres, nursing homes, and hotels. The loss of these jobs has hurt the urban community because they have traditionally provided entry-level employment for relatively low-skilled workers. With the increasing departure of these businesses to the suburbs, low-income people living in center cities (many of them teenagers or young adults) no longer have easy and accessible access to employment.

Globalization of the economy has also had a tremendous impact on cities. In the global economy, companies no longer have a built-in advantage of being located in a particular area. Companies can look for the best price for their materials or labor and can easily ship goods across national boundaries. Many types of jobs have been moved from the United States to other countries, either because labor costs are low (for example, China has gained a large manufacturing sector due to low wages) or because other countries can produce products for the world market at low prices (for example, Korean steel factories are more modern and more efficient than North American steel factories). We frequently hear about low-wage manufacturing jobs being sent overseas (a claim that can be verified by examining labels on clothing, shoes, kitchenware, and other commonly manufactured items). In addition, however, many service-sector jobs are also being moved overseas, especially to areas such as Ireland, Jamaica, India, and other English-speaking countries. Workers in these countries may provide skilled services such as software development, claims processing, accounting, publishing, and telephone and Internet sales and support.

Finally, another important economic trend is the increase in corporate mergers and buyouts called corporate concentration. In particular, large firms are steadily seeking opportunities to grow by buying smaller firms, presumably to compete more successfully in the global economy. These buyouts can negatively impact the economies of the cities in which the smaller firms are located. Larger firms have acquired many companies with long-established ties to particular cities. This trend has been perhaps most apparent in the banking industry, where a few large national (or international) banks have taken over dozens of regional banks, but it has also occurred in such industries as food production, brewing, toys, supermarkets, and health care. Corporate mergers often result in layoffs and job displacement in local economies as the larger company downsizes to streamline its workforce. In addition to job losses, mergers typically result in out-of-town (or out-of-country) ownership and management, as shown in Box 12.1. These absentee managers are often not good corporate citizens because they have no stake in the well-being of the city, no ties with its political and civic leadership, and no feeling of responsibility for the education, services, or transportation of the residents—their employees.

Although the four trends previously cited have caused disinvestment and job loss in many cities, they have spurred growth in jobs and population in selected other cities. This is another example of the pattern of uneven development among geographic areas that we saw in Chapter 7. Some cities show classic signs of deindustrialization, where the decline of entire industries has resulted in job and population loss over the past two decades. Examples of such cities include Buffalo, Detroit, and Cleveland. On the other hand, some cities, such as El Paso, Los Angeles, and Nashville, are growing because of new manufacturing investments. Some cities, including Atlanta, Denver, and Seattle, are growing due primarily to service-sector investment in their region. Finally, several older industrial cities have transitioned from manufacturing to service economies and thus are maintaining stable or growing populations. This group includes Boston, Chicago, and San Francisco (Negrey and Zickel 1994).

The Changing Nature of Jobs

All of these changes in local economies have added up to the increasing gap between rich and poor that we discussed in Chapter 10. This income polarization has resulted not only from the loss of jobs in some communities but also from the shifts in the types of employment available within a given geographic area. In large cities with thriving service sectors, such as New York and Los Angeles, rapid growth has occurred in the high-paying jobs associated with finance, real estate, communications, and other corporate services. In such communities, clusters of companies employing highly educated knowledge workers have provided significant opportunities for a relatively small number of residents (Florida 2002). At the same time, the low-wage service and even manufacturing sectors can also be thriving. To understand the tendency toward income polarization, then, it is important to know both which types of jobs are growing or declining as well as where those changes are occurring.

Former U.S. Secretary of Labor Robert Reich (1991; 2002) analyzed the impact that globalization has had on the availability of jobs in the United States. Instead of categorizing jobs into two groups—manufacturing and services—Reich discovered that today's jobs really fall into three categories:

- Routine production services
- In-person services
- Symbolic-analytic services

B o x 12.1 • Case Study
A Bank in Utica

The Oneida Bank was founded in 1826 as a bank to serve the bustling frontier town that Utica was. One hundred years later, the only major change was a name change to Oneida National Bank and Trust in 1865. After World War II, as it became apparent that America's love of cars was leading to major lifestyle changes, Oneida National began to build branches in other parts of the metropolitan area so their consumers would not have to drive (and find parking) downtown just to cash a check. Enterprising managers realized that they could expand their customer base further by expanding even further afield by buying banks in small towns. In 1957, the first of these mergers was with the First National Bank and Trust of Camden. The following year witnessed another merger with Rome Trust Company, followed by a name change to Oneida National Bank and Trust Company of Central New York. In 1976, the bank acquired Ogdensburg Trust Company and became simply Oneida National Bank in 1982. In 1985, Oneida National was purchased by Norstar Bank of Upstate New York, itself a product of numerous mergers. The headquarters was moved to Albany. Norstar was purchased in 1991 by Fleet Bank, a native of Providence, Rhode Island. Fleet later moved its headquarters to Boston, where it remained until merging with Charlotte, North Carolina–based Bank of America in 2004.

The impact of such mergers was apparent very early on. When Oneida National acquired the First National Bank of Camden it was more than a simple financial transaction: it altered the social relationship between the two communities. Camden had been home to a corporate headquarters and the administrators of that corporation. The community could expect that these neighbors had a stake in the community, and that expectation was normally met in the form of not only corporate investment and charity, but the largesse of the company's managers as well. The merger turned those executives into managers, with major decision making power transferred to Utica. Decisions as to who could get a mortgage or business loan, for instance, went to Utica. The larger organization necessitated a more bureaucratized system that ultimately led to our current system of credit scores fed by computer algorithms and equations—a system that does not necessarily check to see if you can actually pay the debt. Gone was the more personal knowledge of the customer gained through regular interactions and customer—and corporate—loyalty. At the time, the impact was minimal, but over time and across more acquisitions the impact of a centralization of both capital and talent in Utica took place at the expense of the little towns that lost their hometown banks. Instead of a class of bank owners, they would have less powerful and less well reimbursed managers and tellers. This would impact not only decisions by the bank, but the charitable and other community work by the local gentry. Until the merger with Norstar, Utica benefited from this situation at the expense of rural towns in the surrounding area.

With the merger with Norstar, the geographical and social distance between Utica and the headquarters of the new institution became greater and greater. Norstar was based in Albany as a district office and ultimately headquartered in Rochester. This left Utica some low level administrative and "back office" work, but the big money went elsewhere—next to Providence and Boston, more recently to Charlotte. Could London or Hong Kong be next? Or perhaps an up and coming global financial power we have not heard of yet?

SOURCE: Alexander R. Thomas and Polly J. Smith, *Upstate Down: Thinking About New York and Its Discontents* (New York: University Press of America, 2009), pp. 66–67.

Routine production services include all jobs requiring repetitive tasks, whether they are stamping out parts of toasters, making airline reservations, or supervising a payroll office. Such routine jobs during the 1990s accounted for about 25 percent of all jobs, according to Reich. He points out, however, that these routine jobs are being exported most rapidly to other countries. In addition, the routine production workers who remain employed are experiencing substantial decreases in pay and benefits. Reich likens this job sector to a leaky boat.

Providers of **in-person services** also have repetitive jobs, such as preparing and serving food, caring for children and elders, driving buses, and cutting hair. These jobs employ about 30 percent of all workers in the United States and are growing in number. Reich points out that these jobs cannot be moved overseas because they must be provided in person to clients. Pay and benefits to in-person service providers, however, vary widely. Whereas the largest group work at or slightly above the minimum wage and receive no benefits, a small proportion (for example, servers in posh restaurants) may have substantial incomes. These jobs are increasing in number, but Reich thinks that it is unlikely that the pay will increase significantly because of competition for the jobs.

Symbolic-analytic service jobs entail problem solving and strategic thinking rather than routine or repetitive tasks. Reich includes in this group scientists, engineers, attorneys, management consultants, artists, writers, and other people who manipulate ideas and symbols. These are the knowledge workers for the new economy, which is increasingly based on information. Their ranks grew from less than 10 percent of the workforce in the 1950s to about 20 percent in the 1990s. More significantly, their incomes have grown as well, because their skills are in demand both in the United States and abroad.

For Reich, the increasing power of large corporations to shop the world for the lowest labor costs means that individuals in the United States need to be more vigilant than in the past about competing in a global marketplace. This is because new transportation and communication technologies have broken down the barriers that used to protect workers from such competition. Reich fears that this enhanced individualism is replacing a sense of community and of local and national loyalties, with those best able to thrive in this economic reality abandoning the concerns of those less able to compete (Reich 2002; 2008).

Growth of the Informal Economy

If the economy is providing fewer stable, well-paying jobs, but people still need to survive, how do they manage? Sometimes people employed in low-wage positions take second jobs; sometimes additional family members enter the labor force to bring in more income. Sometimes people participate in the **informal sector**, or underground economy, as a supplement to or a substitute for regular employment.

The informal economy includes the ways of earning money or obtaining goods and services that are not recognized by official measures of economic output. Any work that generates unreported income, no matter what the work is, is part of the informal sector. One prominent type of informal sector work is dealing in illegal goods and services. Prostitution, selling drugs, gambling, shoplifting, and selling stolen property fall into this category. Even more widespread than illegal work, however, is unreported work. Many people receive unreported income at some time, from holding a garage sale to being paid under the table for painting a neighbor's house. For some households, though, unreported income is their main form of income. Street vendors may work daily at different locations, folding up their tables and disappearing when the police arrive. Women may run clandestine businesses from their homes: unregistered day-care centers, unlicensed beauty salons, unadvertised tailor shops, or housecleaning businesses. For people whose pay in the regular labor market would be very low, forms of work with almost no overhead (such as rent or equipment) and for which they pay no taxes on their income can provide opportunities for making a living that are reasonably competitive with formal jobs (see Portes, Castells, and Benton 1989). Box 12.2 shows how participation in the underground economy is a means of survival in one poor neighborhood in New York City.

In addition to providing subsistence work for inner-city residents, the informal sector is often linked to the formal economy. In cities like New York, many legitimate companies employ unreported workers. To supplement the regular employees on their formal payroll, they hire a parallel group of workers who work off the books. Paid in cash, they may work within the workplace or in their homes. Some companies do not hire their informal workers directly but subcontract work to a different firm that hires them (Sassen 2001).

Several industries have, at least in part, come to rely on informal workers to supplement their regular workforces. Sassen (2001) reports that in New York City, informal work is prevalent in at least six industries: construction, especially in interior renovation projects that are conducted without building permits; garments, in which homework and sweatshops have become widespread; footwear, including sandals and handbags; furniture making and woodworking; retailing; and electronics assembly. Sassen argues that these industries cluster in New York City partly because of the cheap labor available there. Many of these informal workers are paid a piece rate rather than a minimum wage.

Sassen's study raises the issue of the large number of firms that make an explicit practice of hiring immigrants, particularly undocumented immigrants, as their informal workers. She has uncovered numerous examples of companies preferring immigrant labor because immigrant workers have few choices in employment or are easily intimidated by threats to report them to the authorities. In many cases immigrant entrepreneurs themselves hire their fellow immigrants to perform informal work, and a close association exists between the size of immigrant communities and the size of the informal economy in different cities (Castells and Portes 1989). It would be a mistake, however, to conclude that it is exclusively or even primarily immigration that has caused the growth of the informal sector. Instead, recent researchers have found the informal sector to be an integral component of the economies of the United States and other industrialized countries (Castells and Portes 1989).

The restructuring of manufacturing and rise in services discussed in Chapter 5 is closely related to the growth of the informal economy. The decrease in the

---

B o x 12.2 • Case Study
The Underground Economy in East Harlem

According to the official statistics, my neighbors on the street should have been homeless, starving, and dressed in rags. Given the cost of living in Manhattan, it should have been impossible for most of them to afford rent and minimal groceries and still manage to pay their electricity and gas bills.... The blocks immediately surrounding me were significantly poorer [than the rest of East Harlem] with half of all residents falling below the poverty line. Given New York City prices for essential goods and services, this means that according to official economic measures, well over half the population of El Barrio should not be able to meet their subsistence needs.

In fact, however, people are not starving on a massive scale. Although many elderly residents and many young children do not have adequate diets and suffer from the cold in the winter, most local residents are adequately dressed and reason-ably healthy. The enormous, [unreported], untaxed underground economy allows the hundreds of thousands of New Yorkers in neighborhoods like East Harlem to subsist with the minimal amenities that people living in the United States consider to be basic necessities. I was determined to study these alternative income-generating strategies that were consuming so much of the time and energy of the young men and women sitting on the stoops and parked cars in front of my tenement.

Through the 1980s and 1990s, slightly more than one in three families in El Barrio received public assistance. The heads of these impoverished households have to supplement their meager checks in order to keep their children alive. Many are mothers who make extra money by baby-sitting their neighbors' children or by housekeeping for a paying boarder. Others may bartend at one of the half-dozen social clubs and after-hours dancing spots scattered throughout the neighborhood. Some work "off the books" in their living rooms as seamstresses for garment con-tractors. Finally, many also find themselves obliged to establish amorous relationships with men who are willing to make cash contributions to their household expenses.

Male income-generating strategies in the underground economy are more pub-licly visible. Some men repair cars on the curb; others wait on stoops for unlicensed construction subcontractors to pick them up for fly-by-night demolition jobs or window renovation projects. Many sell "numbers"—the street's version of offtrack betting. The most visible cohorts hawk "nickels and dimes" of one illegal drug or another. They are part of the most robust, multibillion-dollar sector of the booming underground economy. Cocaine and crack, in particular during the mid-1980s and through the early 1990s, followed by heroin in the mid 1990s, have been the fastest growing—if not the only—equal opportunity employers of men in Harlem. Retail drug sales easily outcompete other income-generating opportunities, whether legal or illegal.

SOURCE: Philippe Bourgeois, *In Search of Respect: Selling Crack in El Barrio* (Cambridge, UK: Cambridge University Press, 1996), pp. 2–3.

---

numbers of high-pay, good-benefits, unionized, stable manufacturing jobs has reduced workers' options, and increased their willingness to accept employment that may not be optimal for them. The presence of this "hungrier" labor force has permitted entrepreneurs to establish businesses that might not be able to succeed if they paid regular wages, taxes, and the other expenses that go with the cost of doing business. In addition, new management initiatives have led to decreases in

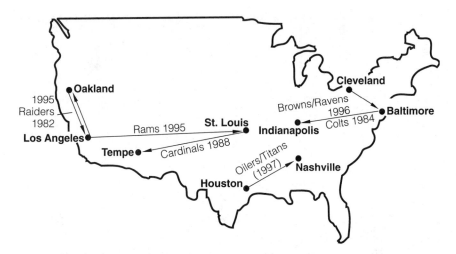

F I G U R E 12.1 **The Home Team?** Cities often invest a substantial amount of public money in athletic facilities, hoping to attract a team from another location. This map shows some of the moves made by National Football League franchises since the 1980s.

firms' permanent workforces and increased use of temporary workers, including, in some cases, informal workers (Bonacich and Appelbaum 2000).

The Arts and the Urban Economy

From the very earliest times, cities have always been centers of artistic and cultural invention. Involvement in the arts—in the broadest sense—is one aspect of cities that makes urban life attractive to people. With the postindustrial restructuring of urban economies after World War II, however, some of the glitter came off the downtowns in North American cities. During the 1960s and 1970s, suburbanization and fear of crime helped depress the number of people who sought their entertainment in downtown areas. Many cities experienced the phenomenon of "rolling up the sidewalks" at 6:00 P.M.

Since the early 1980s, the pattern of the dead downtown has been reversed in a number of cities. An upturn in the economy and a downturn in violent crime helped set the stage for an increase in visitors, both tourists and city residents, to urban downtowns. Both as a conscious strategy and as a consequence of more general demographic and economic changes, many cities have revitalized their artistic and cultural facilities. Cities are rapidly developing high-profile entertainment areas, such as "cultural districts," as well as encouraging the proliferation of cultural spectacle throughout the city in smaller venues, such as neighborhood street fairs.

City governments have fostered some of the increase in artistic and cultural activity as part of their redevelopment strategies. In New York City, for example, public projects have included the reconstruction of Lincoln Center as a venue for high culture (such as the opera), as well as the reconstruction of Times Square. Boston, New York, Baltimore, Milwaukee, and a host of other cities

Mirek Weichsel/First Light/Alamy

F I G U R E 12.2   **Millennium Park in downtown Chicago is a center for recreation and the arts.**

have developed festival marketplaces that combine shopping, restaurants, performing arts, and people watching. Several cities have helped museums, theaters, and ballet companies expand or build new facilities. Elected officials who support public investment in the arts do so chiefly as a way of marketing their cities to tourists and suburban dwellers. (See Judd and Fainstein 1999). This is true for sports complexes as well (see figure 12.1).

Even when city government is not directly involved in fostering the arts, however, several economic trends contribute to the growth in artistic and cultural production in contemporary cities. Cities have what Sharon Zukin (1995) calls **symbolic economies**, or the continual production of spaces that are infused with particular meanings. The buildings, streets, parks, businesses, and other aspects of the built and human environment prompt people to attach meanings to them. The fact that cities are "different" makes them attractive to visitors: the combination of the sights, smells, tastes, experiences, the contrast of different ethnic groups, and different visual stimuli are largely responsible for making cities vital and exciting. In recent years, the increase in immigrants and the growing tendency of the private sector to put its own corporate stamp on public places have transformed the symbolic economies of the larger cities (see figure 12.2).

The arts and culture are a vehicle not only for attracting tourists and suburban dwellers to cities but also for attracting residents. Cities such as Seattle, Portland, and Austin, which are home to large populations of young, educated high-tech workers, have developed arts "scenes" that appeal to that demographic group. The synergy of technological innovation with cultural innovation in music, visual arts, restaurants, and performing arts may be one of the factors helping high-tech companies attract and retain workers. This group is not deterred by the old industrial past of the cities, but sees the gentrification of older manufacturing buildings and working-class neighborhoods as a more sophisticated alternative to sanitized suburbs. Within this context, "grit is glamorous" (Lloyd and Clark 2000).

Some evidence shows that the growth of several cities is the result of their ability to attract large numbers of artists and other creative individuals. Richard Florida (2002) has identified what he terms a "creative class" composed of scientists, writers, artists, musicians, architects, and other workers in the knowledge professions. In Florida's view, this highly educated and mobile class of people tends to locate in cities that they find interesting—cities characterized by three T's: technology, talent, and tolerance. Although the creative class does not work exclusively in the arts, they find a thriving cultural milieu, as well as a high level of diversity in and tolerance of varied ethnicity and sexual preference, to be a large component of their preferred lifestyle. He argues that the creative class has contributed greatly to the growth of cities such as Seattle and Austin, Texas. Box 12.3 explains Florida's research in more detail.

The University and the City

Just as the arts have influenced and been influenced by the city, so have universities and other institutions of learning. Colleges and universities are typically place bound—it is normally not feasible for an institution to relocate all of its buildings and other holdings to another neighborhood or town—and necessarily must consider their relationship with the local community. This is because the local community is often part of the "package" that a potential student considers when shopping for a college. Colleges and universities affect their communities and the wider region in three major ways: the creation of specialized niche markets, entrepreneurialism and technology transfers, and through direct community involvement and investment.

In many cities college students themselves are a significant market for local businesses (Perry, Wiewel, and Menendez 2009). In the cities of Boston and Cambridge, for instance, there are about one hundred thousand college students attending Harvard University, Massachusetts Institute of Technology, Northeastern University, Boston University, and numerous smaller colleges scattered throughout the cities. This creates significant demand for goods and services—such as music, sporting equipment, and even certain types of furniture—by men and women between the ages of eighteen and twenty-five. Harvard Square in Cambridge, for instance, has one of the highest concentrations of bookstores in the United States. This impact is evident in smaller cities as well, and the presence of college students can sometimes mean the difference between a community surviving or failing economically (Thomas and Smith 2009). This "narrow niche" market also applies to those who work in colleges and universities, as administrators and college professors often have significant incomes and urbane tastes in food and art.

Box 12.3 • **Spotlight**
Cities and the Creative Class

The distinguishing characteristic of the creative class is that its members engage in work whose function is "to create meaningful new forms." The super-creative core of this new class includes scientists and engineers, university professors, poets and novelists, artists, entertainers, actors, designers, and architects, as well as the "thought leadership" of modern society: nonfiction writers, editors, cultural figures, think-tank researchers, analysts, and other opinion-makers.... Beyond this core group, the creative class also includes "creative professionals" who work in a wide range of knowledge-based occupations in high-tech sectors, financial services, the legal and health care professions, and business management. These people engage in creative problem-solving, drawing on complex bodies of knowledge to solve specific problems....

In my research I have discovered a number of trends that are indicative of the new geography of creativity. These are some of the patterns of the creative class:

- The creative class is moving away from traditional corporate communities, working class centers, and even many Sunbelt regions, to a set of places I call "creative centers."

- The creative centers tend to be the economic winners of our age. Not only do they have high concentrations of creative class people, they have high concentrations of creative economic outcomes, in the form of innovations and high-tech industry growth....

- The creative centers ... are succeeding largely because creative people want to live there. The companies follow the people—or, in many cases, are started by them. Creative centers provide the integrated habitat where all forms of creativity—artistic and cultural, technological and economic—can take root and flourish....

These shifts are giving rise to powerful migratory trends and an emerging new economic geography. In the leading creative centers, the creative class makes up more than 35% of the workforce, regions such as the greater Washington, DC, region, the Raleigh-Durham area, Boston, and Austin. But despite their considerable advantages, large regions have not cornered the market as creative-class locations. In fact, a number of smaller regions have some of the highest creative-class concentrations in the nation—notably college towns such as East Lansing, Michigan, and Madison, Wisconsin.

The key to understanding the new economic geography of creativity and its effects on economic outcomes lies in what I call the 3Ts of economic development: technology, talent, and tolerance. Creativity and members of the creative class take root in places that possess all three of these critical factors. Each is a necessary but by itself insufficient condition.... I define tolerance as openness, inclusiveness, and diversity to all ethnicities, races, and walks of life. Talent is defined as those with a bachelor's degree or above. And technology is a function of both innovation and high-technology concentrations in a region. My focus group and interview results indicate that talented individuals are drawn to places that offer tolerant work and social environments.

SOURCE: Richard Florida, "Cities and the Creative Class," *City and Community* 2(1) 2003, pp. 8–10.

Often, the ability of universities to transfer new technologies and knowledge of use to the business community is stressed as a function of higher education. For instance, the majority of federal funding for medical research goes to universities and the findings in those institutions are later funneled to pharmaceutical companies who produce the drugs (Office of Technology Assessment 1993). Similarly, graduates of universities, and sometimes even current students, will found companies in the local community. In addition, state and local governments pursue policies that aim to foster a relationship between institutions of higher education and the business community. For instance, Research Triangle Park in North Carolina is situated in the Raleigh-Durham Metropolitan Area near Duke University, the University of North Carolina at Chapel Hill, and North Carolina State University. Similarly, the more recent "Tech Valley" initiative in upstate New York is situated near the University at Albany, Rensselaer Polytechnic Institute, and numerous smaller colleges (Thomas and Smith 2009). Not surprisingly, some of the major high technology centers in the United States, such as Silicon Valley near San Francisco and the Route 128 corridor outside of Boston, are near clusters of research universities.

Direct investment on the part of colleges and universities is becoming more common (Maurrasse 2001). As many students consider the community in which a campus is located and the amenities available nearby, it is often in the best interest of institutions to ensure that their communities appeal to students and their parents. One of the pioneers in this approach was the University of Pennsylvania, an Ivy League university founded by Benjamin Franklin. Situated in West Philadelphia, "Penn" has been influential in the rebuilding of the University City neighborhood. The university has funded programs meant to gentrify the neighborhood and encourage faculty and staff to live nearby, has been involved in building and subsidizing an elementary school, and has been heavily involved in the architecture of the area. While this has been to the advantage of the university, it has also created conflict in a neighborhood that is also home to many poor residents who do not always see the university's motives as pure. Nevertheless, although conflict can arise, the influence of colleges and universities is by and large positive. In University City, for instance, Penn's museums are not only educational but a tourist attraction as well. Other universities, such as San Francisco State University, have also been heavily involved in community service and organizing (University City District 2007).

URBAN ECONOMIC DEVELOPMENT POLICY

In the light of these changes in the national and global economies, what can local communities do to manage their economic growth and decline? The actions that state and local governments undertake to manage and improve their economic conditions are collectively known as economic development policy. In this section we will first examine several traditional economic development policies that localities have pursued, and then we will look at some alternative economic development policies.

Business-Oriented Economic Development

The most common approach to economic development is to attract new businesses and to help existing businesses grow and thrive. Although the money that is spent in such economic development efforts is public money, the profits are almost always returned exclusively to the private companies that benefit from them (Warner and Molotch 2000). There are two main types of business-oriented urban economic development policies: subsidies to companies that lower their costs of doing business, and public–private partnerships, in which the government invests in projects with private businesses.

Subsidies to Business.   City, county, and state governments have adopted numerous programs that subsidize businesses by helping to lower the costs of their operations, especially the costs of taxes, money, land, and regulations.

One form of business subsidy is the **tax abatement**, in which a local government exempts a company from paying part of its property taxes for a given period of time. Cities may use tax abatements to attract companies from other locations or to help companies already in the city to expand. Although tax abatements are helpful to the companies that receive them, they carry some significant disadvantages to the public. First, they shift the tax burden to other taxpayers (including other businesses). Second, when companies receive tax abatements for moving from one location to another, they may not create any new jobs (for example, if they are highly automated or bring their workers with them). To get tax abatements, companies may threaten to move, even when they have no real intention of moving, so cities may spend money unnecessarily on these incentives for fear that their industries will leave town. In addition, there is little evidence that such abatements actually work (Freudenburg 1993; Warner and Molotch 2000).

Cheap land is also an incentive that cities can give to companies. Beginning in the 1950s the federal government initiated the urban renewal program to help cities make land available to businesses, and most cities have participated in this program. Although the urban renewal program ended formally in the mid-1970s, localities have commonly continued with the same types of activities under the more general name, **redevelopment programs**. Most large cities around the country have used redevelopment programs as part of a corporate center strategy for their locality (Hill 1986). Local agencies have used redevelopment to modernize their aging central business districts, to provide land for advanced manufacturing operations, to reorganize traffic and transportation routes, and to provide upscale housing for the corporate-sector workforce in the new central business districts. Critics of these programs have pointed out two important disadvantages of publicly funded redevelopment: first, many of the private construction projects would have happened without the expensive public subsidies, and second, low-income residents and small business owners who were displaced to make way for corporate expansion have absorbed the personal costs of redevelopment.

A final approach to subsidizing business directs subsidies into targeted areas called **enterprise zones**. Cities identify a particular geographic area as an enterprise zone and give businesses special incentives to locate there, including local and state tax reductions, special loans, cheap land, advertising promotion, technical assistance and training, and a reduction in government regulations. The reason the areas are called *enterprise* zones is that they are supposed to promote the entrepreneurial spirit by freeing businesses from government interference such as taxes and regulations. The most common form of relief that cities and states offer to firms in enterprise zones is tax relief. Little evidence supports the belief that enterprise zones actually attract new businesses; in fact, some evidence indicates that they more often encourage existing or newly forming businesses to move to the zone. Another flaw in the program is that few of the enterprise zone programs require that low-income people get preferential treatment in hiring. Overall, the enterprise zone programs function primarily as tax reduction programs that make it somewhat cheaper for businesses operating within the zone than for those outside (Brecher and Costello 1994; Warner and Molotch 2000).

Public–Private Partnerships. In addition to subsidizing businesses to lower their costs, local governments themselves sometimes act as entrepreneurs—that is, those who run enterprises. A publicly run enterprise, however, can be operated for either private or public gain, two significantly different approaches to economic development. In this section on business-oriented strategies, we will discuss the type of entrepreneurial policy that produces private profit, and later in the chapter we will examine some instances of public entrepreneurialism for public benefit.

The principle behind public–private partnerships is that public money is invested in enterprises, with the profits from those enterprises going to private individuals or groups rather than back to the public treasury. These organizations, formed for a specific purpose, are usually governed by boards representing both business and government. Public–private partnerships have existed since at least the 1960s and have increased in prominence since 1980 (Leitner and Garner 1993). Although they are organized for many different economic development purposes, we will consider just two types of projects they frequently oversee: convention centers and sports facilities.

Convention centers represent large investments of public funds, but as ongoing operations, they normally lose money and are even expected to do so. But they are popular with local business leaders because they can attract large numbers of visitors. The visitors who make up this temporary bulge in the population not only require food and lodging but also provide an affluent market for nearby shopping and entertainment. In many cases city officials use convention centers as anchors of their downtown development projects because these centers complement businesses' 9-to-5 schedule with evening activities and populations.

Convention centers are very popular as public-private projects. Despite their enormous cost—on the order of $100 million to $800 million—and despite the controversies they have generated over whether or not they are good uses of public money, city officials promote them as "the smokeless industry that cannot move to the suburbs" (Sanders 1992, 136). Cities are busily expanding their existing centers or constructing new ones to compete with each other for the largest programs and audiences. Between the late 1960s and the late 1990s, the number of square feet of exhibition space in U.S. convention centers more than doubled while the number of convention centers more than tripled (Eisinger 2000).

It is questionable whether convention centers contribute much to local economies. They provide a large number of up-front jobs, mainly in construction, but in the long run create very few permanent jobs. Also, they typically pay no property taxes. Even if we can justify paying out public funds for private benefit, the investment may have too little return to justify itself (Sanders 1992).

A close relative of the convention center is the professional sports facility. Cities with resident professional teams want to keep them, and many cities without major league teams want to get them. Despite the fact that teams are identified by the names of the cities in which they are located, team mobility is common, resulting in such amusingly inappropriate names as the Utah Jazz and Los Angeles Lakers. In recent years team owners have begun to demand more public investment from their home cities. Owners considering a move negotiate with cities for a wide range of financial concessions and subsidies, the costliest being the stadium itself (Euchner 1993). Owners have become so adept at manipulating city governments that "a virtual state of economic warfare exists between cities to capture and keep sports franchises" (Rosentraub 1988, 72).

The types of subsidies that are required to construct major league sports facilities are staggering. A few examples will show the order of magnitude of the public expenditures: during the 1990s, Baltimore and Maryland spent $275 on Camden Yards and Seattle and Washington State spent $275 million on Qwest Field (Rosentraub 1997; Rogus 1997). Not to be outdone, in 2009 New York City and state residents paid $165 million toward a new Mets stadium, almost as much as the $220 million paid toward a new $1.3 billion Yankee Stadium across the street from the original. The return on these massive investments in tax revenues is modest, and the financial demands of the teams grow every year (Ballparks.com 2009).

Evaluation of Business–Oriented Policies. Many critics have pointed out problems with economic development that is fundamentally structured to assist businesses. The first problem they point to is that it is often unclear what help the subsidized companies actually need and what benefits the cities receive in return. As we have seen, business-oriented economic development strategies do not create very many jobs. In addition, the cost of the public subsidy is often higher than the return in jobs generated. The state of Alabama, for example, won a thirty-five-state competition for a Mercedes-Benz plant, but at a cost estimated to be $200,000 per job created (Mahtesian 1994).

Second, businesses have come to expect public subsidies for private projects. Private developers, sports team owners, corporate managers, and other business people routinely seek a package of subsidies from a locality before they commit to constructing a building or locating a branch operation. They often approach several sets of state and local officials, comparing offers and negotiating for the best deal. This bidding pits one community against another in competition that has been compared to the arms race, because each new bid only increases the subsidies that companies expect to receive (Wolman 1988; Brecher and Costello 1994).

Third, the uneven power relationships between the city government and the company lead to cities not asking for paybacks or commitments from the firms they subsidize. One company may have several locations bidding for it. The local government, instead of trying to bargain, may too easily capitulate to the private firm's wishes out of fear of losing it. In a worst-case scenario, some companies, sports teams, or other businesses take the money and run, negotiating a subsidy on the basis that they will stay in the city, then either downsizing, closing, or moving (Warner and Molotch 2000).

It is a bit perplexing that local governments continue to offer subsidies to private businesses. Studies of corporate location decisions have shown that public subsidies are low on the list of factors affecting where firms choose to locate. Taxes constitute a very small proportion of a business's expenditures, especially when you take into account that businesses are weighing the difference in taxes from one jurisdiction to another. Factors such as labor supplies and costs, markets, and transportation costs are more financially significant to firms. Whether or not public subsidies make much of a difference in attracting or retaining companies, most public officials must act as if they do. If a mayor is perceived to have lost a company that has been in a city for decades or to have botched an opportunity to gain a new hotel, sports facility, or factory, he can expect political criticism (Warner and Molotch 2000).

People-Oriented Economic Development

In contrast to the policies just described, cities can adopt policies that focus directly on the needs of local residents. These policies are designed to benefit the taxpayers and working people of the area, treating private investment as a means to an end rather than an end in itself. Thus, businesses receive subsidies only if there is evidence that the subsidy will result in a demonstrable and positive influence on the public good. Rather than simply accepting or attracting growth, the local governments that use people-oriented economic development policies attempt to shape economic growth in the pursuit of wider social goals for the community (Clavel and Kleniewski 1990).

Retaining and Creating Jobs.   As we have seen, giving subsidies to a company does not necessarily mean that it will stay in the city. This situation is particularly a problem with absentee-owned branch plants. To avoid this problem, city economic development funds can be channeled to assist companies that are locally owned and committed to the community such as community-owned enterprises. Funded from a variety of sources, including private investments, foundation grants, public funds, and sometimes employee stock ownership, community-owned enterprises are locally rooted. They employ local residents and tie into local sources of materials and markets. In some cases community-owned enterprises retain manufacturing jobs in the community by taking over ownership of an existing privately owned business whose owners are no longer interested in it. In other cases they start up new businesses that produce a new product but use the skills and experience of the manufacturing workforce. Some of the most common fields for community-owned enterprises are construction, recycling, transportation, and supermarkets. Sometimes the local government itself owns an enterprise, such as a power company (Cleveland) or football team (Green Bay). The city is thus able to sell a product or service at a modest price and still make a profit that benefits the taxpayers (Delaney and Eckstein 2003).

Investing in People. Population is an asset that every city possesses, and local leaders can help residents succeed economically through recognizing and strengthening people's potential. According to theorist Pierre Bourdieu (1986), people can draw on three types of capital to help them meet their goals: economic capital, cultural capital, and social capital. **Economic capital** refers to money, property, and other strictly economic resources an individual possesses. **Cultural capital** refers to two things: knowledge and skills that an individual acquires (through formal education, training, and other means) and the ability to manipulate the symbolic level of manners, aesthetics, and other valued behaviors of a society (for example, "proper" speech and dress). **Social capital** refers to an individual's participation in groups whose members can provide access to resources such as assistance, advice, and other contacts.

Cities can invest in their residents' economic capital very directly, for example, by using the power of local government to promote the creation of good jobs at good wages. Several cities have passed "living wage" ordinances that set a local minimum wage based not on the federal minimum but on the actual cost of living in that city. Other localities require that companies hire a certain number of city residents as a condition of receiving a building permit or other construction licenses. Cities can also help residents purchase homes at a below-market interest rate or with a smaller down payment than normal, thus helping low-wage residents to accumulate equity. When used in combination, these strategies on the part of local government can help mitigate the tendencies toward the proliferation of low-paying jobs that the private economy has generated since the 1970s.

One of the most important strategies public officials can use is to invest in education and training to build cultural capital. Programs that deliver a sound public education for all children while keeping them healthy and safe are the best investment in the population and future urban workforce. For the present time, assisting school dropouts and poorly educated adults to compete for jobs is also an economic development challenge. Cities can establish adult education and training programs that provide job placement for graduates by linking training to a city-run employment service and referring training program graduates to private- and public-sector jobs.

Local government policies cannot do much directly to foster social capital, because informal groups, such as families, neighbors, and religious institutions, typically generate this capital. A great deal of interest among policy analysts has emerged, however, in helping to enhance social ties that already exist by supporting informal groups such as neighborhood associations that can strengthen social ties within local areas. Although residents of poor neighborhoods surely need access to economic and cultural capital, their social capital is another asset that can help them get ahead (Saegert, Thompson, and Warren 2001).

Community Development Corporations.   Thus far, our discussion of economic development focused on the programs and policies that government agencies use to promote their local economies (Green and Haines 2007). In some cases, particularly in poor neighborhoods that private investors have abandoned, neighborhood-based **community development corporations** (CDCs) have been organized to address the community's needs. CDCs are typically not-for-profit corporations (although they may be associated with some for-profit, community-owned enterprises of the type mentioned earlier) organized to raise investment capital, provide community services, and hire local residents. They are not government agencies, although they may receive financial and technical assistance from public agencies. By attracting outside capital in the form of grants and loans and by using volunteers, community development corporations can leverage, or extend, the resources available within the neighborhood. The difference between this investment and strictly private investment is that the neighborhood-based CDC, not the external group, controls the project and the decision-making process.

Community development corporations are often umbrella organizations that have many related activities and subgroups addressing different aspects of the neighborhood's needs. CDCs typically try to link their activities for greater neighborhood impact. An example is housing production, a very common project for CDCs. Because poor inner-city areas often have deteriorated housing and because banks' lending policies often put these areas off limits for mortgages or home improvement loans, housing construction, rehabilitation, and finance may be sorely needed. In addition, residents of the neighborhood may need jobs. So a CDC might form a credit union that will give loans, a job training program that trains people in construction, and a housing development corporation that builds and repairs homes—three related activities that address different aspects of the community's needs (Zdenek 1987).

One of the key differences in the approach of CDCs from the other economic development strategies we have discussed so far is that the CDC strategy is about more than jobs, money, and neighborhood services; it addresses the totality of the neighborhood. CDCs typically address the development of all three types of capital within their neighborhoods: economic, cultural, and social capital (Gittell and Vidal 1998). While some CDCs are primarily organized around economic development, many strive for *community* development, including political empowerment of the residents. These CDCs intertwine education, organization, and political activism with the creation of economic enterprises, or occasionally they use a predominantly political strategy to achieve neighborhood goals and generate resources (Rubin 1994).

As the federal government has deemphasized urban problems and has reduced the amount of money allocated for urban programs, more community groups are forming community development corporations to raise resources from the outside and to utilize the skills of the people within poorer urban neighborhoods. The successes of some CDCs, especially in providing affordable housing and jobs, have led a number of observers to suggest that the solutions to urban economic problems lie in these bootstrap programs, in which neighborhood residents organize themselves, go out and get resources, and solve their problems themselves. We have seen, however, that the problems of poor neighborhoods are not generated within those neighborhoods but are linked to the overall distribution of resources. CDCs can help to address some of the most pressing needs of low-income communities, but they still must address the issue of how to get more resources into those communities (Stoecker 1995).

Evaluation of People-Oriented Policies.   People-oriented policies are often difficult to enact, because they tend to conflict with a private-market, business-oriented outlook. Local officials may fear being accused of ignoring or going against business interests, or they may simply be unaware that a wider range of policy alternatives exists than they realize. But there is also a danger in using public funds to aid businesses rather than people. As we have seen, the private market does generate economic growth, but at the same time it causes problems by concentrating the benefits among those who need them the least. Thus, economic development programs that are designed purely to generate growth in the local economy without concern for who benefits from the growth are wasted programs that simply replicate or reinforce the outcomes of the private economy (Barnekov and Rich 1989: Green and Haines 2007).

People-oriented policies have been enacted in a sufficient number of communities to demonstrate that they can work. They have also been enacted in a wide variety of economic contexts. Some examples have come from cities in the depths of deindustrialization, such as Hartford, others have come from growing service-sector areas such as Berkeley, or diversified restructuring economies such as Chicago. Perhaps surprisingly, the most economically distressed cities are not the most likely to adopt people-oriented economic development policies. Rather, some evidence shows that local governments in cities with strong local economies have more leverage to adopt policies to the benefit of lower-income populations and the public good (Kantor and Savitch 1993).

CONCLUSION

Economic trends such as the shift from manufacturing to services, globalization of the economy, suburbanization of jobs, and firm mergers, have significantly impacted the economies of cities in the United States. Some of these trends have been positive, and some have been negative. Many cities have lost a good deal of their economic base, although others have made a transition to new economic bases.

Local governments routinely attempt to shape the economic resources in their boundaries. They frequently use policies that assist businesses, but a set of policies that assist people is also available to them. What is the proper mix of economic development policies for any particular locality?

A simple way to approach economic development policy is to develop a **public balance sheet** (Feagin and Parker 1990). This tool allows residents to analyze both the costs and the benefits of local economic decisions. Some of the entries might be surprising. When a company invests and builds a new facility, for example, it produces public costs as well as benefits. City officials and residents should consider the hidden costs of increased use of water, roads, housing for the new employees, schools for their children, police protection, and health care for the growing population, as well as the direct public subsidies such as tax relief or low-interest loans. This public balance sheet allows cities and towns to look carefully at all of the consequences of a decision and to alter the balance if it is unsatisfactory. Rather than simply opening up the city to any form of investment, the public balance sheet approach provides a way of assessing whether the costs of investment are worth the benefits.

DISCUSSION QUESTIONS

1. What kind of economic base exists in your community? How many of the jobs do you think fall into the categories of routine production services, in-person services, and symbolic–analytic services? What might the economic structure of your area mean for future job growth?

2. Have any companies in your local area been merged with other companies? What were the results?

3. Does your community have an economic development office? What kinds of programs does it operate? Do people in the community know about its activities?

13

Local Government
and Finances

I am persuaded on this point: that much of the urban problem in the United
States is the result of trying to run cities on the cheap; trying to run cities
without adequate funds for the police, without adequate funds for sanitation,
without adequate funds for housing, without adequate funds for recreation,
without adequate funds for hospitals, without adequate funds for welfare,
without adequate funds for all the peculiar problems, the peculiarly expensive
problems, of the modern metropolis. The one thing we have never
understood was how expensive the very big city is.
JOHN KENNETH GALBRAITH
LOS ANGELES TIMES, OCTOBER 4, 1970

Throughout this book, it has been apparent that politics, in the broadest sense,
matters in what happens to cities, suburbs, and other communities. This
chapter will focus more narrowly on local politics and the political structures
that govern cities and towns. We will address the following questions:

- How are local governments structured?
- How does the political process work at the community level?
- How do local governments finance their activities?
- How have reform movements attempted to change local political processes?

GOVERNMENT AND POLITICAL POWER

Cities in the United States have a slim legal foothold on existence. In fact, the
framers of the U.S. Constitution gave virtually all legal powers to the states and

completely ignored cities. Some municipal governments have petitioned the states in which they are located for their powers and others have been granted broad (but not necessarily permanent) powers by states through home-rule charters (Frug 1999).

Municipal Control, Political Machines, and Reforms

From the very beginning of the nation, urban political leaders have taken initiatives that have tested the limits of the states' tolerance. Local government has sometimes been a hotbed of favoritism, access to wealth, and other privileges of power. Local graft, cronyism, and corruption were so common in the nineteenth century that Lincoln Steffens (1948), writing about local government in 1904, entitled his book *The Shame of the Cities*. How did this "shameful" state of affairs arise?

According to the account by Judd and Swanstrom (2008), cities of the commercial era were sufficiently small and cohesive that they could be governed by volunteers without formal governments. Groups of wealthy merchants organized themselves when they thought that they should act on behalf of the general good. They acted in response to emergencies such as droughts, epidemics, and fires, typically creating committees with limited scopes of authority such as a fire department or a health board. When they needed authority to do more tasks, city and town leaders petitioned the state legislatures for broader authority under their charters. Rather than instituting full-service municipal governments, however, the commercial cities adopted a limited number of committees with narrowly defined duties.

Industrialization and the tremendous growth of cities after the Civil War magnified the problems and tasks for city administrations. With larger and more diverse populations, the sheer physical challenges of making space and resources (such as water) available to residents and businesses increased rapidly. Cities increased in both social and political complexity. No longer small and simple enough to be controlled by a handful of wealthy merchants, urban government became a political arena in which different groups competed for the attention of city officials. As officials gained increased powers, it became common for them to accept bribes for their votes and engage in other types of horse trading with interest groups seeking governmental actions.

In the nineteenth century, most cities and towns were governed by elected councils. Working-class voters in many cities were able to elect majorities to city councils because cities held elections within districts, and working-class voters were the majority of the electorate in most districts. Business leaders and members of the upper class, outnumbered electorally, responded by claiming widespread corruption. They petitioned the state legislatures to remove powers from the city councils and give them to mayors (elected at large throughout the city rather than representing particular neighborhoods) or to appointed boards made up of "upstanding citizens" such as themselves. Thus, in the name of reform, the industrialists and business leaders were able to regain a measure of political control over the cities in the late nineteenth century (Judd and Swanstrom 2008).

Ironically, removing power from council members and centralizing it in strong mayors laid the foundation for another type of organization associated with corruption, the political machine. Political machines are highly organized groups with hierarchical structures that gain political loyalty by distributing material rewards. The rewards cover a wide variety of items: assistance in getting jobs, contracts, or regulatory variances; holiday food or a helping hand in adversity; assistance in confrontations with the law or in transactions with the bureaucracy. In a political machine, an elected official such as the mayor is at the top, but the little person on the bottom (the loyal voter) is connected to the leader through a chain of contacts, beginning with someone from his or her own precinct (a friend or neighbor), who organizes the neighborhood politically. The precinct captain's job is to get the voters to the polls and to ensure their support of the machine's slate of candidates. Social, material, and political interests and activities are closely intertwined to support the machine institution, and loyalty is very important on all sides.

Political machines had the potential to be extremely powerful in local elections. Thus, it is not surprising that they came under fire from political opponents. Several writers and cartoonists, for example, took aim at New York City Supervisor and Deputy Street Commissioner William M. Tweed for his role in New York politics. They accused Tweed of being the leader of a "ring" of cronies who drained money from city projects, particularly the construction of a new courthouse, into their own bank accounts. Thomas Nast, a cartoonist for *Harper's Weekly*, made his career satirizing Tweed, portraying him as a vulture and a thief. Historian Leo Hershkowitz (1977) argues that Nast's cartoons and the anti-Tweed editorials of the *New York Times* were part of an antiurban, anti-immigrant Republican campaign against the urban growth the Democrats supported. Figure 13.1, a cartoon by Nast, shows Tweed's thumb squashing New York City while Republican New Jersey prospers with new homes and public schools.

The early years of the twentieth century saw an increase in the number and power of political machines, but a reform movement soon arose nationwide to address machine control. Largely fueled by wealthy voters and business interests, the good-government groups in different cities pressed for a number of common reforms. They lobbied for nonpartisan elections (where voting is for individuals, not parties), at-large elections (in which candidates must gain the support of voters from the entire city, not just their own district), civil service systems (where city workers receive their jobs without political appointments and cannot be fired when a new administration takes over), and city managers (who would be professional administrators) rather than elected mayors. These reforms again helped business groups regain political power from immigrants, African Americans, and other working-class groups who made up the voting majority and also

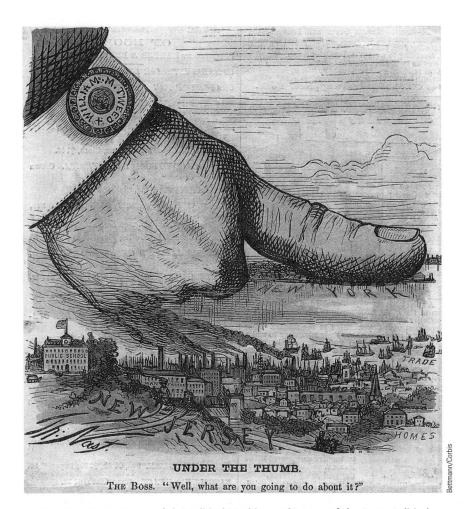

UNDER THE THUMB.

THE BOSS. "Well, what are you going to do about it?"

Bettmann/Corbis

F I G U R E 13.1 **Power of the Political Machine and Power of the Press.** Political cartoonist Thomas Nast helped shape the public's opinion about political figures. This image shows New York City under the thumb of Democrat William M. Tweed while nearby New Jersey prospers under a Republican government.

provided the troops for the political machines. Box 13.1 shows how the very principle of urban self-government through municipal elections came under question during this period.

Studies of Political Power

Today machines no longer dominate local politics in most cities, but a more complicated set of problems and issues characterize local politics. Fewer and fewer eligible people are voting, especially in nonpresidential elections. Do

---

B o x 13.1 • Spotlight
Urban Politics Questioned

By the end of the nineteenth century, accounts of municipal mismanagement across the country were commonplace in an expanding literature on the cities. Many such accounts ... were city-specific, based on the work of local civic organizations and circulated through an emerging national network of local reform organizations. But there were more systematic accounts as well, including comparative financial data on individual cities first published by the U.S. Census in 1890.

More important, reports of widespread municipal mismanagement prompted speculation that the problem was inherent in the very nature of city politics, not simply the result of occasional "defalcations" by a few venal public officials. The speculation centered principally on whether received notions of popular rule and the institutions embodying them were still suitable for governing the modern city—whether the ideas and the institutions could simply be adjusted or, instead, required radical rethinking and restructuring. The issues were crucial to the fate of the democratic experiment. It was not simply that municipal responsibilities had broadened or were being mismanaged. The issues were crucial, as well, because city life was becoming the dominant culture in the United States and because city populations challenged the assumption that suffrage and self-government were suited to all peoples.

SOURCE: Russell D. Murphy, "Politics, Political Science, and Urban Governance: A Literature and a Legacy," Annual Review of Political Science 5 (2002), p. 66.

---

decreases in voting rates mean that citizens do not think they can effect local decisions? To what extent can mayors and other local elected officials shape what happens in cities? Who really holds power and influence over the direction of city government and policies?

The Power Elite and Pluralism.   Beginning in the 1950s, social scientists began the systematic study of local government. They investigated its nature, the level of participation and influence of different groups and individuals, and the impact of political decisions on the lives of community residents. Two opposing perspectives quickly arose: the **power elite**, or power structure, position, and the **pluralist** position. The researchers associated with the power elite, or power structure, position (Hunter 1953, 1980; Mills 1959 Domhoff 1983) found that most cities contained a small number of influential people who devised policy and set new directions for the city, that they tended to be wealthy, and that they formed a cohesive group through their overlapping memberships and frequent interactions with each other. The researchers associated with the pluralist position (Dahl 1961; Polsby 1980) found that many competing groups influenced city governments, that the pattern of who won and who lost on each contested issue had little consistency, and that alliances shifted from one issue to another.

The debate between the power elitists and the pluralists is still unresolved. Looking back on these studies, researchers pointed out that the two perspectives examined different aspects of city government and used different methodologies, thus finding different answers to their questions. Therefore, neither side can claim victory over the other. This body of research, however, created an important legacy by providing social scientists with a great deal of data about how decisions have been made in a wide range of cities.

The studies of power also started a debate that would eventually lead social scientists to ask different and more subtle questions about local politics, questions about who holds power in what circumstances, what leaders can do with the power they have, and what relationships exist among elected officials, business leaders, and citizens' groups.

Recent Directions in the Study of Local Government

Beginning in the 1970s, a number of researchers writing within the general framework of political economy tackled the analysis of local governments. Although they disagree on particulars, their work shares a number of themes. They study entire social and political systems as well as their parts, they look at significant and long-term outcomes of government actions rather than focusing on each decision, and they examine the interplay between the government and the interest groups that relate to it.

Pro-Growth Politics. The early studies of community power asked the question, "Who governs?" Later researchers, such as John Logan and Harvey Molotch (2007) added a second question, "To what end?" Logan and Molotch's research focuses on economic growth as the primary outcome of local political decisions. They argue that the city can be seen as a **growth machine** that benefits those groups that stand to profit from growth. This pro-growth elite includes property owners, developers, business owners, newspapers and media, sports franchises, bankers, and investors in public utilities. These groups all work together in **pro-growth coalitions** to promote growth and to portray growth as noncontroversial on the basis that it supposedly benefits all residents, not just a small number of elite groups. The pro-growth policies backed by such groups include construction of roads, airports, and water supplies; expansion of schools, hospitals, and social services; urban renewal; tax incentives; and advertising a good business climate to attract investment.

The group that provides the core of the pro-growth coalition in cities, according to Logan and Molotch, is property entrepreneurs, or **rentiers**. As we saw in Chapter 4, rentiers make their incomes from property by buying, selling, renovating, renting, or otherwise handling real estate and buildings. Because growth fosters a strong demand for real estate, the rentiers benefit most directly from a growing population and also from economic growth and development. They also employ or are closely associated with other businesspeople, such as attorneys, brokers, and financial service providers. But outside of this core group, the pro-growth coalitions involve most local businesses. They have established in most communities the assumption that growth is good for the population at large while skirting or suppressing questions about the considerable public costs of growth, or how equally the benefits of growth are distributed.

John Mollenkopf (1983) expanded on the notion of the pro-growth coalition by looking at the differential impact it has had over time and in different places. In a study of San Francisco and Boston, he argues that growth coalitions did not always exist and that they did not just appear. Rather, in the context of federal policies that facilitated growth (such as the urban renewal program that we will examine in Chapter 14), a small number of urban leaders helped to organize growth coalitions at the local level. Mollenkopf particularly cites the role of **political entrepreneurs**, local leaders who raised the issue of growth, sold the idea to others, and forged local pro-growth coalitions. Mollenkopf's account of the pro-growth coalitions differs from Logan and Molotch's because each emphasizes a different core group of actors involved in initiating the coalitions. Logan and Molotch's version of growth politics stresses the involvement of economic elites; Mollenkopf's version stresses political leaders.

Although these writers argue that pro-growth coalitions are always active in urban politics, if sometimes in the background, at certain times the pro-growth coalitions have been visible and dominant in setting the urban agenda. During the decades of the 1950s through 1980s, for example, dozens of cities, spurred by coalitions of business, civic, and political groups, undertook massive rebuilding programs. Using federal funds from urban renewal and highway programs, Boston, New York, Philadelphia, Chicago, Detroit, Hartford, Newark, Cincinnati, New Orleans, Denver, and San Francisco systematically destroyed and rebuilt large areas of their central cities to attract investment and draw new types of businesses. Box 13.2 describes the intertwining of the business and political interests in San Francisco that pushed for the redevelopment of the South of Market neighborhood and its establishment as a convention and high-rise office complex.

Studies of local politics show, however, that pro-growth and pro-business coalitions have not always held free rein on the decision-making process. In fact, the urban redevelopment and highway projects displaced so many residents and small businesses and consumed so many local resources that in many cities community organizations arose to stop further demolition and to rechannel resources from the downtowns to other city neighborhoods. In many cases, these neighborhood movements (often coalitions of low-income white, African-American, or Latino neighborhood organizations) organized politically to back their own candidates for mayor, city council, and other local offices. The visible resistance, protest, lobbying, and mobilization tactics drew public attention through the press and in many cases helped the counter-business movements succeed in redirecting the course of public funding and development toward low-income housing, neighborhood economic development, and strengthening community organizations (Ferman 1996).

Limits of Political Action.   Once candidates win an election and take control of city government, to what extent can they influence what happens in their cities? Despite their intentions and personal ideologies, are they obligated to respond to the "needs" of business? In other words, how much leeway do elected officials have in creating the political agenda, and to what extent do factors over which they have no control constrain their decisions? Political analysts spend considerable time discussing this question.

B o x 13.2 • Case Study
Politics in San Francisco

Note: The following selection is from the concluding chapter of a book in which Chester Hartman describes how the process of urban redevelopment transformed central San Francisco from a series of charming small-scale, diverse neighborhoods to a high-rise corporate center.

San Francisco's development history in the post–World War II period has been overwhelmingly dominated by business interests, those in the position to reap the largest profits from this development. They have controlled and peopled the City's government at all levels. They have established their own planning and watchdog mechanisms and agencies, and funded others, to ensure the kind of future they want. The connections between the business community and public policy run the gamut from massive plans to intimate personal ties....

Although much of this private sector planning and manipulation are done out of public view, it would be incorrect to describe the transformation of San Francisco as a large-scale secret conspiracy. Rather, it is a confluence of powerful public and private sector actors operating in their class and personal interests. Much of what transpires is and must be done openly....

In concrete local terms, San Francisco city government overall has been extremely supportive of what the corporate community wants to do in and to the city. The individuals elected and appointed to major positions in city government ... have come overwhelmingly from or are closely linked, economically and socially, with the business community. The oil of this electoral politics machine—cash—has flowed easily, in quantities which overwhelm what other organizations, individuals, and sectors can provide, to elect or retire individual candidates and office holders, and most notably to determine the results of the ballot initiative form of law-giving, which is used quite extensively and creatively in San Francisco and California generally. The money represents an infinitesimal portion of business profits, wisely invested. The business community has a collective sense of itself and its needs, and directly influences the plans prepared by government agencies. Should local government, pressed by popular protest movements, challenge business hegemony too greatly, threats of capital flight, and abandonment, with its attendant job and tax revenue loss, serve to discipline the public sector. It is not a contest of equals.

SOURCE: Chester Hartman, The Transformation of San Francisco (Totowa, NJ: Rowman & Allanheld, 1984), pp. 319–321 *passim*.

The most extreme position holds that local governments have little or no discretion in the conduct of their affairs. Paul Peterson's book *City Limits* (1981) most succinctly sets forth this view. Peterson argues that the market economy is the underlying institution that structures urban patterns. He says that local governments are like businesses competing against each other to attract private investment. Thus, if officials adopt policies that businesses view as too directive or regulatory, they will lose out in the competition with other cities for capital investment.

Peterson's approach has been criticized for overemphasizing the degree to which economic rules of the game bind political actors and institutions (Gottdiener 1983 Logan and Swanstrom 1990). These critics say that different local and global conditions affect political directions and decisions differently. They argue that political processes and outcomes are not economically determined but *contingent*—that is, within a given set of circumstances, political actors have a number of directions that they can choose. As Jones and Bachelor (1986) put it, business interests may have a privileged position in city governments, but they do not outright control those governments; rather, elected officials normally operate in an environment where they can make choices—within certain bounds.

The idea that political power is contingent on a number of contextual factors has led to the study of political **regimes**. The term *regime* refers to the relatively stable coalition of elected officials and behind-the-scenes influencers who run cities. The perspective acknowledges the role of both the set of groups that come together to help officials win elections (electoral coalitions) and the often quite different set of groups that officials must work with to run their cities (governing coalitions). For example, former mayor of Atlanta and former top aide to Martin Luther King, Jr., Andrew Young, faced what mayors and other elected officials experience when forging these different coalitions: the day after he was elected mayor in 1981 he told Atlanta's assembled business leaders, "I didn't get elected with your help, but I can't govern without you" (quoted in Dreier, Mollenkopf, and Swanstrom 2004 153).

A comprehensive study identified three primary types of political regimes: *liberal, progressive,* and *conservative* (Dreier, Mollenkopf, and Swanstrom, 2004). The authors found that each type of regime is characterized by support from a different kind of political coalition, a distinctive philosophy about the role of government, and a different set of approaches toward addressing urban issues such as poverty. In their view, liberal regimes try to "incorporate poor and working-class people, especially minorities, by expanding government services without challenging business influence over other aspects of the urban agenda, especially downtown development" (Dreier, Mollenkopf, and Swanstrom 2001, 197). Progressive regimes go further to empower and distribute resources to low-income groups and challenge business dominance of development issues. Conservative regimes court businesses by stripping away regulation, cutting taxes to create a "healthy business environment," and cutting direct services to the poor.

Clarence Stone (1993) has conducted extensive research on urban political regimes to see how different regime types come to power and what they can do once in office. Stone identifies two major factors by which the environments of local governments differ: the amount of resources at their disposal and the difficulty of the governing task they have chosen to undertake. He argues, for example, that a regime mainly concerned with the relatively unchallenging task of delivering routine services can operate successfully under conditions of *either* abundant or scant resources. On the other hand, Stone argues that a regime must act within a context of abundant economic resources if it attempts to carry out the more challenging task of mobilizing the poor for redistributive programs. This means that progressive regimes have a better chance of success, both in being elected and in being effective politically, when the economic context is already one of growth.

The Contingent Nature of Urban Government.   What have we learned from reviewing the findings of recent research on city government? The early studies of the power elitists and pluralists tended to take an all-or-nothing approach to urban power: Either it was monopolized by an economic elite or it was diffused broadly among the citizenry. By examining cities from different perspectives, we see the emergence of a more complex view: economic elites may shape the outer limits of the political debate, but they do not hold a monopoly on political power. Business owners and other members of the economic elite are not always unified internally on specific issues, even when they agree more generally on the larger issues. In addition, political leaders have their own agendas that may overlap with the interests of the business elite, particularly on certain key issues such as growth, but that at times set them in opposition to key interest groups. It is also important to remember that political leaders usually need to seek reelection, which encourages them to respond to well-organized citizens' groups whether or not they have a great deal of financial resources.

From these studies, we see that the actions of local officials are contingent on the economic and political context in which they operate as well as on their own political strategies. In the end, local officials can exercise some creative management and decision making, but only within limits. What are those limits? To address this issue, we now turn to a more detailed analysis of progressive regimes that have tried to make some changes in local power structures.

Progressive Urban Politics and Urban Reform

Throughout the past few decades, some local activists and political leaders have attempted to locate, test, and extend the limits of action that local officials can take. Stephen Elkin (1987) described the central issue as an attempt to create regimes that are dedicated to popular control, that respect individual liberties, and that promote a commercial society that serves the public interest. This approach contrasts with the conservative notion that city government's primary role is to maintain a good business climate.

Pierre Clavel (1986) studied the policies of local governments during the 1970s and 1980s in five communities that he called "progressive cities": Hartford, Connecticut; Berkeley and Santa Monica, California; Burlington, Vermont; and Cleveland, Ohio. In each of these cities, a group of elected officials carried out a program that attempted to redistribute the benefits of the city to less powerful groups: renters, small businesses, racial minorities, unemployed people, and women. The policies and programs they enacted varied, but they had several common themes, all of them challenging local governments' business-as-usual approach, including:

- Initiating or supporting municipally owned enterprises
- Fostering the development of cooperative businesses
- Making taxes and fees more progressive (based on income)
- Restructuring services during cutbacks so that the poor would not disproportionately bear the cuts
- Regulating the private sector to manage development
- Encouraging citizen participation (Clavel 1986, 11–12).

F I G U R E 13.2 Harold Washington. The first African-American mayor of Chicago, Harold Washington, supported racial equality and community involvement in his urban development programs.

The regimes in the five progressive cities were the first visible and long-lasting of a number of efforts within local governments to carry out policies with similar goals.

Chicago, for example, elected a progressive regime oriented toward social and economic change in 1982. The administration of Mayor Harold Washington (see Figure 13.2) incorporated many political ideas that had been developed and field-tested elsewhere and produced many new ideas. The decline of the political machine in Chicago and the growth of the neighborhood movement—including groups of many ethnicities and racial backgrounds—provided the political support for a progressive candidacy. Once in office, Washington (an African American) made it clear that his government was not to be just another machine for a different ethnic group but was going to provide open access, information, and resources on a democratic basis. Many of the reforms Washington made were institutionalized in the city government structure and persisted after his death in 1987 (Clavel and Wiewel 1991).

In 2009, a mayor with a progressive urban agenda was elected for his second term in Los Angeles. Mayor Antonio Villaraigosa had a strong base of support in labor organizations and community groups as well as the Latino and Catholic voters. He sought to redefine a "healthy business climate" as one that is good for working people and city residents as well as for investors. The issues he has addressed include improving wages for low-income workers, reducing pollution (a legendary problem in Los Angeles), increasing the stock of affordable housing, and expanding public transportation. Box 13.3 outlines the accomplishments of Mayor Villaraigosa's first term of office.

As in the case of Los Angeles, most administrations in progressive cities were elected by issue-oriented coalitions that used an electoral strategy to create change. By forming a coalition and working for a slate of candidates, groups such as liberals, members of racial minorities, union members, religious people, and neighborhood-based groups merged their interests and constructed programs that supported their common vision. Like Chicago's Harold Washington, Boston's Mayor Ray Flynn and Cleveland's Mayor Dennis Kucinich were elected in populist campaigns based on social movements. A survey of cities (Kantor and Savitch 1993) shows that cities where popular control is strong are more able to enact policies that favor the common good over corporate interests.

Several cities with growing service sectors have elected progressive local governments that have sought to manage and redistribute economic growth. As we have seen, when the corporate service sector (banks, insurance companies, law firms, advertising agencies, stockbrokerages, and so on) grows, it can begin to dominate the city, both in the types of land use and the growing class of up-scale residences and businesses in the city. Some local governments may welcome this economic investment, but progressive officials realize that rapid economic development and the resulting gentrification can squeeze out small businesses as well as poor and middle-class residents. Their strategy is not to stop the growth but to harness it by capturing some of the growth through taxes or fees and using it to offset the potentially harmful effects. Progressive leaders in Boston adopted a program called **linkage** that taxed downtown development projects to provide funds for the construction of affordable housing for low-income residents. The City of Berkeley instituted a **First Source hiring program** that trained unemployed people, women, citizens of color, and people with disabilities and placed them in positions with private companies. In return for participating in the program, the city gave the companies special benefits such as loans and expedited permits. Burlington, Vermont, adopted a host of programs to harness growth including a land trust to deter speculation in real estate and a revolving loan fund to assist small businesses (Clavel and Kleniewski 1990).

Studies of urban reform regimes show that local governments indeed have a range of space for their policies and a fairly wide repertoire of actions from which they can choose. But progressive officials cannot act alone; they must be supported by a sympathetic electorate and be able to assemble an administration that both agrees with their vision and is competent in finding ways to operationalize it. By closely analyzing the resources in their localities and creatively negotiating with formerly entrenched interests, reform governments have been able to make some significant changes in their cities.

FINANCING LOCAL GOVERNMENT

A good example of how economics and politics are intertwined in local government is the issue of government finances. Local discussions and decisions about

B o x 13.3 • Case Study
Mayor Villaraigosa's Agenda for Los Angeles

[Antonio] Villaraigosa, the first Latino mayor in LA's modern history, inherited a city where the divide between the rich and everyone else was widening. (LA had more millionaires than any other city, but was also the nation's capital of the working poor). Housing costs were skyrocketing. Traffic congestion, inadequate public transit, and the Port made LA the most polluted metro area in the country. The schools were overcrowded and underfunded, with a huge drop-out rate.
   He asked to be judged on whether he could address these issues, especially the plight of the poor and the struggling lower-middle class, as well manage basic municipal services. He wanted to promote what activists call a "growth with justice" agenda.
   During his first four-year term, Villaraigosa has sought to be a new kind of progressive pro-business mayor—by redefining a "healthy business climate" to mean prosperity that is shared by working people, one that lifts the working poor into the middle class. He has tried to promote a more enlightened view of business's responsibility to the broader community. He has encouraged, even pushed, employers to support workers' rights to unionize. Building on the living wage model, his Community Redevelopment Agency and other departments have focused municipal subsidies on industries and firms that provide decent pay, benefits and a career path with upward mobility and create "green" jobs. He has advocated for a mixed-income housing law that requires developers to set aside units for working families.
   On the basic matters of "civic housekeeping" LA has been well-served by Villaraigosa. Crime is down significantly. Traffic flows have improved and new rapid bus routes are in place. Villaraigosa led the campaign for Prop R, which voters approved, and which will provide $40 billion for public transit. Despite the usual griping by some residents, potholes get fixed and the garbage gets collected with reasonable efficiency. In his four years in office, the number of summer jobs for youth has increased from 3,000 to 16,000.

taxes and spending are often among the most controversial of political issues. Taxes are a hot issue because they address the question of redistribution—that is, government takes money away from citizens in the form of taxes and then gives it back to them in the form of services. Questions about taxing and spending are directly related to the issues of what government does, who pays, and who benefits.

If we think of the city's finances as a ledger book, the *income* side would include several items such as property tax, sales and income taxes, fees charged for services, and federal and state aid. Figure 13.3 shows the aggregate of all local government income in the United States from all sources in the Fiscal Year 2005. (These figures refer to all local governments, including cities, towns, and counties.) Note that state and federal aid make up the largest category of income (more than one-third), while property taxes make up only about a quarter of the total revenue. This is a big change from the past, when

On housing, Villaraigosa has funded the $100 million Housing Trust Fund to create more affordable units, strengthened tenants' rights, improved code inspection to fix slum buildings, and partnered with nonprofit community groups like ACORN, One LA, and Neighborhood Housing Services to help homeowners facing foreclosure. Housing advocates have been pushing for a mixed-income housing law in LA for a decade, one that (like those in 170 other California cities) would require developers to include units for nurses, secretaries, security guards, garment workers, school teachers and other low- and moderate-income people. Villaraigosa has been an ally in that effort.

No big-city mayor in the entire U.S. has been as fervent a champion for the working poor—and for the rights of workers—as Villaraigosa. He played a central role in helping the city's low-wage security guards win a union campaign by getting major office building owners to the bargaining table. He utilized the leverage of the Community Redevelopment Agency to create a pipeline of young people prepared for jobs in the construction trades. Against the strong opposition of the city's business community, he supported a dramatic expansion of the city's "living wage" law to lift several thousands of workers who work at a dozen hotels near the LAX airport out of poverty. He has shown up at union picket lines and been a key behind-the-scenes mediator in several labor disputes.

Some agenda items—like the rewriting of the city's comprehensive zoning plan (needed to combat sprawl), the expansion of the regional subway (which will require substantial state and federal funds), the reform of public schools (ditto), and the planting of a promised one million trees (behind schedule)—are still works in progress, projects that will take many years to complete. The jury is still out on how, or whether, they will succeed.

SOURCE: Peter Dreier, "*LA* Magazine's Failure: Irresponsible Journalism," The Huffington Post, July 25, 2009, *passim*.

property taxes were the main source of income for local governments. The proportion of local revenues contributed by the property tax steadily decreased during the twentieth century, from 73 percent in 1902 to 50 percent in 1962 to only 25 percent in 2005. The reasons for the proportional decline of the property tax are complex, including the substitution of relatively less visible sales taxes, the adoption of income taxes levied not only city residents but suburban residents who work in the city, and the increasing contribution of state and local aid as city tax bases failed to keep up with growing needs (Judd and Swanstrom 2008).

On the *expense* side of the local government ledger book would be items in the **operating budget**, such as the pay of city employees (teachers, police, street crews, etc.), office supplies, utilities, and other day-to-day expenses of government agencies. Also on the *expense* side is the capital budget, the expensive but long-lasting items, such as schools, water treatment plants, firehouses, bridges,

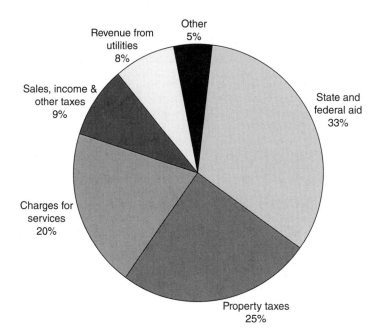

F I G U R E 13.3 **Local Government Revenues.** This chart shows the sources of revenue for all local governments. Note that the largest source is federal and state aid. Property taxes account for only a quarter of all revenues.

SOURCE: Derived from U.S. Census Bureau, Statistical Abstract of the United States 2009, Table 437.

sewers, and so on. Figure 13.4 shows the aggregate pattern of local government expenses in the United States in the Fiscal Year 2005. Note that more than half of all money spent by local governments went to education, health, and social services. Along with public safety (police and fire departments) and sanitation (here included in "environment"), these are the core services that cities provide to their residents on a daily basis.

In addition to collecting taxes and fees, local governments must borrow money to fund their activities. Capital expenditures are almost always financed through borrowed money, raised by issuing bonds to lenders such as individuals, financial institutions, and pension funds. If financial experts think that a local government is financially sound and able to pay back its loans, they give it a high rating. Cities with good bond ratings normally have more demand for their bonds than cities with lower bond ratings. Cities sometimes also issue short-term notes, borrowing funds to meet their operating budget when they are temporarily short of cash but expect to receive revenues in the near future (for example, just before residents are due to pay their property taxes). These bonds constitute a debt for the locality in that they must pay back both principal and interest to lenders over a stated number of years. Localities have increased their borrowing, and thus their indebtedness, steadily over the past twenty-five years, as shown in Figure 13.5.

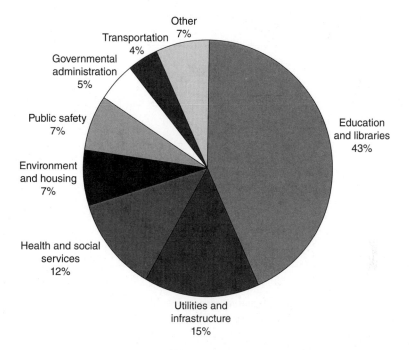

F I G U R E 13.4 Local Government Expenditures. This chart shows how local governments spend their funds. Note that education, health, and social services account for approximately half of all local expenditures.

SOURCE: Derived from U.S. Census Bureau, *Statistical Abstract of the United States*, 2009, Table 438.

A good deal of the task of managing large cities lies in managing the complex and controversial issues related to the budget. How much will the city receive in tax revenues? When shortfalls occur, are they temporary or long term? What is an appropriate level of debt for a city to carry? When expenditures must be cut, where should the cuts be made and what "essential" services should be protected? The decisions public officials make will have both economic and political impacts on their cities.

Fiscal Distress

City officials must balance their localities' revenues against their expenditures. This is often a difficult balancing act. As Dreier, Mollenkopf, and Swanstrom (2004) point out, tax revenues are limited and unpredictable. They are limited because cities can only raise taxes to an amount that will be acceptable to residents and property owners and because a great deal of urban property is tax-exempt (for example, hospitals, universities, and museums). Tax revenues are unpredictable because revenues from all sources (property, sales, and income tax, as well as fees and government transfers) fluctuate with the ups and downs of the economy. On the other hand, expenses keep rising steadily because of steady increases in the demand for services and the costs of doing business. A growing low-income population

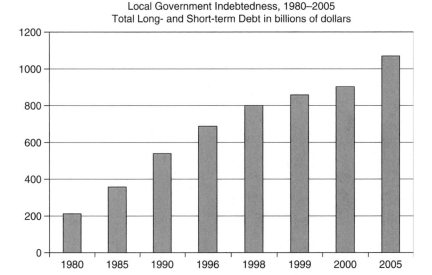

FIGURE 13.5 **Local Government Indebtedness.** As this chart indicates, local governments have taken on increasingly large debt burdens to finance their activities.
SOURCE: Derived from U.S. Census Bureau, Statistical Abstract of the U.S. 2009, Table 438.

needs social services; the public demands additional police protection; municipal employees must receive negotiated wage increases; changing federal and state laws mandate costly changes in education for special populations and in Medicaid payments. Even in relatively prosperous times, city governments struggle to raise sufficient income to meet expenditures.

When a city's expenditures are substantially greater than its revenues over a sustained period of time, the resulting gap produces fiscal distress. Fiscal distress is characterized by a combination of a high debt burden and/or declining revenues compared to expenses. The most extreme examples are those that result in a fiscal crisis, a condition in which a city may not meet its payroll, may default on its bond payments, or may declare bankruptcy.

Economic conditions in the1970s generated well-publicized fiscal crises in two major cities, New York and Cleveland. In 1975 New York City suddenly found itself unable to borrow money, and in 1978 the city of Cleveland went into default, meaning that it was unable to repay the city's lenders when its bonds came due. Both crises were based on the fact that the cities' budgets were reliant on borrowed money, which the local banks refused to lend. New York City ended up in **receivership**, with city officials having to answer to a board appointed by the banks. This board put New York on an **austerity program**, making the city reduce its level of expenditures while holding taxes down. The austerity program resulted in wholesale closings and cutbacks in schools, hospitals, parks and recreation, police and fire protection, and other city services (Shefter 1985). In the case of Cleveland, the city's bankers refused to lend money to the city because of a dispute with the mayor over the control of a public utility company (Swanstrom 1985).

Research on these two prominent cases of fiscal crisis revealed that they were not isolated incidents but simply exaggerated examples of a problem that affects local governments throughout the United States. The 1990s brought the recurrence of fiscal distress in a number of cities as the economy waned. Since 2000, we have witnessed sharp increases in local tax revenues during the boom times and precipitous declines during recessionary times. During 2005, for example, New York City's "superheated" real estate and stock market brought in $3.4 billion to city coffers over what the city had expected (McIntire 2005). On the other hand, in 2009, a steep decline in housing prices and sales taxes (from the drop-off in automobile sales) cost local governments in Los Angeles County an estimated $11 billion for the Fiscal Year 2009. In response, localities had to freeze hiring, impose work furloughs, postpone repairs, and reduce services (Zavis 2009).

Taxpayers' Movements. A final factor helps explain the fiscal problems of local government. Since the late 1970s local taxpayers have commonly rejected tax increases or voted for tax limitation measures. The first tax limitation movement that gained national attention was Proposition 13 in California, a law that limited increases in local property taxes. Subsequently, tax protest movements have been organized in Massachusetts, Connecticut, New Jersey, Illinois, Michigan, Oregon, Idaho, Arizona, and other states—all aimed at reducing taxes on homeowners and small businesses. But one year after the California tax limitation was passed, studies showed that homeowners and small businesses had received only modest reductions in their tax bills, whereas large corporations and landlords had received the lion's share of the benefits (Furlong 1979). Thus, Proposition 13 redistributed the tax burden so that homeowners and small businesses paid proportionately more taxes while having their services cut.

The irony of the California taxpayers' revolt, according to Clarence Lo (1990), was that it was originally organized by working-class and middle-class homeowners who felt squeezed between their stagnating wages and increasing local property taxes. The movement initially had a decidedly anticorporate and anti–big government agenda. As time passed, however, more suburban, upper middle-class voters and business owners became involved in the movement, changing its goals and rhetoric. The idea of downward tax redistribution and justice for "the little person" was gradually replaced with a more antigovernment rhetoric. Not only did this result in an initiative passed that helped businesses more than small property owners, but it also set the stage for further reductions and limitations on taxes on the national and local levels. These tax reduction measures, including massive income tax cuts in the 1980s as well as local and state limitations, have overwhelmingly benefited the wealthy and the business sector (Lo 1990).

Capping property taxes may have slowed the growth of spending, but it has certainly not stopped it. To get around the restrictions on property taxes, cities and towns have increasingly turned to other sources of revenue. Bartle (2003) points out that during the past twenty years, the proportion of local revenues contributed by state aid and property taxes has decreased, while during the same period the proportion of local revenues contributed by sales taxes, excise taxes, and user fees has increased sharply. He notes that even though controlling property taxes is politically popular, spending on items such as schools, public safety, and infrastructure is also popular. To meet the ever-increasing demand for services, local governments have simply raised sales taxes, which they find is more favorably received than property tax increases.

POLITICAL FRAGMENTATION
AND REGIONAL STRATEGIES

As we saw in Chapter 5, metropolitan areas are now the actual, or functional, cities in our society. Yet they are most often not the political or legal city. Instead, most metropolitan areas are fragmented into numerous cities, towns, school districts, and other jurisdictions. The Chicago metropolitan area, for example, contains 1,458 governmental units, Philadelphia's contains 877, and the St. Louis area contains 789 governments (Dreier, Mollenkopf, and Swanstrom 2001, 39).

One of the problems with political fragmentation is its inefficiency. When each city, town, and village has its own police, fire, water, highway, and sanitation departments, its own school systems, and its own social service agencies, serious problems of duplication of effort arise. In addition, the costs of providing infrastructure (including roads, water and sewer lines, schools, and hospitals) are higher in low-density, small communities than in high-density, more centralized areas (Williamson, Imbroscio, and Alperovitz 2002).

The second problem with political fragmentation is that it can be environmentally harmful. Political fragmentation encourages suburban sprawl because each municipality has incentives to increase tax revenues by fostering development, whether or not it is in the long-term best interest of the community. Because each independent municipality controls its own zoning and its own taxes, the tendency is to develop as much land as possible for homes (preferably large homes on large lots) and businesses, thereby reducing open space, which does not bring in tax revenues. Sprawl in turn promotes road construction and longer commutes for residents, which in turn brings additional traffic congestion and air pollution.

The third problem with fragmentation is that much of the economic growth within metropolitan areas is captured by the outlying communities at the expense and to the detriment of the central cities. As we saw in the last section, many cities are experiencing fiscal distress due to declining tax revenues. Cities' tax revenues have decreased compared to their costs partly because much of the growth in our urban areas is located in the smaller communities outside of the central cities. Residents of the outlying communities may work in the city, use its roads or transit services, and patronize its museums without contributing to the tax base of the city.

The fourth, and potentially most challenging, problem with political fragmentation is that it contributes to growing social inequality. As we saw in

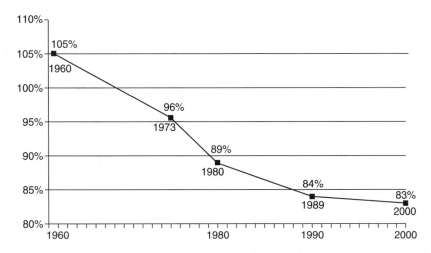

F I G U R E 13.6 **Ratio of Central City–Suburban Per Capita Income, 1960–2000.** The proportion of the average income that central city residents make compared to the average income that suburban residents make dropped from 105 percent to 83 percent in forty years.

SOURCE: Dreier, Mollenkopf, and Swanstrom 2004, p. 46.

Chapter 10, our society has been dividing geographically by social class. Dreier, Mollenkopf, and Swanstrom (2001) document the increasing geographic separation of the different social classes not only into separate neighborhoods but into separate municipalities and school districts. They show that although economic segregation is an ongoing pattern in the development of the United States—much more than in other nations—the degree and scope of economic segregation have grown at a startling pace since 1970. We can see this by tracking changes in the difference between the incomes of city residents compared to the incomes of suburban residents. Figure 13.6 shows how rapidly the average income of central-city residents has fallen when compared with suburban residents in the same metropolitan area. In 1960 city dwellers earned on average more than suburban dwellers; however, by 1999 they earned only 87 percent of their suburban neighbors.

As we saw in Chapter 4, where municipal boundaries are drawn is a political decision that can be changed. Some analysts argue that politically consolidating metropolitan areas and sharing both the revenues and expenses of the municipalities would help solve the problem of economic segregation and would strengthen metropolitan areas as a whole. Although this is a radical idea in some areas, it has happened naturally in other areas. Some metropolitan areas such as Indianapolis, Nashville, Houston, and Jacksonville, Florida, have acknowledged that cities and suburbs are part of the metropolitan whole by merging the various local governments into metropolitan governments or by expanding the central city's boundaries to encompass the adjacent suburban communities.

David Rusk (1993, 1999) argues that the metropolitan areas that have consolidated their urban and suburban jurisdictions into metropolitan governments have fared much better on a host of social and economic indicators than have those metropolitan areas that have chosen to remain politically divided. Rusk cites higher economic growth, lower income inequality, and less concentrated poverty as benefits of metropolitan consolidation. He points to Minneapolis, Minnesota, and Portland, Oregon, as cities that developed regional strategies that foster collaboration between the central cities and their suburbs. He shows how cities can gain by focusing on their "inside game" of city-oriented programs, complemented by an "outside game" of sharing resources and authority across their metropolitan regions. Former Minnesota State Senator Myron Orfield (2002), credited with the development of the regional plan for Minneapolis, advocates "metropolitics" as a solution to problems of both central cities and regions.

Evidence from other cities, however, indicates that metropolitan collaborations may not be effective or even appropriate as a solution to urban problems. The case of Louisville's regionalization, as recounted by David Imbroscio (2006) resulted in a decided shift of political power from the core city to the more diffuse metropolitan region. Imbroscio argues that the city was not in such bad shape to begin with, and now city residents have lost power to suburban voters and interest groups. He makes a plea for returning from regionalism to a focus on the city as the site of policy efforts and political activity.

Still other analysts argue that suburban communities have in many cases outgrown their need for central cities because they have become sufficiently large and varied to allow them to exist independently. In *Edge City* for example, Joel Garreau (1991) describes a number of suburban communities complete with housing, schools, industrial and office parks (sometimes containing skyscrapers), recreational facilities, shopping centers, and transportation hubs. Garreau argues that such communities thrive precisely because they have become disconnected from their central cities. They may have sprung up initially because of their proximity to a central city, but over the years their growth and development have made the central city less and less relevant to the functioning of the edge city. In his view, residents of such suburbs have no need for the central city, and by implication have nothing to gain or lose if the central city succeeds or fails.

CONCLUSION

Political structures and political power have an enormous impact on life in cities. Local governments have often been exploited for private economic gain, from the political machines that benefited individuals, to the organized growth machines that benefit local business as a whole. Reforms in the political process can shift power from one group to another and give access to previously disenfranchised groups. Progressive regimes in a number of cities have instituted policies that mitigate the problems caused by the market.

The study of urban finances shows that urban officials are in a difficult position. They must provide the services that residents need while keeping taxes within an acceptable range for homeowners and businesses. Many local governments experience fiscal distress stemming from the imbalance between revenues and expenses, and a few cities have experienced outright fiscal crises in which they fall seriously short of the income they need to provide the most basic city services.

The political fragmentation of metropolitan areas into hundreds of jurisdictions characterizes local government in the United States. The separation of the wealthy from the poor and the suburbanization of business have left urban officials with little room to develop policies to address their local problems. Some central city mayors have formed coalitions with their suburban colleagues to take a regional approach to metropolitan issues. These regional initiatives have become increasingly popular as federal aid to cities has declined, putting more of the burdens of government on the local officials. In the next chapter, we will see just how much the federal government does to aid cities and the kinds of activities it supports.

DISCUSSION QUESTIONS

1. Political machines encouraged corruption, but they also encouraged political participation by voters. What gets people out to vote today? Could the turnout in local elections be improved? What kinds of measures do you think would lead to increased voter participation?

2. Do you see articles and letters about property taxes and public services in your local newspaper? What kinds of issues do they raise?

3. Some studies contrast a conservative pro-business local government policy with a pro-people, or progressive, policy. What kinds of activities flow from each orientation? Could you characterize your local government's policies as more pro-business or more progressive? What indicators would you choose to examine to do so?

14

Federal Urban Policy

The clock is ticking, time is moving ... we must ask ourselves every night
when we go home, are we doing all that we should do in our nation's capital,
in all other big cities of the country.
PRESIDENT LYNDON JOHNSON
IN A SPEECH AFTER THE WATTS RIOT, AUGUST, 1965

Throughout this book, we have seen that a number of different factors shape
cities and urban life. We have weighed the extent to which actions of individuals and actions of institutions influence cities. Individuals' decisions to buy or
sell property, to locate businesses in particular places, and to sell or rent space for
particular purposes help to shape the city. These actions occur in what economists think of as the market. But the actions of individuals in the market are not
the full extent of the factors that shape urban form. Government intervention
through planning, regulation, and other actions also has a significant impact on
cities. In Chapter 13, we saw how cities are governed and how local government
affects cities. This chapter will explore how the federal government shapes cities.

It will focus on the following four questions:

- What policies has the federal government implemented that have affected
  cities?

- How and why have government policies changed over time?

- What are the effects of urban policies on cities?

- What political factors affect the government's choice of urban policies?

Not all of the government actions that affect cities are included in what are
officially called *urban policies*. Some significant changes in cities have come about
through the creation of national policies that simply happen to have a concentrated effect on cities. In this chapter, therefore, we will begin with a brief discussion of several **indirect urban policies** before moving to the bulk of the
chapter, which will focus on direct, or **explicit urban policies**.

INDIRECT URBAN POLICY

Urban policy is not the only type of government activity that impacts cities and urban dwellers. Other federal actions have an indirect impact on cities and can therefore be considered implicit urban policy (Wolman 1986). These include federal economic policy, spending patterns, tax policy, and regulations.

An important type of policy that has an enormous impact on communities is **macroeconomic policy**, or the set of actions the federal government takes to regulate the ups and downs of the business cycle. The goal of macroeconomic policy is to prevent either inflationary overheating of the economy on the one hand, or unemployment-causing recessions on the other. Depending on which is thought to be the more significant problem at the time, federal agencies take opposite actions. If recession is a problem, federal agencies can stimulate the economy by reducing interest rates, cutting taxes, and increasing government spending. These actions give businesses more resources to expand and give people more money to spend. If inflation is a problem, the federal government can raise interest rates, raise taxes, and cut government spending, thus putting the brakes on economic expansion and slowing inflationary growth.

Macroeconomic policy is a general policy rather than a specific policy. Comparing it to medicine, it is more of a tonic that keeps the patient well, rather than a surgical procedure that corrects a problem in a specific organ. In general, when the national economy is growing, urban economies are healthiest, even though not all cities do equally well during growth periods. In addition to a general policy of economic growth, then, specific policies are needed to address inner-city areas and cities in slowly growing regions. Several anti-inflationary policies that the federal government adopted in the early 1980s created a deep recession on the national level. But the impact of that recession on inner cities was far greater than on other areas, fostering more rapid and more dramatic increases in rates of unemployment, poverty, homelessness, infant mortality, and violence than occurred elsewhere (Dreier 1993; Wolman 1986). This macroeconomic action that was only mildly detrimental to the national economy was devastating to poor urban areas.

Similarly, federal spending on social service programs such as Medicare (medical assistance for senior citizens), Medicaid (medical assistance for low-income households), and Temporary Assistance to Needy Families (public assistance), has a disproportionate impact on cities, although not geographically targeted toward cities. The reason for the disproportionate impact is that higher concentrations of the programs' participants live in urban areas than in other types of communities, so the urban areas benefit from the federal funds their residents receive. Cuts in these federally funded programs, therefore, reduce the incomes and services that citydwellers receive, leaving a greater burden on the city governments to fill the gap.

Housing policy, although it affects all types of communities, also has a special impact on cities. Federal income tax policy allows taxpayers to deduct a proportion of their income to offset the amount that they pay each year in property taxes and in mortgage interest payments. The homeowners' income tax

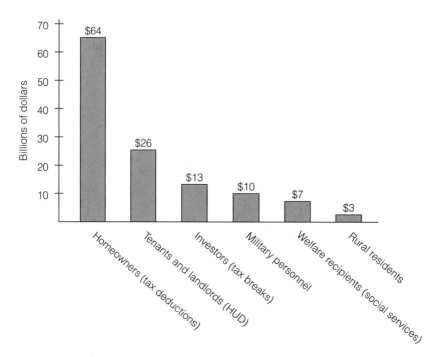

F I G U R E 14.1 **Government Housing Programs: Who Benefits?** The homeowners' tax deduction for middle- and upper-income households far outstrips spending for low-income groups.

SOURCE: Adapted from Peter Dreier and John Atlas, "Housing Policy's Moment of Truth," *The American Prospect* (Summer, 1995): 68–77.

deduction is actually the nation's largest housing program, costing more than $90 billion in 2004 (Dreier 2005). It dwarfs other housing programs, for example, subsidized rental housing, as shown in Figure 14.1.

The homeowners' tax deduction has two important consequences for cities. First, the subsidy has helped to build the suburbs. It encourages families to buy larger homes and pay higher property taxes than they could without the tax deduction. Second, the subsidy is a kind of Robin Hood in reverse. The largest tax deductions go to the households with the largest homes, the largest mortgages, and the largest taxable incomes. Although it is unlikely that all of the federal money spent through these tax deductions could be used for other housing programs, it is nonetheless a commentary on the nature of the policy-making process that the lion's share of our national housing subsidies go to the groups who need it the least.

How the federal government chooses to spend money also affects communities. One study (Joassart-Marcelli and Musso 2001) examined how federal spending affected cities in the Southern California region during the 1980s and 1990s. The authors found that the cities with the highest average incomes received the largest proportions of money from federal programs. Although cities with poorer populations received larger amounts of funding from programs specifically targeted toward alleviating poverty, once all of the other federal programs were considered, the cities with the wealthier populations received considerably more federal dollars. A decrease in Medicaid funding is another example of how the federal government chooses not to spend money. The federal government initiated Medicaid, a program to provide basic medical services to low-income people, but federal funding has not kept up with soaring health care costs. Instead, the costs have been shifted to the states and cities, which are obligated by federal law to provide the services, even if they do not receive funding adequate to the task. Such "unfunded mandates" have contributed to the fiscal stress we discussed in the previous chapter.

EMERGENCE OF URBAN POLICY

True, or explicit, urban policy is a relatively new phenomenon. Problems of poverty, poor housing, and urban unrest have been present in cities of the United States since colonial times, but, to the extent that the government addressed them at all, they were the responsibility of local jurisdictions until about a century ago. The first time that the federal government took any action targeted toward urban problems was in 1892, when Congress appropriated $20,000 to investigate slum conditions in large cities. The resulting study described the conditions of slum dwellers but recommended no actions to address their problems. In a statement that today would be called "blaming the victim," the study noted that slum areas had more saloons and arrests than other parts of cities, implying that slum conditions were due to the immoral behavior of the inhabitants (Judd and Swanstrom 2008).

Public Housing

The Great Depression of the 1930s prompted the first concentrated urban policy, which addressed the problem of slum housing. In 1933 Congress created the Works Progress Administration, whose housing division assisted local agencies in clearing slums and constructing subsidized rental units. It was a timid beginning, because only a small number of communities participated in this initial effort. In 1937, the passage of the federal Housing Act launched the **public housing** program, the first major urban program. Although public housing today serves both urban and rural areas, it was initially confined to cities (Bratt 1990). The central idea of the program was that the government could compete with private landlords in providing housing, not for everyone, but for the poor who were not well served by the private housing market.

The legislation that created public housing was supported by a coalition of reformers and labor unions with different goals. Housing reformers wanted to improve poor people's living conditions. Social welfare advocates wanted social justice for the poor. Labor unions wanted to get construction jobs. President Franklin D. Roosevelt wanted to get the nation's stalled economy moving again. The opponents of public housing, however, were unified. These private landlords and housing industry leaders feared that the competition from government-built housing would drive down rents in the private sector (Jackson 2009, 1985). The resulting legislation was a compromise that established a public housing program but limited it so it would not become a threat to privately owned rental housing.

The basic operating procedure of public housing has changed little since its inception. Cities and counties run agencies called *housing authorities* that receive federal funds to build and operate rental housing. Once the projects are built, they are supposed to support themselves through rents. Federal program guidelines spell out the types of housing that can be built, the size of households and income levels of eligible tenants, and most other conditions of the program's operation (see Figure 14.2).

In some ways, however, public housing has changed dramatically over the past thirty years. The initial tenants of public housing during the Depression were the "submerged" middle class, the respectable but temporarily poor people who needed publicly subsidized housing until their fortunes improved. As time passed, the conditions of the housing market changed and so did the nature of the poor population living in cities. Many members of the submerged middle class surfaced from poverty and moved to the suburbs during the prosperity of the post–World War II period. Congress then changed the guidelines for tenants' income levels to include more of the very poor, and public housing projects gained increasing numbers of extremely low-income households. In addition, segregated projects that had been built for white families (including most of the projects up to the 1950s) were desegregated in the 1960s, leading to a rapid transformation in the racial composition of many public housing projects (Friedman 1980).

These changes, along with a severe shortage of funds and the difficulties of maintaining buildings that were constructed cheaply in the first place, added up to the transformation of a sizeable number of public housing projects into virtual warehouses for the minority poor. Although the impersonal, superblock-type projects shown in Figure 14.2 (a) gave public housing a negative public image, many other projects continued to be safe, well maintained, successful alternatives to the private housing available to low-income tenants.

Congress, however, has become increasingly critical of public housing and has made a number of changes to the operation and funding of the program. The Housing Bill of 1990 aimed at radically transforming if not eliminating public housing. The bill provided funds for rebuilding selected "distressed" projects, removing some apartments to decrease housing density, and redesigning the buildings to resemble surrounding neighborhoods. The bill also encouraged local authorities to mix different types of housing, including both owner-occupied and rental units at both subsidized and market rates in the same project. In addition, the section of the legislation called HOPE (Home Ownership for People Everywhere) set up a program to sell public housing units to tenants wherever feasible. Finally, the bill included a "self-sufficiency" provision, requiring tenants to participate in counseling, education, community service, and case management programs as a condition of remaining in public housing. This requirement was designed to wean residents from all forms of public assistance, including public housing (Hays 1995). The current version of the legislation, HOPE VI,

(a)

(b)

F I G U R E 14.2   Public Housing. (a) Many people associate public housing with large-scale projects such as Philadelphia's Raymond Rosen Homes, which was demolished in 1995. (b) Less visible types of public housing include scattered-site units that are indistinguishable from the other homes in the surrounding neighborhoods.

(a)

(b)

F I G U R E 14.3 HOPE VI. The principle behind HOPE VI is to demolish "distressed" public housing developments such as (a) above and replace them with mixed-income developments as seen in (b).

emphasizes the renovation of older public housing units and their transformation into mixed-income developments with a combination of rental and owner-occupied units.

The HOPE VI program is a companion to the Moving to Opportunity program discussed in Chapter 9. Both programs have the ultimate goal of reducing concentrations of low-income racial minority households by "dispersing" them to areas where they will have nonpoor, white neighbors. The mechanism of MTO is the use of rental vouchers to enable tenants to move to nonpoor neighborhoods. The mechanism of HOPE VI is to demolish large public housing developments and rebuild them, reducing the number of low-income units in the mix. (See Figure 14.3.) These policies have raised a number of issues about how best to provide housing for disadvantaged households. Goetz (2003) for example, details the political controversy that arose from the implementation of a public housing development in Minneapolis under HOPE VI. The residents there did not perceive themselves as having a choice when they were evicted from public housing and argued that there were few places they could go where they would be welcome, where they had the family and social network support of their old neighborhood, and where transportation, schools, and day care were accessible. Goetz asks whether the policies that aim to deconcentrate poverty represent a retreat from attempts to solve the problems of poverty as opposed to moving it around.

Changes in the operation of public housing since 1990, then, continued the trend begun in the 1980s: the federal government supporting fewer public housing units and increasingly relying on the private rental market to house low-income people. The reduction in public housing creates severe problems for the very poor, and in many cities it causes increased homelessness as low-cost housing becomes scarcer and scarcer. On the positive side, because of changes including reconstruction and new services, some of the public housing developments that remain in operation are gradually becoming better places to live. Many contextual factors go into making a successful as opposed to an unsuccessful redevelopment of a public housing project, including how well organized the tenants are, how responsive the management is, and how economically viable the surrounding community is (Salama; Vale 2002 1999).

Urban Renewal

The urban renewal program was a variation on the slum clearance approach to urban policy. Originally called *urban redevelopment*, the strategy behind this program was for government agencies to obtain land by **eminent domain**, demolish the structures on it (and often replace the infrastructure such as roads and sewers), and then replan and redevelop the land for a different use. The idea was not for the government bodies to take possession permanently, but to assemble buildable parcels of land and sell them to private developers at a subsidized price. The federal government provided funds but local agencies, called *redevelopment authorities*, identified deteriorated properties, bought them, cleared the land, and resold it to private buyers.

The real estate lobby and other private groups enthusiastically supported the urban renewal program. For example, the Central Business District Council of the Urban Land Institute and the National Association of Real Estate Boards promoted urban renewal and helped write the law that Congress passed. Largely at the urging of these lobbying groups, several states had passed urban renewal legislation prior to the national act in 1949. Throughout the debates on the legislation, there was a great deal of tension between the supporters of urban renewal, who wanted to make cities more profitable for private interests, and the supporters of public housing, who wanted to improve housing opportunities for the poor. Ultimately, despite the contradictory goals, both urban renewal and an updated public housing program were included in the 1949 law (Weiss 1980; Judd and Swanstrom 2008).

Urban renewal proved to be a controversial program. A number of cities' downtowns were revitalized or even "saved" through the rebuilding program, but the costs of demolition—both human and economic—were high. Understandably, slum clearance affected mostly very low-income households. They were displaced from their homes with either no payment (for the vast majority who were tenants) or with a fair market value payment for homeowners, which normally meant less than would be necessary to buy a replacement home. Not surprisingly, a large number of deteriorated neighborhoods selected for the program turned out to be low-income African-American neighborhoods. In some cities, local officials chose urban renewal sites for the express purpose of moving such ghettos away from the central business districts (Judd and Swanstrom 2008). During the life of the program, 1949 to 1974, 63 percent of families relocated by urban renewal were minorities (mostly African American) and only 37 percent were white (Sanders 1980). By the mid-1960s urban renewal had acquired the epithet "Negro removal" in the inner cities. The National Commission on Urban Problems (1968), convened to find the causes of the ghetto riots of the 1960s, cited the failures of the urban renewal program, particularly the problem of displacement, as one of the factors contributing to urban unrest.

Department of Housing and Urban Development

Both public housing and urban renewal were bricks and mortar programs aimed at changing the physical nature of the cities by building and/or demolishing structures. In the 1940s and 1950s, when the urban crisis was thought of as a crisis of physically aging and deteriorating cities, such physical approaches to urban revitalization made sense. But during the 1960s, the nature of the urban crisis came to be understood as a culmination of the problems of poverty and racial inequality—a general social and economic crisis—that just happened to be highly visible in cities. In 1965 President Lyndon Johnson responded by reorganizing urban programs into a new agency, the Department of Housing and Urban Development (HUD), with Cabinet status for its director.

The goals of the new agency were to integrate existing urban programs and to develop new initiatives for urban social and economic development. One of HUD's most interesting experiments was the model cities program, a cross between an antipoverty program and a more traditional urban program. The model cities approach was ambitious and comprehensive, addressing the education, health, recreation, public safety, and employment needs of urban residents as well as their housing needs. The model city neighborhoods were areas of innovation, where new and complementary community development efforts could be instituted. In principle, the model cities program had the potential to address some of the major problems faced by poor urban residents, but its accomplishments were limited due to a lack of specific program goals and the severe shortage of funding (Lemann 1991; Judd and Swanstrom 2008).

In addition to initiating new programs, HUD instituted some changes in existing programs. The Federal Housing Administration home mortgage program, which had previously been targeted to middle-class households buying new, single-family, detached homes was revamped to provide funding for low-income households buying existing housing, including both single-family and multifamily housing. It also created a number of new programs to support subsidized homeownership for moderate-income families.

Efforts to Direct Urban Policy from Washington

From the Depression to the 1960s, urban policy consisted of a number of separate programs funded and administered from Washington. These programs did not flow from a single philosophy but were the result of compromises among many different political interest groups. The programs had some successes: they provided low-cost housing, helped revitalize some cities, and prevented some urban areas from slipping even more deeply into poverty. The urban policies of this era, however, did not solve some of the most pressing urban problems, either because they were not designed to solve them, or because they lacked the resources to address them adequately. The public housing program, for example, could have greatly reduced the problem of private slum housing by building more units and providing for better maintenance. Political pressure simply prevented this policy option from being adopted, because it would have put government-run housing directly into competition with privately run housing.

Wilson (2009) points out that government policy frequently had unplanned negative impacts on the cities. He argues that many social policies of the 1960s and 1970s had the unintended consequence of increasing concentrated poverty. These policy directions included the housing and highway programs that spurred the growth of the suburbs and a decrease in federal aid to the cities. In combination with the movement of employment to the suburbs, he argues, these federal programs resulted in the impoverishment of many urban centers.

TRANSFORMATION OF URBAN POLICY

New Federalism

In recent decades, the philosophy of the federal government has shifted toward a less-directive approach to urban policy. This new policy approach that came to be known as the **new federalism** allows state and local governments to spend federal money with few restrictions. Instead of money for specific programs, the federal government now gives states and localities a **block grant** to spend on urban programs of their own choosing.

The Community Development Block Grant (CDBG) program began in 1974 to replace seven federal programs that had given aid to cities for urban development projects. The major selling point of the block grant program was decentralized decision making. Instead of telling cities how to run their programs, the federal government began to allow local governments to develop their own directions (Hays 1995; Dommel 1984).

The new federalism is also oriented toward fine-tuning the market rather than giving government direction. Rental assistance programs, for example, help people find housing in the private market rather than in government-owned developments. The housing voucher program gives subsidies to low-income tenants looking for housing, and to developers who set aside a certain portion of their rental units for low-income households. These rental assistance programs are designed to replace the public housing program. Rental assistance programs have been successful in helping many low-income households gain access to housing. But these programs are severely underfunded, leaving many low-income households on waiting lists for years. They also keep rents higher than they might otherwise have been and thus may help landlords more than tenants.

Urban policy through the mid-1970s was based on the philosophy that cities and the people who lived in cities were valuable national resources. Thus, it was deemed the government's responsibility to invest federal funds in cities to keep them viable. Investing in cities also made a great deal of political and economic sense, because cities were the society's centers of population and of business—the society's growth machine. Beginning in the late 1970s, however, the idea of investing tax money in cities became more controversial. Opponents of urban aid argued that because the urban programs of the 1960s had failed to eliminate poverty or slums, there was little point in continuing to spend money on them. Additionally, news headlines of the 1970s highlighted the problems of the national economy—not the urban slums—as the crisis that government needed to address. With the massive suburbanization of the population, cities no longer contained as much of the voting population as they had just twenty years before, thus reducing their political influence on national policy and rendering them "politically invisible" (Waste 1998).

The emphasis in Washington began to shift from giving aid to *places* to giving aid to *people*. Proponents of the people-based approach argued that the federal government should not concern itself with cities because the growth and decline of communities were the result of natural, inevitable, market-driven processes. Their new strategy would assist individuals in finding employment, even if that meant helping them move to other parts of the country to do so (President's Commission for a National Agenda for the Eighties 1981). Critics, including many urban planners and elected officials, argued that because existing cities contain valuable resources in buildings and infrastructure, it is wasteful to let them deteriorate. In addition, they said that the people-based strategy overlooks the fact that most people are part of social communities of family, neighborhood, religious, and other social networks that provide some of their sense of identity. Thus, the human cost of uprooting people from their customary place of living and social community should be included in the calculation of program costs.

Urban Policy in the 1980s

During the 1980s urban issues were low on the list of national priorities. Federal spending was consistently reduced and federal funds began to disappear from urban areas. Congress passed several pieces of legislation that consolidated urban programs into block grants and reduced their overall funding by 20 percent. Rather than directing urban policy on a national level, Congress authorized the **devolution** of policy initiatives to the states and cities. President Reagan's administration (1981–1989) believed that the federal government's main responsibility toward cities and states was simply to keep the national economy healthy and that targeted urban programs were unnecessary. Critics were quick to point out, however, that even when the national economic indicators were positive, the benefits of national economic growth were unevenly spread. The cities' boats were not lifted as high on the rising tide as the suburban boats, and growth in the Sunbelt was outstripping growth in the Frostbelt (Wolman 1986).

The administration of the first President Bush (1989–1993) continued with the approach of his predecessor, cutting back on urban programs or outright eliminating them. The major urban development grant program, federal assistance for local public works, and general revenue sharing payments were eliminated. As well, community development block grant funding was decreased by 54 percent; job training was decreased by 69 percent: economic development assistance was decreased by 78 percent; and mass transit funding was decreased by 25 percent—all occurring between 1980 and 1990 (Caraley 1992).

Although the new federalism was supposed to provide the cities and states with the freedom to make choices about how to solve their own urban problems, critics have noted that the poorest communities, those with the most problems, are the least able to solve their problems by themselves. For example, Caraley (1992) argues that the notion that every community could choose what was best for itself is actually a myth, because poor communities have more limited resources and therefore more limited choices than do wealthy communities. Unfortunately for poorer communities, the new federalism gave them more freedom but simultaneously took away an enormous amount of the outside assistance that had previously supplemented their own meager funds.

Thus, in the span of less than twenty years, the urban crisis was dramatically redefined. From a problem of racial and class inequality and unequal opportunity for some groups, the crisis became a problem of overall economic performance. In addition, federal policy was changed to emphasize the market, federal and state funds committed to addressing urban problems were reduced, and many urban programs were eliminated.

Urban Policy in the 1990s

In the 1990s, urban policy was back on the agenda in Washington. President Clinton (1993–2001), a proponent of "reinventing government," also reinvented urban policy. The Clinton administration proposed an urban policy that addressed many of the urban problems common in cities since the 1960s but attempted to address them in a new way. The administration redefined cities to include metropolitan areas, redefined urban policy to include indirect as well as explicit urban policy, and asked cities to compete for funds rather than simply giving them grants based on the population size. The administration's policy proposals emphasized the importance of education, access to well-paying jobs, better housing opportunities, economic development, and making cities safer (U.S. Department of Housing and Urban Development 1995).

The Clinton administration combined liberal and conservative approaches in its policy proposals, partly to obtain political support. Perhaps best known and most controversial was the initiative to "end *welfare* as we know it" by eliminating the federal entitlement to public assistance and converting it to a block grant to the states. Under the new program, Temporary Assistance to Needy Families, states were required to enforce strict time limits and work requirements for welfare recipients. Another initiative that was implemented was the *empowerment zone* program, which targeted poor neighborhoods not just for tax relief (as the enterprise zone programs did) but also for expanded services, neighborhood planning, and strengthening of local organizations. A third initiative was the *crime bill* that provided for funding for adding 100,000 police in the nation's cities and implementing community policing programs to encourage police responsiveness to the communities with which they work. A fourth direction for urban policy under Clinton was the emphasis on *fair housing*, including enhanced enforcement of the Community Reinvestment Act that monitors banks' mortgage lending practices. A fifth area was increased funds for and consolidation of programs directed toward *homelessness* (Waste 1998, Hays 1995).

Urban Policy Since 2000

From 2001 to 2009, both the presidency and Congress were controlled by conservative Republicans. Their direction for urban policy continued the trend of retreat from urban programs that began in the 1980s. The most prominent initiative of the George W. Bush administration was to encourage "faith-based" religious groups to sponsor urban programs such as homeless shelters, food banks, and social services. President Bush's education policy, encoded in the No Child Left Behind Act, required school districts to test all children and report their scores annually. The legislation, however, did not provide additional funding to school districts for either the testing itself nor for any initiatives to improve learning in low-scoring schools. The administration also made dramatic cuts in housing subsidies (Dreier 2004).

Urban policy must be seen within the context of national priorities. Peter Dreier (2004) argues that the most important priorities of the Bush administration and Congress were to cut taxes, especially for the wealthy, to cut government regulation of business, and to increase military spending. A combination of an economic recession, sizeable tax cuts, and military spending on the wars in Iraq and Afghanistan resulted in a massive federal deficit. The deficit contributed to a continued reduction in federal spending on social needs such as health, education, housing, and transportation. Although federal assistance to states and cities was decreased, federal legislation increasingly required states and cities to pay for certain activities, including Medicaid expenses and welfare-to-work programs.

A new policy direction since 2000 is the prevention of and response to terrorism. The unfortunate attack on the World Trade Center on September 11, 2001, alerted the nation to the fact that cities are attractive targets and potentially vulnerable to terrorist actions. Congress mandated changes and improvements to security in public facilities, including airports, train stations, ports, water supplies, communications systems, and hospitals. Cities received some federal assistance to improve security of these critical facilities, but the funding formula that Congress finally approved spreads the money throughout the country instead of concentrating it on the most likely targets of terrorism, the larger cities.

At the time of this writing (2009), President Obama has been in office for less than a year. His administration has indicated that it will take an aggressive approach to urban issues. According to his website (www.change.gov), the key elements of the Obama program for urban development include a wide range of policy directions. Some of the goals his staff enumerates include the following:

- Create a White House Office on Urban Policy
- Fully fund the Community Development Block Grant program
- Support job creation and access to jobs
- Increase access to capital for underserved businesses
- Convert our manufacturing centers into clean technology leaders
- Increase the supply of affordable housing throughout metropolitan regions
- Establish "Promise Neighborhoods" for areas of concentrated poverty
- Build more livable and sustainable communities
- Support teachers in urban schools
- Reduce the high school dropout rate
- Support local law enforcement
- End the dangerous cycle of youth violence
- Address gun violence in cities

Of course to obtain the desired changes in urban policy the president must have the cooperation of Congress. At the current time, the focus of attention in Congress is on the overall economic crisis, and some of the solutions to that crisis will undoubtedly affect the cities. Whether a clear focus on urban issues will emerge is to be seen.

Politics and Urban Policy

How is policy formulated? Through the political process, business groups such as banks, real estate associations, builders, and other private interest groups actively try to shape urban policy to their benefit. They do so sometimes as a unified large group and sometimes as a series of subgroups with different interests, agendas, and proposals. Nonbusiness groups, such as labor unions, churches, and community organizations, also lobby, but their generally less powerful position affords them a smaller influence on the outcome of urban policy and programs.

Another perspective on urban policy is that of Myron Orfield (2002) who argues that urban policy has always been a reaction to acute problems. Orfield attributes the establishment of public housing to the economic woes of the Depression, antipoverty and revitalization programs as resulting from the ghetto riots of the 1960s, and empowerment zones as a response to the Los Angeles riot of 1992. In each case, he holds, Congress rushed to address a prominent problem without committing to a thorough understanding of the causes or consequences of the policies it enacted.

Government policies redistribute income and resources within the society. The urban programs of the 1960s redistributed income downward by giving it to poor people or by providing goods and services for them. This was loosely based on the notion that the underlying urban problem was poverty. But in the 1980s the underlying urban problem was redefined as the inability of the economy to produce and of American businesses to compete in the global economy. In response, the federal government began to redistribute income to businesses. Will we see a return to urban policy under President Obama? Time will tell.

Why Is the United States Different?

Studies of urban policy consistently find that the policy choices and directions in the United States are quite different from those of other countries. The general direction of the difference has been summed up in the title of David Popenoe's book, *Private Pleasure, Public Plight* (1985). In comparing Sweden, England, and the United States, Popenoe finds that the public sector receives much less attention and funding in the United States than it does in the other two countries. The differences in national approaches pervade urban life, from the amount of space devoted to public and private use in our cities; to the level of funding for public services such as health, education, transportation, and child care; to the amounts of public and private interaction citizens have with each other.

In Popenoe's view, the excessive privatization of American cities is partly the result of personal choices influenced by long-standing cultural norms. But it is also due in part to a series of policy choices and directions that have reinforced the privatization trend and, in effect, left few public alternatives available. If the land in a particular subdivision is used totally for house lots, leaving no space for a park or playground, children are unlikely to experience public play areas on a regular basis. If the public schools of a community are underfunded, many more families will choose to send their children to private schools than will those who live in a community that invests more (or has more to invest) in its public schools. If a state or county has chosen not to invest in convenient, high-quality public transportation, commuters are left with no choice but to drive to work. People help make these policy choices, but once they are made, these past choices shape future choices.

Approaches to government housing policy, for example, differ greatly among the industrialized nations of the world. A comparative study of the housing policies of six nations found that the United States far outstrips the other five countries (the Netherlands, Sweden, Great Britain, France, and Germany) in its emphasis on supporting private housing and homeownership. The study found that public housing in the United States is provided almost exclusively for the poorest of the poor, whereas in all of the other countries studied, public housing is provided for a range of income groups and is treated as a normal part of communities' housing stock. In addition, in the other countries studied, government subsidies help to support nonprofit housing, cooperatives, and a range of alternative housing forms that have been overlooked in the United States. Although the housing policy approaches of different countries overlap a great deal, what varies greatly is the mix and the general direction of the programs (Harloe 1995).

Studies of our close neighbor, Canada, show that even a country extremely similar to our own has adopted very different housing policies. Since the early 1970s, the Canadian government has helped to support the growth of a nonprofit housing sector. Called *social housing*, it consists of housing developed, built, and managed by local community groups, including, in many cases, the tenants themselves. Interestingly, support for social housing in Canada was prompted in the 1960s by dissatisfaction with the type of public housing common at the time, a type very similar to U.S. public housing. Rather than turning to a market-based approach, as the U.S. government did, Canadians developed the alternative **third sector** of nonprofit housing. As a result, Canadian social housing usually consists of low-rise apartments, grouped in modestly-sized developments and spread throughout metropolitan areas, in both cities and suburbs. Some social housing developments are managed with the help of local government; others are run by churches or other private groups with no government direction except for funding; still other developments are cooperatives managed by the tenants (Dreier and Hulchanski 1993).

Several analysts have addressed the issue of why housing and other urban policy choices of the United States are more market-oriented and more likely to favor the private sector than the policy choices of other countries. One reason they cite is that the political culture of the United States simply does not allow as much government action as in other countries because of a deep distrust of government on the part of American citizens (Dreier and Hulchanski 1993). Another explanation they offer is that the historical circumstances of several European countries—especially countries that survived the destruction of World War II—made it necessary for the government to provide publicly funded housing for a large portion of the population. These nations tried several different approaches to government housing programs and developed more of a middle-class constituency for public housing (Harloe 1995). A third factor that makes the United States different is the higher degree of business influence on the planning and policy-making process in the United States, even over questions about what policy options are debatable (Fainstein and Fainstein 1978). Finally, a related factor is that the political power of cities has been reduced as our society has become more suburbanized and politically fragmented (Dreier 1993).

CONCLUSION

The federal government implements many policies that affect cities, both indirectly and directly. An explicitly national urban policy emerged in the 1940s, grew substantially in the 1960s, and has been curtailed and refocused since the

1980s as national attention has turned to other issues and the cities have lost power politically.

Political interests strongly shape the direction of urban policy. The United States has a narrower scope of urban policy than most other industrialized countries because of the strength of business and property interests and the weakness of other social groups. Prevailing ideology in the United States also supports individualistic, market-based strategies rather than collective, government-funded strategies for advancement. The experience of the cities since the 1980s shows us that the private market can indeed result in growth in some urban areas such as the downtown financial districts of certain large cities. But if government policy does not intervene to shape and redistribute growth, the results are highly unequally distributed. Whether this is good or bad and who benefits from it are the philosophical and political questions underlying the debate over policy.

DISCUSSION QUESTIONS

1. When urban policy was first formulated, it was directed from Washington. Recently it has been implemented more at the local level. What do you think are the advantages and disadvantages of each approach?

2. Does your community contain public housing units? Where are they located, and what is their condition? Is there a waiting list for them? For other housing assistance? What are the options for low-income households in private housing compared to public housing?

3. What urban policy issues are being discussed in your local newspaper? Do they involve federal programs? Which ones?

15

Urban Unrest
and Social Control

Hardly a day goes by, you know, that some innocent bystander ain't shot in
New York City. All you got to do is be innocent and stand by and they're
gonna shoot you. The other day, there was four people shot in one day—four
innocent people—in New York City. Amazing. It's kind of hard to find four
innocent people in New York. That's why a policeman don't have to aim.
He just shoots anywhere. Whoever he hits, that's the right one.
WILL ROGERS

In the United States, cities, especially big cities, have a reputation for being
violent and disorderly. Many of the images associated with urban life include
violence, crime, and disrespect for rules, authority, or fellow-citizens. Why does
this reputation exist? Is it deserved? If cities are really more violent and disruptive
than other types of communities, what makes them so?

This chapter will explore several related questions about order and conflict
in urban areas:

- How do sociologists view social unrest, lawbreaking, and violence?
- What kinds of unrest are characteristic of urban areas?
- What are the causes of urban violence and unrest?
- What can be done to reduce social unrest?

HOW ORDERLY IS SOCIETY?

Theories Stressing Order

Sociologists disagree about how much order is "normal" in societies. Going back
to the time of the classical theorists, sociologists have pondered the question of

how social order exists. Most of the classical theorists saw societies as fundamentally stable but capable of being disrupted under certain circumstances. Tönnies, Durkheim, and Simmel all thought that social ties among urban dwellers were different and weaker than social ties in rural communities. These classical theorists questioned whether the weaker, less personal relationships between individuals in modern cities would provide the same level of stability and cohesiveness found in traditional villages. In addition, Durkheim (1964) argued that during periods of rapid social change, societies would temporarily be characterized by anomie (French for "normlessness"), or a lack of agreement about what the social norms are. To the classical theorists, social order and stability were normal but fragile and easily disturbed by changing social conditions.

Urban sociologists of the twentieth century have investigated the question of social order through their observations of life in large cities. Lyn Lofland, for example, pointed out that living in cities means learning to live with strangers. Her book *A World of Strangers* (1985) shows the social mechanisms that different types of urbanized societies have evolved for dealing with the fact that most of the people we meet every day are people we do not know. Erving Goffman (1971) makes the point even more strenuously. He argues that there are unspoken social rules for public behavior that are so widely obeyed that most of the time we do not even notice that we are following them. These norms or rules for public behavior include when to look at someone, when to ignore them, where to walk, and under what circumstances it is permissible to speak to a stranger. Because most strangers obey the rules of order most of the time, strangers can normally trust each other to behave properly. William H. Whyte (1988), reporting on a sixteen-year study of public life in New York City, found that not only do people on city streets, in parks, and in other public places have very little trouble dealing with strangers, but paradoxically that the presence of other people (most if not all of them strangers) makes urban areas safe. Whyte's study showed repeated instances of people congregating in areas containing other people but avoiding deserted spaces. These studies stress that social order is possible, even usual, in cities.

What about disorder and disruption? Several Chicago School ecologists studied neighborhoods that had high rates of crime, juvenile delinquency, sales of illegal drugs and alcohol, and prostitution to see what was different about those areas. They found that neighborhoods with high rates of unlawful or disruptive behavior also tended to have high rates of poverty, high levels of immigrant and African-American population, and a greater than average incidence of broken families (Reckless 1926; Thrasher 1928). Many ecologists characterized this entire package of urban social ills as social disorganization (Shaw and McKay 1931), implying that social ties and mechanisms for regulating the behavior of individuals had broken down in these areas—an argument similar to Durkheim's anomie.

The term *social disorganization* fell out of use after later studies showed that many inner-city neighborhoods characterized by poverty and violence were, in fact, highly organized with strong group ties (Suttles 1968; Gans 1962). But a similar analysis of urban life has persisted to recent times, namely the culture-of-poverty argument. Derived from studies of poor ethnic ghettos, the argument is that many inner-city neighborhoods have a distinctive culture that includes norms and values different from those of the mainstream culture. Proponents argue that a subculture arises in many poor neighborhoods as a response to the lack of economic opportunities and isolation from mainstream society. Such "pathological" cultural values as the avoidance of work and marriage, a fascination with toughness, a propensity for risk taking, and a lack of concern about the future lay the groundwork for potentially higher rates of disruptive behavior in these areas than in other urban neighborhoods. Cultural arguments hold that the inner-city urban subculture develops because of the residents' isolation from mainstream social values and attitudes (See Katz 1989; Auletta 1999.)

To summarize, theories that stress order tend to see social stability as normal and social disruptions as a temporary, abnormal, or pathological state of affairs. Causes for disruption might include social change, disorganized communities, or subcultural norms that differ from mainstream ideas of proper behavior.

Theories Stressing Conflict

Some theorists see conflict and change as intrinsic to social systems, sometimes as overt, disruptive conflicts and sometimes as hidden but nonetheless real conflicts. Theorists who stress conflict and change often use Marx and Weber as their points of departure. Their definition of conflict includes the institutionalized competition and opposition of different social groups such as social classes, ethnic groups, or even different age groups. They argue that powerful actors in societies generally can establish the rules of the game to benefit themselves and also control the distribution of rewards and punishments. Thus, a certain amount of conflict is the result of those groups with less access to power struggling to get some rewards (Vold 1958; Turk 1969).

Social conflicts are often economic struggles or conflicts. John Hagan (1994) reviewed studies of high-crime areas in the United States and Canada and found a repeated pattern of high rates of crime, violence, and other unrest in neighborhoods characterized by concentrated poverty. He does not attribute these disruptions to the social disorganization of the people who live in these neighborhoods nor to their cultural values. Instead, he looks at the wider context and asks how these neighborhoods became so poor in the first place. The most important answer he finds is massive disinvestment in these communities by outsiders, such as companies and government agencies that control economic resources. Without the legitimate means of getting ahead, Hagan argues, residents of concentrated poverty areas frequently find other ways of making money that put them in conflict with each other and with the law. The fundamental conflict, in Hagan's view, is simply the struggle for economic resources. Similarly, Reid (2003) found that shifts in the economic base of a city can impact the city's crime rate. In Boston, the rise of high-skill service sector jobs after a period of deindustrialization led to lower rates of crime, whereas in Atlanta an increase in low-skill service sector jobs led to higher crime rates.

Social conflicts may also be political struggles. Although the premise of democratic electoral systems is "one person, one vote," actual analyses of the political process indicate that not everyone has equal political power. Wealth and income give some actors more power than their single vote, and many people who lack wealth and income are effectively disenfranchised. They might (or might not) be able to vote, but often find that their vote has no effect on their lives because they are seldom able to vote for a candidate who represents their interests. Piven and Cloward (1977) argue that the poor are so effectively disenfranchised from the regular political channels in the United States that one of the few effective means of political participation available to them is disruptive protest. Low-income groups are not the only ones that engage in social protest; other disenfranchised groups (women, African Americans, young people) have also mounted protest movements. Urban areas, however, provide both the reasons and the means for their low-income residents to organize for social change.

Clearly, these theorists who stress the "normality" of conflict do not mean that conflict is always at an obvious boiling point. They mean that conflict, in one form or another, is an ongoing characteristic of social life, but that under some circumstances it intensifies or takes on different forms. Rather than seeing conflict as simply destructive or disturbing, they argue that it can lead to social change. Sometimes, conflicts can lead directly to a significant redistribution of power or resources. Think, for example, of revolutions in which common people dethrone a king or unseat a dictator. At other times, overt conflicts can serve as a signal that something is seriously wrong with the current social arrangements or a threat that potentially more violent disruptions could be ahead. Such disruptions can serve to pressure the powerful groups toward reforms.

SOME TYPES OF URBAN UNREST

Cities do not have to be violent, disorderly, or disruptive. It is simply wrong to think that just because millions of people are living in close proximity with strangers they will interact inappropriately with each other. On the contrary, some of the largest, most densely populated cities of the world, such as Hong Kong, are extremely safe and quiet (Michelson 1970). It is highly unlikely that something about the urban environment itself encourages social unrest.

Cities of the United States, in fact, rank far above the cities of the other industrialized countries in their rates of violence, lawbreaking, and other forms of disruptive activity. The United States is an exceptionally violent and crime-prone country overall; and within this violent and unruly society, cities and metropolitan areas have higher rates of many kinds of disruptive behavior than do rural areas. Although we will be focusing on urban violence and unrest, we should take this social context into account: violence, crime, and lawbreaking are traits characteristic of American society (Messner and Rosenfeld 2006).

In this section we will examine four particularly urban types of unrest: crime, gang activity, riots, and social movements. In each case we will look at the relationship between the behavior and urban life: how common is this activity, how disruptive is it, and how do we account for it?

T A B L E   15.1   Crime Rates per 1,000 Inhabitants by Type of Community, 1980–2007

	Violent Crime			Property Crime		
	1980	1998	2007	1980	1998	2007
U.S. Total	5.8	5.7	4.7	53	40	33
Metropolitan Areas	7.0	6.3	5.0	61	43	34
Other Cities	3.5	4.4	4.0	50	45	38
Rural Areas	1.8	2.3	2.1	21	18	17

SOURCE: Data from Federal Bureau of Investigation, 1980, Table 1, Federal Bureau of Investigation, 1999, Table 2, and Federal Bureau of Investigation, 2008, Table 2.

Crime

How much crime is there in cities, what kind of crime is it, and what do the trends show about increases and decreases in crime? First, let us consider a few definitions. Crimes are acts that violate the law, and *known crimes* are those that someone reports to the police. The crime rate that the Federal Bureau of Investigation (FBI) publishes is an index of the reported rates (number per one hundred thousand population) of eight common and serious crimes: murder, rape, robbery, aggravated assault, burglary, auto theft, arson, and larceny.

Is the crime rate in the United States increasing or decreasing? According to FBI statistics, overall crime has decreased steadily since 1991, and by 2007 it was lower than it had been in 1980. As Table 15.1 shows, both cities and rural areas experienced decreases in crime rates during this period. Although crime fell overall, the types of crimes committed changed somewhat; property crimes decreased much more substantially than did violent crimes.

Are cities more crime-prone than rural areas? They certainly appear to be. Table 15.1 shows the breakdown of crime rates by type of community—metropolitan areas, other cities not in metropolitan areas, and rural areas. (The FBI reports crime by metropolitan area rather than city because metropolitan areas are more comparable to each other than are central cities.) By looking down each column you can see that cities have higher crime rates than rural areas. These aggregate data support the view that cities are indeed more dangerous than rural areas.

If cities have higher crime rates than do rural areas, do the largest cities have the highest crime rates? Perhaps surprisingly, they do not. According to the U.S. Department of Justice statistics (2008), cities with populations over one million had property crime rates lower than cities with populations in any size category from 50,000 to 999,999. Population is obviously not always a good predictor of crime; for instance, in 2007, the violent crime rate of Sumter, South Carolina, a metropolitan area of 105,369, was 1,457.7 per 100,000 people, about three times as high as that found in the Washington, D.C. metropolitan area (494.7) (Federal Bureau of Investigation 2008).

The public *perception* of crime, on the other hand, is that crime is a serious and major problem in cities, one that threatens virtually everyone. Studies of

---

B o x 15.1 • Spotlight
Fear of Crime

"The killing of innocent bystanders, particularly in the cross fires of this nation's drug wars, has suddenly become a phenomenon that greatly troubles experts on crime," began a front page story in the *New York Times*. It is "the sense that it could happen to anybody, anywhere, like a plane crash" that makes these attacks so scary, the reporter quoted Peter Reuter from the RAND Corporation. According to the *New York Daily News*, "spillover" crime from the drug wars even affected people in "silk-stocking areas." In fact, a *New York* magazine article revealed, thanks to a crack cocaine epidemic, "most neighborhoods in the city by now have been forced to deal with either crack or its foul by-products: if not crack houses and street dealers or users, then crackhead crimes such as purse snatchings, car break-ins, burglaries, knife-point robberies, muggings, and murders." TV newscasts, needless to say, breathlessly report much the same, with pictures at eleven.

One expert eventually became skeptical of the reporting and set out to examine whether New Yorkers were truly at equal and random risk of falling victim to drug-related violence. What Henry Brownstein, a researcher with the New York State Division of Criminal Justice Services, found when he looked at data available from the police was almost exactly the opposite. About two out of one hundred homicides in New York City involved innocent bystanders, and most drug-related violence occurred between people connected to the drug trade itself. When innocent people did get hurt, Brownstein discovered, often they were roughed up or shot at not by drug users but by police officers in the course of ill-conceived raids and street busts.

SOURCE: Barry Glassner, *The Culture of Fear* (New York, Basic Books, 1999), pp. 110–111.

---

fear of crime relative to actual rates of crime show two interesting findings. First, people seem to form their fear of crime not from their own experiences but from secondhand information, including news accounts, TV shows, and friends' anecdotes (Glassner 2000). Media sensationalization of specific crimes creates a generalized atmosphere of fear even when there is little real danger. (See Box 15.1 for an example of this phenomenon.) Second, people's fear of crime bears little relationship to the likelihood that they will be victimized. The group most likely to become victims of crime is young African-American males. The groups most fearful of crime, namely elderly people and white women, are the least likely to be victimized by crime (Madriz 1997). Yet fear, even when unrealistic, often acts as a deterrent for people to leave their homes, interact with others, and participate in community life (Klinenberg 2002).

The use and sale of illegal drugs have added another dimension to the urban crime profile in recent years. Neither the use nor the sale of illegal drugs is an index crime, that is, one reported in FBI statistics. Yet arrests for drug offenses have risen sharply in recent years. Although there is little evidence that either drug use or drug sales are actually increasing, the war on drugs being waged in many cities has resulted in a sharp increase in the number of drug arrests police make. Because of federal and state mandatory sentences for drug offenders (based on the amount and type of illegal drugs involved in the offense), drug offenders are much more likely to be incarcerated in jail or prison than are other types of offenders. By the early 1990s, drug offenses became the single largest category of people admitted to state prisons (Tonry 1994).

A study by Tonry (1994) pointed out a disturbing relationship between drug arrests and race. He tracked the proportion of whites and African Americans arrested for different types of crime from 1976 to 1992. As a consequence of the changes in arrest and sentencing patterns, by 1990 African Americans outnumbered whites among the ranks of those being sent to prison, even though their rates of violent crimes had not increased. The change in the proportions of African Americans and whites in the prison population was almost totally attributed to drug offenses.

Randall Kennedy (2001) documents three ways in which the criminal justice system treats African Americans differently from whites. He provides evidence of widespread **racial profiling**, or the practice of using a person's race in part to determine whether the individual is likely to engage in criminal activity. Kennedy reports that even many educated, professional African Americans have experienced the phenomenon of being stopped by law enforcement officers because they were "driving while black." A second way in which the legal system treats the races differently, according to Kennedy, is in the much larger proportion of peremptory challenges that attorneys use to disqualify African Americans from serving on juries compared to potential white jurors. These challenges and other methods of forming pools of jurors result in a severe underrepresentation of African Americans in jury pools nationally, thus making it more difficult for African-American defendants to be tried by their peers. The third way in which the criminal justice system treats African Americans differently from whites is in punishment, according to Kennedy. He shows that African Americans are far more likely to be sentenced to death than are whites convicted of the same crimes. In addition, he cites the widely criticized law that makes the penalty for selling a single gram of crack cocaine (a cheap drug primarily used by poor people) equal to the penalty for selling one hundred grams of powder cocaine (an expensive drug primarily used by affluent people).

What are we to conclude about crime in cities? According to the official statistics, the crime rate has leveled off and is going down, even more rapidly in cities than in other types of communities. The rates of arrest and incarceration—borne disproportionately by African Americans—however, are rapidly growing (Walker et al. 2006). Are these increased arrests and penalties helping to solve the crime problem? We will return to this question later in the chapter.

Gang Activity

Gangs of young males, hanging on street corners, fighting, and breaking the law, have been part of the urban scene since the mid-1800s. In the mid-1980s gang visibility increased after waning somewhat in the 1970s. Through media accounts, many people form stereotypes about gang members, such as that described by Joan Moore (1993, 28): "[Gang members are seen as] violent, drug- and alcohol-soaked,

F I G U R E 15.1 Gang Symbols. Gang members and "wanna-bes" can be identified by their distinctive clothing, hand signals, tattoos, and other subcultural symbols.

sexually hyperactive, unpredictable, confrontational, drug-dealing criminals.... All gangs are thought to have a high potential for developing the worst behavior displayed by any one of them."

Fortunately, sociologists have a rich tradition of research on gangs that allows us to examine these stereotypes. Like most stereotypes, they contain a kernel of truth, some dramatic confirming examples, and many counterexamples that tend to be overlooked. Several recent studies of street gangs (summarized in Coughlin and Venkatesh 2003) address how and why gangs form, what activities they do, and their members' relationship to crime and violence.

Gangs (sometimes called clubs or crews) are overwhelmingly composed of teenagers or young adults who live in the same neighborhood. They usually have strong geographical ties, and in some cities it is common for gangs to take the name of a neighborhood or street. Gangs are often racially or ethnically homogeneous and can be of any color or ethnicity, but they are more commonly found in nonwhite, non-Anglo neighborhoods. Gangs form subcultures with distinctive languages, symbols, and dress, as shown in Figure 15.1. Violence and crime are only minor parts of most gangs' activities; hanging around, dancing or showing off, graffiti "tagging," playing sports, drinking, and looking for girls occupy a much greater proportion of gang members' time. Members cite many different reasons for joining gangs, including economic gain, protection, fun or social activity, access to drugs and alcohol, and wanting to live a different sort of life than that of their parents (Hagedorn and Macon 1998; Jankowski 1991; Cummings and Monti 1993). Box 15.2 describes several ways in which gangs recruit new members.

B o x 15.2 • Spotlight
Gang Recruitment

As old members die, fade away, or go to prison, the gang struggles to maintain its membership.... The street gangs look for members all the time, but the best times for recruiting are during summer vacations and at the start of the school year. Individuals join gangs for different reasons, and they are drawn into the gangs through three styles of recruitment—fraternity, obligation, and commitment.

Fraternity-style membership recruitment requires that a street gang appear very desirable to potential recruits. Prized recruits ... are drawn into the gang through social events. The benefits of gang life, such as drugs, alcohol, money, excitement, power, influence, and access to members of the opposite sex, are displayed at these events. The recruits see the gang as a path to the better things in life that they may feel are unavailable through legitimate channels.

Street gangs that are territorial in nature will use an individual's sense of obligation as a method of recruitment. The gang's strong identification with a neighborhood can work to its benefit in attracting new members.... Failure to join the gang is considered a betrayal and thought to show a lack of respect. Individuals living in the neighborhood may have family members who have been in the gang and done their service for the neighborhood. These individuals grow up with a sense of responsibility and desire to join the local gang.

[Coercion as a recruitment method] relies on intimidation and fear. Individuals who do not actually want to join a gang may find themselves threatened with physical harm to themselves or family members if they do not join. Gangs using this method of recruitment must maintain a level of fear to ensure continued gang loyalty and cohesion. They must make a strong example of any member straying from the gang. This least desirable method of recruiting may be necessary if a gang has a high turnover rate due to incarceration or death of members.

SOURCE: Rick Landre, Mike Miller, and Dee Porter, *Gangs: A Handbook for Community Awareness* (New York: Facts on File Books, 1997), pp. 19–20.

Street gangs sometimes engage in entrepreneurial activities such as selling drugs or fencing stolen property (Padilla 1992). In particular, some gangs have been accused of drug trafficking, perhaps with ties to large-scale organized crime rings. According to Coughlin and Venkatesh (2003), however, numerous studies illustrate that street gang organization is typically too loose and locally based to be part of organized crime, that only a small proportion of gangs engage in drug trafficking, and that even when gang members sell drugs, this activity is only a minor part of the gang's scope of activities. In short, they conclude that gangs generally should not be compared to businesses or to organized crime.

Gangs are often known for violence. The best-known type of gang violence is associated with intergang rivalry, motivated by turf battles, revenge for past wrongs, or the desire to bond the group more closely and test the loyalty of the members. In these cases, Jankowski shows, violence can be carried further than the group originally intended. Gang members' reports of their most violent involvements often include two factors: gang discipline and sophisticated weapons. Leaders of hierarchically organized gangs sometimes order their subordinates to attack a rival group, a situation that relieves the members who do the fighting of personal responsibility for the attack and frees them to go overboard with the rationale that they "are just following orders" (Jankowski 1991, 171). In addition, the availability of automatic weapons has permitted gang members who do engage in violence to become more destructive. In the words of one member, "I had this automatic rifle, and when I started to shoot, man, it was easy. That's what makes it easy, it's fast and there's nothing personal in it like when you use a knife" (Jankowski 1991, 172).

In recent years more reports and studies have shown gang activity among young women (Campbell 1984; Chesney-Lind and Hagedorn 1999). These so-called "girl gangs" can be either independent or linked to young men's gangs. Although it is difficult to count exact numbers, female members may constitute approximately 30 percent of the total gang membership (Coughlin and Venkatesh 2003). Although female gang members tend to engage in violent and illegal actions less often than male gang members, they have higher levels of criminal and violent activity than comparable females who are not gang members.

Gangs are primarily an urban phenomenon, given the fact that they are territorially based and bounded within certain areas. The majority of gang members are drawn from the poorer, racially segregated neighborhoods of the central cities. But evidence shows that gangs may be growing more rapidly in suburban and rural areas than in the cities (Coughlin and Venkatesh 2003).

Riots

Riots, more formally known as civil disorders, have erupted in cities from time to time throughout American history. Riots take place in many settings and among many populations, but those we will consider here are urban riots. These episodes of spontaneous mob formation, unrest, violence, and destruction are unpredictable but show certain similarities. Many riots have begun as conflicts between groups of different racial or ethnic backgrounds. New York's Astor Place Riot of 1849 left thirty-one people dead and over one hundred wounded after a theater performance by an English actor who had become a focus for anti-English sentiment. An anti-Chinese mob numbering over five thousand people ransacked and burned much of San Francisco's Chinatown in 1877. Chicago's race riot of 1919, which left thirty-eight people dead, was motivated by whites trying to "put Negroes back in their place" after a black youth swam across the color line that divided whites and blacks at a public beach. New York's draft riot of 1863, in which over one hundred people were killed, is still considered to be the most serious civil insurrection of U.S. history. This uprising, which lasted for three days, began as an attack on an Army draft office by young Irish-American men who then turned their violence on African Americans (Glaab and Brown 1976; Lewis 1966).

The hundreds of riots and disturbances of the 1960s differed from many of the earlier riots in that most participants were members of the African-American minority rather than the white majority. So many riots occurred between 1964 and 1967 that President Johnson appointed a National Advisory Commission on Civil Disorders to investigate the causes of the riots and to propose policy measures. The report of the National Advisory Commission on Civil Disorders (1968) concluded that there was no single cause for the riots but pointed to several contributing factors: a history of racial oppression that blacks were beginning to challenge, mass migrations of black people from the rural South to the urban North, an economic structure of blocked or limited opportunities for urban blacks, and less than positive conditions in urban ghetto neighborhoods, including tense police-community relations. The targets of rioters' violence were more often than not symbols of white authority or economic control, and participants in the riots appeared to be seeking "fuller participation in the social order and the material benefits enjoyed by the majority of Americans" (1968, 7).

The best-known conclusion of the National Advisory Commission's report, an issue that emerges repeatedly in studies of riots, is that racial and class inequality are primary causes of riots. In the words of the Commission's report: "Our nation is moving toward two societies, one black, one white,—separate and unequal" (1968, 1).

The two most prominent riots in the United States since the 1960s are the 1980 uprising in Miami's Liberty City and the 1992 uprising in Los Angeles. The Miami riot took sixteen lives, resulted in $80 million worth of property damage, lasted for several days, and spread to Orlando and Chattanooga. The Los Angeles riot lasted six days and left fifty-two people dead and over $1 billion in damaged property. Both incidents were precipitated by jury verdicts in police abuse cases. In the Miami case, an all-white jury acquitted four police officers of the death of African-American businessman Arthur McDuffie, despite the legal and medical evidence that showed he had been beaten to death. In the Los Angeles case, four white police officers—whom millions of television viewers had seen on videotape savagely beating African-American motorist Rodney King—were acquitted of assault charges (see Figure 15.2). In both Miami and Los Angeles, the perception of racial injustice was the primary precipitating factor in the disturbance (Fukurai, Krooth, and Butler 1994; Sears 1994).

Studies of the 1992 Los Angeles riot have addressed two questions: (1) What were the long-term causes of the riot? and (2) How does the 1992 riot differ from the last major race riot that took place in Los Angeles, the Watts riot of 1965? Researchers have identified three long-term factors: the enduring poverty of the black underclass, racial tensions between blacks and whites, and interethnic tensions among blacks, Latinos, and Asians. The economic position of Los Angeles's poor African-American residents, their experiences with housing and job discrimination, and the dwindling of economic opportunities due to economic restructuring and a loss of manufacturing jobs have persisted and even intensified since the 1960s (Baldassare 1994). Similarly, tensions between African Americans and Anglos (white English-speaking groups), already high in the 1960s, have persisted and played a key role in both uprisings.

The new element in the Los Angeles social and cultural situation that fed into the 1992 riot is the changing ethnic composition of Los Angeles. The white Anglos of Los Angeles are declining as a percentage of the population; as of 1990, less than half of the population of Los Angeles is white. Growth of the immigrant population, particularly Latino and Asian immigrants, has greatly

F I G U R E   15.2   Rodney King's Beating. The not-guilty verdict handed down to four police officers who had been videotaped beating motorist Rodney King was the spark that ignited the Los Angeles riot of 1992.

outstripped growth of the African-American population; the new mix of population has created a new set of ethnic relationships that became visible during the 1992 riot (Morrison and Lowry 1994).

Unlike the 1965 Watts riot, in which most of the participants were African American, more than half of the people arrested for rioting in 1992 were Latinos. In addition to the change in the participants' race or ethnicity, the race or ethnicity of their victims changed as well. During the 1965 riot, whites owned most of the businesses targeted for looting; but in 1992, Koreans owned most of the targeted businesses. This change occurred for two reasons. First, most white merchants had abandoned the inner-city areas, with Koreans taking over many of the small businesses, so they were simply more available as targets. Second, just a year before the King-police case, a Korean shop owner had shot and killed a young black woman shopper (again in a case that was replayed on video for all to see) and had received no jail sentence from the courts. To African-American and Latino residents, already suspicious of the economic success of the Koreans, this trial was evidence that poor, darker-skinned people were worth less than whites and Asians in the eyes of the criminal justice system (Baldassare 1994; Sears 1994; Fukurai, Krooth, and Butler 1994).

To understand fully the Los Angeles riot of 1992, then, we need to consider three background factors. First, the economy of Los Angeles is thriving, but not all groups are benefiting from the prosperity. Second, racial and ethnic differences deepen divisions between rich and poor. Third, the police force is a symbol of racial oppression and control, not peace and order, in inner-city neighborhoods. This is particularly true when most of the police force is white, as was the case in the Rodney King affair (Levin and Thomas 1997). Within this context it is easy to see how an event like the police officers' acquittal in the King case would confirm the worst fears of people of color regarding police misconduct and the racial biases of the criminal justice system.

Is political or social protest the main factor that motivates people's participation in riots? Don't some people simply want to join in a fight, destroy a police car, or perhaps steal a new TV or case of liquor? From studies of previous riots, we know that, once riots are started, some people participate because of the general holiday atmosphere or the opportunity to get material goods. In the case of the Los Angeles riot, surveys afterward found that about two-thirds of the African-American respondents viewed the rioters as primarily motivated by political protest and only one-third viewed them as primarily motivated by economic gain. Among other racial and ethnic groups, however, the majority of survey respondents viewed the motivations as mainly self-interest (Bobo et al. 1992).

Social Movements

A **social movement** is an organized attempt to bring about or resist large-scale social change by noninstitutionalized means (Piven and Cloward 1977; Garner 1996). In simpler terms, noninstitutionalized means are group tactics that fall outside of official channels for action. Take, for example, a neighborhood group whose homes are threatened by the proposal to build a highway ramp through their area. In addition to writing letters of protest (an institutionalized avenue of action), they may stage sit-ins in city council offices, clog the highway department's switchboard with coordinated phone calls, or even lie down in front of bulldozers at a highway construction site. Some of these noninstitutionalized tactics are simply outside of normal channels; others are clearly outside of the law.

Social movements include many organizations, but the movement is wider than any single organization. To distinguish between the two concepts, sociologists have adopted the term social movement organization (SMO) to describe the organizations that make up a social movement. In urban areas several related organizations may be part of the same or overlapping social movements. For example, a tenants' organization, a community development corporation, and a women homeowners' coalition are all organizations that might participate in a movement to improve housing opportunities for low-income households.

Regardless of the goal of a specific social movement, the underlying logic of all social movements is to challenge and change the distribution of power and resources in the society. Not surprisingly, wealthy groups with more access to the resources of money and political power are more likely to work within the system, whereas middle-class and poor people, with fewer options open to them, are far more likely to engage in extralegal tactics. In fact, Piven and Cloward (1977) argue that because poor people are rarely allowed to pursue their own interests through socially approved means, they regularly turn to social movements as their best option for action.

Urban social movements have been prominent not only in the history of the United States but throughout the world. In his book *The City and the Grassroots*, Manuel Castells (1983) discusses social movements in Europe, North America, and Latin America. According to Castells's analysis, urban social movements most often address three types of issues:

1. **Collective consumption**, or the movement to maintain high-quality, publicly supported goods and services, such as subsidized housing and parks, and to preserve historic areas.

2. **Community**, or the search for cultural identity that affirms ethnically or socially based ties within a neighborhood.

3. **Citizens' movements**, or movements organized to gain political influence or self-management.

One of the most pressing urban problems today is the problem of the loss of political and economic resources from U.S. cities. Throughout this book we have seen repeated examples of the withdrawal of investment from cities in general and from lower-income neighborhoods in particular. It should not surprise us, then, that the most prominent urban social movements in recent years have organized in response to the withdrawal of resources from urban neighborhoods. Urban residents organize with their neighbors to develop housing and job opportunities as well as to demand better services from local governments. They also put pressure on the private firms that influence the quality of life in urban areas—firms such as banks, insurance companies, and even supermarket chains—whose actions can make or break a local community. In their approaches to community action, many of the community groups combine two of Castells's issues: maintaining a high quality of collective consumption (particularly good housing) and gaining political influence and control over their neighborhoods.

One well-known social movement is ACORN (the Association of Community Organizations for Reform Now). This national organization is composed of dozens of affiliated branches in different cities. The group, founded in Arkansas in 1970, is a "mass-based, multi-issue, multitactical, community organization" (Delgado 1986, 3). It is the largest national organization dedicated to community organizing, and it specializes in organizing among poor and minority populations. When ACORN leaders decided to address housing issues, they worked with neighborhood leaders in low-income areas to pressure local housing agencies to provide additional housing resources. In addition to the legal means of letter writing, lobbying, and so on, ACORN initiated a squatters campaign that used the extralegal means of breaking into abandoned, government-owned houses and taking possession of them. This direct-action approach had two benefits: it provided some immediate results and a sense of progress to the people who moved into the homes, and, the high-publicity campaign put pressure on local and federal officials to change the policies that had caused the stockpile of abandoned housing.

In addition to housing itself, another resource in short supply in urban neighborhoods is mortgage investment money. As we saw in Chapter 9, many urban areas, particularly those with heavy concentrations of minority residents, are redlined by banks and savings and loan companies. As defined by Gregory Squires (1992, 2), redlining is "a process by which goods and services are made unavailable, or are available only on less than favorable terms, to people because of where they live regardless of their relevant objective characteristics." Community groups in many cities have mobilized to pressure their local banks and other lenders to make mortgage money available in neighborhoods where banks do not usually make loans.

The community reinvestment movement began in the 1970s when a number of community activists researched their local housing markets and discovered that it was impossible to get mortgages in many urban neighborhoods. Although banks and other lenders were not obligated to reveal where they gave mortgages, researchers pieced together loan patterns from tax rolls and sales records, revealing huge geographic disparities in lending patterns. Some community groups targeted individual banks and convinced organizations to stop doing business with them if they would not agree to lend in city neighborhoods. Activists from several cities successfully sued the Federal Deposit Insurance Corporation and other agencies that regulate banks on the grounds that the agencies were not properly overseeing the banks to prevent racial discrimination in lending, as past fair housing laws had required. They then succeeded in getting Congress to pass the Home Mortgage Disclosure Act in 1976, which required banks to make their lending data public, and the Community Reinvestment Act of 1978, which required banks to address the needs of the communities in which they are located. As the movement grew, multi-issue organizations such as ACORN joined National People's Action and a national network of housing and neighborhood groups to support reinvestment on both the local and the national levels (Squires 1992; Adamson 1993).

Organizing as part of a social movement might sound like a tremendous amount of effort and might lead you to wonder whether social movements actually can produce social change. In their book *Poor People's Movements*, Piven and Cloward (1977) describe several movements that had a major impact on our society: the movement of unemployed workers in the Depression that resulted in the founding of the Social Security system; the movement of employed workers, also during the Depression, that gained legal recognition and rights for trade unions; the civil rights movement of the 1950s and 1960s that challenged and finally defeated legal segregation; and the welfare rights movement of the 1960s and 1970s that pressured the federal government to raise the level of public assistance to a livable rate.

Has the community reinvestment movement made any impact on urban areas? To understand just how much it has done, it is important to remember that up to the 1960s, racial discrimination in housing was legal. Banks, landlords, realtors, and government housing agencies routinely and legally treated individuals differently because of race. A series of laws and executive orders in the 1960s (resulting from pressure brought by the civil rights movement) banned individual discrimination in sales and rental of housing but did not address the issue of how institutions discriminate against whole urban neighborhoods by simply not investing in them. The community reinvestment movement is significant because its activists have identified a root cause of the major social problems in urban areas—the availability of resources—and have begun a systematic struggle to reverse patterns of urban disinvestment.

Terrorism

On September 11, 2001, Americans were reminded of the threat of terrorism in dramatic fashion. Four airplanes were hijacked by nineteen men brandishing nothing more than box cutters. One plane, United Airlines flight 93, crashed into a field in rural Shanksville, Pennsylvania, after its passengers attempted to regain control of the plane. The three other planes were each crashed into buildings symbolic of American economic and military power: the twin towers of the World Trade Center in New York and the Pentagon near Washington, D.C. Nearly three thousand people died and over six thousand were injured in the deadliest foreign attacks on American soil in history. Although 9/11 is considered by many to be the beginning of the "War on Terror," it was not the first time a terrorist attack had occurred on American soil (Wright 2006).

Criminologists distinguish between at least two types of terrorism: domestic terrorism and international terrorism. The events of 9/11 are an example of international terrorism. The World Trade Center was first bombed on February 26, 1993, an incident of international terrorism that resulted in six dead and over a thousand injured. As with 9/11, the 1993 bombing involved a group of militant Islamic fundamentalists. The attackers were from several different countries, but shared a hostile view of American economic power and its support of nondemocratic regimes in the Middle East. On the day of the attack, two men drove a rented van into the parking garage and ignited a 1,500-pound bomb. The bomb severely damaged the structure, cutting electricity and disrupting phone service to lower Manhattan for over a week (Lance 2003).

Domestic terrorism is also normally motivated by political or cultural issues. Such groups as the Ku Klux Klan, the Black Liberation Army, and the Animal Liberation Front are often classified, at least by some scholars and law enforcement, as domestic terrorist organizations. Prior to 9/11, the deadliest terrorist attack in American history was the bombing of the Oklahoma City federal office building on April 19, 1995. Three men connected to the Militia Movement were convicted of the crime. The bombing was in revenge for the way in which the government handled standoffs between law enforcement and suspects at Ruby Ridge, Idaho, and Waco, Texas, in 1993. Although the perpetrators of the Oklahoma City bombings were religious, the primary motivation appears to have been political. In contrast, consider the Centennial Park bombing at the 1996 Olympic Games in Atlanta. After bombings at two abortion clinics and a lesbian night club, the FBI identified Eric Robert Rudolph as the bomber. A fundamentalist Christian, Rudolph chose his targets on the basis of his religious beliefs that declared abortion, homosexuality, and socialism to be immoral and punishable by death.

The threat of terrorism in many cities, particularly larger cities home to such symbols of government power or cultural diversity, has influenced urban policy and planning. Major events, such as concerts and major athletic events, now normally include provisions for enhancing security. Today the design of new buildings is more likely to consider the threat of terrorist attack than those built in the past, and major buildings, such as the United Nations in New York and the White House in Washington, D.C., have been retrofitted to defend against attack.

CAUSES OF URBAN DISRUPTIONS

Crime, gang activity, riots, social movements, and terrorism are all disruptive to social order in cities. What do these phenomena have in common? Why do we find them concentrated in cities rather than spread evenly throughout different types of communities? Let us quickly survey the thoughts of a few major sociologists who have tackled these questions.

Research since the 1980s has shown that crime rates are closely related to the lack of adequate employment in communities (Currie 1985; Wilson 1997, 2009a). Crime is not related directly to the unemployment rate, however, but rather people's prospects for obtaining a decent life through work. Young people are most likely to commit crimes when they are unable to find high-quality, satisfying work; that is, when they lack economic viability (Padilla 1992; Hagedorn and Macon 1998). As we have seen previously, in many inner-city areas, what work is available is unstable, low-paying, boring, or difficult, with little or no opportunity for advancement. It should not be surprising that some people in these circumstances use property crime as an alternative or a supplement to these dead-end jobs (Walker, Spohn, and DeLone 2006).

Sociologists Jay MacLeod (1995) and Philippe Bourgeois (1995) have explored how the community and family setting in some job-poor neighborhoods can encourage crime. In neighborhoods characterized by a scarcity of good jobs, many young people try working at legitimate jobs but cannot get ahead. They feel powerless to achieve success through socially acceptable channels. Their own families can serve as negative role models in one of two ways. Many teenagers have parents or older siblings who, despite years of hard work, are still deeply mired in poverty. They have also seen some people take a criminal route to a degree of economic success. This is not necessarily a culture of poverty with different values, as some theorists have argued, but rather people's response to an economic setting that has different opportunities, rewards, and risks for legitimate work compared with illegal "work," such as dealing drugs or selling stolen goods.

Mercer Sullivan's (1989) study of the young males growing up in three New York City neighborhoods put it even more bluntly. He found that when the young men had difficulty finding legitimate jobs that paid decently, they sometimes used street crime (for example, mugging people or snatching their gold chains) as a way of supplementing their incomes. They thought of such petty crime as either "getting over" (beating the system) or "getting paid" (Sullivan 1989, 2).

Researchers who study gang activity (e.g., Cummings and Monti 1993; Hagedorn and Macon 1998; Jankowski 1991) have found three general reasons that young people join gangs. The first is to have something to do, a sense of identity, and a degree of fun, prestige and friendship that is not available in school or in their families. The second is to get tangible rewards such as alcohol, drugs, and money (in those gangs that sell drugs, steal cars, or otherwise have illegal businesses). The third is to get protection or avoid harassment. The reason that gangs flourish in poor communities is that the **opportunity structure** encourages gang formation. Young men living in poor communities with inadequate schools, few recreation opportunities, and no prospects for part-time jobs have lots of time on their hands. They have nothing to lose by joining a gang because they think they have no future anyway, and it might be fun or profitable. They understand and accept the possibility that they might get shot. Studies of gangs stress that these attitudes are not simply generated out of thin air but are young people's responses to the real and perceived conditions in the communities where they live.

Studies of urban riots also show that this particular type of violence has, since the 1960s, occurred overwhelmingly in low-income minority ghetto neighborhoods. Riot participants in Los Angeles were predominantly Latino and African-American young adults. A typical study found that the South Central area of Los Angeles was ripe for a disturbance because of two conditions: "a long accumulation of grievances against ethnically different neighbors [Korean merchants] who were accessible for reprisal, combined with the availability of a large pool of idle young men who had little stake in civil order" (Morrison and Lowry 1994, 41). This analysis is consistent with the report of the National Advisory Commission on Civil Disorders (1968) that explained urban riots as a result of two trends: the racial and class segregation of lower-income African-American households in inner cities and the steady decline in adequate housing, jobs, health care, and education in those same areas.

What about the relationship between social movements and urban areas? According to Piven and Cloward (1977), poor people who organize social movements do so because they lack not only their fair share of the nation's resources but also access to the political and economic power they need to change their situation. They correctly perceive that, as long as they act within the approved channels of established institutions, they cannot change their situation. Neighborhoods where the residents are not in control of the resources they need and have no way of getting those resources can understandably look for noninstitutionalized ways of getting the resources. There are two main differences between lawbreaking that we call *street crime* and lawbreaking that we call a *social movement*. First, street crime is an individualistic and largely predatory activity, whereas social movements involve a large segment of the community cooperating for a common purpose. Street crime pits resident against resident and can undermine community cohesion; social movements bind residents together and support community cohesion. Second, unlike individually motivated crime, social movements are self-consciously organized to bring about social change, often involving a renegotiation or redefinition of laws and public policies.

In the case of the squatters campaign, activists persuaded local and federal authorities to change laws and policies regarding the ownership of abandoned housing.
In the case of the community reinvestment movement, low-income groups
successfully challenged the role of the banking industry in mortgage lending
both by direct pressure on specific banks and by indirect pressure on Congress
and on the government agencies that regulate banks.

What all of these activities—crime, gang association, riots, and urban social
movements—have in common is that each is in some way a response to urban
disinvestment. Hagan (1994) discusses three ways that disinvestment leads to crime:
first, through the concentrated poverty that results when jobs are withdrawn from
urban communities; second, through the residential segregation that keeps people
of different social classes and ethnic groups separate and that has resulted in the
creation of inner-city neighborhoods populated chiefly by the poorest of the
poor; third, through the inequality in access to employment and access to information about employment such as job referrals. Corporate and social disinvestment
has caused highly concentrated poverty and, more important, has eroded the opportunity structure for economic success formerly available to lower-income
groups in cities.

As responses to disinvestment, the four activities of crime, gang association,
riots, and social movements may not seem to have much in common. Economic
crime is an individualistic response (except for the case of organized crime) that
gives people increased access to resources. Gangs substitute for community resources and activities by providing alternative activities and rewards for the group.
Riots have the peculiar characteristic of being individualistic and collective at the
same time; as an expression of the politically powerless, they at least can draw public attention to their communities' needs. Social movements, most directly, address
the lack of political and economic power and are self-consciously aimed at changing the system rather than simply the individual's place in it. Although these responses differ, seeing them as connected to disinvestment helps us understand their
prominence on the urban landscape.

APPROACHES TO REDUCING URBAN
DISRUPTIONS

What can be done to address urban unrest, crime, and other disruptions of urban
life? The answer, at least in part, is found in the system of social control that
every society creates.

All social systems, including communities, contain mechanisms that generally
keep people following the rules. These are **social control** mechanisms, or
arrangements that encourage people to obey rules and discourage them from
disobeying rules. Some social control mechanisms are informal, or simply part
of the social fabric; others are formal, or codified in laws or written rules
and regulations. But, as we will see, social control is only part of the solution
to urban disorder.

Informal Social Control

Informal social control is the most common and most powerful form of social control. In the simplest terms, informal social control refers to people watching out for each other and noticing rule violations. Settings in which people know each other, where social networks are highly developed, and where there is a good deal of public activity, typically have high levels of informal social control. Jane Jacobs (1961) discussed the street life of urban neighborhoods such as Greenwich Village in New York City, noting that at almost any time of the day or night, people were out on the street. Whether walking to work, watching their kids play, running errands, or just looking out of the window, they were observing other people. In Jacobs's words, there were always "eyes on the street" (1961, 35).

Informal social control mechanisms work in three ways. First, simply being in public view is a powerful deterrent to crime or violence, because people engaging in illegal acts strongly prefer anonymity. Second, informal mechanisms require a low level of intervention to be effective; challenging a stranger who "doesn't belong" in a particular place or reprimanding kids who are acting disruptively can prevent more serious incidents that would require police intervention. Third, informal control mechanisms are often integrated into other community processes. In areas where it is common for neighbors to do favors for each other, watching out for each other's houses and children is a simple extension of borrowing, gossiping, and other neighboring activity.

Although informal social control is powerful, it may not be as widespread as it was in the past due to changing social conditions. Do people know their neighbors? Are they willing to intervene when other people's property is threatened or when other people's children are misbehaving? Merry (1981) found in a study of a low-income neighborhood in Boston that two factors had interfered in people's willingness to exert informal social control in their neighborhood: fear and ethnic barriers. In the low-income development Merry studied, many people who did not know their neighbors or who said they avoided interacting with strangers cited fear as the main problem. In particular, residents feared making contact with people of different racial and ethnic groups, whether they were strangers or neighbors. This lack of social interaction among neighbors contributed to the danger of the neighborhood, because residents often had no way of knowing whether strangers in their buildings were friends of their neighbors or potential burglars.

Informal social control can be a powerful force for order, but conditions such as fear of weapons, fear of strangers, anonymity, and a reluctance to take personal responsibility for public space can reduce its effectiveness in some urban neighborhoods. Nevertheless, Innes (2003) points out that the line between informal social control and formal social control (below) is blurred in that many formal situations are also dealt with informally (Innes 2003, p. 7).

Formal Social Control

Formal social control mechanisms are those that are institutionalized through laws, usually involving complex sets of rules, regulations, and penalties.

F I G U R E 15.3   Community Policing. Many cities have instituted community policing programs that place officers in the community to act as a resource to residents and work with them to prevent crime.

The most prominent are the criminal law and the criminal justice system, including police, courts, jails and prisons. Formal social control has emerged to fortify, supplement, and in some places substitute for informal social control mechanisms. Police forces, for example, were created in most cities of the United States just before the Civil War, during the 1830s and 1840s. During the same time period, many laws were passed to regulate public behavior and morality (such as laws against Sunday drinking, shopping, and mail delivery). Public officials initiated these increases in formal social control in an attempt to address the (largely urban) violence, riots, and conflicts of an urbanizing, changing society deeply divided by differences in religion, ethnicity, and social class (Feldberg 1980).

How well do laws, police, and prisons work as social control mechanisms? A police presence, especially when incorporated into the everyday functioning of the community, may be somewhat effective in deterring crime. During the 1980s, a number of urban police departments instituted an approach called **community policing**, based on the philosophy that attacking the root causes of crime is more effective than attacking individual criminals. In community policing programs, police are partners rather than adversaries with neighborhood residents. They identify and attempt to deal with potential problems before they become more serious (Greene and Mastrofski 1988). Figure 15.3 shows an example of community policing.

The more traditional approach to policing, however, is oriented toward controlling crime by apprehending and punishing violators. This form of social control has only a limited impact on crime, as recent efforts to strengthen it have revealed. Since about 1980, police, courts, and legislatures have instituted a multitude of practices designed to toughen law enforcement, from adding police officers, to removing constraints on police, to decreasing prosecutors' flexibility in charges (plea bargaining), to lengthening sentences and restoring the death penalty. Although these measures may reassure the public that our society is tough on crime, several studies have shown that such measures have little impact on actual crime, either on the number of crimes committed, the number of people caught, or the likelihood of conviction (Spelman and Brown 1984; Walker 1989).

Why is the crime control approach to urban crime deficient? First, it does nothing to address the underlying causes of urban crime, such as the fact that economic opportunities are badly distributed in relation to where they are needed most. Without addressing the root causes, crime control policy cannot make any inroads into actually reducing crime. Second, crime control is expensive. As a nation we have diverted billions of dollars from health, education, and other supportive services to assemble a larger criminal justice system, build additional prisons, and incarcerate people for longer periods of time, all with little return on the investment (Currie 1985).

In addition to those problems, policing and formal social control can paradoxically make the crime problem seem worse than it is. Police–gang relations in Los Angeles are an excellent example. Belonging to a gang is not a crime (although the City Attorney's office has attempted to get the law changed to criminalize gang membership). Yet police in the 1980s routinely established antidrug operations, consisting of roadblocks or sweeps of playgrounds and hangouts. Here they detained teenagers, entering their names in a computerized database on suspicion of gang membership. This suspicion could be based on a minor signal, such as red shoelaces or a high-five with the wrong person. Although not charged with a crime, when these youths have another encounter with the police (perhaps for a traffic violation) and their name is found in the database, they are considered a suspected gang member, which adds to the gravity of their offense and makes it more likely that they will be charged with a crime (Davis 1990).

One reason that police action can be a problem is that the criminal justice system is characterized by a great deal of discretion in handling offenses. Discretion can lead to two negative consequences: labeling and abuse. Police officers, prosecutors, judges, prison guards, and parole officers continually make judgments based in large part on their definition of the situation (Reid 1993). They have the power to label individuals as harmful or harmless. Unfortunately, the record shows that age, race, sex, and ethnicity are factors that the police routinely rely on when they label people. Their biases stem from attitudes about who is likely to be a criminal, rooted in police subcultures (Chambliss 1994). Once labeled, the police treat the person as the label ("suspected gang member") suggests. In Los Angeles, aggressive policing toward Latino and African-American males between fifteen and twenty-five years old has led to a history of abuse complaints against the Los Angeles Police Department, few of them resolved in favor of the complainants. As we saw, the history of minority community grievances against the police was at the heart of the 1992 riot (Fukurai, Krooth, and Butler 1994; Levin and Thomas 1997).

Formal social control is a necessity in modern cities. As our communities become more complex and diverse, we rely on it more. Diana Gordon and colleagues (1992, 366) argue that the "justice system is a last-resort mechanism that comes into play when all other mechanisms of social control, private and public, [have] failed." Not only does formal social control not address the causes of social unrest, it may add to them. Yet we use it because we have been persuaded that crime and disruptions such as gang violence cannot be cured, so they must be controlled.

Strategic Reinvestment

How, then, do we understand the root causes of social unrest and what can we do to address them? The most powerful overall explanation of urban unrest, including street crime, gang formation, ghetto riots, and urban social movements, is that they are all responses to community disinvestment (Hagan 1994). Given the overall opportunity structure and the inequality of the distribution of resources in our society, people living in poor neighborhoods often find it difficult to get ahead through legitimate channels. To understand urban disruptions, we must examine the structure of urban inequality. To understand inequality, we must understand who controls resources and where they invest them.

Throughout this book we have seen repeated examples of investors, both private (corporations) and public (governments) moving resources from inner-city residential neighborhoods to central business districts, from cities to suburbs, and from one region of the country to another. This mobile pattern of investment and disinvestment results in an uneven geography of economic and political winners and losers. The areas with the least investment, or the greatest disinvestment, in our society are inner-city, low-income, segregated districts of cities.

Although it may not look like it on the surface, this pattern reveals a major societal conflict between those who control resources and those who do not. Wealthy individuals and communities with economic capital to invest have the most control over their own future actions and usually a good deal of influence over others as well. Middle-class individuals and communities typically have less money capital but have the cultural capital of good educations, professional skills, and knowledge of the political system that positions them to take advantage of opportunities for advancement. Low-income individuals and communities have little of either economic capital or **cultural capital**. Consequently, they may attempt to recapitalize their communities by drawing resources (illegally) from other people or by using noninstitutionalized means to pressure the political or economic institutions to gain additional access to resources (Hagan 1994; Piven and Cloward 1977). The conflict between those who control resources and those who do not becomes apparent in the disruptions we have examined; and all evidence shows that as social inequality worsens, the conflicts become more apparent.

What alternatives exist to illegal and disruptive ways of residents of disinvested neighborhoods "getting paid"? A program of strategic reinvestment in cities is the most likely route to a more peaceable and prosperous urban future. This includes investment in both the cities and their residents: in the infrastructure such as housing and transportation, in services such as education and health care, and, most importantly, in providing opportunities for employment that is respectable, meaningful, and decently paid. But do we have the resources to accomplish this feat? It would take some redistribution of resources, although not as much as some might fear. Ironically, simply redistributing the funds that we now spend on maintaining our prison system would provide enough of an income to bring every poor family out of poverty or to create decent jobs for one million young people (Currie 1985).

Rather than ask, What is the cost of a strategic reinvestment program?, we should ask, What is the cost of the current policy? Is it worth the billions of dollars spent every year just to hold the line and control crime at its current level? Do we want to lose any more of our young people to gang violence? How many more riots will spring up as responses to social inequality? Perhaps if ordinary people understood that strategic investments in job development, education, and housing were the real crime-reduction program, they would support the redirection of corporate and government resources in the direction of greater equity and opportunity.

CONCLUSION

Social unrest and disruption are sometimes part of urban life. As we have seen, however, disruptions such as crime are not exclusively urban-based phenomena but are characteristic of our society as a whole. Within that context, cities of the United States are, for the most part, stable and orderly.

Sociologists studying urban crime and disorder have found a consistent pattern of relationships. The neighborhoods with the highest levels of street crime tend to be those with the highest rates of poverty and the least access to economic resources. They are the areas of the greatest disinvestment of businesses, jobs, mortgage loans, and other components of a healthy economy. To be sure, not everyone living in these disinvested neighborhoods engages in criminal behavior. Property crime, drug sales, and gang activity, however, are some residents' responses to living in areas of concentrated poverty and limited opportunities.

Another set of responses to disinvestment include civil disorders (riots) and social movements. These activities frequently test the flexible boundary between legal and illegal protest. Precisely because they shock the community or targeted institutions (such as banks and government agencies), such disruptions can be an effective avenue to social change, particularly for those groups that lack access to power through the approved channels. In addition to pressuring for social change, social movements can create social networks, strengthening residents' sense of identity and control over their neighborhoods.

Although informal social control mechanisms are normally sufficient to keep communities safe, we have turned increasingly to formal social control mechanisms such as police and prisons. These agencies seldom address the root causes of many crimes and disruptions: concentrated poverty and community disinvestment. Instead, criminal justice agencies are organized to punish individual violators in the hope of deterring other individuals. If we as a society want to address the real roots of disorder, we need to take steps to reduce the inequality and fragmentation of social class, race, and ethnicity that characterize our communities. Public funds spent on strategic reinvestment in schools and decent jobs will in the long run do more for social peace than funds spent on even the best trained peace officers.

DISCUSSION QUESTIONS

1. Ask several of your friends to generate a list of words they associate with the concepts crime and disorder. Do they associate these events with any particular social groups or geographic areas?

2. Why do you think that states and counties are building prisons and incarcerating people at a record rate? What are the reasons for the growing prison population? What alternatives exist to imprisonment, and what are their advantages and disadvantages?

3. Have you ever participated in or read about a social movement? What was it trying to change? What tactics did it use? What kinds of changes did it bring about? Did it change your thinking about power and social structures? If so, how?

PART V

Conclusion

16

Planning for the Future
of Cities

People come together in cities for security;
they stay together for the good life.
ARISTOTLE

Cities and towns grow in patterns that are partly the result of individual decisions—often based on economic considerations—and partly the result of planning. From the earliest settlements described in Chapter 3, archaeologists have found evidence of collective efforts to make the urban setting work. Whether it was a street pattern, walls surrounding the city, or public spaces, someone thought out a pattern that others followed to a greater or lesser degree.

Cities are located in the physical environment. Once they are constructed, the buildings, roads, and other improvements that people add to the landscape become part of the environment too. The built environment is just as influential as the natural environment in shaping how people use the city. Once roads, bridges, sewers, and buildings are constructed, they channel people's activities. So how they are built is important to the social as well as the physical life of the city.

This chapter will focus on four questions:

- How has urban planning been carried out in the past?
- What ideas have modern planners advanced regarding urban design and function?
- How and where have their ideas been implemented?
- What implications does planning have for the future of cities?

URBAN PLANNING IN HISTORY

Most cities have historically been planned to one degree or another. The degree to which they have been planned, however, varies greatly. If you look at a map of ancient Athens, for example, you see that the districts containing the monumental public buildings were laid out geometrically, while the residential districts were a hodgepodge of narrow, winding streets. The Aztec city of Teotihuacán, on the other hand, was rigorously planned and laid out in alignment with the constellations.

Many cities have been planned for defensive purposes. In ancient times, many cities were surrounded by high, thick walls that could be entered only by one or two gates. Walls are the most common, but not the only, physical feature that city builders have used to defend the residents against attacks from outsiders. Other defense strategies include strategically locating the city where it is easy to protect (for example, on a cliff or next to a river), building a moat or ditch around the city, or building towers for observation posts. Location was also an important consideration: early American colonial capitals, such as Albany, New York, and Hartford, Connecticut, were located far upstream on river in part for defensive purposes. Similarly, Washington, D.C. is located upstream on the Potomac River.

In the United States, commerce and profit have often been the guiding force behind city planning. We have numerous examples of how trade and commerce have shaped the internal structure of our cities. The most important is the adoption of the grid street pattern in virtually every section of the country. In colonial times, the streets of most cities tended to follow the natural contours of the land, weaving around such topographical features as creeks and hills. In Philadelphia, however, William Penn laid out a rectangular street grid because he thought the physical order of the town would lead to an orderly social life. Not coincidentally, the grid also made it easy to subdivide and sell property.

Urban planning has also been utilized as a way of demonstrating political power. In the middle of the nineteenth century, Napoleon III decided to have Paris rebuilt to reflect its proper place as the center of the Napoleonic Empire. He commissioned Baron Haussmann to create an impressive design. Haussmann razed acres of housing and small shops, replacing them with majestic boulevards such as the Champs-Élysées, substituting a star-shaped street pattern over the existing streets. At the center of the most prominent star, he placed the emblem of the Empire's conquests, the Arc de Triomphe, or arch of triumph. In addition to the goal of publicizing the Empire's political power, Napoleon also sought to remake the city for defense purposes. Haussmann's street plan allowed for two strategic military advantages: the broad boulevards of the rebuilt Paris allowed troops to move through the city and allowed canons to fire for long distances in a straight line. The star-shaped streets allowed entire sections of the city to be cordoned off so that disturbances in a neighborhood could quickly be isolated.

In the United States, where the impulse for grandeur is perhaps less well developed than in Europe, we nonetheless find that the capital city, Washington, D.C., was planned with the idea that it would underscore the power of the government. Originally planned by Pierre L'Enfant in 1791 but taken over by other designers, the plan was revived a century later and married to elements of the City Beautiful movement. Washington's planners adopted the same star-shaped street scheme as Paris, allowing long vistas and broad boulevards that show off its many monuments and neoclassical buildings. The importance and power of government is obvious in Washington. As a seat of government, the Capitol is situated prominently on a hill, and the most important presidents such as Washington, Jefferson, and Lincoln all have their impressive memorials.

URBAN PLANNING: THE VIEW FROM THE GROUND

What does it mean to the individual if streets are grid-shaped or star-shaped? Do monumental buildings really make people react the way the political leaders think they will react? After planners and architects have designed spaces, how do ordinary people use them? These are the questions that one asks when looking at planning "from the ground" rather than in charts and drawings.

In the past fifty years, planners, geographers, sociologists, and psychologists have conducted a great deal of research on how people interact with space. We will discuss two of the better-known approaches, one that examines how people think about city spaces and one that examines how people live in and use city spaces.

Imaging the City

One of the key thinkers in urban planning and design is Kevin Lynch, author of *The Image of the City* (1960). Lynch set out to understand how people make sense of cities and how they find their way around in cities. He interviewed dozens of residents and asked them to describe the neighborhoods where they lived and the city districts that they saw on a regular basis. His findings fascinated social scientists because they were so unexpected, yet they seemed to make perfect sense. By interviewing residents of three different cities, Boston, Los Angeles, and Jersey City, Lynch determined that certain areas of cities are more memorable—and therefore more useful—to people than other areas. He found that what makes an area memorable is its "legibility," or the ease with which people can recognize the parts of an urban landscape and reassemble them into a whole. A legible area has well-defined components, whereas an area that is not legible is usually less well defined. (See Figure 16.1.)

Lynch provided planners with some building blocks of design that would assist those who use cities in "reading" their component parts. His building blocks include:

- *Paths:* linear areas for pedestrians or vehicles (roads, sidewalks, stairways)
- *Edges:* boundaries of areas (railroad tracks, a river bank, a lakefront, a concrete wall)
- *Districts:* distinctive areas with an identifying, unified, or coherent look (a downtown, a skid row)
- *Nodes:* strategic spots formed by the coming together of roads, railroads, or other traffic (a square, a train station)

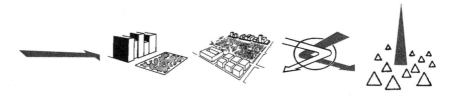

F I G U R E 16.1 Elements of Design Form. Kevin Lynch identified five types of elements that help people make sense of urban landscapes. From left to right, they are paths, edges, districts, nodes, and landmarks.
SOURCE: Kevin Lynch, *The Image of the City.* Copyright ©1960, MIT Press.

- *Landmarks:* points that stand out sufficiently from the surroundings and are sufficiently prominent that they can orient people to a location or direction (a church steeple, monument, or skyscraper)

In designing "good" spaces for people to use, Lynch argues, planners must recognize that sameness is not a desirable quality, because it provides little legibility. Rather, some visual differences in the landscape should be apparent, and elements should be clearly differentiated from each other to give a sense of the whole. Lynch's studies of people's perceptions show that attractive cities are not just orderly but also vivid and varied, with texture and unique visual stimuli.

The Social Life of the Street

Can cities be designed to foster constructive and pleasant social interactions? What do we know about spaces that "work" socially?

William H. Whyte spent sixteen years researching behavior in public places in New York City. Beginning in the 1970s, he organized students as his research assistants to observe people on the streets, in stores, cafes, train stations, and parks. He set up dozens of video cameras to record public interactions. Whyte published the results of his research in the 1988 book, *City: Rediscovering the Center.*

According to Whyte's videos, many of our commonsense ideas about how people behave in public places are simply wrong. Take the idea that people avoid dense crowds, for example. On the contrary, crowds seem to draw people (at least, people in Manhattan). Whyte observed office workers on their lunch hours sitting in crowded plazas and on busy steps while shunning empty parks, plazas, and streets. Crowds on the street grew ever larger as entertainers, hawkers, and other spectacles drew even more onlookers. Most surprisingly, when two friends met by chance on the street or in the doorway of a store, instead of stepping to the side, more often than not they held their conversation in the middle of the pedestrian traffic.

Whyte's observations show that some design elements repel people, for example, plazas invisible from the street get little use. Other elements that attract people include water, light, food, and places to sit. The biggest attraction of all seems to be viewing other people. The conclusion Whyte drew is that people are attracted to social life as one of the positive aspects of city life. Yet he found that many urban property owners, especially business owners, discouraged people from using their spaces. They installed spikes to prevent people from sitting on walls; they removed chairs from plazas; they tried to banish vendors from the sidewalks. Whyte argues that signs of "disorder" such as people sitting on steps or walls are actually signs of urban vitality.

To make social life more viable in cities, Whyte advocates stopping or reversing two trends now occurring in New York and other cities. One is the practice of building megastructures, large buildings that include interior malls or atria. These structures remove life from the public street by moving indoors such amenities as benches and coffee shops. Rather than being democratically open to everyone, the amenities inside megastructures are available only to those who know about them, and anyone who clearly "does not belong" can be removed because the space is private property. The other negative trend, in Whyte's view, is the practice of building structures with blank walls facing the streets, as we find in downtown shopping malls, parking garages, and convention centers. The problem with the blank walls is that people avoid streets when there is nothing to see on them, and an empty street is likely to feel like (and be) a dangerous street.

In *The Great Good Place* (1989), sociologist Ray Oldenburg makes a related observation. He argues that urban space need not be rigidly separated into public and private. As a way of fostering social life, Oldenberg looks to places that have some of the characteristics of both public and private life, spaces he calls **third places**. These might include a doughnut shop in Chicago, a taverna in Greece, a sidewalk cafe in Paris, an Austrian coffee shop, or a London pub. The characteristics these third places share are not necessarily the availability of food and beverages. Rather, Oldenburg says, they have an atmosphere that encourages sociability and conversation, while providing safety from interactions that might get out of hand. The truly great gathering places attract a regular, loyal group of patrons who come for the interaction with each other as much as for the food and drink. Third-place patrons develop and nurture the "habit of association," a characteristic that is in danger of extinction, as people increasingly turn to their home entertainment centers and microwave dinners.

URBAN PLANNING: VISIONS AND REALITIES

To some extent, cities grow and change by virtue of thousands of decisions individuals make about properties and buildings. That is, they are shaped by *market forces*. Other aspects of cities are *planned* by design professionals, in accordance with an overall strategy. In this section, we will examine several of the ideas that inspired urban planners and some of the results of planning gone awry.

Utopian Visions

Utopia (which literally means, "no place") was a vision of the perfect society written by Sir Thomas More over 500 years ago. Since that time, other writers have expressed utopian ideas about the perfectibility of humanity. Most utopian plans run on the theme that improving social arrangements can overcome human and social ills. Religious beliefs inspired some utopian thinkers, as they sought to create God's kingdom on earth. Others were secular reformers, grappling with the issue of how to get people to live in harmony with each other and with nature. Whatever their motivation, these planners designed innovative ways of living, working, worshipping, and raising children.

The Industrial Revolution was a major spur to utopian experimentation in the nineteenth century. The rapid pace of industrialization and urbanization in Europe and the United States caused a major transformation from the traditional way of life that had prevailed in small towns since the Middle Ages. Critics of industrial capitalism pointed to the long hours, unhealthy working conditions, and poor wages common among large-scale industrial cities such as the Manchester of Engels's time. As a response to the perceived evils and degradation of industrial capitalism, several utopian thinkers proposed to create communities that would provide a better balance among work, family life, and community life. One of the most famous was the French industrialist Charles Fourier. Intrigued by the socialist ideas of shared ownership and shared work, Fourier advocated the construction of new industrial communities that would give the workers the recognition and humanity they lacked in cities such as Manchester.

Robert Owen.   In the 1820s, Robert Owen, an associate of Fourier, came to the United States from Scotland. Owen planned to build a community in Indiana that he called New Harmony. As the name implies, it was to be a small, humanistic community, providing all the needs for one thousand residents. Owen proposed that everyone in the community should receive an education and that children would be raised cooperatively. To have access to the outdoors, the scale of industry would be kept deliberately small. This plan enunciated a radically different set of conditions than was commonly found in industrial cities.

Owen drew up detailed plans for New Harmony. The city was laid out in a square, with public buildings such as a school, church, meeting hall, and shops in the center. Around the sides of the square was housing for adults on three sides and for children on the fourth side. (Like many utopian communities, children lived apart from their parents for at least part of their lives.) To give the greatest possible access to the natural landscape, manufacturing was located at the outskirts of the town, as were farming areas. Unfortunately, Owen was never able to bring his vision to reality. Before he could construct New Harmony, his followers dissolved the group, but his writings and plans inspired others to create their own experiments.

Ebenezer Howard.   In addition to creating new economic and social relations with their fellow humans, another prominent theme in the writings of the utopian visionaries was improving relations between humans and the environment. Reacting to the congestion, pollution, and grime of the industrial cities, a number of thinkers designed plans that took the integrity of the natural environment as a central principle. The most influential of these early ecological writers was Ebenezer Howard, an amateur planner who spent most of his life in London.

Like other critics of industrialization, he attacked the problem of overcrowding in cities and proposed a new solution. Howard argued that working people were compelled to live in crowded cities because employment opportunities were concentrated there, and that the biggest cities continued to grow because they contained the most jobs. Howard thought that a better type of environment would combine the amenities of the city with the beauty and cleanliness of the country in a "marriage of the town and country." His book, *Garden Cities of Tomorrow* (1902), laid out plans for the ideal community, the garden city.

In Howard's scheme, communities would be limited to about 30,000 residents. The *garden cities* would be built in rural areas to take advantage of the pastureland and forests already available. The areas surrounding the city would form a permanent greenbelt, preventing the city from taking over the land for additional growth. Howard laid out only schematic diagrams for his communities rather than full plans. He thought that the city plan should be modified to take into account the natural features of the terrain, rather than the terrain being changed to follow a plan, as often occurs.

In principle, however, Howard recommended a fan-shaped city plan, with a series of circular roads culminating in a park at the center with boulevards radiating outward. Each boulevard defined a wedge-shaped district in which residents lived, worked, worshipped, played and attended school. Around the central park Howard placed major public buildings such as a theater, gallery, library, concert hall, and hospital. Howard planned for manufacturing shops and other workplaces to be on the outside of the circle, adjacent to small family farms. As its name implies, the garden city plan was generous with trees and open space, and the city was forever surrounded by forests, pastures, and orchards.

Unlike Owen, Howard was able to see his plans become a reality. Because he viewed capitalism as a main source of both social and environmental ills, Howard was interested in socialist ideas and drew inspiration from Edward Bellamy's *Looking Backward*, a futuristic novel about how cooperative socialism could transform modern societies. Howard spoke to many of Bellamy's followers and with a group of them founded a Garden City Association to promote the construction of new communities. With the help of the Garden City Association, Howard raised the money to build two garden cities, Letchworth (begun in 1902) and Welwyn (1920), both on the outskirts of London.

Le Corbusier. One of the most influential architects and planners of the twentieth century was Swiss-born Charles-Édouard Jeanneret, known simply as Le Corbusier. Le Corbusier, like Howard, was a critic of modern city life. Rather than following the idea of the garden city, however, Le Corbusier proposed what he called a *radiant city*, a series of towers in open parkland. Le Corbusier argued that by increasing the number of people accommodated in a building, the amount of land covered could be reduced and the amount of open space maximized, thus giving the city its green "lungs." The skyscraper in the park, intersected by the highway, is the signature Le Corbusier left on the design of twentieth-century cities. His architecture, part of the Modernist movement in art, became known as the International Style. (See Figure 16.2.)

F I G U R E 16.2 Le Corbusier's Radiant City. As an alternative to dense coverage of urban land with low-rise buildings, Le Corbusier proposed building tall towers. By increasing the density in the building, the surrounding land could be kept open. His International Style greatly influenced construction around the world after World War II.

SOURCE: LeCorbusier, *The Radiant City* (New York: Onion Press, 1967), p. 284.

Planning Realities in the United States

With the exception of a handful of cities, no utopian visions guided the early development of cities in the United States. Rather, they were mostly laid out by surveyors, in grids that were simply extended as the populations of the cities grew. Overall, then, the free market was the original driving force in shaping American cities.

By the late nineteenth century, it was apparent that the free-market approach to urban development had created many physical and social ills. Reformers advocated planning to solve urban problems such as high population densities, unsanitary streets, air and water pollution, lack of open space, rigid repetition of the grid street patterns, intermixing of industrial and residential land use, and traffic congestion. Their critique contained three points: unplanned cities were inefficient, ugly, and inequitable.

The inefficiency of cities had its most damaging impact on public health and cleanliness. Free-enterprise construction meant that cities did not supply water and sewers; every house had to find its own water supply and dispose of its own wastes. In practical terms, this meant a well and a pit toilet in each backyard—often right next to each other. As a result, epidemics from contaminated water periodically ravaged cities. Gradually, municipal governments built water pumping plants and extended pipelines to all residential neighborhoods (if not to every house) in the city. Later, urban planners imported from England

Stock Montage

F I G U R E 16.3 The White City. Architect Daniel Burnham designed elaborate, monumental buildings within expansive parks for the 1893 World Columbian Exhibition. This style, which became the signature of the City Beautiful movement, was adopted by cities all over the world.

the practice of building sanitary sewers to carry waste from each house for central disposal (Peterson 1983).

The ugliness of the city was also a public issue. Reformers addressed it by a new way of thinking about architecture and building. The so-called **City Beautiful movement** endeavored to raise the standards of design in public spaces and to bring art into the consciousness of the ordinary citizen. Imported from Paris, the City Beautiful movement gained public awareness in the United States during the 1893 World's Columbian Exposition in Chicago. Architect Daniel Burnham designed a "White City" of some 700 acres with broad avenues, majestic pools, and marble buildings in the neoclassical style designed to replicate Greek and Roman temples. The site included thousands of trees in a parklike setting with lakes and fountains. (See Figure 16.3.) The exposition was so successful that Burnham was later commissioned to draw up a plan for the entire city of Chicago.

The City Beautiful movement had an enormous impact on urban planning and architecture. Dozens of cities adopted City Beautiful plans in the early 1900s, sometimes tearing down dense, old neighborhoods and replacing them with wide boulevards of massive, columned buildings lined with stately trees. San Francisco's Civic Center and Philadelphia's Benjamin Franklin Parkway are prominent City Beautiful sites that retain their attractiveness today. Even in cities that did not adopt an overall City Beautiful plan, the fashion of using neoclassical architecture for prominent public buildings persisted right up into the 1950s.

Cities built by free enterprise were also inequitable: whereas richer areas had good living conditions and access to services, poor neighborhoods had dilapidated housing and few or no services. Reformers who advocated better living conditions for the poor thus added another element to the impetus for planning. They publicized an agenda focused on women and children: improved housing, access to open space for recreation, and the construction of schools for all children. They argued that government had to step in to correct the ills and chaos that the free market had created in the cities. Many of these reformers were associated with the Settlement House movement and often were opposed to the City Beautiful movement. According to one historian of city planning,

> Settlement workers were not opposed to making the city more
> beautiful.... Usually, however, they were more concerned with
> promoting playgrounds than elaborate, formal parks, and were more
> interested in clean streets and tenement houses than in grand tree-lined
> boulevards or elaborate ceremonial buildings. (Davis 1967, 214)

The origins of urban planning, then, were prompted by a mix of practical realities about public health and safety, desires for aesthetic surroundings, and aspirations to improve social conditions. At times these practical problem-solving impulses collided with the plans and designs of the visionaries.

The Vision Implemented

As the twentieth century has proceeded into the twenty-first, realities of economics and politics have constrained the actions that planners (who generally work for city governments) can take. In some of the planned developments that have actually been implemented, it is possible to see elements of the visionary proposals made by the "big-picture" thinkers. In many cases, however, the built reality that a particular thinker may have inspired was implemented in a way that the idea's originator, such as Ebenezer Howard or Le Corbusier, would have barely recognized.

Garden Cities and New Towns.   Howard's garden city concept drew the attention of federal officials during the Great Depression of the 1930s. Congress passed legislation to construct three *new towns* on the garden city principle: Greenbelt, Maryland; Greendale, Wisconsin; and Green Hills, Ohio. This legislation represented a vote of confidence in public planning as well as an attempt to infuse some money into the economy and provide jobs for construction workers. The projects did not have the consistent support of Congress, however. At first, World War II diverted federal funds away from housing investment; later, a fear of communism turned legislators against government enterprises and prompted them to sell the developments to private owners.

Despite the federal government's withdrawal of support for garden cities, Howard's ideas filtered into the private real estate market. Private developers built several garden city–type new towns after World War II. The best known of these are Radburn, New Jersey; Reston, Virginia; and Columbia, Maryland. Reston provides an interesting example of a private new town that succeeded after some difficulty. Although construction began in the early 1960s, the city initially attracted few residents and was sold twice. The original developer,

Robert Simon, had planned Reston to be an economically diverse community with middle- and upper-income families interspersed throughout. Later owners changed this part of the plan so that the neighborhoods are now relatively homogeneous. Although Reston is primarily an upper middle-class community, it has a degree of racial diversity and also includes several hundred units of federally subsidized low-income housing. In recent years, Reston has experienced steady growth, not just in residents but also in the number of businesses locating there. In that way, it is a greater success than the other garden city communities, including Howard's own Letchworth, because the presence of business makes it a complete town rather than simply a commuter suburb.

The British government has been more supportive of new towns than the U.S. government. After World War II, partly because of the terrible housing shortage caused by wartime destruction and partly because of the desire to reduce population growth in London, Parliament approved a program to build new towns in rural areas. The New Towns Act of 1946 provided for the establishment of new communities planned somewhat along the lines of garden cities. Although the new towns were allowed to vary in their physical characteristics, the principles on which they were founded were consistent. These included strong government control over the location of new industries, limits on the size and population density allowed in each community, and mechanisms to ensure diversity in land use and social class composition in each town. Eventually thirty-four new towns were built, but the towns in reality did not all work out as planned. One deviation from the plan was that Howard's goal of 30,000 residents per town was pushed upward to 60,000, and then up to as many as 250,000 residents, as great population growth and a scarcity of undeveloped land hampered efforts to keep densities low. Another deviation was that the original goal of social diversity in neighborhoods was not achieved. Planners had thought that mixing different housing types (apartments and houses of different sizes and prices, subsidized and market-rate) on each block would help mix social classes, but the dynamics of the housing market soon sorted people out into more homogeneous neighborhoods (LaGory and Pipkin 1981).

The International Style.   Compared to Ebenezer Howard, Le Corbusier had a very different perspective on what made a city healthy. His vision of cities as open space punctuated by high-rise, densely populated buildings contrasted sharply with Howard's vision of the town that mixed agriculture, industry, and housing. While Howard's goal was to reduce the size and density of towns and have people in close contact with the land, Le Corbusier's goal was to minimize the amount of land covered by buildings, retain as much open space as possible, and spread out development over larger areas to avoid the congestion caused by cities having a single central business district. Although only one city (Chandigarh, India) was actually constructed according to an overall plan that Le Corbusier developed, his ideas became architectural lore in the postwar period and thus had a major impact on contemporary cities. A glance at the developments built around the world since 1950 shows many examples of the "tower in the park" architecture.

The International Style, while inspiring many successful developments, also contributed to an unfortunate experiment with public housing. When the federal government began constructing public housing projects for poor families during the 1930s, they were almost universally two-story garden apartment-style buildings arranged around courtyards, each apartment with its own entrance. After 1950, government architects adopted Le Corbusier's reasoning that if they increased the density in the buildings by constructing high-rises, they could leave more open space for recreation. Not incidentally, by covering less land, this construction plan would also make each housing unit substantially cheaper to build. Beginning in the early 1950s, a number of high-rise "tower in the park" public housing projects were constructed. Perhaps the best known was a St. Louis project called Pruitt-Igoe. Built in 1955, its design won awards for creativity, but it was declared a disaster and demolished only nineteen years later. During the intervening years, it had quickly become a segregated high-rise ghetto, a warehouse for the poorest citizens of St Louis.

The physical structure of the Pruitt-Igoe buildings, designed along the International Style lines, compounded the problems of poverty and unemployment among the project's residents. The eleven-story buildings offered few inside places for children to play, encouraging them to congregate in stairways and out on the pavement, where adults had few opportunities to supervise them. Based on sociological studies of the project, the architect Oscar Newman investigated the design and identified a major flaw, which he says exists in most high-rise public housing. It is the lack of what Newman (1973) calls **defensible space**, space that is watched and cared for by people who have a legitimate interest in its use. According to Newman, the old-style garden apartment projects have lower rates of crime and vandalism because people can see what is going on outside their front doors. In the high-rises, too much space is a no-man's-land without opportunities for social control.

If Pruitt-Igoe was so bad that it was demolished, does that mean that Le Corbusier's vision is dangerous? Not necessarily. Tower-in-the-park developments have been successfully constructed throughout the world. Sociologists have concluded that not every social class or age group, however, are appropriate residents for such developments. The federal government continues to build high-rise developments for elderly citizens, and private developers continue to build them for the wealthy. For families with children, however, and particularly for low-income, single-parent families with children, high-rise housing is probably not an appropriate living space because of the few opportunities it offers for supervising children's activities.

The New Urbanism.   One of the newest trends in urban planning stems not from the supposed evils of the congested city but from the supposed evils of suburban sprawl. The New Urbanism, as it is called, is an effort to retain the feel of older cities and towns in new suburban communities. The New Urbanism is in some ways reminiscent of Howard's garden city, and it also echoes what Kevin Lynch and William Whyte wrote about how people actually use urban space.

The Celebration Company/The Walt Disney Company

F I G U R E 16.4 The New Urbanism. Planners and architects who subscribe to the New Urbanism design neighborhoods to encourage walking and neighborhood social interaction. They favor design features such as small front yards, porches, sidewalks, and narrow streets.

Peter Calthorpe (1994), an architect and proponent of the New Urbanism, writes:

> Sprawl is destructive in any growth strategy. Contemporary suburbs have failed because they lack ... the fundamental qualities of real towns: pedestrian scale, an identifiable center and edge, integrated diversity of use and population, and defined public space. They may have diversity in use and user, but these diverse elements are segregated by the car. They have none of the places for casual and spontaneous interaction which create vital neighborhoods, quarters, or towns.... In every context, therefore, the quality of new development in a region should follow town-like principles—housing for a diverse population, a full mix of uses, walkable streets, positive public space, integrated civic and commercial centers, transit orientation, and accessible open space. (p. xv)

Suburban communities designed according to the principles of the New Urbanism mimic the physical characteristics of cities or towns rather than the more common low-density, sprawling suburb. Planners deliberately re-create the narrow streets, sidewalks, smaller yards, and mixed residential, commercial, and recreational land-use characteristic of the 1920s. (See Figure 16.4.) Houses have porches in front and garages in back. Schools and shops are located within walking distance of most homes. Streets and sidewalks encourage pedestrian traffic rather than automobile traffic.

Some critics call these design features "nostalgic." Todd Bressi (1994), however, points out that they can be functional. He writes,

> The New Urbanism is not a romantic movement; it reflects a deeper agenda. The planning and design approaches ... revive principles about building communities that have been virtually ignored for half a century: public spaces like streets, squares, parks should be a setting for the conduct of daily life; a neighborhood should accommodate diverse types of people and activities; it should be possible to get to work, accomplish everyday tasks (like buying fresh food or taking a child to day care), and travel to surrounding communities without using a car. (p. xxv)

One of the most controversial aspects of the New Urbanism is the debate over whether such diverse living environments foster more of a sense of community than traditional, more homogeneous suburbs. New Urbanist developers claim that their towns are more "community-oriented" than ordinary suburbs. Their marketing materials appeal to values such as knowing one's neighbors, diversity, child-friendliness, and environmental consciousness. They promise an alternative way of life.

Probably the most famous community built on the principles of the New Urbanism is Celebration, Florida, near Orlando. Developed by The Walt Disney Company, Celebration's popularity is largely based on the promise of community spirit aided by good design. However, two books by residents of Celebration (Ross 1999; Frantz and Collins 1999) raise many questions about the gaps between theory and practice in the New Urbanism. For example, every house in Celebration is designed with a front porch to encourage social interaction. According to Frantz and Collins, however, residents rarely sit on their front porches in the evening, preferring instead to watch TV inside. As another example, many residents are drawn to Celebration by the focus on activities for their kids. Yet, according to Ross, the teenagers who are supposed to find lots of activities and friends in the community still feel disaffected. He says, "This could have been a group of white adolescents anywhere in suburban America ..." (Ross 1999, 99). Even the pedestrian-friendly layout and mixed land use that supposedly facilitates walking is not always effective. Ross reports that although it was possible to live in Celebration without a car, and although he walked to most places, most other residents drove, even to destinations that were clearly within walking distance.

If the New Urbanism does not necessarily live up to all of its proponents' claims and hopes in creating community in new suburban towns, it still holds promise in terms of improving existing cities. Revitalization efforts in many older cities are based on New Urbanist principles. Plans for Montreal, Boston, Baltimore, Providence, Los Angeles, and several smaller cities have incorporated the ideas of mixing land uses, favoring pedestrians, supporting public transportation, and increasing usable public spaces to make their downtown areas more attractive and livelier. By incorporating these design elements, cities can provide people with interesting alternatives to the homogeneity of suburban malls and housing developments.

Planning and Politics

How much impact can urban planning have on urban life? In the United States, planning can be a highly politicized process. The reality is that professional planners are normally employed by city and state governments, under the supervision of mayors, council members, governors, and legislators. Several facts of political life serve to restrict the amount of freedom that planners have to do their jobs. First, elected officials who run state and local governments (including planning departments) must be sensitive to the considerations of their constituencies, including voters, property owners, and businesses. Second, officials' views can be influenced by those in a position to contribute to their campaigns. Third, as elections are won or lost, the priorities of a city or state can change. Finally, there is a tension between goals that may be desirable on an abstract basis (for example, the principles of "a clean environment" or "economic development") and how powerful interests can shape the interpretation and implementation of those goals. In the case studies that follow, we will briefly explore some of the political aspects of planning.

Equity Planning in Cleveland.   Cleveland was among the industrial cities that fared worst after World War II. By the late 1960s, its population was rapidly declining and its industry leaving. Rates of welfare and unemployment were far higher than the national average, and the crime rate was soaring. The city was called "a basket case" and "the mistake by the lake." On the other hand, the mostly white suburbs surrounding the city were growing and prosperous, with low unemployment and low crime rates.

Cleveland made news when the voters elected Carl Stokes, the first black mayor of a large city in the United States. Stokes hired a new planning director, Norman Krumholz, who set out to address Cleveland's problems using an approach called **equity planning**. In Krumholz's words, "We altered the planner's traditional posture as an apolitical technician serving a unitary public interest. Instead, we devoted ourselves to 'providing more choices to those who have few, if any, choices'" (Krumholz 1982, 165).

Rather than concern itself with zoning, land use, and other small scale issues, the Cleveland planning commission took on several projects that addressed the big picture of the regional inequalities in the Cleveland area. The planning commission initiated a study of the mass transit system, pointing out that public subsidies increasingly supported automobile use while cutting back on support for those without cars. The city administration used this information to negotiate some important (although temporary) changes in fares and schedules of mass transit. Another initiative was convincing the county and state to share the financial support for parks that the city could no longer afford to support alone. Probably the most controversial issue the city planners took on was the attempt to prevent the sale of the city-owned electrical utility to the major private utility in the region. The argument the planners made was that it was important to both low-income residents and small businesses to provide cheaper electricity than was available through the private company.

TABLE 16.1   Santa Barbara and Ventura, California

	Santa Barbara	Ventura
City Population	88,978.0	103,119.0
Median Household Income	58,073.0	63,147.0
Percent High School Graduates	83.9	87.3
Percent College Graduates	41.3	29.5
Percent of Individuals living In Poverty	14.7	10.6

SOURCE: U.S. Census Bureau, 2005–2007, American Community Survey Factsheets for Santa Barbara and Ventura, California.

After Stokes (a Democrat) left office, the Cleveland planning commission continued to follow the principles of equity planning under the next two mayors, one a Republican and one a self-styled populist. Krumholz points out that the philosophy of equity planning can be compatible with many different city administrations because there is a good deal of slack in local government that gives municipal departments room to innovate. He encourages planners to be less timid and to take the initiative toward enunciating important goals (such as class and racial equity) and developing ways of meeting them.

These two case studies show how closely entwined planning is with politics. Planning can be a political tool, and politics can be a planning tool. In both case studies, the reason that planners had an impact is that they were able to make proposals that transcended business as usual and that they (mostly) had the political support to innovate. As we will see below, the decisions made in a city's history can have long-term planning implications.

Comparing Ventura and Santa Barbara.   Located only thirty miles apart, the two small metropolitan areas of Santa Barbara and Ventura, California, are statistically very similar, as shown in table 16.1 (Warner and Molotch 2000; Molotch et al. 2000). As noted by Molotch et al. (2000):

> Both cities are the government seats and historic centers of their counties (of the same names). They have nearly identical (and ideal) climates, with little variation from the year-round average high temperature of 70 degrees in Ventura and 72 in Santa Barbara. Both cities have low humidity and many days of sunshine (an annual average of 252 in Ventura and 308 in Santa Barbara; by comparison, Seattle has 55), and they support an extraordinary diversity of natural and exotic fauna and flora (e.g., oak, palm, eucalyptus, citrus, hibiscus, cacti). The adjacent ocean waters of the Santa Barbara Channel, on which both cities front, are protected by a shield of scenic offshore islands-accessed by recreational boat service from Ventura (the closer of the two cities). Most of the coast is beach front, although Ventura's beaches stretch a greater distance than Santa Barbara's and are more consistently wide and sandy, like the idealized California beaches of travel brochures. The Los Padres

National Forest provides a mountainous backdrop to both places, more visually dramatic from Santa Barbara. (795)

Nevertheless, although by most indicators the two cities appear quite similar, most people familiar with both would consider the two cities quite different. Santa Barbara "approximates development experts' contemporary ideal—a 'learning economy' on the forefront of information, technology, and leisure services dubbed "Silicon Beach" to celebrate its emergence as a center of computer and internet innovations" (Molotch et al. 2000, 797). In contrast, Ventura is more similar to the types of problematic urban development found in many if not most American cities, with a struggling downtown area and suburban competition (Molotch et al. 2000, 797). How did two cities thirty miles apart with approximately the same natural advantages turn out so different? The answer lies in planning and the political pressures that influence planning.

Ventura was the first of the two cities to grow, with commercial oil development beginning in 1861—fifteen years before that development in Santa Barbara. Oil production was continuous through the 1950s, and an "oil district" developed around Ventura's waterfront. This gave the city an industrial character, and as the twentieth century continued, new functions sought to avoid the downtown: retail shopping migrated to the city's east, the county government followed suit, and the political interest groups that would have advocated for Ventura's downtown and waterfront did not materialize. As a result, when the state built a freeway through the downtown, local residents advocated for a downtown exit, but gave little resistance to the highway cutting the city off from its waterfront or the visual impact the highway would have.

In contrast, Santa Barbara's oil industry developed during a time period when wealthy residents were concerned about preserving the visual allure of the waterfront, and "through gifts and public action, industrial facilities at the beach were gradually removed" (Molotch et al. 2000, 804). By 1922 a local planning committee had been advocating a "Spanish style" architectural theme for the city, a goal brought to fruition by the fortuitous earthquake of 1925. After the quake, the city created the nation's first architectural review board, which strictly enforced the Spanish style. As the city was rebuilt, an emphasis on architectural integrity, city beautification, and good planning was instituted that is still evident today.

The cases of Ventura and Santa Barbara point to two considerations in urban planning. The first is that initial conditions are important. Ventura arguably had the more favorable natural environment with its wider beaches and access to offshore islands, but the initial importance of the oil industry and the transformation of its waterfront into an industrial zone has been a persistent theme in the subsequent development in the city. In Santa Barbara, the early political pressure from wealthy residents and civic boosters interested in beautifying the waterfront and downtown has also been a continuous theme in development decisions in the city's history. The result is two very different cities that, on paper, appear quite similar. The second theme is the importance of community groups in shaping local cultural attitudes toward development. The growth machine in Ventura viewed its downtown as "industrial" for much of its history, and without groups of equivalent power advocating for alternative uses of the waterfront and downtown this group won out. In Santa Barbara, groups advocating for beautification of its downtown and the waterfront acted as a counterforce against those who would place industrial uses on the waterfront or construct building not conforming to the Spanish style of architecture downtown. Perhaps as important, however, is the fact that past practice and political powers need not dictate future development decisions: today, officials in Ventura are trying to learn from the success of Santa Barbara. The reason is that the "perception of what is ideal—(and) that Santa Barbara is closer to ideal than Ventura—is shared by numbers of Ventura officials, citizens group leaders, and business activists, many of whom explicitly hope to emulate what they refer to as Santa Barbara's 'success'" (Molotch et al. 2000, 798).

CITY AND ENVIRONMENT

The 1990s and early twentieth century have witnessed a new interest in environmental concerns as global warming and pollution received renewed attention from the media and from politicians. The 1992 Earth Summit in Rio de Janeiro, Brazil, followed by the 1997 Kyoto Protocol limiting greenhouse gas emissions, increased public awareness of environmental issues. Although the United States has signed the Kyoto Protocol, it remains one of only a handful of countries not to have ratified the treaty and implemented its requirements. Besides pollution and its contribution to global warming, cities impact the natural environment in a variety of ways.

In *The Ecology of Fear*, Mike Davis (1998) discusses the multiple ways in which Los Angeles is vulnerable to a variety of cataclysms: earthquake, flood, fire, wind, animals, and cultural destruction in books and movies. In Southern California, the environment is of course the primary mechanism for such disasters. For instance, earthquakes are caused by a variety of faults extending deep below the city. Similarly, the great basin that is Los Angeles is particularly vulnerable to flooding because it is so flat. However, the way in which humans have urbanized the region also contributes to how these disasters are experienced; indeed, if they are disasters at all. For instance, Davis points out that human contact with mountain lions is becoming more common because new subdivisions are now more likely to be adjoining natural areas than in the past. Farmland used to form a buffer between cities and wildlife, but as farmland is less common and people move to places close to nature, their chances of encountering dangerous animals has increased. As he notes:

> As white flight and an antiurban ethos drive the tract house frontier deeper into rugged foothills and interior valleys, suburbanites have acquired wild carnivores as unexpected and capricious neighbors. The result is a greater intimacy with nature than many had bargained for when purchasing their view lots or country estates. (Davis 1998, 201–202)

Similarly, wildfires in forested areas have long been a feature of the southern California landscape, but are now more disastrous because humans are moving into those areas. One cultural consequence of this "ecology of fear" is that Los Angeles has been destroyed in film and novels over 138 times!

Cities require a physical infrastructure that provides basic goods and services to residents, including shelter, food, water, and sanitation services like waste removal and sewers. Many people commonly think of the provision of such services in terms of the energy used in their provision; this is referred to as the **carbon footprint**. A broader account of natural resources is the **ecological footprint**, which includes all the space, energy, and biologically productive land and sea to sustain the population and absorb its wastes. Most modern cities have an ecological footprint many times its actual land area. For example, an American city of about one million residents has an ecological footprint about the size of Ohio. This is particularly apparent when one considers a basic resource such as water. The city of New York, for instance, has only a small fraction of the amount of freshwater consumed by its residents within the city limits. In order to supply fresh water, the city has constructed seventeen reservoirs and hundreds of miles of tunnel and aqueducts that bring water from up to one hundred miles away in the Catskill Mountains (Koeppel 2000). The construction for this included flooding hundreds of square miles of land as well as displacing thousands of residents from their villages. In some cases, the reservoirs were named after those villages destroyed for water, such as the Cannonsville Reservoir and the Gilboa Dam (Galusha 1999). Even after several generations, conflict between the city and local residents continues to be an issue in the Catskills (Thomas 2005).

Although the provision of an urban infrastructure can inflict a considerable cost on the natural environment, the lack of infrastructure can be far more severe. The concentration of people in a small area creates problems of pollution that might be manageable at a smaller scale. For instance, many nineteenth-century American farmhouses had "outhouses" in their backyards through which human waste was deposited and filtered into the environment. At such a small scale, damage to the natural environment was minimal and easily handled. However, the concentration of thousands or even millions of residents in a small area results in a serious problem in regard to human waste, both in terms of the pollution of groundwater supplies and the more open breeding grounds for such diseases as cholera. Similarly, other household and industrial waste is often deposited in landfills that concentrate waste into a small area (Boone and Modarres 2006).

Urban planners today attempt to consider environmental factors in developing new areas or redeveloping old ones. For instance, New Urbanism attempts to mitigate environmental damage from the automobile by providing access to walking and bike paths. Sustainable urban development often calls for a return to mass transit to reduce greenhouse gases, the development of higher density communities—more like "urban" neighborhoods and less like "suburban" neighborhoods—in which goods and services are within walking or biking distance, and increased reliance on such "green" technologies as solar power, rooftop gardens, and wind energy (Register 2006). In general, the goal is to build cities that do not so much alter nature but seek to exist in harmony with nature (Farr 2007).

SOCIAL JUSTICE AND THE CITY

At least as early as the 1960s, writers in the popular press were asking the question, "Are cities obsolete?" (Weissbourd 1964). In the 1960s and 1970s, that question was prompted by two issues: the physically decaying infrastructure of many cities, and the growing concentration of low-income and minority population in cities. By the 1980s, another set of issues shaped the question: With the decline of manufacturing, the growth of services, and the information economy, why does economic production have to be tied to cities or to any *place* at all? Could it be that cities will disappear in the future as the service-and-information economy matures?

Several researchers have argued strenuously against the proposition that cities are dispensable. Mollenkopf (1995) argues that, in addition to supporting local economic growth, cities are engines for national economic growth. Several of the economic sectors that have been growing rapidly, and probably will continue to do so for at least the near future, are disproportionately urban-based. These include information services, corporate services, health care, higher education, and research. Persky, Sclar, and Wiewel (1991) argue that cities represent substantial investments in resources, including capital assets such as buildings, but also human assets such as workforces and knowledge bases. To disperse these resources, they claim, would be inefficient and would destroy a national strength. Sassen (1994) argues that cities have new functions in the global economy, functions such as command and innovation that benefit from agglomeration. So there seem to be several good arguments in favor of the persistence of cities into the future.

But Sassen's analysis raises a second question: Even if cities exist, what will urban life be like? Sassen points out that the new role of cities implies the redistribution of people and resources. At the same time that corporations and the managerial workforce are gaining bigger shares of the income distribution, low-income workers, particularly those who are members of minority racial and ethnic groups, are becoming increasingly marginalized. As economic polarization and social isolation between groups increase, the have-nots have begun making claims on cities' resources through the political process. If these trends toward social inequality continue, will cities face a future of outright class warfare? Do we have and can we have a vision for urban society that goes beyond the self-interested rationalizations of "greed is good" for the corporate manager, "I'm just getting paid" for the mugger, and "not in my backyard" for the suburban homeowner?

With these questions, we are leaving the realm of social science and entering the realm of values. Social science can describe the way things are and can analyze the reasons why they are, but it cannot tell us how things should be. When we discuss possible futures, we must recognize that what we think should happen is based on our values and beliefs as much as on facts and scientific predictions. Thus, we will conclude this book with a discussion of social justice and the value of community.

In 1973 David Harvey began an important discussion of social justice and the city with his book of the same name. Harvey's definition of social justice is "a just distribution justly arrived at" (1973, 98). This notion of justice challenges the issues Sassen raised, both increasing income inequality and political marginalization. But how do we come to a consensus about how much people *should* have, how much is the necessary minimum, and how much those with "extra" should give up? These are the questions that political actors discuss daily: questions about taxes, welfare, and corporate subsidies. Since the late 1970s, this political discussion has moved away from policies that would reverse the tendency toward income inequality. *Justice* has increasingly been defined not as a just distribution but as individual reward: If people make a lot, it's because they deserve it; if they make nothing, it's because they deserve it.

In this author's view, Harvey's definition of social justice is a good beginning and can be improved by adding another dimension: the sharing of resources. In addition to a just distribution among individuals, social justice includes an expanded shared, or social, sector. Most communities already have a basis for shared land (in parks), shared facilities (schools, hospitals), and some shared services (sanitation, transit). Yet how much do we value and support these shared resources? The public debate on this question reveals that support for shared resources is uneven. Some people, for example, oppose school taxes because they don't have any children in the schools and oppose mass transit funding because they don't use it. This narrow view ignores the public benefits they gain—some people without children paid for their education and someone without an automobile is paying to maintain the city streets. There can also be powerful institutional opposition to shared resources. Many private schools and private hospitals see it in their interests to reduce support for public schools and public hospitals, and some property developers advocate the sale of parklands and waterfronts for private rather than public use. What portion of the total wealth should be for the "common wealth" and what portion should be reserved for individual use would also make an interesting discussion.

Finally, questions about what constitutes the good city can go beyond economic, political, and physical resources to notions of social and political participation. How should people relate to each other? How should they think about each other? Has the slow growth of the economy so preoccupied people with "getting their own" that competition and mean-spiritedness routinely prevail over cooperation and neighborliness? Has the media coverage about crime convinced us that we cannot trust each other? Have people focused on finding scapegoats for problems instead of solutions for them? Is it hopelessly nostalgic and unrealistic to think that urbanites can be civil and cooperative? After all, isn't conflict one of the fundamental principles of social relations?

One answer is that conflict exists on different levels. An argument over who got to a parking space first is a conflict (over a resource) expressed on an individual level. A community organization's lobbying for a new public parking lot is a conflict (over how public resources will be distributed) expressed through local institutions. A corporation's efforts to buy up all of the parking lots in the city so it can have a monopoly is an economic conflict (with consumers), although the parties on the opposite side may not even realize it exists. Because conflict can exist at different levels, it is not at all incompatible with cooperation. The members of that community organization, for example, cooperate for a goal, united by their common interest, but they are in conflict with other groups that are in turn united by their common interests. Community organizers tell us that it is important to recognize what the real problem is and who the real enemy is rather than being distracted by individual or intragroup conflicts.

What of future conflicts? In the context of increasing social inequality, it will be interesting to see which groups cooperate with each other and which groups fight with each other. For example, will a threatened middle class support policies to aid corporate growth at the expense of the poor? Or will they support policies to assist the poor, even if it means an increase in corporate taxes? As another example, will individuals' identification with their own racial and ethnic groups result in cohesive communities whose members can enter into coalitions with other groups on common economic issues? Or will the result be racial and ethnic exclusion, scapegoating, and increased intergroup conflict?

Some of the most important questions about the future of cities are less about reality than about perceptions: How do people perceive cities and urban residents? What do cities provide for their residents? For the society? These questions are significant because when people define situations as real, their consequences are real (Thomas and Thomas 1928). If people dismiss cities as there and the people who live there as them, they can, in the words of Beauregard (1993), "disconnect" from urban issues. They can happily avoid taking responsibility for cities, while still enjoying the benefits of the cities' cultural and economic products. If, however, more people define cities as socially, economically, and culturally beneficial to the society—that is, if they see them as a resource for everyone—they are more likely to become engaged and supportive of urban needs and contributions. Whether you currently live in a city, a suburb, a town, or a rural area, you are connected to urban issues in many ways.

DISCUSSION QUESTIONS

1.   The large populations of cities makes them big consumers of energy; but at the same time their density and compactness provide opportunities for energy conservation. If fossil fuels such as oil and coal become scarcer in the future, what advantages might cities have over suburbs in their use of energy? What disadvantages might they have?

2.   Read your local newspaper or that of a nearby sizeable community for a week, noting stories (or letters to the editor) that involve planning issues such as urban redevelopment or public construction projects. What interest groups are identified as taking positions on these issues?

3.   What is your vision of a good city or good community? On what values and beliefs do you base your description? How do you think values are reflected in urban planning?

Glossary

acculturation The process by which an immigrant group adopts some of the practices of the dominant culture (for example, speaking the language), although the group still maintains its distinctiveness.

agglomeration The pattern that results when many similar businesses locate near each other.

agricultural revolution The historic process of change from food consuming to food producing, which was accompanied by changes in human living arrangements.

annexation The process by which central cities incorporate adjacent communities, making them part of the city.

assimilation The process by which an immigrant group is absorbed into the dominant culture, becoming virtually indistinguishable from the dominant group.

austerity Severe restrictions on spending money.

bid rent curve A theory that assumes a trade-off between the cost of land and the distance from the center of the city.

biotic order In human ecology, the changing pattern of land use resulting from the ways in which populations adapt to territory.

block grant The federal government's practice of giving cities and states a block or pool of money for a general purpose (such as community development or human services) rather than giving funds for specific programs (such as public housing or school lunches).

built environment The buildings, streets, and other structures that make up the physical city, as distinct from the natural environment.

capital budget The part of a government's budget that is reserved for the construction of buildings and other long-lasting projects.

census statistical area A region that is integrated with the central city and composed of all the metropolitan and micropolitan areas in the region.

central place functions Retail and administrative functions provided by a community to its surrounding residents.

chain migration The practice of several members of a single family or community following each other as immigrants to a new country.

Chicago School The perspective in urban sociology developed first at the

University of Chicago associated with the human ecology perspective.

citadel (According to Marcuse and van Kempen 2000) A high-tech, high-rise development within globalizing cities.

citizens' movements Social movements organized to gain political power or self-government.

City Beautiful movement A late nineteenth-century movement to rebuild and beautify cities, often by constructing monumental Greek-revival buildings in prominent central locations.

class society A society containing persistent group differences in income and control over resources, but in which the position of each individual may change over time.

cognitive map The method by which the human mind understands the arrangement of physical and geographical spaces and orients itself to places.

cohousing A form of housing in which several households jointly own property, share space and facilities, and often cooperate on some household tasks such as cooking and child care.

collective consumption The provision of public goods and services such as education, housing, and parks.

commercial city A city organized around trade or commerce.

commodification The process of turning a thing (such as food) or activity (such as cooking) into a commodity by selling it (in a market or restaurant, for example).

commodity An object or service that is sold for money or traded for other goods.

community (1) A group that perceives itself as having strong and lasting bonds, particularly when the group shares a geographic location. (2) A city or town.

community development corporation A community-based group organized to foster economic and social development of a neighborhood.

community-owned enterprises Publicly owned and operated businesses.

community policing Programs in which the police work with community residents to address the causes of crime.

concentrated poverty area A neighborhood with greater than 40 percent of the households having incomes below the federally set poverty level

concentric zone model The theory developed by Ernest Burgess that depicts urban land use as a series of concentric circles surrounding a central business district.

contradiction Marx's theory that each social arrangement both supports and undermines its own existence.

core-based statistical area A collection of settlements, grouped by counties in most of the United States but by townships in New England, judged to be highly integrated with one another on the basis of commuting patterns.

core countries In world system theory, those countries that are the most central to the world-economy; the richest and most economically dominant countries.

corporate city A city organized around the presence of corporate offices and services to corporations.

criminalize To make an activity illegal by passing a law against it.

cultural capital According to Pierre Bourdieu, the assets a person has by virtue of education and training (sometimes called human capital) as well as the ability to use significant symbols such as language, behavior, and dress to convey status.

defensible space A semipublic area such as a shared walk, hallway, or terrace that can be watched and protected by the people who live nearby.

dependency The situation of a country or region forced to rely on the infusion of resources from the outside.

development perspective A theory stating that the poorer countries of the world are capable of industrialization and economic development if they use their resources properly.

disinvestment The withdrawal of resources from an area by powerful actors such as banks, insurance companies, corporations, and government agencies.

devolution The practice of delegating responsibility for policy from the national level (Congress) to the state and local level.

displacement The process by which a social or economic change removes people involuntarily, such as from their homes or from employment.

dual housing market A housing market in which individuals' access to housing differs depending on their race.

economic capital Money, property, and other tangible resources, as distinct from human capital or social capital.

economic restructuring Widespread changes in investment patterns that affect entire industries and communities.

economies of agglomeration A principle in economics that states that as firms of similar function locate near each other, the presence of such firms attracts other related firms and customers, creating increased competition and lowering prices.

economies of scale A principle in economics that states that as the size of a company or other economic unit increases, the cost per unit of providing goods and services decreases.

edge cities Self-contained communities located on the outskirts of metropolitan areas whose residents do not rely on the core city for employment and other economic functions.

emigration Leaving one country to settle in another.

eminent domain The right of a government to take private property for public use.

empire A number of territories or nations under a single centralized power.

enclave economy A local economy in which a high percentage of workers are employed by members of their own ethnic group, normally within a few industries.

enterprise zones Areas targeted to attract private investment by providing government incentives such as reduced taxes.

entrepreneur A business owner or someone who acts like a business owner.

environmental racism A policy or practice that differentially affects environmental quality for individuals, groups, or communities based on their race or color; these effects can be either intended or unintended.

equity planning An approach to urban planning that emphasizes providing additional choices for people with the fewest resources.

ethnic enclave A neighborhood in which a large proportion of the residents share the same ethnic background, usually resulting from a high level of immigration.

ethnic identification The extent to which an individual identifies as a member of a culturally distinctive group.

ethnic solidarity The extent to which an ethnic group thinks of itself and acts as a unit.

ethnography A descriptive study of a social group, emphasizing its ways of life and cultural practices.

European Union An alliance of countries in Europe formed to promote mutual economic goals.

exchange value The worth of an object or service based on the price it could bring if it were sold.

excluded ghetto (According to Marcuse and van Kempen 2000) A neighborhood where the poor are concentrated, with few services and few connections to middle-class groups.

exclusionary enclave (According to Marcuse and van Kempen 2000) A wealthy neighborhood that is isolated and protected from the intrusion of outsiders, for example, a gated community or secure high-rise apartment building.

exclusionary zoning The practice of excluding lower and moderately priced housing in a community through specific zoning regulations, such as requiring large lots and certain building materials, or prohibiting apartments.

explicit urban policy Government policies that are designed to affect cities in some way.

feminization of poverty The trend for an increasing proportion of the poor population to be made up of women.

feudalism An economic system based on holding the property rights to agricultural land.

first-source hiring programs Job development programs encouraging companies doing business with local governments to hire through city employment services.

fiscal crisis A severe incidence of a local government's income being insufficient to pay for its expenditures, often resulting in a government shutdown.

fiscal distress An ongoing imbalance between local government's income and expenditures.

flexible production A system of manufacturing using small-batch techniques to produce nonstandardized products.

Fordism A system of economic and political organization in which large-scale companies that produce standardized products dominate the economy.

Garden Cities A planning movement begun by Ebenezer Howard to build new communities in which people worked harmoniously with the natural environment.

gemeinschaft A term introduced by Ferdinand Tönnies to describe a small, close-knit community, in which tradition, family, and religion govern social life; sometimes translated as *community*.

gender The socially defined distinction between men and women and the connotations of masculinity and femininity that accompany it.

gendered spaces Differences in the spaces that men and women have access to and use in daily life; a spatial expression of the inequalities of gender.

gentrification The pattern of wealthier residents moving into a poorer neighborhood in sufficient numbers to transform its social identity.

gesellschaft A term introduced by Ferdinand Tönnies to describe a large, impersonal social setting in which formal social institutions such as the law govern social relations; sometimes translated as *society*.

Great Migration The large-scale migration of African Americans from the rural South to work in northern cities between 1916 and 1930.

growth machine The theory that urban growth is supported by a coalition of interest groups that stand to benefit from growth.

global cities A small number of cities, including New York, London, and Tokyo, that serve as the command posts of the global economy and production sites for corporate services.

globalization The increased interdependence of the world's economies, shown by the circulation of information, money, people, and goods across national boundaries.

hinterlands The nonurban areas that surround a city.

housing tenure The relationship of a household to their housing, for example, homeowner, renter, condominium owner, cooperative member.

incipient homelessness Being on the verge of homelessness; living in circumstances that could easily lead to homelessness.

indirect urban policy Government policies that, although not designed to affect cities, nonetheless have important urban impacts.

industrial capitalism An economic system in which profits are made primarily from the production and sale of manufactured goods.

industrial city A city organized around manufacturing.

informal sector The hidden part of the economy in which transactions are not officially recorded or reported.

International Style A type of architecture associated with Le Corbusier, characterized by sweeping gardens containing high-rise structures.

in-person services Those jobs consisting largely of personal services, such as health care, beauty care, table service.

Iron Curtain The name for the imaginary line between the communist countries of Eastern Europe and the Western democracies during the Cold War.

leveraging The process of using a relatively small investment to create a much larger one by obtaining loans based on the original investment.

linkage A program that requires developers constructing new projects to contribute money or other resources for public projects.

Los Angeles School The perspective in urban sociology largely developed by the study of Los Angeles as the "city of the future." It is associated with the postmodernist perspective.

macroeconomic policy Government actions that attempt to influence the overall performance of the economy, particularly those related to controlling the balance between unemployment and inflation.

marginalization The process by which a group or individual is prevented from full participation in the life of the society.

material feminism A movement of the late nineteenth century in which women challenged the boundaries between home and community by organizing to work in groups and share domestic duties.

mechanical solidarity Durkheim's concept that simple societies are integrated through social bonds stemming from the similarities among the members.

merchant capitalism An economic system based on trade in which profits are generated through the buying and selling of commodities.

metropolitan area The unit formed by a central city and its adjacent suburban communities. It is defined as a core-based statistical area with an urbanized area of at least fifty thousand residents. Some metropolitan areas cross state boundaries, for example, New York City, Chicago, and Portland, Oregon.

metropolitan division A grouping of communities within a metropolitan area of at least two and a half million residents who are highly integrated with one another as measured by commuting patterns.

micropolitan area A core-based statistical area with a central settlement of at least ten thousand but less than fifty thousand residents.

model cities program The federal program that allocated money to cities to assist targeted inner-city neighborhoods both in rebuilding the physical neighborhood and in strengthening public services such as education and public safety.

moral order In human ecology, the norms and values of a given social group.

multiple nuclei model A theory of urban land use developed by Harris and Ullman that identifies homogeneous urban districts but finds no regular pattern to where those districts are located in relation to each other.

native-born The term used by the U. S. Census Bureau to refer to people born in the United States, as opposed to immigrants.

nativism The belief that native-born residents of a country are superior to immigrants and thus deserve special privileges.

Natufian The period preceding the Neolithic during which the tools of agriculture were developed but the domestication of plants had not yet taken place.

natural area In human ecology, the name given to a specialized district of a city, for example, a slum or a factory district.

neoclassical economics An approach to economics that explains the location of various land uses and social groups by relating the cost of land to the ability of different groups to pay for land.

Neolithic The period during which the domestication of plants took place and the first true agricultural societies evolved.

New Federalism An approach to urban policy reducing the level of direction and support from the federal government.

New Urbanism An approach to urban planning that emphasizes mixed land use and public spaces while favoring pedestrian traffic and public transportation over automobile use.

nongovernmental organizations Organizations established across national boundaries to promote solutions to social problems, such as environmental issues, women's issues, and health problems.

operating budget The part of a government's budget that pays for regularly recurring expenses such as payroll and utilities.

opportunity structure The presence or absence of channels by which individuals may advance economically.

organic solidarity Durkheim's concept that complex societies are integrated by social bonds created through a division of labor; the interdependence that occurs when individuals play different roles in a group.

overurbanization The situation in which urban populations grow more rapidly than does industrialization, resulting in high unemployment.

paradigm A set of linked concepts that a group of researchers finds most useful for understanding the world; also, those research questions, theories, and assumptions that are related to the core concepts. Examples of paradigms in urban studies include human ecology and political economy.

peripheral countries In world system theory, those countries that have the least favored positions in the world-economy; the poorest countries.

physical restructuring Changes in the built environment of a city as its economy changes.

pluralism The theory that political power is distributed among numerous competing groups that form temporary coalitions around specific issues without becoming permanently aligned.

polarization The tendency for a group to become more divided and unalike rather than more centralized and alike; for example, polarization of income refers to a growing gap between rich and poor; racial polarization refers to an increasing division between races.

political economy A theory stressing the impact of political and economic institutions on the physical form and social life of cities.

political entrepreneurs Political actors who actively shape urban political decisions and policy; they may be elected or appointed officials or may act in less formal capacities.

political machine A hierarchical form of local politics in which people at lower levels support a political boss in return for material incentives such as jobs and administrative favors.

postmodernism A philosophical and theoretical school in the social science and humanities that refers to social, economic, and artistic conditions after the modernist period.

power (1) The ability to get people to do things they would not otherwise do. (2) Control over resources.

power elite (power structure) A theory that political power is concentrated among a small number of relatively cohesive groups.

primacy The situation in which a single city contains an extremely large portion of the nation's population.

primary group A group that has frequent face-to-face interaction and a high degree of group cohesion and identity.

primate city A single city containing an extremely large proportion of a country's population.

private troubles The problems we have as individuals, especially if we think of them as affecting only ourselves.

producer services Services provided to companies rather than individuals, often replacing functions that companies choose not to do themselves, for example, advertising, accounting, human resource management, legal services, and consulting.

profit cycle A theory that industries grow and decline based on the success of new products and reduced profits from established products.

pro-growth coalitions Those groups with an interest in supporting urban growth.

public balance sheet An account to the press and media of the funds that the local government spends on aid to private corporations and the public goods it receives in return.

public housing The program that allocates federal funds to construct and operate rental housing through local housing authorities.

public issues Problems that affect many people and that people recognize as requiring collective action.

public–private partnership A corporation or group formed by representatives of both government and private companies.

racial profiling The practice of using race as a factor in determining whether an individual should be suspected of criminal activity.

racial zoning The former practice in which local governments identified certain geographic boundaries within which residents of a certain race must live, for example, Chinatowns and "black belts."

racially restrictive covenants Clauses in deeds for property specifying the racial groups permitted to live on the property. Although these are no longer legally enforceable, they still exist in many deeds.

rank-size order A principle in geography that states that the population of a town multiplied by its rank will be equal to the population of the largest city in a nation or territory.

redevelopment programs Efforts by government to revitalize cities by demolishing older buildings and making the land available for new construction. Redevelopment often also includes rebuilding roads, utilities, and other infrastructure.

redlining Occurs when institutional actors (banks, insurance companies) withhold access to resources such as mortgages and insurance policies from specific geographic areas; named for the former practice of drawing red lines around "unfavorable" neighborhoods; also known as disinvestment.

refugee A person who emigrates to flee political, ethnic, or religious persecution.

regime The coalition of elected and appointed officials as well as related powerful actors who direct a city's government.

rentiers The people who buy, renovate, and make property available for others to use, sometimes called *property capitalists*.

routine production services Jobs consisting largely of repetitive tasks, such as working on an assembly line or processing forms.

sanctions Rewards and punishments associated with social norms.

scapegoat An individual or group blamed for problems he she or it did not cause.

sector model The theory developed by Hoyt that describes urban land use as clustered within wedge-shaped sectors of cities.

sending country The country from which a person emigrates.

service sector The part of the economy that is neither resource extraction (farming, fishing, mining, lumbering) nor manufacturing. Major service sector jobs include personal services (cutting hair), health services, restaurant services, financial services, professional services (attorney) and education.

settlers Immigrants who enter a country with the intention of staying for the remainder of their lives.

shelter poverty The term referring to a household that, although not technically poor, pays so much for its housing that it cannot meet its other needs such as food, transportation, clothing, and health care.

social area analysis An approach to studying urban populations based on the income, ethnicity, and family status of the residents.

social capital The sum of relationships people have by virtue of their membership in different groups such as family, neighborhood, and voluntary organizations.

social control Sanctions designed to encourage people to obey social norms and discourage them from disobeying norms.

social disorganization An early explanation for poverty and social problems.

social geography The spatial patterns resulting from the distribution of different social groups (especially social classes) within geographic areas.

social housing Housing owned and operated on a nonprofit basis by groups such as local city councils, housing associations, and cooperatives (as distinct from private housing).

socially excluded groups The European term for groups excluded from mainstream society, whether by virtue of poverty, ethnicity, addiction, or other social or economic factors.

social mobility The possibility of changing social class membership, either improving or worsening one's social class position.

social movement A self-conscious, collective attempt to bring about or resist social change, often through noninstitutionalized means.

sociological imagination According to C. Wright Mills, the quality of mind that allows people to link their experiences to broader social patterns.

sociospatial perspective A theoretical perspective that emphasizes the reciprocal relationship between people and space, as well as the symbolic meaning of space.

sojourners Immigrants who enter a country with the intention of staying only for a specified length of time or until they have reached a certain economic goal, then returning to their country of origin.

speculator Someone who buys property and holds it without improving it, in the hope that the value of the land will rise.

status A term introduced by Max Weber to refer to social standing or prestige.

subprime mortgage A mortgage loan that charges higher interest than a standard mortgage and typically charges a substantial fee for prepayment or changes. Subprime mortgages were originated to serve homebuyers who could not obtain standard mortgages because their income or credit history did not allow them to qualify for a standard bank loan.

symbolic analytic services Employment largely consisting of manipulating symbols and ideas.

symbolic economy The production of symbols and meanings through the creation of and changes in urban spaces.

tax abatement A reduction or forgiveness of local or state taxes to a company, normally as an inducement to perform a particular activity.

taxpayers' movements Organized efforts by local residents to limit the taxing power of local governments.

third places Places that have characteristics of both private and public space.

third sector Housing run by neither government nor the private sector but by nonprofit corporations; social housing.

uneven development perspective The theory that the gap between the richer countries and poorer countries is relatively permanent.

urban cluster A settlement or settlements that has a population density of at least one thousand residents per square mile, and can include a surrounding "fringe" with a population density of at least five hundred residents per square mile, and a total population of less than fifty thousand residents.

urban ecology An approach to studying cities that stresses the links between urban social patterns and the patterns of the natural world; a subset of human ecology.

urbanism The theory developed by Louis Wirth that urban areas have a distinctive way of life due to population size, density, and heterogeneity.

urbanized area A settlement or settlements that has a population density of at least one thousand residents per square mile, and can include a surrounding "fringe" with a population density of at least five hundred residents per square mile, and a minimum population of fifty thousand residents.

urban political economy An approach to studying cities that stresses the conflicts and competition of groups over resources.

urban renewal The program through which the federal government assists local authorities in buying deteriorated properties, demolishing the buildings, and reselling the land to private developers.

urban–rural continuum A scale of urban development whereby the "rural" is characterized by a natural landscape and "urban" is characterized by nearly total development.

use value The value derived from using an object—for example, living in a house—apart from its monetary value.

vertical integration A corporate structure in which the corporation controls all of the processes involved in the manufacture and sale of a product.

welfare state A set of policies adopted by most Western European countries in the twentieth century that provides government support for the basic needs of life: education, health care, housing, and pensions; these services are supported by national taxes.

world cities Cities recognized for their prominence throughout the world, especially as it relates to their historical and cultural dominance.

world-economy According to world system theory, the economic system that emerged between A.D. 1400 and 1700 and still exists today, linking different nations into a global economy in which different countries have different positions.

world system theory A theory that the countries of the world are related to each other through a division of labor in which different countries play different roles. (*See* core countries, peripheral countries.)

xenophobia An extreme and irrational fear of foreigners.

zone in transition In the concentric zone model, the area surrounding the central business district, which is particularly prone to speculation and deterioration.

zoning The process by which a local government body limits certain kinds of building (single-family residential, commercial, industrial, etc.) to specific areas of the city.

References

Abrahamson, Mark. 2004. *Global Cities.* New York: Oxford University Press.

———. 1996. *Urban Enclaves: Identity and Place in America.* New York: St. Martin's Press.

Abu-Lughod, Janet. 1991. *Changing Cities.* New York: HarperCollins.

———. 1999. *New York, Chicago, Los Angeles: America's Global Cities.* Minneapolis: University of Minnesota Press.

Acker, Joan. 1992. From Sex Roles to Gendered Institutions. *Contemporary Sociology* 21: 565–569.

Adams, Carolyn. 1988. *The Politics of Capital Investment.* Albany: State University of New York Press.

Adams, Carolyn, D. Bartelt, D. Elesh, I. Goldstein, N. Kleniewski, and W. Yancey. 1991. *Philadelphia: Neighborhoods, Division, and Conflict in a Post-Industrial City.* Philadelphia: Temple University Press.

Adamson, Madeleine. 1993. The ACORN Housing Agenda. *Shelterforce* 15(2): 8–11.

Akkermans, P. M., and G. M. Schwartz. 2003. *The Archaeology of Syria.* New York: Cambridge University Press.

Alba Richard D., John Logan, and Brian J. Stults. 2000. How Segregated Are Middle-Class African Americans? *Social Problems* 47(4): 543–58.

Aldana, Carolyn and Gary A. Dymski. 2004. Urban Sprawl, Racial Separation, and Federal Housing Policy. In *Up Against the Sprawl,* edited by J. Wolch, M. Pastor, Jr., and P. Dreier. Minneapolis: University of Minnesota Press.

Algaze, G. 1993. *The Uruk World System.* Chicago: University of Chicago Press.

Alihan, Milla. 1938. *Social Ecology: A Critical Analysis.* New York: Columbia University Press.

Alonso, William. 1964. *Location and Land Use.* Cambridge, Mass.: MIT Press.

Anas, Alex, and Richard Arnott. 1993. Development and Testing of the Chicago Prototype Housing Market Model. *Journal of Housing Research* 4(1): 73–129.

Anderson, D. 2005. *Histories of the Hanged: The Dirty War in Kenya and the End of Empire.* New York: Norton.

Anderson, Elijah. 1990. *Streetwise: Race, Class, and Change in an Urban Community.* Chicago: University of Chicago Press.

Anderson, Perry. 1974. *Passages from Antiquity to Feudalism*. London: Verso.

Arrighi, Giovanni. 1991. World Income Inequalities and the Future of Socialism. *New Left Review* 189: 39–65.

Atlas, John, and Peter Dreier. 1992. Why a National Housing Policy Is Not on the Agenda. *Shelterforce* 15(5): 18–20.

Auletta, K. 1999. *The Underclass*, revised edition. Woodstock, N.Y.: Overlook Press.

Babcock, Richard. 1966. *The Zoning Game*. Madison: University of Wisconsin Press.

Bailey, Conor, Charles Faupel, and James Gundlach. 1993. Environmental Politics in Alabama's Black Belt. In *Confronting Environmental Racism: Voices from the Grassroots*, edited by R. Bullard. Boston: South End Press.

Baldassare, Mark. 1994. Introduction. In *The Los Angeles Riots*, edited by M. Baldassare. Boulder: Westview Press.

Ballparks.com. 2009. *Ballparks*. Retrieved May 15, 2009, from http://www.ballparks.com/baseball/.

Baltzell, E. Digby. 1958. *Philadelphia Gentlemen: The Making of a National Upper Class*. New York: Free Press.

Bar Yosef, O. 1986. The Walls of Jericho: An Alternative Explanation. *Current Anthropology* 27: 157–162.

Barber, Benjamin. 2000. Globalizing Democracy. *The American Prospect* (September 11): 16–19.

Barnekov, Timothy, and Daniel Rich. 1989. Privatism and the Limits of Local Economic Development Policy. *Urban Affairs Quarterly* 25(2): 212–238.

Barnes, Sandra L. 2005. *The Costs of Being Poor: A Comparative Study of Life in Poor Urban Neighborhoods in Gary, Indiana*. New York: State University of New York Press.

Barr, Kenneth. 1991. From Dhaka to Manchester: Factories, Cities, and the World Economy, 1600–1900. In *Cities in the World-System*, edited by R. Kasaba. New York: Greenwood Press.

Bartle, John R. 2003. Trends in Local Government Taxation in the 21st Century. *Spectrum: Journal of State Government* 76(1): 26–30.

Baum, Alice, and Donald Burnes. 1993. *A Nation in Denial: The Truth About Homelessness*. Boulder: Westview Press.

Bean, Frank D. and Gillian Stevens. 2003. *America's Newcomers and the Dynamics of Diversity*. New York: Russell Sage Foundation.

Beauregard, Robert. 1993. *Voices of Decline: The Postwar Fate of U.S. Cities*. Cambridge, Mass.: Blackwell.

———. 2003. City of Superlatives. *City and Community* 2(3): 183–199.

———. 2006. *When America Became Urban*. Minneapolis: University of Minnesota Press.

Beecher, Catherine, and Harriet Beecher Stowe. 1869. *The American Woman's Home*. Hartford, Conn.: Stowe-Day Foundation.

Bell, W., and M. Force. 1956. Urban Neighborhood Types and Participation in Formal Associations. *American Sociological Review* 21 (February): 25–34.

Bellwood, P. 2005. *First Farmers: The Origins of Agricultural Societies*. New York: Blackwell.

Bernard, Jessie. 1973. *The Sociology of Community*. Glenview, Ill.: Scott Foresman.

Bettencourt, L. M. A., J. Lobo, D. Helbing, C. Kuhnert, and G. B. West. 2007. Growth, Innovation, Scaling, and the Pace of Life in Cities. *Proceedings of the National Academies of Science* 104: 7301–7306.

Blacksell, Mark. 1998. Redrawing the Political Map. In *The New Europe: Economy, Society, and Environment*, edited by D. Pinder. New York: Wiley.

Blau, Joel. 1992. *The Visible Poor: Homelessness in the United States*. New York: Oxford University Press.

Bluestone, B., and B. Harrison. 1984. *The Deindustrialization of America*. New York: Basic Books.

Bluestone, Barry, and Mary Huff Stevenson. 2000. *The Boston Renaissance*. New York: Russell Sage Foundation.

Bobo, Lawrence, J. Johnson, M. Oliver, J. Sidanius, and C. Zubrinsky. 1992. Public Opinion Before and After a Spring of Discontent. Los Angeles: UCLA Center for the Study of Urban Poverty.

Bobo, Lawrence D., Melvin L. Oliver, James H. Johnson, Jr., and Abel Valenzuela, Jr., eds. 2000. *Prismatic Metropolis: Inequality in Los Angeles*. New York: Russell Sage Foundation.

Bocharov, Yuri. 1997. Political Myths and the Alteration of Moscow. In *The Architecture and Building of Moscow*, edited by A. Grushina. Moscow: Voznesenski Pereulok.

Body-Gendrot, Sophie and Marco Martiniello, eds. 2000. Introduction. In *Minorities in European Cities: The Dynamics of Social Integration and Social Exclusion at the Neighborhood Level*. New York: St. Martin's Press.

Bonacich, Edna, and Richard Appelbaum. 2000. *Behind the Label: Inequality in the Los Angeles Apparel Industry*. Berkeley: University of California Press.

Boone, Christopher G., and Ali Modarres. 2006. *City & Environment*. Philadelphia: Temple University Press.

Borchert, John R. 1967. American Metropolitan Evolution. *Geographical Review* 57(3): 301–332.

Bourdieu, Pierre. 1986. The Forms of Capital. In *Handbook of Theory and Research for the Sociology of Education*, edited by J. G. Richardson. New York: Greenwood Press.

Bourgeois, Philippe. 1995. *In Search of Respect: Selling Crack in El Barrio*. Cambridge: Cambridge University Press.

Bouvier, Leon. 1992. *Peaceful Invasions: Immigration and Changing America*. Lanham, Md.: University Press of America.

Bowlby, Sophie. 1988. From Corner Shop to Hypermarket: Women and Food Retailing. In *Women in Cities*, edited by J. Little, L. Peake, and P. Richardson. New York: New York University Press.

Bowles, Samuel. 1982. The Post-Keynesian Capital-Labor Stalemate. *Socialist Review* 65 (September): 45–74.

Brady, James. 1983. Arson, Urban Economy, and Organized Crime: The Case of Boston. *Social Problems* 31: 1–27.

Bratt, Rachel. 1990. *Rebuilding a Low-Income Housing Policy*. Philadelphia: Temple University Press.

Brecher, Jeremy and Tim Costello. 1994. *Global Village or Global Pillage: Economic Reconstruction from the Bottom Up*. Boston: South End Press.

Bressi, Todd. 1994. Planning the American Dream. In *The New Urbanism*, edited by Peter Katz. New York: McGraw-Hill.

Brooks-Gunn, Jeanne, Greg J. Duncan, and Lawrence Aber, eds. 1997. *Neighborhood Poverty, Volume I: Context and Consequences for Children*. New York: Russell Sage Foundation.

Bryant, Bunyan, and Paul Mohai. 1992. Environmental Racism: Reviewing the Evidence. In *Race and the Incidence of Environmental Hazards*, edited by B. Bunyan and P. Mohai. Boulder: Westview Press.

Bullard, Robert. 1993. Anatomy of Environmental Racism and the Environmental Justice Movement.

In *Confronting Environmental Racism: Voices from the Grassroots*, edited by R. Bullard. Boston: South End Press.

———. 1990. *Dumping in Dixie*. Boulder: Westview Press.

Bullard, Robert, Glenn Johnson, and Angel Torres, eds. 2000. *Sprawl City: Race, Politics, and Planning in Atlanta*. Washington, D.C.: Island Press.

Bullard, Robert, and Maxine Waters. 2005. *The Quest for Environmental Justice: Human Rights and the Politics of Pollution*. New York: Sierra Club.

Burgess, Ernest W. 1925. The Growth of the City: An Introduction to a Research Project. In *The City*, edited by R. E. Park, E. W. Burgess, and R. D. McKenzie. Chicago: University of Chicago Press.

Burnier, DeLysa. 1987. Urban Policy in the New Federalism Era: The Emergence of Enterprise Zones. Paper presented at the Urban Affairs Association annual meeting.

Calthorpe, Peter. 1994. The Region. In *The New Urbanism*, edited by Peter Katz. New York: McGraw-Hill.

Campbell, A. 1984. *The Girls in the Gang*. New York: Basil-Blackwell.

Campbell, Karen, and Barrett Lee. 1990. Gender Differences in Urban Neighboring. *Sociological Quarterly* 31: 495–512.

Caraley, Demetrios. 1992. Washington Abandons the Cities. *Political Science Quarterly* 107(1): 1–30.

Carr, James, and Isaac F. Megbolugbe. 1993. The Federal Reserve Bank of Boston Study on Mortgage Lending Revisited. *Journal of Housing Research* 4(2): 277–313.

Castells, Manuel. 1983. *The City and the Grassroots*. Berkeley: University of California Press.

———. 1985. High Technology, Economic Restructuring and the Urban-Regional Process in the U.S.

In *High Technology, Space, and Society*, edited by M. Castells. Thousand Oaks, Calif.: Sage.

———. 1989. *The Informational City*. Oxford: Blackwell.

———. 1996. *The Rise of the Network Society*. Oxford: Blackwell.

Castells, Manuel, and Alejandro Portes. 1989. World Underneath: The Origin, Dynamics, and Effects of the Informal Economy. In *The Informal Economy*, edited by A. Portes, M. Castells, and L. Benton. Baltimore: Johns Hopkins University Press.

Castro, Max. 2007. Miami Vise. *The Nation* (May 14): 26–32.

Cauvin, Jacques. 2000. *The Birth of the Gods and the Origins of Agriculture*, translated by T. Watkins. New York: Cambridge University Press.

Chambliss, William, 1994. Policing the Ghetto Underclass. *Social Problems* 41(2): 177–194.

Change.gov. 2009. The Obama-Biden Plan. http://change.gov/agenda/urban_policy_agenda.

Charles, Camille Zubrinsky. 2003. The Dynamics of Racial Residential Segregation. *Annual Review of Sociology* 29: 167–207.

———. 2001. Processes of Racial Residential Segregation. In *Urban Inequality: Evidence from Four Cities*, edited by Alice O'Connor, Chris Tilly, and Lawrence D. Bobo. New York: Russell Sage Foundation.

Chase-Dunn, Christopher. 1982. Socialist States in the Capitalist World Economy. In *Socialist States in the World System*, edited by C. Chase-Dunn. Thousand Oaks, Calif.: Sage.

———. 1985. The System of World Cities, A.D. 800–1975. In *Urbanization in the World Economy*, edited by M. Timberlake. Orlando: Academic Press.

———. 2000. Globalizing from Below: Toward a Collectively Rational and Democratic Commonwealth. Paper presented at the annual meeting of the American Sociological Association, Washington, D.C., August.

Checkoway, Barry. 1980. Large Builders, Federal Housing Programmes and Postwar Suburbanization. *International Journal of Urban and Regional Research* 4: 21–45.

Chen, Hsiang-Shui. 1992. *Chinatown No More: Taiwan Immigrants in Contemporary New York.* Ithaca, N.Y.: Cornell University Press.

Cheng, Te-K'un. 1982. *Studies in Chinese Archaeology.* Hong Kong: Chinese University Press.

Cheshire, Paul. 1999. Some Causes of Western European Patterns of Urban Change. In *Urban Change in the United States and Western Europe*, edited by A. Summers, P. Cheshire, and L. Senn. Washington, D.C.: The Urban Institute Press.

Chesney-Lind, M., and J. M. Hagedorn. 1999. *Female Gangs in America: Essays on Girls, Gangs and Gender.* Chicago: Lake View Press.

Childe, V. Gordon. 1950. The Urban Revolution. *Town Planning Review* 21: 3–17.

Christaller, W. [1933] 1966. *Central Places in Southern Germany*, translated by C. W. Baskin. New York: Prentice Hall.

Citizens' Commission on Civil Rights. 1983. *A Decent Home.* Washington, D.C.: Citizens' Commission on Civil Rights.

Clampett-Lundquist, Susan and Douglas S. Massey. 2008. Neighborhood Effects on Economic Self-Sufficiency: A Reconsideration of the Moving to Opportunity Experiment. *American Journal of Sociology* 114(1): 107–143.

Clavel, Pierre. 1986. *The Progressive City.* New Brunswick, N.J.: Rutgers University Press.

Clavel, Pierre, and Nancy Kleniewski. 1990. Space for Progressive Local Policy: Examples from the U.S. and the U.K. In *Beyond the City Limits*, edited by J. Logan and T. Swanstrom. Philadelphia: Temple University Press.

Clavel, Pierre, and Wim Wiewel, eds. 1991. *Harold Washington and the Neighborhoods: Progressive City Government in Chicago, 1983–1987.* New Brunswick, N.J.: Rutgers University Press.

Clay, Philip. 1992. The (Un)Housed City: Racial Patterns of Segregation, Housing Quality, and Affordability. In *The Metropolis in Black and White*, edited by G. Galster and E. Hill. New Brunswick, N.J.: Center for Urban Policy Research.

Coontz, Stephanie. 1992. *The Way We Never Were: American Families and the Nostalgia Trap.* New York: Basic Books.

Corbier, Mireille. 1991. City, Territory and Taxation. In *City and Country in the Ancient World*, edited by J. Rich and A. Wallace-Hadrill. London: Routledge.

Coughlin, Brenda and Sudhir Venkatesh. 2003. The Urban Street Gang after 1970. *Annual Review of Sociology* 29: 41–64.

Cowan, Ruth S. 1983. *More Work for Mother.* New York: Basic Books.

Cowie, J., and J. Heathcott, eds. 2003. *Beyond the Ruins: The Meanings of Deindustrialization.* New York: Cornell University Press.

Cummings, Scott, and Daniel J. Monti, eds. 1993. *Gangs: The Origins and Impact of Contemporary Youth Gangs in the U.S.* Albany: State University of New York Press.

Currie, Elliott. 1985. *Confronting Crime: An American Challenge.* New York: Pantheon Press.

Dahl, Robert. 1961. *Who Governs? Democracy and Power in an American City.* New Haven, Conn.: Yale University Press.

Daniels, P. W. 1998. Advanced Producer Services and Economic Development. In *The New Europe: Economy, Society, and Environment*, edited by D. Pinder. New York: Wiley.

Danielson, Michael N. 1976. *The Politics of Exclusion*. New York: Columbia University Press.

Danziger, Sheldon, and Peter Gottschalk. 1995. *America Unequal*. New York: Russell Sage.

Darden, Joe T. 1987. Choosing Neighbors and Neighborhoods. In *Divided Neighborhoods*, edited by G. Tobin. Thousand Oaks, Calif.: Sage.

Davie, Maurice R. 1938. The Pattern of Urban Growth. In *Studies in the Science of Society*, edited by G. P. Murdock. New Haven, Conn.: Yale University Press.

Davis, Allen. 1967. *Spearheads for Reform: The Social Settlements and the Progressive Movement, 1890–1914*. Oxford: Oxford University Press.

Davis, Diane E. 1994. *Urban Leviathan: Mexico City in the Twentieth Century*. Philadelphia: Temple University Press.

Davis, Mike. 1998. *The Ecology of Fear: Los Angeles and the Imagination of Disaster*. New York: Vintage.

———. 2002. *Dead Cities and Other Tales*. New York: The New Press.

———. 2006. *City of Quartz*. New York: Verso.

———. 2007. *Planet of Slums*. New York: Verso.

Dawkins, Casey J. 2004. Recent Evidence on the Continuing Causes of Black–White Residential Segregation. *Journal of Urban Affairs* 26 (3): 379–400.

Dawson, Andrew. 1998. Industrial Restructuring in the New Democracies. In *The New Europe: Economy, Society, and Environment*, edited by D. Pinder. New York: Wiley.

Dear, Michael J. 2002. Los Angeles and the Chicago School: Invitation to a Debate. *City and Community* 1(1): 5–32.

———. 2003. Response to Beauregard— Superlative Urbanisms: The Necessity for Rhetoric in Social Theory. *City and Community* 2(3): 201–204.

Dear, Michael J. and Steven Flusty. 1998. Postmodern Urbanism. *Annals of the Association of American Geographers* 88(1): 50–73.

Dear, Michael J. and Jennifer R. Wolch. 1987. *Landscapes of Despair: From Deinstitutionalization to Homelessness*. Princeton: Princeton University Press.

Deckman, Melissa. 2007. Gender Differences in the Decision to Run for School Board. *American Politics Research* 35(4): 541–563.

Defreitas, Gregory. 1994. Fear of Foreigners: Immigrants as Scapegoats for Domestic Woes. *Dollars and Sense* (January/February): 8–9, 33–35.

Delaney, K. J., and R. Eckstein. 2003. *Public Dollars, Private Stadiums: The Battle over Building Sports Stadiums*. New York: Rutgers University Press.

Delgado, Gary. 1986. *Organizing the Movement: The Roots and Growth of ACORN*. Philadelphia: Temple University Press.

DeNavas-Walt, Carmen, Bernadette Proctor, and Jessica Smith. 2009. Income, Poverty and Health Insurance Coverage in the United States, 2006. *Current Population Reports* P60–233. Washington, D.C.: U. S. Census Bureau.

Denemark, Robert. 2000. *World System History: The Social Science of Long-Term Change*. New York: Routledge.

DeSena, Judith. 1994. Women: The Gatekeepers of Urban Neighborhoods. *Journal of Urban Affairs* 16(3): 271–284.

Devine, Joel, and James Wright. 1993. *The Greatest of Evils: Urban Poverty and the American Underclass*. New York: Aldine de Gruyter.

Diehl, Richard A. 2004. *The Olmecs: America's First Civilization*. New York: Thames & Hudson.

Dillon, David. 1994. Fortress America. *Planning* 60(6): 8–12.

Dixey, Rachel. 1988. A Means to Get Out of the House: Working Class Women, Leisure, and Bingo. In *Women in Cities*, edited by J. Little, L. Peake, and P. Richardson. New York: New York University Press.

Dolbeare, Cushing. 1986. How the Income Tax System Subsidizes Housing for the Affluent. In *Critical Perspectives on Housing*, edited by R. Bratt, C. Hartman, and A. Meyerson. Philadelphia: Temple University Press.

Dolbeare, Cushing, and Don Ryan. 1997. Getting the Lead Out. *Shelterforce* 19(5): 24–27.

Domhoff, G. William. 1983. *Who Rules America Now? A View for the '80s*. Englewood Cliffs, N.J.: Prentice-Hall.

Dommel, Paul R. 1984. Local Discretion: The CDBG Approach. In *Urban Economic Development*, edited by R. D. Bingham and J. P. Blair. Thousand Oaks, Calif.: Sage.

Downs, Anthony. 1981. *Neighborhoods and Urban Development*. Washington, D.C.: Brookings Institution.

———. 1999. Contrasting Strategies for the Economic Development of Metropolitan Areas in the United States and Western Europe. In *Urban Change in the United States and Western Europe*, edited by A. Summers, P. Cheshire, and L. Senn. Washington, D.C.: The Urban Institute Press.

Drakakis-Smith, D. (2000). *Third World Cities*, 2nd ed. New York: Routledge.

Dreier, Peter. 1993. America's Urban Crisis: Symptoms, Causes, Solutions. *North Carolina Law Review* 71(5): 1351–1370.

———. 2004. George W. Bush and the Cities. *Planners Network Magazine*, Fall.

http://www.plannersnetwork.org/. www/pub/archives/fall2004/dreier. htm.

———. 2005. Will President Bush Reform the Mansion Subsidy? *Shelterforce* 144 (November–December).

———. 2009. *LA* Magazine's Failure: Irresponsible Journalism. *The Huffington Post*, July 25, 2009.

Dreier, Peter, and J. David Hulchanski. 1993. The Role of Nonprofit Housing in Canada and the United States: Some Comparisons. *Housing Policy Debate* 4(1): 43–80.

Dreier, Peter, John Mollenkopf, and Todd Swanstrom. 2004. *Place Matters: Metropolitics for the 21st Century*, 2nd ed. Lawrence, KS: University Press of Kansas.

DuBois, W. E. B. 1967. *The Philadelphia Negro*. New York: Schochen Books. Originally published in 1899.

Duncan, Greg. 1984. *Years of Poverty, Years of Plenty*. Ann Arbor: University of Michigan Institute for Survey Research.

Duncan, Otis D. 1961. From Social System to Ecosystem. *Sociological Inquiry* 31: 140–149.

Duneier, Mitchell. 1992. *Slim's Table: Race, Respectability, and Masculinity*. Chicago: University of Chicago Press.

Durand, Jorge and Douglas S. Massey, eds. 2004. *Crossing the Border: Research from the Mexican Migration Project*. New York: Russell Sage Foundation.

Durkheim, Émile. 1964. *The Division of Labor in Society*. New York: Free Press. Originally published in 1893.

Economist, The. 1993. Live by the Sword, Die by the Sword. *The Economist* 326 (7802): A32–34.

———. 1995. California Again in the Picture. *The Economist* 337 (7943): 21–23.

———. 1997. The West Is Best Again. *The Economist* 344 (8029): 19–21.

Edin, Kathryn, and Laura Lein. 1997. *Making Ends Meet: How Single Mothers Survive Welfare and Low-Wage Work.* New York: Russell Sage.

Eisenstadt, S. N., and A. Shachar. 1987. *Society, Culture, and Urbanization.* Thousand Oaks, Calif.: Sage.

Eisinger, Peter. 2000. The Politics of Bread and Circuses: Building the City for the Visitor Class. *Urban Affairs Review* 35(3): 316–333.

Elkin, Stephen. 1987. *City and Regime in the American Republic.* Chicago: University of Chicago Press.

Ellen, Ingrid G. 2000. *Sharing America's Neighborhoods: The Prospects for Stable Racial Integration.* Cambridge, Mass.: Harvard University Press.

Ellwood, David. 1988. *Poor Support: Poverty in the American Family.* New York: Basic Books.

Emerson, Michael O., Karen J. Chai, and George Yancey. 2001. Does Race Matter in Residential Segregation? Exploring the Preferences of White Americans. *American Sociological Review* 66 (6): 922–935.

Engels, Friedrich. 1958. *The Condition of the Working Class in England.* Stanford, Calif.: Stanford University Press.

Euchner, Charles. 1993. *Playing the Field: Why Sports Teams Move and Cities Fight to Keep Them.* Baltimore: Johns Hopkins University Press.

Ewen, Elizabeth. 1980. City Lights: Immigrant Women and the Rise of the Movies. *Signs* 5(3S): S45–S66.

Fainstein, Norman, and Susan Fainstein. 1983. Regime Strategies, Communal Resistance, and Economic Forces. In *Restructuring the City*, edited by S. Fainstein, N. Fainstein, R. C. Hill, and M. P. Smith. London: Longman.

Fainstein, Susan. 1992. The Second New York Fiscal Crisis. *International Journal of Urban and Regional Research* 16(1): 129–141.

———. 2001. *The City Builders*, 2nd ed. Lawrence, KS: University Press of Kansas.

Fainstein, Susan, and Norman Fainstein. 1978. National Policy and Urban Development. *Social Problems* 26: 125–146.

Fainstein, Susan, and Michael Harloe. 1992. Introduction: London and New York in the Contemporary World. In *Divided Cities*, edited by S. Fainstein, I. Gordon, and M. Harloe. London: Blackwell.

———. 1983. Economic Change, National Policy, and the System of Cities. In *Restructuring the City*, edited by S. Fainstein, N. Fainstein, R. C. Hill, D. Judd, and M. P. Smith. London: Longman.

Fall, Patricia L., Lee Lines, and Steven E. Falconer. 1998. Seeds of Civilization: Bronze Age Rural Economy and Ecology in the Southern Levant. *Annals of the Association of American Geographers* 88(1): 107–125.

Farley, John. 1987. Segregation in 1980: How Segregated Are America's Metropolitan Areas? In *Divided Neighborhoods*, edited by G. Tobin. Thousand Oaks, Calif.: Sage.

Farley, Reynolds, C. Steeh, T. Jackson, M. Krysan, and K. Reeves. 1993. Continued Racial Residential Segregation in Detroit: Chocolate City, Vanilla Suburbs Revisited. *Journal of Housing Research* 4(1): 1–38.

Farr, Douglas. 2007. *Sustainable Urbanism: Urban Design with Nature.* New York: Wiley.

Fasenfest, David. 1986. Community Politics and Urban Redevelopment: Poletown, Detroit, and General Motors. *Urban Affairs Quarterly* 22: 101–121.

Fava, Sylvia F. 1988. Residential Preferences in the Suburban Era: A New Look? In *Women, Housing, and Community*, edited by W. Van Vliet. Aldershot, England: Avebury.

Feagin, Joe. 1988. *Free Enterprise City: Houston in Political and Economic Perspective.* New Brunswick, N.J.: Rutgers University Press.

Feagin, Joe, and Robert Parker. 1990. *Building American Cities: The Urban Real Estate Game.* Englewood Cliffs, N.J.: Prentice-Hall.

Federal Bureau of Investigation. 2008. *Crime in the United States 2007.* Washington: United States Department of Justice.

Feldberg, Michael. 1980. *The Turbulent Era: Riot and Disorder in Jacksonian America.* New York: Oxford University Press.

Feldman, Roberta. 1995. Architect. Personal communication (e-mail), August 3.

Feldman, Roberta, and Susan Stall. 1994. The Politics of Space Appropriation: A Case Study of Women's Struggles for Homeplace in Chicago's Public Housing. In *Women and the Environment,* edited by I. Altman and A. Churchman. New York: Plenum Press.

———. 2004. *The Dignity of Resistance: Women Residents' Activism in Chicago Public Housing.* Cambridge, UK: Cambridge University Press.

Fennelly, Katherine. 2008. Prejudice Toward Immigrants in the Midwest. In *New Faces in New Places: The Changing Geography of American Immigration,* edited by D. Massey. New York: Russell Sage Foundation.

Ferman, Barbara. 1996. *Challenging the Growth Machine: Neighborhood Politics in Chicago and Pittsburgh.* Lawrence, KS: University Press of Kansas.

Ferro, M. 1997. *Colonization: A Global History.* New York: Routledge.

Firey, Walter. 1945. Sentiment and Symbolism as Ecological Variables. *American Sociological Review* 10: 140–148.

Fischer, M. J. 2003. The Relative Importance of Income and Race in Determining Residential Outcomes in U.S. Urban Areas, 1970–2000. *Urban Affairs Review* 38: 669–696.

Fitzpatrick, Kevin and Mark LaGory. 2000. *Unhealthy Places: The Ecology of Risk in the Urban Landscape.* New York: Routledge.

Fix, Michael, and Jeffrey Passel. 1994. *Immigration and Immigrants: Setting the Record Straight.* Washington, D.C.: The Urban Institute.

Flanagan, William G. 1993. *Contemporary Urban Sociology.* New York: Cambridge University Press.

Flannery, K. J. 1972. The Origins of the Village as a Settlement Type in Mesoamerica and the Near East. *Man, Settlement, and Urbanism,* edited by P. J. Ucko. London: Duckworth.

Flannery, K. V., and J. Marcus. 2003. The Origin of War: New C14 Dates from Ancient Mexico. *Proceedings of the National Academies of Science* 100 (20): 11801–11805.

Florida, Richard. 2002. *The Rise of the Creative Class.* New York: Basic Books.

———. 2003. Cities and the Creative Class. *City and Community* 2: 3–19.

Florida, Richard L., and Marshall Feldman. 1988. Housing in U.S. Fordism. *International Journal of Urban and Regional Research* 12(2): 187–209.

Foner, Nancy. 2000. *From Ellis Island to JFK: New York's Two Great Waves of Immigration.* New Haven: Yale University Press.

Form, William. 1954. The Place of Social Structure in the Determination of Land Use: Some Implications for a Theory of Urban Ecology. *Social Forces* 32: 317–323.

Forman, Robert. 1971. *Black Ghettos, White Ghettos and Slums.* Englewood Cliffs, N.J.: Prentice-Hall.

Frantz, Douglas, and Catherine Collins. 1999. *Celebration, USA: Living in*

Disney's Brave New Town. New York: Henry Holt.

Frazier, E. Franklin. 1932. *The Negro Family in Chicago*. Chicago: University of Chicago Press.

Freeman, Jo. 1980. Women and Urban Policy. *Signs* 5(3S): S4–S22.

Freeman, Lance. 2006. *There Goes the 'Hood: Views of Gentrification from the Ground Up*. Philadelphia: Temple University

Freudenburg, W. 1993. A "Good Business Climate" as Bad Economic News. *Society and Natural Resources* 3(4): 313–330.

Friedman, John. 2005. *China's Urban Transition*. Minneapolis: Minnesota Press.

Friedman, Lawrence M. 1980. Public Housing for the Poor. In *Housing Urban America*, 2nd ed., edited by J. Pynoos, R. Schafer, and C. Hartman. Chicago: Aldine.

Frug, Gerald E. 1999. *City Making*. Princeton, N.J.: Princeton University Press.

Fukurai, Hiroshi, Richard Krooth, and Edgar Butler. 1994. The Rodney King Beating Verdicts. In *The Los Angeles Riots*, edited by M. Baldassare. Boulder: Westview Press.

Funnell, Charles E. 1983. *By the Beautiful Sea*. New Brunswick, N.J.: Rutgers University Press.

Furlong, Tom. 1979. The Rich Got Richer Throughout the State. In *State and Local Tax Revolt*, edited by D. Tipps and L. Webb. Washington, D.C.: Conference on Alternative State and Local Policies.

Fustel de Coulanges, Numa D. n.d. *The Ancient City*. Garden City, N.Y.: Doubleday. Originally published in 1864.

Gale, Dennis. 1987. *Washington, DC: Inner-City Revitalization and Minority Suburbanization*. Philadelphia: Temple University Press.

Galster, George. 1988. Residential Segregation in American Cities: A Contrary View. *Population Research and Policy Review* 7: 93–112.

———. 1990. Racial Discrimination in Housing Markets During the 1980s: A Review of the Audit Evidence. *Journal of Planning Education and Research* 9(3): 165–175.

Galster, George, and Ronald Mincy. 1993. Understanding the Changing Fortunes of Metropolitan Neighborhoods: 1980 to 1990. *Housing Policy Debate* 4: 303–352.

Galusha, D. 1999. *Liquid Assets: A History of New York City's Water System*. Fleischmanns, N.Y.: Purple Mountain Press.

Gans, Herbert. 1962. *The Urban Villagers*. New York: Free Press.

———. 1967. *The Levittowners*. New York: Vintage Books.

———. 2008. Involuntary Segregation and the *Ghetto*: Disconnecting Process and Place. *City & Community* 7(4): 353–357.

Ganshof, F. L. 1996. *Feudalism*, translated by P. Grierson. Toronto: University of Toronto Press.

Garner, Roberta. 1996. *Contemporary Movements and Ideologies*. New York: McGraw-Hill.

Garraty, John A., and Peter Gay, eds. 1972. *The Columbia History of the World*. New York: Harper and Row.

Garreau, Joel. 1991. *Edge City*. New York: Doubleday.

Gates, Charles. 2003. *Ancient Cities: The Archaeology of Urban Life in the Ancient Near East and Egypt, Greece and Rome*. New York: Routledge.

Gibbon, Edward. 1879. *The Decline and Fall of the Roman Empire*. New York: Dell.

Gilbert, Alan, and Josef Gugler. 1992. *Cities, Poverty, and Development*, 2nd ed. Oxford, England: Oxford University Press.

Gittell, Ross, and Avis Vidal. 1998. *Community Organizing: Building Social Capital as a Development Strategy.* New York: Sage.

Glaab, Charles, and A. Theodore Brown. 1976. *A History of Urban America,* 2nd ed. New York: Macmillan.

Glassner, Barry. 2000. *The Culture of Fear.* New York: Basic Books.

Goetz, Edward. 2003. *Clearing the Way: Deconcentrating the Poor in Urban America.* Washington, D.C.: Urban Institute Press.

Goffman, Erving. 1971. *Relations in Public.* New York: Basic Books.

Goode, Judith, and Jo Anne Schneider. 1994. *Reshaping Ethnic and Racial Relations in Philadelphia: Immigrants in a Divided City.* Philadelphia: Temple University Press.

Goodman, Martin. 2007. Rome and Jerusalem: The Clash of Ancient Civilizations. New York: Knopf.

Gordon, David. 1978. Capitalist Development and the History of American Cities. In *Marxism and the Metropolis,* edited by W. Tabb and L. Sawers. New York: Oxford University Press.

Gordon, Diana R., J. G. Greene, D. Steelman, and S. Walker. 1992. Urban Crime Policy. *Journal of Urban Affairs* 14(3/4): 359–375.

Gordon, Milton. 1964. *Assimilation in American Life.* New York: Oxford University Press.

Gottdiener, Mark. 1977. *The Decline of Urban Politics.* Thousand Oaks, Calif.: Sage.

———. 1983. Understanding Metropolitan Deconcentration: A Clash of Paradigms. *Social Science Quarterly* 64(2): 227–246.

Gottdiener, Mark, and Joe Feagin. 1988. The Paradigm Shift in Urban Sociology. *Urban Affairs Quarterly* 24(2): 163–187.

Gottdiener, Mark, and Ray Hutchison. 2000. *The New Urban Sociology,* 2nd ed. New York: McGraw-Hill.

Gottman, Jean. 1964. *Megalopolis: The Urbanized Northeastern Seaboard of the United States.* Cambridge, Mass.: MIT Press.

Grasmuck, Sherri, and Patricia Pessar. 1991. *Between Two Islands: Dominican International Migration.* Berkeley: University of California Press.

Greed, Clara. 1994. *Women and Planning: Creating Gendered Realities.* London: Routledge.

Green, Constance McLaughlin. 1965. *The Rise of Urban America.* New York: HarperCollins.

Green, G. P., and A. Haines. 2007. *Asset Building and Community Development,* 2nd ed. New York: Sage.

Greene, J. R., and S. Mastrofski. 1988. *Community Policing: Rhetoric or Reality?* New York: Praeger.

Grenier, Guillermo, A. Stepick, D. Draznin, A. LaBorwit, and S. Morns. 1992. On Machines and Bureaucracy: Controlling Ethnic Interaction in Miami's Apparel and Construction Industries. In *Structuring Diversity,* edited by L. Lamphere. Chicago: University of Chicago Press.

Grushina, A., ed. 1997. *The Architecture and Building of Moscow.* Moscow: Voznesenski Pereulok.

Hagan, John. 1994. *Crime and Disrepute.* Thousand Oaks, Calif.: Pine Forge Press.

Hagedorn, John M. 1998. *People and Folks: Gangs, Crime and the Underclass in a Rustbelt City.* Chicago: Lake View Press.

Hall, Derek. 1998. Urban Transport, Environmental Pressures, and Policy Options. In *The New Europe: Economy, Society, and Environment,* edited by D. Pinder. New York: John Wiley & Sons.

Hall, Peter. 2001. *Cities in Civilization.* New York: Fromm International.

Halle, David. 1984. *America's Working Man.* Chicago: University of Chicago Press.

Hanson, Susan, Geraldine Pratt, Doreen Mattingly, and Melissa Gilbert. 1994. Women, Work, and Metropolitan Environments. In *Women and the Environment,* edited by I. Altman and A. Churchman. New York: Plenum Press.

Hardy-Fanta, Carol. 1993. *Latina Politics, Latino Politics.* Philadelphia: Temple University Press.

Hareven, Tamara, and Randolph Langebach. 1978. *Amoskeag.* New York: Pantheon.

Harloe, Michael. 1995. *The People's Home? Social Rented Housing in Europe and America.* Oxford: Blackwell.

Harris, Chauncey, and Edward Ullman. 1945. The Nature of Cities. *Annals of the American Academy of Political and Social Science* 242: 7–17.

Harrison, Bennett. 1984. Regional Restructuring and "Good Business Climates": The Economic Transformation of New England Since World War II. In *Sunbelt, Snowbelt,* edited by L. Sawers, and W. Tabb. New York: Oxford University Press.

Hartman, Chester. 1984. *The Transformation of San Francisco.* Totowa, N.J.: Rowman and Allanheld.

Hartman, Chester, Dennis Keating, and Richard LeGates. 1982. *Displacement.* Berkeley, Calif.: National Housing Law Project.

Harvey, David. 1973. *Social Justice and the City.* Baltimore: Johns Hopkins University Press.

———. 1974. Class-Monopoly Rent, Finance Capital, and the Urban Revolution. *Regional Studies* 8: 239–255.

———. 1978. The Urban Process Under Capitalism: A Framework for Analysis. *International Journal of Urban & Regional Research* 2: 101–131.

———. 2006. *Spaces of Global Capitalism: A Theory of Uneven Geographical Development.* New York: Verso.

Harvey, David L. 1993. *Potter Addition.* New York: Aldine de Gruyter.

Häussermann, Hartmut, and Anne Haila. 2005. The European City: A Conceptual Framework and Normative Project. In *Cities of Europe,* edited by Yuri Kazepov. Oxford, UK: Blackwell Publishing.

Hawley, Amos. 1944. Ecology and Human Ecology. *Social Forces* 22: 398–405.

Hayden, Dolores. 1981. *The Grand Domestic Revolution.* Cambridge, Mass.: MIT Press.

———. 1984. *Redesigning the American Dream.* New York: Norton.

———. 2003. *Building Suburbia: Green Fields and Urban Growth, 1820–2000.* New York: Vintage Books.

Hays, R. Allen. 1995. *The Federal Government and Urban Housing.* Albany: State University of New York Press.

Haywoode, Terry. 1999. Working-Class Women and Local Politics: Styles of Community Organizing. In *Community Politics and Policy,* edited by N. Kleniewski and G. Rabrenovic. Greenwich, Conn.: JAI Press.

Helper, Rose. 1969. *Racial Policies and Practices of Real Estate Brokers.* Minneapolis: University of Minnesota Press.

Herbers, John. 1986. Use of Private Suits in Housing Bias Cases in Federal Courts Is Increasing. *New York Times,* February 16, p. A36.

Hershberg, Theodore, A. Burstein, E. Ericksen, S. Greenberg, and W. Yancey. 1979. A Tale of Three Cities: Blacks and Immigrants in Philadelphia, 1850–1880, 1930, 1970. *The Annals of the American Academy of Political and Social Science* 441: 55–81.

Hershkowitz, Leo. 1977. *Tweed's New York: Another Look.* Garden City, N.Y.: Anchor Press.

Hill, Richard C. 1986. Crisis in the Motor City: The Politics of Urban

Development in Detroit. In *Restructuring the City*, 2nd ed., edited by S. Fainstein, N. Fainstein, R. Hill, D. Judd, and M. Smith. New York: Longman.

Hoch, Charles. 1984. City Limits: Municipal Boundary Formation and Class Segregation. In *Marxism and the Metropolis*, edited by W. K. Tabb and L. Sawers. New York: Oxford University Press.

Hodder, I. 2006. *The Leopard's Tale: Revealing the Mysteries of Catalhoyuk*. New York: Thames & Hudson.

Hoefer, Michael, Nancy Rytina, and Bryan C. Baker. 2009. Estimates of the Unauthorized Immigrant Population Residing in the United States: January 2008. *Population Estimates*. Washington, D.C.: U.S. Department of Homeland Security.

Hoffman, Lily, and Jiri Musil. 1999. Culture Meets Commerce: Tourism in Postcommunist Prague. In *The Tourist City*, edited by D. Judd and S. Fainstein. New Haven, Conn.: Yale University Press.

Hollingshead, A. B. 1947. A Re-examination of Ecological Theory. *Sociology and Social Research* 31: 194–204.

———. 1949. *Elmtown's Youth: The Impact of Social Classes on Adolescents*. New York: John Wiley & Sons.

Horowitz, Irving Louis. 1966. *Three Worlds of Development*. New York: Oxford University Press.

Horton, John. 1992. The Politics of Diversity in Monterrey Park, California. In *Structuring Diversity*, edited by L. Lamphere. Chicago: University of Chicago Press.

Howard, Ebenezer. 1965. *Garden Cities of Tomorrow*. Cambridge, Mass.: MIT Press. Originally published in 1902.

Hoyt, Homer. 1933. *One Hundred Years of Land Values in Chicago*. Chicago: University of Chicago Press.

———. 1939. *The Structure and Growth of Residential Neighborhoods in American Cities*. Washington, D.C.: Federal Housing Administration.

Hummon, David. 1990. *Commonplaces: Community Ideology and Identity in American Culture*. Albany: State University of New York Press.

Hunter, Floyd. 1953. *Community Power Structure: A Study of Decision Makers*. Chapel Hill: University of North Carolina Press.

———. 1980. *Community Power Succession: Atlanta's Policy Makers Revisited*. Chapel Hill: University of North Carolina Press.

Huttman, Elizabeth. 1991. Housing Segregation in Western Europe: An Introduction. In *Urban Housing Segregation of Minorities in Western Europe and the United States*, edited by E. Huttman, W. Blau, and J. Saltman. Durham, N.C.: Duke University Press.

Imbroscio, David L. 2006. Shaming the Inside Game: A Critique of Liberal Expansionist Approaches to Addressing Urban Problems. *Urban Affairs Review* 42(2): 224–248.

Innes, M. 2003. *More than Just Race: Being Black and Poor in the Inner City*. New York: Open University Press.

Jackson, Kenneth. 1985. *Atlas of American History*, 2nd ed. New York: Scribners.

Jackson, Kenneth. 2009. *Crabgrass Frontier*, 2nd ed. New York: Oxford University Press.

Jacobs, Jane. 1961. *The Death and Life of Great American Cities*. New York: Vintage Books.

Jankowski, Martin Sanchez. 1991. *Islands in the Street*. Berkeley: University of California Press.

Jargowsky, Paul. 1997. *Poverty and Place: Ghettos, Barrios, and the American City*. New York: Russell Sage.

———. 2003. *Stunning Progress, Hidden Problems: The Dramatic Decline of*

Concentrated Poverty in the 1990s. Washington, D.C.: The Brookings Institution.

———. 2006. The "Underclass" Problem Revisited: A Social Problem in Decline. *Journal of Urban Affairs* 28(1): 55–70.

Joassart-Marcelli, Pascale, and Juliet A. Musso. 2001. The Distributive Impact of Federal Fiscal Policy: Federal Spending and the Southern California Cities. *Urban Affairs Review* 37: 163–183.

Johnson, Kevin. 2003. The "Huddled Masses" Myth: Immigration and Civil Rights. Philadelphia: Temple University Press.

Johnston-Anumonwo, Ibipo, Sara McLafferty, and Valerie Preston. 1995. Gender, Race, and the Spatial Context of Women's Employment. In *Gender in Urban Research*, edited by J. Garber and R. Turner. Thousand Oaks, Calif.: Sage.

Jones, Bryan, and Lynn Bachelor. 1984. Policy Discretion and the Corporate Surplus. In *Urban Economic Development*, edited by R. Bingham and J. Blair. Thousand Oaks, Calif.: Sage.

———. 1986. *The Sustaining Hand.* Lawrence: University Press of Kansas.

Judd, Dennis, and Susan Fainstein, eds. 1999. *The Tourist City.* New Haven, Conn.: Yale University Press.

Judd, Dennis and Todd Swanstrom. 2008. *City Politics: Private Power and Public Policy* (6th edition). New York: Longman.

Kandel, William, and Emilio A. Parrado. 2005. Restructuring of the U.S. Meat Processing Industry and New Hispanic Migrant Destinations. *Population and Development Review* 31(3): 447–471.

Kain, John. 1967. The Distribution and Movement of Jobs and Industry. In *The Metropolitan Enigma*, edited by J. Q. Wilson. Washington, D.C.: U.S. Chamber of Commerce.

———. 1987. Housing Market Discrimination and Black Suburbanization in the 1980s. In *Divided Neighborhoods*, edited by G. Tobin. Thousand Oaks, Calif.: Sage.

———. 2004. A Pioneer's Perspective on the Spatial Mismatch Literature. *Urban Studies* 41(1): 7–32.

Kantor, Paul. 1993. The Dual City as Political Choice. *Journal of Urban Affairs* 15(3): 231–244.

Kantor, Paul, and H. V. Savitch. 1993. Can Politicians Bargain with Business? A Theoretical and Comparative Perspective on Urban Development. *Urban Affairs Quarterly* 29(2): 230–255.

Kasarda, John D. 1989. Urban Industrial Transformation and the Underclass. *Annals of the American Academy of Political and Social Science* 501: 26–47.

Kasinitz, Philip. 1992. *Caribbean New York: Black Immigrants and the Politics of Race.* Ithaca, N.Y.: Cornell University Press.

Katz, Michael. 1989. *The Undeserving Poor.* New York: Pantheon Books.

Kazepov, Yuri, ed. 2005. *Cities of Europe: Changing Contexts, Local Arrangements, and the Challenge to Urban Cohesion.* Oxford, UK: Blackwell Publishing.

Keating, W. Dennis. 1994. *The Suburban Racial Dilemma: Housing and Neighborhoods.* Philadelphia: Temple University Press.

Kennedy, Randall. 2001. Racial Trends in the Administration of Justice. In *America Becoming*, edited by N. Smelser, W. J. Wilson, and F. Mitchell. Washington, D.C.: National Academy Press.

Kessler-Harris, Alice. 1982. *Out to Work.* New York: Oxford University Press.

King, Russell. 1998. From Guestworkers to Immigrants: Labour Migration from the Mediterranean Periphery. In *The New Europe: Economy, Society, and Environment*, edited by D. Pinder. New York: Wiley.

Kleniewski, Nancy. 1981. From Industrial to Corporate City: The Role of Urban Renewal. In *Marxism and the Metropolis*, edited by W. Tabb and L. Sawers. New York: Oxford University Press.

———. 1987. Local Business Leaders and Urban Policy: A Case Study. *Insurgent Sociologist* 14(1): 33–56.

Klinenberg, Eric. 2002. *Heat Wave: A Social Autopsy of Disaster in Chicago*. Chicago: University of Chicago Press.

Koegel, Paul. 1996. The Causes of Homelessness. In *Homelessness in America*, edited by J. Baumohl. Phoenix: Oryx Press.

Koeppel, G. T. 2000. *Water for Gotham: A History*. Princeton, N.J.: Princeton University Press.

Kornblum, William. 1974. *Blue Collar Community*. Chicago: University of Chicago Press.

Kotkin, J. 2005. *The City: A Global History*. New York: Random House.

Kozol, Jonathan. 1988. *Rachel and Her Children*. New York: Fawcett Columbine.

———. 1991. *Savage Inequalities*. New York: HarperCollins.

Kreider, Rose M. 2007. *Living Arrangements of Children: 2004*. Current Population Reports, P70–114. Washington, D.C.: U. S. Census Bureau.

Krieg, Eric J. 1998. The Two Faces of Toxic Waste: Trends in the Spread of Environmental Hazards. *Sociological Forum* 13(1): 3–20.

Kritz, Mary, and Hania Zlotnik. 1992. Global Interactions: Migration Systems, Processes, and Policies. In *International Migration Systems*, edited by M. Kritz, L. Lim, and H. Zlotnik. Oxford: Clarendon Press.

Krumholz, Norman. 1982. A Retrospective View of Equity Planning: Cleveland 1969–1979. *Journal of the American Planning Association* 48: 163–183.

Krysan, Maria and Reynolds Farley. 2002. The Residential Preferences of Blacks: Do They Explain Persistent Segregation? *Social Forces* 80(3): 937–980.

Kusmer, Kenneth L. 1976. *A Ghetto Takes Shape: Black Cleveland, 1870–1930*. Urbana: University of Illinois Press.

Lacy, Karyn. 2007. *Blue Chip Black: Race, Class, and Status in the New Black Middle Class*. Berkeley: University of California Press.

LaGory, Mark, and John Pipkin. 1981. *Urban Social Space*. Belmont, Calif.: Wadsworth Publishing Company.

Lamarche, François. 1976. Property Development and the Economic Foundations of the Urban Question. In *Urban Sociology: Critical Essays*, edited by C. G. Pickvance. New York: St. Martin's Press.

Lane, Roger. 1986. *Roots of Violence in Black Philadelphia 1860–1900*. Cambridge, Mass.: Harvard University Press.

Lance, Peter. 2003. *1,000 Years for Revenge*. New York: HarperCollins.

Landre, Rick, Mike Miller, and Dee Porter. 1997. *Gangs: A Handbook for Community Awareness*. New York: Facts on File Books.

Larsen, Luke J. 2004. *The Foreign-Born Population in the United States: 2003*. Current Population Reports P20–551. Washington, D.C.: U. S. Census Bureau.

Larson, Magali Sarfatti. 1993. *Behind the Postmodern Facade*. Berkeley: University of California Press.

Lawless, Jennifer and Richard Fox. 2008. Why Are Women Still Not Running for Office? *Issues in Governance Studies* 16 (May): 1–20.

Lazarus, Emma. 1944. *Emma Lazarus: Selections from Her Poetry and Prose*. New York: Cooperative Book League. Originally published in 1883.

Leavitt, Jacqueline. 1989. Two Prototypical Designs for Single Parents: The Congregate House and the New American House. In *New Households, New Housing*, edited by K. Franck and S. Ahrentzen. New York: Van Nostrand Reinhold.

LeCorbusier. 1967. *The Radiant City*. New York: Onion Press.

Lee, Jennifer. 2002. *Civility in the City: Blacks, Jews, and Koreans in Urban America*. Cambridge, Mass.: Harvard University Press.

LeGates, Richard, and Chester Hartman. 1986. The Anatomy of Displacement in the U.S. In *Gentrification of the City*, edited by N. Smith and P. Williams. Boston: Allen and Unwin.

Leitner, Helga, and Mark Garner. 1993. The Limits of Local Initiatives: A Reassessment of Urban Entrepreneurialism for Urban Development. *Urban Geography* 14(1): 57–77.

Lemann, Nicholas. 1991. *The Promised Land*. New York: Vintage Books.

Lenski, Gerhard. 1966. *Power and Privilege*. New York: McGraw-Hill.

Levin, Jack, and Alexander R. Thomas. 1997. Experimentally Manipulating Race: Perceptions of Police Brutality in an Arrest. *Justice Quarterly* 14(3): 577–86.

Levitt, Peggy. 2001. *The Transnational Villagers*. Berkeley: University of California Press.

Lewis, Carol. 1994. Municipal Bankruptcy and the States. *Urban Affairs Quarterly* 30(1): 3–26.

Lewis, Oscar. 1966. *San Francisco*. Berkeley, Calif.: Howell-North.

Lieberson, Stanley. 1980. *A Piece of the Pie: Blacks and White Immigrants Since 1880*. Berkeley: University of California Press.

Liebow, Elliot. 1967. *Tally's Corner*. Boston: Little, Brown.

———. 1993. *Tell Them Who I Am: The Lives of Homeless Women*. New York: Free Press.

Light, Ivan, and Edna Bonacich. 1988. *Immigrant Entrepreneurs: Koreans in Los Angeles, 1965–1982*. Berkeley: University of California Press.

Liverani, M. 2006. *Uruk: The First City*, translated by Z. Bahrani and M. van de Mieroop. London: Equinox.

Lloyd, Richard, and Terry Clark. 2000. The City as an Entertainment Machine. Paper presented at the American Sociological Association annual meeting, Washington, D.C., August.

Lo, Clarence. 1990. *Small Property vs. Big Government: Social Origins of the Property Tax Revolt*. Berkeley: University of California Press.

Loewen, James. 2005. *Sundown Towns: A Hidden Dimension of American Racism*. New York: The New Press.

Lofland, Lyn. 1985. *A World of Strangers*. Prospect Heights, Ill.: Waveland Press.

Logan, John. 1976. Industrialization and the Stratification of Cities in Suburban Regions. *American Journal of Sociology* 82: 333–348.

———. 2000. Still a Global City: The Racial and Ethnic Segmentation of New York. In *Globalizing Cities: A New Spatial Order?*, edited by P. Marcuse and R. Van Kempen. Oxford: Blackwell.

Logan, John, and Richard Alba. 1999. Minority Niches and Immigrant Enclaves in New York and Los Angeles: Trends and Impacts. In *Immigration and Opportunity*, edited by F. Bean and S. Bell-Rose. New York: Russell Sage.

Logan, John, and Harvey Molotch. 2007. *Urban Fortunes: The Political Economy of Place*, 20th anniversary ed. Berkeley: University of California Press.

Logan, John, Brian J. Stults, and Reynolds Farley. 2004. Segregation of Minorities in the Metropolis: Two Decades of Change. *Demography* 41(1): 1–22.

Logan, John, and Todd Swanstrom. 1990. Urban Restructuring: A Critical View. In *Beyond the City Limits*, edited by J. Logan and T. Swanstrom. Albany: State University of New York Press.

Low, Setha. 2003. *Behind the Gates: Life, Security, and the Pursuit of Happiness in Fortress America*. New York: Routledge.

Luttrell, Wendy. 1988. The Edison School Struggle: The Reshaping of Working-Class Education and Women's Consciousness. In *Women and the Politics of Empowerment*, edited by A. Bookman and S. Morgan. Philadelphia: Temple University Press.

Lynch, Kevin. 1960. *The Image of the City*. Cambridge, Mass.: MIT Press.

Lynch, K. 2005. *Rural-Urban Interaction in the Developing World*. New York: Routledge.

Lynd, Robert S. and Helen M. Lynd. 1937. *Middletown in Transition: A Study in Cultural Conflicts*. New York: Harcourt, Brace, & World.

———. 1929. *Middletown: A Study in American Culture*. New York: Harcourt, Brace & World.

MacLeod, Jay. 1995. *Ain't No Makin' It*, 2nd ed. Boulder: Westview Press.

Mackensen, Rainer. 1999. Urban Decentralization Processes in Western Europe. In *Urban Change in the United States and Western Europe*, edited by A. Summers, P. Cheshire, and L. Senn. Washington, D.C.: The Urban Institute Press.

Madriz, Esther. 1997. *Nothing Bad Happens to Good Girls: Fear of Crime in Women's Lives*. Berkeley: University of California Press.

Maher, Timothy. 1990. Community and Upper Class Consciousness. In *Research in Community Sociology*, edited by D. Chekki. Greenwich, Conn.: JAI Press.

Mahtesian, Charles. 1994. Romancing the Smokestack. *Governing* (November): 36–40.

Maisels, Charles Keith. 1990. *The Emergence of Civilization*. New York: Routledge.

Maisels, Charles Keith. 1999. *Early Civilizations of the Old World*. New York: Routledge.

Mann, C. C. 2006. *1491: New Revelations of the Americas Before Columbus*. New York: Vintage.

Marcuse, Peter, and Ronald van Kempen. 2000. Conclusion: A Changed Spatial Order. In *Globalizing Cities: A New Spatial Order?*, edited by P. Marcuse and R. Van Kempen. Oxford: Blackwell.

Marks, Carole. 1989. *Farewell—We're Good and Gone: The Great Black Migration*. Bloomington: Indiana University Press.

Markusen, Ann. 1987. *Regions: The Economic and Politics of Territories*. Totowa, N.J.: Rowman and Littlefield.

Marx, Karl. 1970. *A Contribution to the Critique of Political Economy*. New York: International Publishers.

———. 1971. *The Grundrisse*, edited and translated by D. McLellan. New York: Harper and Row.

Massey, Doreen. 1994. *Space, Place, and Gender*. Minneapolis: University of Minnesota Press.

Massey, Douglas S. 2005. *Strangers in a Strange Land: Humans in an Urbanizing World*. New York: W. W. Norton.

Massey, Douglas, R. Alarcon, J. Durand, and H. Gonzalez. 1987. *Return to Aztlan: The Social Process of International Migration from Western Mexico*.

Berkeley: University of California Press.

Massey, Douglas S. 2001. Residential Segregation and Neighborhood Conditions in U.S. Metropolitan Areas. In *America Becoming*, edited by N. Smelser, W.J. Wilson, and F. Mitchell. Washington, D.C.: National Academy Press.

Massey, Douglas S. and Chiara Capoferro. 2008. The Geographic Diversification of American Immigration. In *New Faces in New Places: The Changing Geography of American Immigration*, edited by D. Massey. New York: Russell Sage Foundation.

Massey, Douglas, and Nancy Denton. 1993. *American Apartheid: Segregation and the Making of the Underclass.* Cambridge, Mass.: Harvard University Press.

Maurrasse, David J. 2001. *Beyond the Campus: How Colleges and Universities Form Partnerships with Their Communities.* New York: Routledge.

McCamant, Kathryn, and Charles Durrett. 1989. Cohousing in Denmark. In *New Households New Housing*, edited by K. Franck and S. Ahrentzen. New York: Van Nostrand Reinhold.

McIntire, Mike. 2005. Unexpected Rise in Tax Revenue Cuts City's Budget Gap in Half. *New York Times*, November 23, p. B3.

McIntyre, Robert. 1987. Tax the *Forbes* 400! *New Republic*, August 31, pp. 15–18.

McLanahan, Sara, and Christine Percheski. 2008. Family Structure and the Reproduction of Inequalities. *Annual Review of Sociology* 34: 257–276.

McLemore, S. Dale. 1994. *Racial and Ethnic Relations in America*, 4th ed. Boston: Allyn & Bacon.

McMichael, Philip. 2000. *Development and Social Change.* Thousand Oaks, Calif.: Pine Forge Press.

Megacities Project. 2009. *Innovations for Urban Life.* Retrieved March 30, 2009, from http://megacitiesproject.org.

Meggers, Betty. 1975. The Transpacific Origins of Mesoamerican Civilizations. *American Anthropologist* 77: 1–23.

Merry, Sally Engle. 1981. *Urban Danger: Life in a Neighborhood of Strangers.* Philadelphia: Temple University Press.

Messner, Steven F., and Richard Rosenfeld. 2006. *Crime and the American Dream*, 4th ed. Belmont, Calif.: Wadsworth.

Meyer, Karl E. 1973. *Teotihuacán.* New York: Newsweek Books.

Michelson, William. 1970. *Man and His Urban Environment.* Reading, Mass.: Addison-Wesley.

Mills, C. Wright. 1959. *The Sociological Imagination.* New York: Oxford University Press.

Mishel, Lawrence, Jared Bernstein, and John Schmitt. 1999. *The State of Working America, 1998–1999.* Ithaca, N.Y.: Cornell University Press.

Mishel, Lawrence, Jared Bernstein, and Heidi Shierholz. 2008. *The State of Working America 2008-09.* Washington, D.C.: Economic Policy Institute.

Mitchell, Christopher, ed. 1992. *Western Hemisphere Immigration and U.S. Foreign Policy.* University Park: Penn State University Press.

Mitchell, R. E. 2005. The Definition of Patres and Plebs: An End to the Struggle of the Orders. In K. A. Raaflaub, *Social Struggles in Archaic Rome.* Malden, Mass: Blackwell, pp. 128–167.

Mollenkopf, John. 1983. *The Contested City.* Princeton, N.J.: Princeton University Press.

———. 1995. What Future for Federal Urban Policy? *Urban Affairs Review* 30(5): 657–660.

Mollenkopf, John, and Manuel Castells. 1991. Introduction. In *Dual City,*

edited by J. Mollenkopf and
M. Castells. New York: Russell Sage.

Molotch, Harvey. 1976. The City as a
Growth Machine: Toward a Political
Economy of Place. *American Journal
of Sociology* 82: 309–332.

———. 1993. The Political Economy of
Growth Machines. *Journal of Urban
Affairs* 15(1): 29–53.

Moore, A. M. T., G. C. Gillman, and
A. J. Legge. 2000. *Village on the Euphrates:
From Foraging to Farming at Abu Hureyra.*
New York: Oxford University Press.

Moore, Joan. 1993. Gangs, Drugs, and
Violence. In *Gangs*, edited by
S. Cummings and D. Monti. Albany:
State University of New York Press.

Morley, Neville. 1996. *Metropolis and Hin-
terland: The City of Rome and the Italian
Economy, 200 BC–AD 200*. New
York: Cambridge University Press.

Morrison, Peter, and Ira Lowry. 1994.
A Riot of Color. In *The Los Angeles
Riots*, edited by M. Baldassare.
Boulder: Westview Press.

Muller, Thomas. 1993. *Immigrants and the
American City*. New York: New York
University Press.

Mumford, Lewis. 1938. *The Culture of
Cities*. New York: Harcourt, Brace &
World.

———. 1961. *The City in History*. New
York: Harcourt, Brace, and
Jovanovich.

Munnell, Alicia, L. Browne, J. McEneaney,
and G. Tootell. 1996. Mortgage
Lending in Boston: Interpreting
HMDA Data. *American Economic
Review* 86: 25–53.

Murphy, Russell D. 2002. Politics, Politi-
cal Science, and Urban Governance:
A Literature and a Legacy. *Annual
Review of Political Science* 5: 63–85.

Murray, M. J., and G. A. Myers. 2007.
Cities in Contemporary Africa, edited by
M. J. Murray, and G. A. Myers. New
York: Palgrave MacMillan.

Murie, Alan. 1991. Introduction to the
Policies in European Countries. In
*Urban Housing Segregation of Minorities
in Western Europe and the United States*,
edited by E. Huttman, W. Blau, and
J. Saltman. Durham, N.C.: Duke
University Press.

Musterd, Sako, and Wim Ostendorf. 2005.
Social Exclusion, Segregation, and
Neighborhood Effects. In *Cities of
Europe*, edited by Yuri Kazepov.
Oxford, UK: Blackwell Publishing.

Nadel, D. 2003. The Ohalo II Brush Huts
and the Dwelling Structures of the
Natufian and PPNA Sites in the
Jordan Valley. *Archaeology, Ethnology &
Anthropology of Eurasia* 1(13): 34–48.

Nagel, Joane. 1994. Constructing Ethnicity: Creating and Recreating Ethnic
Identity and Culture. *Social Problems*
41(1): 152–176.

Naples, Nancy. 1992. Activist Mothering:
Cross-Generational Continuity in the
Community Work of Women from
Low-Income Urban Neighborhoods.
Gender & Society 6: 441–463.

National Advisory Commission on Civil
Disorders. 1968. *Report*. New York:
Bantam Books.

National Commission on Urban
Problems. 1968. *Building the American
City*. Washington, D.C.: U.S.
Government Printing Office.

National Fair Housing Alliance. 2008.
2008 Fair Housing Trends Report.
Washington, D.C.: National Fair
Housing Alliance.

———. 2005. *2005 Fair Housing Trends
Report*. Washington, D.C.: National
Fair Housing Alliance.

National Law Center on Homelessness
and Poverty. 1999. *Out of Sight—Out
of Mind?* Washington, D.C.: Author.

National Law Center on Homelessness
and Poverty. 2006. *A Dream Denied:
The Criminalization of Homelessness in
U.S. Cities*. Washington: National

Law Center on Homelessness and Poverty.

Negrey, Cynthia, and Mary Beth Zickel. 1994. Industrial Shifts and Uneven Development: Patterns of Growth and Decline in U.S. Metropolitan Areas. *Urban Affairs Quarterly* 30(1): 27–47.

Newman, Katherine S. 1991. *Falling from Grace.* New York: Vintage Press.

Newman, Oscar. 1973. *Defensible Space.* New York: Collier Books.

Newman, Peter, and Andy Thornley. 1996. *Urban Planning in Europe.* London: Routledge.

Noyelle, Thierry, and Thomas Stanback. 1984. *The Economic Transformation of American Cities.* Totowa, N.J.: Rowman and Allanheld.

Oakley, Ann. 1974. *Women's Work.* New York: Random House.

O'Brien, William. 1999. Philadelphia Campaign Reshapes Homelessness Debate. *Shelterforce* 106 (July–August), 8–9.

O'Connor, James. 1998. *Natural Causes: Essays in Ecological Marxism.* New York: Guilford.

Office of Management and Budget. 2000. *Standards for Defining Metropolitan and Micropolitan Statistical Areas.* Washington, D.C.: United States Office of Management and Budget.

Office of Technology Assessment. 1993. *Pharmaceutical R&D: Costs, Risks and.* Washington, D.C.: Office of Technology Assessment.

Oldenburg, Ray. 1989. *The Great Good Place: Cafes, Coffee Shops, Community Centers, Beauty Parlors, General Stores, Bars, Hangouts, and How They Get You Through the Day.* New York: Paragon House.

Orfield, Myron. 2002. *American Metropolitics: The New Suburban Reality.* Washington, D.C.: The Brookings Institution.

Osofsky, Gilbert. 1963. *Harlem: The Making of a Ghetto.* New York: Harper & Row.

Padilla, Felix, M. 1992. *The Gang as an American Enterprise.* New Brunswick, N.J.: Rutgers University Press.

Pahl, R. E. 1989. Is the Emperor Naked? Some Questions on the Adequacy of Sociological Theory in Urban and Regional Research. *International Journal of Urban and Regional Research* 13: 709.

Pager, Devah, and Hana Shepherd. 2008. The Sociology of Discrimination: Racial Discrimination in Employment, Housing, Credit, and Consumer Markets. *Annual Review of Sociology* 34: 181–209.

Palen, J. John. 1995. *The Suburbs.* New York: McGraw-Hill.

Park, Robert E. 1915. The City: Suggestions for the Investigation of Human Behavior in the City Environment. *American Journal of Sociology* 20: 577–612.

———. 1936. Human Ecology. *American Journal of Sociology* 42: 1–15.

Parrillo, Vincent. 1994. *Strangers to These Shores,* 4th ed. New York: Macmillan.

Pastor, Manuel Jr., Jim Sadd, and John Hipp. 2001. Which Came First? Toxic Facilities, Minority Move-In, and Environmental Justice. *Journal of Urban Affairs* 23(1):1.

Pattillo, Mary 2007. *Black on the Block: The Politics of Race and Class in the City.* Chicago: University of Chicago Press.

Pearce, Diana. 1978. The Feminization of Poverty: Women, Work, and Welfare. *Urban and Social Change Review* 10: 28–36.

———. 1979. Gatekeepers and Homeseekers: Institutional Patterns in Racial Steering. *Social Problems* 26: 325–342.

Perez, Lisandro. 1992. Cuban Miami. In *Miami Now!,* edited by G. Grenier and A. Stepick. Gainesville: University Press of Florida.

Perry, D. C., W. Wiewel, and C. Menendez. 2009. The University's

Role in Urban Development: From Enclave to Anchor Institution. *Land Lines* (July): 2–7.

Persky, Joseph, Elliott Sclar, and Wim Wiewel. 1991. *Does America Need Cities?* Washington, D.C.: Economic Policy Institute.

Peterson, Jon. 1983. The Impact of Sanitary Reform on American Planning. In *Introduction to Planning History in the United States*, edited by D. A. Kreuckeberg. New Brunswick, N.J.: Center for Urban Policy Research.

Peterson, Paul. 1981. *City Limits.* Chicago: University of Chicago Press.

Philpott, Thomas L. 1991. *The Slum and the Ghetto: Neighborhood Deterioration and Middle Class Reform, Chicago 1880–1930.* New York: Oxford University Press.

Pickup, Laurie. 1988. Hard to Get Around: A Study of Women's Travel Mobility. In *Women in Cities*, edited by J. Little, L. Peake, and P. Richardson. New York: New York University Press.

Pickvance, C. G. 1984. The Structuralist Critique in Urban Studies. In *Cities in Transformation*, edited by M. P. Smith. Beverly Hills, Calif.: Sage.

Pinder, David, and Julia Edwards. 1998. Transport, Economic Development, and the Environment. In *The New Europe: Economy, Society, and Environment*, edited by D. Pinder. New York: Wiley.

Piore, Michael, and Charles Sabel. 1984. *The Second Industrial Divide.* New York: Basic Books.

Pirenne, Henri. 1956. *Medieval Cities.* Garden City, N.Y.: Doubleday.

Pitcoff, Winton. 2000. No Place to Call Home: America's Housing Crisis. *Dollars and Sense* 21(2): 24–47.

Piven, Frances Fox, and Richard Cloward. 1977. *Poor People's Movements.* New York: Vintage Books.

PlanetArk. n.d. *Your Daily Guide to Helping the Planet.* Retrieved April 12, 2009, from http://www.planetark.org/.

Pollock, Susan. 1999. *Ancient Mesopotamia.* New York: Cambridge University Press.

Polsby, Nelson. 1980. *Community Power and Political Theory.* New Haven, Conn.: Yale University Press.

Ponting, Clive. 1991. *A Green History of the World.* New York: Penguin Books.

Popenoe, David. 1985. *Private Pleasure, Public Plight: American Metropolitan Community Life in Comparative Perspective.* New Brunswick, N.J.: Transaction Books.

Porter, Eduardo. 2005. Not on the Radar: Illegal Immigrants Are Bolstering Social Security. *Generations* 29(1): 100–102.

Portes, Alejandro. 1985. The Informal Sector and the World Economy: Notes on the Structure of Subsidized Labor. In *Urbanization in the World Economy*, edited by M. Timberlake. Orlando: Academic Press.

———. 2003. Symposium. *Contemporary Sociology* 31 (5): 522–525.

———. 2007. The Fence to Nowhere. *The American Prospect* 18(10): 26–29.

Portes, Alejandro, M. Castells, and L. Benton, eds. 1989. *The Informal Economy: Studies in Advanced and Less Developed Countries.* Baltimore: Johns Hopkins University Press.

Portes, Alejandro, and Ruben Rumbaut. 2006. *Immigrant America: A Portrait*, 3nd ed. Berkeley: University of California Press.

Portes, Alejandro, and Alex Stepick. 1993. *City on the Edge: The Transformation of Miami.* Berkeley: University of California Press.

President's Commission for a National Agenda for the Eighties. 1981. *A National Agenda for the Eighties.* New York: Mentor.

Pula, James S., and Eugene E. Dziedzic. 1991. *United We Stand: The Role of Polish Workers in the New York Mills Textile Strikes, 1912 and 1916.* New York: Columbia University Press.

Rabrenovic, Gordana. 1995. Women and Collective Action in Urban Neighborhoods. In *Gender in Urban Research*, edited by J. Garber and R. Turner. Thousand Oaks, Calif.: Sage.

————. 1996. *Community Builders.* Albany: State University of New York Press.

Reckless, Walter. 1926. The Distribution of Commercialized Vice in the City: A Sociological Analysis. *Publications of the American Sociological Society* 20: 164–176.

Reich, Robert. 1983. *The Next American Frontier.* New York: Penguin Books.

————. 1991. *The Work of Nations.* New York: Knopf.

————. 2002. *The Future of Success: Working and Living in the New Economy.* New York: Vintage.

————. 2008. *Supercapitalism: The Transformation of Business, Democracy, and Everyday Life.* New York: Vintage.

Reid, Lesley Williams. 2003. *Crime in the City: A Political and Economic Analysis of Urban Crime.* El Paso, TX.: LFB Scholarly Publishing.

Reid, Sue Titus. 1993. *Criminal Justice*, 3rd ed. New York: Macmillan.

Register, Richard. 2006. *EcoCities: Rebuilding Cities in Balance with Nature.* Gabriola Island, B.C.: New Society Publishers.

Reskin, Barbara, and Irene Padovic. 1994. *Women and Men at Work.* Thousand Oaks, Calif.: Pine Forge Press.

Richard, J.-C. 2005. Patricians and Plebians: The Origins of a Social Dichotomy. In K. A. Raaflaub, *Social Struggles in Archaic Rome.* Malden, Mass: Blackwell, pp. 107–126.

Rieder, Jonathan. 1985. *Canarsie: The Jews and Italians of Brooklyn Against Liberalism.* Cambridge, Mass.: Harvard University Press.

Ritzdorf, Marsha. 1994. A Feminist Analysis of Land Use and Residential Zoning in the United States. In *Women and the Built Environment*, edited by A. Churchman and I. Altman. New York: Plenum.

Roberts, Bryan. 1978. *Cities of Peasants.* Thousand Oaks, Calif.: Sage.

Rogus, Deborah. 1997. America's Sports Stadiums: How Much Do They Really Cost You? *Your Money* (June/July): 70–77.

Roscigno, Vincent, Diana Karafin, and Greg Tester. 2009. The Complexities and Processes of Racial Housing Discrimination. *Social Problems* 56(1): 49–69.

Rosenbaum, James. 1995. Expanding the Geography of Opportunity by Expanding Residential Choice: Lessons from the Gautreaux Program. *Housing Policy Debate* 6: 231–270.

Rosentraub, Mark. 1988. Public Investment in Private Businesses: The Professional Sports Mania. In *Business Elites and Urban Development*, edited by S. Cummings. Albany: State University of New York Press.

————. 1997. *Major League Losers.* New York: Basic Books.

Ross, Andrew. 1999. *The Celebration Chronicles: Life, Liberty, and the Pursuit Property Values in Disney's New Town.* New York: Ballantine Books.

Ross, Robert J. S., and Kent C. Trachte. 1990. *Global Capitalism: The New Leviathan.* Albany: State University of New York Press.

Rostow, Walter W. 1960. *The Stages of Economic Growth: A Non-Communist Manifesto.* Cambridge, England: Cambridge University Press.

————. 1978. *The World Economy: History and Prospect.* Austin: University of Texas Press.

Rubin, Herbert. 1994. There Aren't Going to Be Any Bakeries Here If There Is No Money to Afford Jellyrolls: The Organic Theory of Community Based Development. *Social Problems* 41(3): 401–424.

Rusk, David. 1993. *Cities Without Suburbs.* Baltimore: Johns Hopkins University Press.

———. 1999. *Inside Game, Outside Game: Winning Strategies for Saving Urban America.* Washington, D.C.: Brookings Institution Press.

Rytina, Nancy and John Simanski. 2009. Apprehensions by the U.S. Border Patrol: 2005–2008. *Fact Sheet.* U.S. Department of Homeland Security Office of Immigration Statistics. http://www.dhs.gov/ immigrationstatistics.

Saegert, Susan. 1988. The Androgynous City: From Critique to Practice. In *Women, Housing and Community,* edited by Willem Van Vliet. Aldershot, England: Avebury.

Saegert, Susan, J. Philip Thompson, and Mark Warren, eds. 2001. *Social Capital and Poor Communities.* New York: Russell Sage Foundation.

Saiko, Tatyana. 1998. Environmental Challenges in the New Democracies. In *The New Europe: Economy, Society, and Environment,* edited by D. Pinder. New York: Wiley.

Salama, Jerry. 1999. The Redevelopment of Distressed Public Housing: Early Results from HOPE VI Projects in Atlanta, Chicago, and San Antonio. *Housing Policy Debate* 10(1): 95–142.

Saltman, Juliet. 1990. *A Fragile Movement: The Struggle for Neighborhood Stabilization.* Westport, Conn.: Greenwood Press.

Sanders, Heywood. 1980. Urban Renewal and the Revitalized City: A Reconsideration of Recent History. In *Urban Revitalization,* edited by D. Rosenthal. Thousand Oaks, Calif.: Sage.

———. 1992. Building the Convention City: Politics, Finance, and Public Investment in Urban America. *Journal of Urban Affairs* 14(2): 135–159.

Sassen, Saskia. 1990. Economic Restructuring and the American City. *Annual Review of Sociology* 16: 465–490.

———. 1994. *Cities in a World Economy.* Thousand Oaks, Calif.: Pine Forge Press.

———. 2001. *The Global City: New York, London, Tokyo,* 2nd ed. Princeton, N.J.: Princeton University Press.

———, ed. 2002. *Global Networks, Linked Cities.* New York: Routledge.

———. 2008. *Territory, Authority, Rights: From Medieval to Global Assemblages.* Princeton, N.J.: Princeton University Press.

Sassen-Koob, Saskia. 1987. Growth and Informalization in the Core: A Preliminary Report on New York City. In *The Capitalist City,* edited by M. P. Smith and J. R. Feagin. New York: Blackwell.

Sawers, Larry. 1975. Urban Form and the Mode of Production. *Review of Radical Political Economics* 7: 52–68.

Sears, David. 1994. Urban Rioting in Los Angeles: A Comparison of 1965 with 1992. In *The Los Angeles Riots,* edited by Mark Baldassare. Boulder: Westview Press.

Seeley, John R., R. A. Sim, and E. W. Loosley. 1956. *Crestwood Heights: A Study of the Culture of Suburban Life.* New York: Wiley.

Sennott, Charles. 2004. As European Union Moves East, Not All on Vanguard Are Cheering. *Boston Globe* April 25, A10.

Service, Elman R. 1978. Classical and Modern Theories of the Origins of Government. In *Origins of the State,* edited by R. Cohen and E. Service. Philadelphia: Institute for the Study of Human Issues.

Shannon, Thomas, Nancy Kleniewski, and William Cross. 1991. *Urban Problems in Sociological Perspective*, 2nd ed. Prospect Heights, Ill.: Waveland Press.

Shaw, Clifford, and Henry McKay. 1931. *Social Factors in Juvenile Delinquency*. Washington, D.C.: National Commission on Law Observance and Enforcement.

Shefter, Martin. 1985. *Political Crisis/Fiscal Crisis: The Collapse and Revival of New York City*. New York: Basic Books.

Shelton, Beth Anne, N. Rodriguez, J. Feagin, R. Bullard, and R. Thomas. 1989. *Houston: Growth and Decline in a Sunbelt Boomtown*. Philadelphia: Temple University Press.

Shevky, Eshref, and Wendell Bell. 1955. *Social Area Analysis*. Stanford, Calif.: Stanford University Press.

Shlay, Anne. 1989. Financing Community: Methods for Assessing Residential Credit Disparities, Market Barriers, and Institutional Reinvestment Performance in the Metropolis. *Journal of Urban Affairs* 11(3): 201–223.

Short, John Rennie. 1996. *The Urban Order*. Oxford, UK: Blackwell Publishers.

Simmel, Georg. 1905. The Metropolis and Mental Life. Reprinted in *The Sociology of Georg Simmel*, edited by K. Wolff. New York: Free Press, Originally published in 1905.

Sinclair, Upton. [1920] 1984. *The Jungle*. Cutchogue, N.Y.: Buccaneer Books.

Sjoberg, Gideon. 1960. *The Preindustrial City*. New York: Free Press.

Small, Mario Luis. 2004. *Villa Victoria: The Transformation of Social Capital in a Boston Barrio*. Chicago: University of Chicago Press.

Smith, David A. 1965. The Origin and Evolution of Cities. In *Cities*, edited by Scientific American. New York: Knopf.

——. 1987. Overurbanization Reconceptualized: A Political Economy of the World-System Approach. *Urban Affairs Quarterly* 23: 270–294.

——. 1995. The New Urban Sociology Meets the Old: Rereading Some Classical Human Ecology. *Urban Affairs Review* 30(3): 432–457.

Smith, Neil. 1979. Toward a Theory of Gentrification. *Journal of the American Planning Association* 45: 538–548.

——. 2008. *Uneven Development*. 3rd Edition. New York: Blackwell.

——. 1986. Gentrification, the Frontier, and the Restructuring of Urban Space. In *Gentrification of the City*, edited by N. Smith and P. Williams. London: Allen and Unwin.

Smith, Polly J. 2007. *The Impact of Military Desegregation on Segregation Patterns in American Cities: A Case Study of Colorado Springs, New London and Fayetteville*. Lewiston, N.Y.: Edwin Mellon Press.

Snow, David, and Leon Anderson. 1993. *Down on Their Luck: A Study of Homeless Street People*. Berkeley: University of California Press.

Soja, Edward. 1987. Restructuring the Internationalization of the Los Angeles Region. In *The Capitalist City*, edited by M. Smith and J. Feagin. New York: Basil-Blackwell, pp. 113–137.

Soja, Edward and Allen Scott. 1996. Introduction to Los Angeles: City and Region. In *The City: Los Angeles and Urban Theory at the End of the Twentieth Century*, edited by A. Scott and E. Soja. Berkeley: University of California Press.

Spain, Daphne. 1992. *Gendered Spaces*. Chapel Hill: University of North Carolina Press.

——. 1993. Built to Last: Public Housing as an Urban Gendered Space. Paper presented at the annual meeting of the Urban Affairs Association.

Spain, Daphne and Suzanne Bianchi. 1996. *Balancing Act: Motherhood, Marriage, and Employment Among American Women.* New York: Russell Sage.

Spates, James, and John Macionis. 1987. *The Sociology of Cities.* Belmont, Calif.: Wadsworth.

Spear, Allen H. 1967. *Black Chicago: The Making of a Ghetto, 1890–1920.* Chicago: University of Chicago Press.

Spelman, W., and D. K. Brown. 1984. *Calling the Police.* Washington, D.C.: U.S. Government Printing Office.

Squires, Gregory D., ed. 1992. *From Redlining to Reinvestment: Community Responses to Urban Disinvestment.* Philadelphia: Temple University Press.

———. 1994. *Capital and Communities in Black and White.* Albany: State University of New York Press.

———. 2002. *Urban Sprawl: Causes, Consequences, and Policy Responses.* Washington, D. C.: The Urban Institute.

———. 2003. Racial Profiling, Insurance Style: Insurance Redlining and the Uneven Development of Urban America. *Journal of Urban Affairs* 24 (4): 391–410.

Squires, Gregory, W. Velez, and K. Taeuber. 1991. Insurance Redlining, Agency Location, and the Process of Urban Disinvestment. *Urban Affairs Quarterly* 26(4): 567–588.

Stack, Carol. 1974. *All Our Kin.* New York: Harper & Row.

Stack, John, and Christopher Warren. 1992. The Reform Tradition in Ethnic Politics: Metropolitan Miami Confronts the 1990s. In *Miami Now!*, edited by G. Grenier and A. Stepick. Gainesville: University Press of Florida.

Stark, R. 2006. *Cities of God.* New York: HarperOne.

Steffens, Lincoln. 1948. *The Shame of the Cities.* New York: Peter Smith. Originally published in 1904.

Steinaker, Annette. 1998. Economic Restructuring of Cities, Suburbs, and Nonmetropoplitan Areas, 1977–1992. *Urban Affairs Review* 34(2): 212–240.

Stoecker, Randy. 1995. The Myth of Community Empowerment: Rethinking the Community Development Corporation Model. Paper presented at annual meeting of the American Sociological Association.

Stone, Clarence. 1993. Urban Regimes and the Capacity to Govern: A Political Economy Approach. *Journal of Urban Affairs* 15(1): 1–28.

Stull, Donald, Michael Broadway, and Ken Erickson. 1992. The Price of a Good Steak: Beef Packing and Its Consequences in Garden City, Kansas. In *Structuring Diversity*, edited by L. Lamphere. Chicago: University of Chicago Press.

Sullivan, Mercer. 1989. *Getting Paid: Youth Crime and Work in the Inner City.* Ithaca, N.Y.: Cornell University Press.

Susser, Ida. 1982. *Norman Street.* New York: Oxford University Press.

Suttles, Gerald. 1968. *The Social Order of the Slum.* Chicago: University of Chicago Press.

———. 1972. *The Social Construction of Communities.* Chicago: University of Chicago Press.

Swanstrom, Todd. 1985. *The Crisis of Growth Politics: Cleveland, Kucinich, and the Challenge of Urban Populism.* Philadelphia: Temple University Press.

———. 1993. Beyond Economism: Urban Political Economy and the

Postmodern Challenge. *Journal of Urban Affairs* 15(1): 55–78.

Szelenyi, Ivan. 1983. *Urban Inequalities Under State Socialism*. Oxford: Oxford University Press.

Szymanski, Albert. 1981. *The Logic of Imperialism*. New York: Praeger.

Tabb, William K. 1982. *The Long Default: New York City and the Urban Fiscal Crisis*. New York: Monthly Review Press.

Taeuber, Karl E. 1968. The Effect of Income Redistribution on Racial Residential Segregation. *Urban Affairs Quarterly* 4: 5–14.

Taeuber, Karl, and Alma Taeuber. 1965. *Negroes in Cities*. New York: Atheneum.

Takaki, Ronald. 1989. *Strangers from a Different Shore: A History of Asian Americans*. New York: Penguin Books.

Tauxe, Caroline S. 1993. *Farms, Mines, and Main Streets: Uneven Development in a Dakota County*. Philadelphia: Temple University Press.

Taylor, Dorceta. 1993. Environmentalism and the Politics of Inclusion. In *Confronting Environmental Racism: Voices from the Grassroots*, edited by R. Bullard. Boston: South End Press.

Taylor, Monique M. 2002. *Harlem: Between Heaven and Hell*. Minneapolis: University of Minnesota Press.

Thomas, Alexander R. 2003. *In Gotham's Shadow: Globalization and Change in Central New York*. Albany: SUNY Press.

———. 2005. *Gilboa: New York's Quest for Water and the Destruction of a Small Town*. New York: University Press of America.

Thomas, Alexander R., and Polly J. Smith. 2009. *Upstate Down: Thinking about New York and its Discontents*. New York: University Press of America.

Thomas, William I., and Dorothy Thomas. 1970. *The Child in America*. New York: Johnson. Originally published in 1928.

Thrasher, Frederic. 1928. *The Gang*. Chicago: University of Chicago Press.

Tomaskovic-Devey, D., and S. M. Miller. 1982. Recapitalization: The Basic Urban Policy of the 1980s. In *Urban Policy Under Capitalism*, edited by N. Fainstein and S. Fainstein. Thousand Oaks, Calif.: Sage.

Tönnies, Ferdinand. 1963. *Community and Society*. New York: Harper and Row. Originally published in 1887 as *Gemeinschaft und Gesellschaft*.

Tonry, Michael. 1994. Racial Politics, Racial Disparities, and the War on Crime. *Crime and Delinquency* 40(4): 475–494.

Turk, Austin. 1969. *Criminality and the Legal Order*. Chicago: Rand McNally.

Turner, Margery Austin. 1998. Moving Out of Poverty: Expanding Mobility and Choice through Tenant-Based Housing Assistance. *Housing Policy Debate* 9(2): 373–394.

Turner, Margery A., Stephen L. Ross, George C. Galster, and John Yinger. 2002. Discrimination in Metropolitan Housing Markets: National Results from Phase 1 HDS 2000. Washington, D.C.: Urban Institute and U.S. Department of Housing and Urban Development.

Tyner, Christopher. 2003. Don't Believe All You Hear About the California Economy. *Christian Science Monitor*, August 27, p. 2.

United Nations. 1991. *World Urbanization Prospects 1990*. New York: UNO Sales.

United Nations Conference on Trade and Development (UNCTAD). 2009. *The Least Developed Countries Report 2009*. New York: United Nations.

University City District. 2007. *University City Report Card 2007*. Philadelphia: University City District.

Ur, Jason. 2002. Settlement and Landscape in Northern Mesopotamia: The Tell Hamoukar Survey 2000–2001. *Akkadica* 123: 57–88.

U.S. Bureau of Labor Statistics. 2004. *Labor Force Statistics from the Current Population Survey*. Washington, D.C.: U.S. Government Printing Office.

———. 2008. *Women in the Labor Force: A Databook*. Washington, D.C.: U.S. Government Printing Office.

U. S. Census Bureau. 1990. *Statistical Abstract of the U.S., 1990*. Washington, D.C.: U.S. Government Printing Office.

———. 2000(a). *The Foreign-Born Population in the United States*. Washington, D.C.: U.S. Government Printing Office.

———. 2000(b). *Statistical Abstract of the United States, 1999*. Washington, D.C.: U.S. Government Printing Office.

———. 2001. *Census of Population, 2000*. Washington, D.C.: U.S. Government Printing Office.

———. 2003. *Current Population Survey Detailed Tables*, Table POV02. Washington, D.C.: U.S. Government Printing Office.

———. 2004. *Statistical Abstract of the U.S., 2004*. Washington, D.C.: U.S. Government Printing Office.

———. 2009(a). *Statistical Abstract of the United States, 2009*. www.census.gov.

———. 2009(b). *The 2009 Statistical Abstract of the United States: Table 39: Native and Foreign-Born Population by State*. www.census.gov/compendia.

———.n.d. *American Factfinder*. Retrieved March 3, 2009, from http:\\www.census.gov.

———.n.d. California Quick Facts. http://quickfacts.Census.gov/qfd/states/066000.htm/.

U.S. Department of Agriculture. 2009. *Economic Research Service*. Retrieved February 4, 2009, from http://www.ers.usda.gov/.

U.S. Department of Housing and Urban Development. 1995. *Empowerment: A New Covenant with America's Communities*. President Clinton's National Urban Policy Report. Washington, D.C.: U.S. Government Printing Office.

U.S. Department of Justice, Bureau of Justice Statistics. 2008. *Criminal Victimization in the United States, 2007*. Washington, D.C.: U.S. Government Printing Office.

U.S. Immigration and Naturalization Service. 1999. *Statistical Yearbook of the Immigration and Naturalization Service, 1997*. Washington, D.C.: U.S. Government Printing Office.

U.S. Office of Management and Budget. 2000. *Standards for Defining Metropolitan and Micropolitan Statistical Areas; Notice*. Federal Register, Vol. 65, No. 249.

Vale, Lawrence. 2002. *Reclaiming Public Housing: A Half Century of Struggle in Three Public Neighborhoods*. Cambridge, Mass.: Harvard University Press.

Van de Mieroop, Marc. 1999. *The Ancient Mesopotamian City*. New York: Oxford University Press.

Vandell, Kerry. 1995. Market Factors Affecting Spatial Heterogeneity Among Urban Neighborhoods. *Housing Policy Debate* 6(1): 103–139.

Van Kempen, Ronald. 2005. Segregation and Housing Conditions of Immigrants in Western European Cities. In *Cities of Europe*, edited by Yuri Kazepov. Oxford, UK: Blackwell Publishing.

Van Valey, Thomas, W. C. Roof, and J. E. Wilcox. 1977. Trends in Residential Segregation: 1960–70. *American Journal of Sociology* 82: 826–844.

Vesselinov, Elena. 2008. Members Only: Gated Communities and Residential Segregation in the Metropolitan United States. *Sociological Forum* 23(3): 536–555.

Vold, George. 1958. *Theoretical Criminology.* New York: Oxford University Press.

von Thünen, Johan. 1826. Der Isolierte Staat in Beziehung auf Landwirtschaft und Nationalekonomie.

Wacquant, Loic, and William J. Wilson. 1989. The Cost of Racial and Class Exclusion in the Inner City. *The Annals of the American Academy of Political and Social Science* 501: 8–25.

Waldinger, Roger. 1990. Immigrant Enterprise in the United States. In *Structures of Capital,* edited by S. Zukin and P. DiMaggio. Cambridge: Cambridge University Press.

———. 1996. *Still the Promised City? African-Americans and New Immigrants in Postindustrial New York.* Cambridge, Mass.: Harvard University Press.

Waldinger, Roger and Michael Lichter. 2003. *How the Other Half Works: Immigration and the Social Organization of Labor.* Berkeley: University of California Press.

Walker, Richard A. 1978. Two Sources of Uneven Development Under Advanced Capitalism: Spatial Differentiation and Capital Mobility. *Review of Radical Political Economics* 10: 28–37.

Walker, Richard, and Michael Heiman. 1981. Quiet Revolution for Whom? *Annals of the Association of American Geographers* 71(1): 67–83.

Walker, Samuel. 1989. *Sense and Nonsense About Crime.* Pacific Grove, Calif.: Brooks/Cole.

Walker, Samuel, Cassis Spohn, and Miriam DeLone. 2006. *The Color of Justice: Race, Ethnicity, and Crime in America,* 4th edition. Belmont Hills, Calif.: Wadsworth.

Wallace, Anthony. 1972. *Rockdale.* New York: Norton.

Wallace-Hadrill, Andrew. 1991. Introduction. In *City and Country in the Ancient World,* edited by J. Rich and A. Wallace-Hadrill. London: Routledge.

Wallerstein, Immanuel. 1976. *The Modern World System.* New York: Academic Press.

Walton, John. 1987. Theory and Research on Industrialization. *Annual Review of Sociology* 13: 89–108.

———. 1993. Urban Sociology: The Contribution and Limits of Political Economy. *Annual Review of Sociology* 19: 301–320.

Ward, David. 1971. *Cities and Immigrants: A Geography of Change in Nineteenth Century America.* New York: Oxford University Press.

Warner, Kee, and Harvey Molotch. 2000. *Building Rules.* Boulder, Co.: Westview Press.

Warner, Sam Bass, Jr. 1962. *Streetcar Suburbs.* New York: Athenaeum Press.

———. 1968. *The Private City.* Philadelphia: University of Pennsylvania Press.

Warner, W. Lloyd, ed. 1963. *Yankee City.* New Haven: Yale University Press.

Waste, Robert. 1998. *Independent Cities: Rethinking U.S. Urban Policy.* New York: Oxford University Press.

Watkins, Alfred J., and David C. Perry. 1977. Regional Change and the Impact of Uneven Urban Development. In *The Rise of the Sunbelt Cities,* edited by D. Perry and A. Watkins. Thousand Oaks, Calif.: Sage.

Weber, Adna. 1965. *The Growth of Cities in the Nineteenth Century.* Ithaca, N.Y.: Cornell University Press.

Weber, Max. 1946. Class, Status, Party. Reprinted in *From Max Weber,* edited and translated by H. Gerth and C. W. Mills. New York: Oxford University Press.

———. 1958. *The City*. Edited and translated by D. Martindale and G. Neuwirth. New York: Free Press.

Weisman, Leslie Kanes. 1992. *Discrimination by Design: A Feminist Critique of the Man-Made Environment*. Urbana: University of Illinois Press.

Weiss, Marc A. 1980. The Origins and Legacy of Urban Renewal. In *Urban and Regional Planning in an Age of Austerity*, edited by Pierre Clavel et al. New York: Pergamon Press.

Weiss, Michael. 1982. *The Clustering of America*. New York: Tilden Press.

———. 2000. *The Clustered World: How We Live, What We Buy, and What It All Means About Who We Are*. London: Little, Brown.

Weissbourd, Bernard. 1964. Are Cities Obsolete? *Saturday Review* 47 (December 19): 15.

Wekerle, Gerda. 1980. Women in the Urban Environment. *Signs* 5(3): S188–S214.

West, Troy. 1989. Alternative Architecture for the 1990s. *Shelterforce* 11(4): 16–18.

White, Michael. 1987. *American Neighborhoods and Residential Differentiation*. New York: Russell Sage.

White, Morton, and Lucia White. 1961. *The Intellectual vs. the City*. New York: Mentor.

White, Paul. 1984. *The West European City: A Social Geography*. London: Longman.

———. 1998. Urban Life and Social Stress. In *The New Europe: Economy, Society, and Environment*, edited by D. Pinder. New York: Wiley.

Whyte, William H. 1956. *The Organization Man*. Garden City, N.Y.: Doubleday-Anchor.

———. 1988. City: *Rediscovering the Center*. New York: Doubleday-Anchor.

Wiese, Andrew. 1995. Neighborhood Diversity: Social Change, Ambiguity, and Fair Housing since 1968. *Journal of Urban Affairs* 17(2): 107–129.

Wilder, Margaret, and Barry Rubin. 1988. Targeted Redevelopment Through Urban Enterprise Zones. *Journal of Urban Affairs* 10(1): 1–17.

Wilhelm, Sidney. 1964. The Concept of the Ecological Complex: A Critique. *American Journal of Economics and Sociology* 23: 241–248.

Williams, Richard, Reynold Nesbia, and Eileen Diaz McConnell. 2005. The Changing Face of Inequality in Home Mortgage Lending. *Social Problems* 52(2): 181–208.

Williamson, Thad, David Imbroscio, and Gar Alperovitz. 2002. *Making a Place for Community: Local Democracy in a Global Era*. New York: Routledge.

Wilson, Elizabeth. 1992. *The Sphinx in the City: Urban Life, the Control of Disorder, and Women*. Berkeley: University of California Press.

Wilson, Richard A. 2001. *The Politics of Truth and Reconciliation in South Africa: Legitimizing the Post-Apartheid State*. New York: Cambridge University Press.

Wilson, William J. 1987. *The Truly Disadvantaged*. Chicago: University of Chicago Press.

———. 1997. *When Work Disappears: The World of the New Urban Poor*. New York: Alfred A. Knopf.

———. 2009a. *More than Just Race: Being Black and Poor in the Inner City*. New York: Norton.

———. 2009b. The Political and Economic Forces Shaping Concentrated Poverty. *Political Science Quarterly* 123(4): 555–571.

Wilson, William J., and Kathryn Neckerman. 1986. Poverty and

Family Structure: The Widening Gap Between Evidence and Public Policy Issues. In *Fighting Poverty: What Works and What Doesn't*, edited by S. Danziger and D. Weinberg. Cambridge, Mass.: Harvard University Press.

Wilson, William J., R. Aponte, J. Kirschenman, and L. Wacquant. 1988. The Ghetto Underclass and the Changing Structure of Urban Poverty. In *Quiet Riots*, edited by F. Harris and R. Wilkins. New York: Pantheon Books.

Wirth, Louis. 1938. Urbanism as a Way of Life. *American Journal of Sociology* 44: 1–24.

Wright, Lawrence. 2006. *The Looming Tower: Al Qaeda and the Road to 9/11*. New York: Knopf.

Wolch, Jennifer, Manuel Pastor, Jr., and Peter Dreier, eds. 2004. *Up Against the Sprawl: Public Policy and the Making of Southern California*. Minneapolis: University of Minnesota Press.

Wolman, Harold. 1986. The Reagan Urban Policy and Its Impacts. *Urban Affairs Quarterly* 21: 311–335.

———. 1988. Local Economic Development Policy: What Explains the Divergence Between Policy Analysis and Political Behavior? *Journal of Urban Affairs* 10(1): 19–28.

Yanitsky, Oleg. 1986. Urbanization in the USSR: Theory, Tendencies, and Policy. *International Journal of Urban and Regional Research* 10(2): 243–287.

Young, Michael, and Peter Willmott. 1957. *Family and Kinship in East London*. London: Routledge.

Zavis, Alexandra. 2009. Steep Drop in Property Tax Forecast. *Los Angeles Times* (March 10): A1.

Zdenek, Robert. 1987. Community Development Corporations. In *Beyond the Market and the State*, edited by S. Bruyn and J. Meehan. Philadelphia: Temple University Press.

Zeder, Melinda A., and Brian Hesse. 2000. The Initial Domestication of Goats (Capra hircus) in the Zagros Mountains 10,000 Years Ago. *Science, New Series* 287 (5461): 2254–2257.

Zhou, Min. 1992. *Chinatown: The Socioeconomic Potential of an Urban Enclave*. Philadelphia: Temple University Press.

Zlolniski, Christian. 2006. *Janitors, Street Vendors, and Activists: The Lives of Mexican Immigrants in Silicon Valley*. Berkeley: University of California Press.

Zorbaugh, Harvey. 1929. *The Gold Coast and the Slum*. Chicago: University of Chicago Press.

Zukin, Sharon. 1982. *Loft Living: Culture and Capital in Urban Change*. Baltimore: Johns Hopkins University Press.

———. 1991. *Landscapes of Power: From Detroit to Disney World*. Berkeley: University of California Press.

———. 1995. *The Cultures of Cities*. Cambridge, Mass: Blackwell Publishers.

Zunz, Olivier. 1982. *The Changing Face of Inequality*. Chicago: University of Chicago Press.

Index

Decision making, 88
Defended neighborhoods, 248
Deindustrialization, 207, 221, 226, 261
Denationalization, 67
Denver, 106
Department of Homeland Security, 177
Department of Housing and Urban
    Development (HUD), 310–311
Determinism, 32
Detroit
    description of, 5, 77, 106
    eminent domain controversy in, 231
    profit cycles in, 88
    Renaissance Center in, 13
Developing regions
    Africa, 148–149
    China, 151–152
    colonial status of, 147
    colonization of, 147–148
    East Asia, 150–151
    empire influences on, 147
    India, 152–153
    inequality in, 147
    Latin America, 153–156
Developing world cities, 143–163
    characteristics of, 143–144
    development of, 156–162
    overurbanization of, 144–145
    population trends in, 144–156
    primacy in, 144
Development
    community, 277–278
    concentration of, 5
    economic. *See* Economic development
    urban. *See* Urban development
Development perspective, 156–161
    uneven, 156
Die Stadt (Weber), 34
Discriminatory lending, 203
Disinvestment, 201, 204, 262, 337
Division of labor, 53, 253
Division of Labor in Society
    (Durkheim), 24
Domestic terrorism, 334
Dominican immigrants, 179
Dot.com businesses, 91–92
Down on Their Luck (Snow and
    Anderson), 233
Drugs, illegal, 324–325
Dual city, 109, 140

Dual housing market, 200
DuBois, W. E. B., 192
Duncan, Otis D., 31
Durkheim, Émile, 24, 320

E

East Asia, 150–151
East Harlem, 266
Eastern European cities, 129–135
    economic restructuring in, 133–134
    environmental challenges in, 134–135
    housing in, 132–137
    urban planning in, 130–132
Eastern Roman Empire, 59
Ecological footprint, 365
Ecology, 22
    factorial, 216
    human, 26, 42
    urban, 22, 37
Ecology of Fear, The, 364
Economic activity, 80–81
Economic capital, 276
Economic development, 157
    business subsidies and, 272–273
    business-oriented, 272–275
    CDCs in, 277–278
    people-oriented, 275–278
    policy for, 272
    public balance sheet in, 279
    public–private partnerships and,
        273–274
    retaining and creating jobs in, 275–276
Economic restructuring, 38, 42–44, 106–107
Economic stimulus programs, 116
Economics, neoclassical school of, 27
Economies of agglomeration, 5
Economies of scale, 5
Economy, 36, 259–279
    arts and, 267–269
    changing, 116
    and changing nature of jobs, 262–264
    corporate mergers and buyouts in,
        261–262
    deindustrialization and, 261
    disinvestment in, 262
    feudal, 65
    globalization of, 38, 261
    government response to changes in, 116
    growth of, through government
        spending, 116